S0-CFU-209

PAGEMAKER® 4 FOR
THE MACINTOSH MADE EASY

PAGEMAKER® 4 FOR THE MACINTOSH

Marty Matthews

Osborne **McGraw-Hill**

Berkeley   New York   St. Louis   San Francisco
Auckland   Bogotá   Hamburg   London   Madrid
Mexico City   Milan   Montreal   New Delhi   Panama City
Paris   São Paulo   Singapore   Sydney
Tokyo   Toronto

Osborne **McGraw-Hill**
2600 Tenth Street
Berkeley, California 94710
U.S.A.

For information on translations and book distributors outside of the U.S.A., please write to Osborne **McGraw-Hill** at the above address.

A complete list of trademarks appears on page 557.

PageMaker® 4 for the Macintosh Made Easy

Copyright © 1990 by Martin S. Matthews and Carole Boggs Matthews. All rights reserved. Printed in the United States of America. Except as permitted under the Copyright Act of 1976, no part of this publication may be reproduced or distributed in any form or by any means, or stored in a database or retrieval system, without the prior written permission of the publisher, with the exception that the program listings may be entered, stored, and executed in a computer system, but they may not be reproduced for publication.

4567890 DOC 9987654321

ISBN 0-07-881650-5

Information has been obtained by Osborne McGraw-Hill from sources believed to be reliable. However, because of the possibility of human or mechanical error by our sources, Osborne McGraw-Hill, or others, Osborne McGraw-Hill does not guarantee the accuracy, adequacy, or completeness of any information and is not responsible for any errors or omissions or the results obtained from use of such information.

To Carole Boggs Matthews,
a partner in the fullest sense of the word

CONTENTS
AT A GLANCE

CONTENTS

ACKNOWLEDGMENTS

Over a couple of years, several friends have been insistent that my wife (who is also a computer book author) and I should write about Macintosh products. For those gentle prods, thanks to Marsha Buxton, Nancy Johnson, Barbara Vange, Art Hyland, and John and Marilyn Hannahs. John and Marilyn also helped in several ways to make writing this book easier.

Jim Kerr and Greg Hall of Apple's Bellevue, Washington office did a yeoman's effort, with much patience, to try to get a PC-based mind to think Macintosh.

At Aldus, Jeff Harmon, Freda Steven, and Whitney McCleary all went out of their way to provide much needed assistance.

Peter Gariepy of Zedcor, Inc., publishers of the excellent desktop accessory and graphics products, DeskPaint and DeskDraw, gave a lot of his time to try to explain the intricacies of handling Macintosh graphics. Zedcor's address and phone number are listed in Appendix E.

The screen shots in this book were produced by Capture 2, a product from Mainstay. (See Appendix E for their address and phone number.) Their product worked flaw-lessly and provided the means to make a point where words alone could not.

The newsletter produced in Chapter 7 is an actual quar-terly, *The Orator,* published by Opinion Movers for The Churchill Club. Rich Karlgaard, of Opinion Movers, who is a founder of The Churchill Club, gave us permission to use the newsletter and graciously provided us with information and materials.

Frank Stapleton, of McPherson's, provided a similar ser-vice in giving permission to use his catalog, "McPherson's Wholesale Art Supplies/Graphic Arts/Drafting and Engi-neering Catalog," as the sample project in Chapter 8.

Osborne/McGraw-Hill always manages to assemble an excellent team to produce a book. From that set of stars, one superstar truly stands out. Ilene Shapera, pulling dou-ble duty as both associate editor and copy editor, not only turned gibberish into deft prose but also used a consider-able insight to make a number of very material additions to this book. Thanks, as always, to Elizabeth Fisher, acquisi-tions editor, for her patience and calming influence.

INTRODUCTION

In the five years that PageMaker has been on the market, it has proven that it uniquely combines ease of use with tremendous production capability. As a result, it has become the layout tool of choice for a broad range of printed materials, including newsletters, brochures, forms, catalogs, and manuals. A rapidly growing group of professionals and nonprofessionals have found that PageMaker solidly enhances their ability to produce a printed product while reducing costs.

Now, with the release of PageMaker 4, PageMaker's legendary ease of use and production capabilities are significantly improved. The new and robust word processing features, including search and replace and spell checking, add greatly to PageMaker's text capabilities. The new typographic controls, including the ability to rotate, expand, and condense text and to enhance leading and kerning, further streamline text manipulation. Finally, enhanced long-document capabilities, which include table of contents- and index-generation, in-line graphics affixed to text, and new link management features that allow you to track external text and graphics files, increase PageMaker's versatility.

Originally a very serviceable desktop publishing package, PageMaker is now an exceptionally powerful product that can easily be employed in a multitude of publishing projects.

ABOUT THIS BOOK

As easy as it is to use, there are many desktop publishing concepts, shortcuts, and tricks involved in learning Page-Maker. This book has been written to provide the necessary explanations and to demonstrate how to use these shortcuts and tricks to unleash the power of Page-Maker 4.

PageMaker 4 for the Macintosh Made Easy complements the PageMaker manuals and tutorials by continuing where they leave off. While it is not assumed that you have read through the manuals and done the tutorials, doing so is encouraged. If you have not, pay particular attention to the first three chapters of this book to learn the basics of PageMaker, the Macintosh, and desktop publishing.

HOW THIS BOOK IS ORGANIZED

PageMaker 4 for the Macintosh Made Easy is organized into three parts, each containing increasingly advanced applications of PageMaker, and a set of appendixes at the end of the book. Although the projects are separate and can be created independently of each other, you will get a good overall understanding of PageMaker's capabilities by creating them all. However, you can also concentrate on just those examples that you are interested in developing for yourself.

Part I is more a tutorial than the rest of the book. It explains the basic concepts of operating PageMaker so that you can comfortably use the remaining chapters even if you have not read the PageMaker tutorial. Part I discusses the essential elements of desktop publishing, the Macintosh, and PageMaker. If you are already familiar with Page-Maker and Macintosh concepts, simply scan the chapters to review the basics and the terminology. If you are new to PageMaker, carefully read Part I so that you will be able to get more out of the other chapters.

Chapter 1, "Desktop Publishing and Pagemaker," introduces desktop publishing and compares it to traditional publishing. You will quickly learn the essential concepts and terminology that are important in understanding Page-Maker. In Chapter 2, "Using the Macintosh and Its Mouse," you will become acquainted with important Macintosh terminology and concepts as they apply to PageMaker. In Chapter 3, "Getting Started with a Flyer," you will learn the fundamentals of using PageMaker by actually creating an advertising publication. You will be led through the production more slowly and with more guidance than you will be in later chapters.

Part II addresses three common needs of businesses: creating business forms, advertising brochures, and formal financial reports—all of which benefit from the professionally typeset appearance of finished PageMaker publications. These applications, more advanced than the ones you create in Part I, use most of the basic capabilities of Page-Maker.

Chapter 4, "Making a Sales Order Form," illustrates how to use PageMaker to create a business form. You will learn to create custom forms that have a "typeset" look that adds a professional touch to most business documents. In Chapter 5, "Creating a Brochure," you will create a two-page advertising brochure containing columns. The text for the brochure will be taken from Microsoft Word and then placed into the PageMaker publication. Also, a graphic will be created in Aldus FreeHand and placed in the publication. Chapter 6, "Generating an Annual Report," illustrates how to dress up financial reports that you distribute to people outside your own company. You will compose this formal, multipage document with word processing text from MacWrite II and financial worksheets and charts from Microsoft Excel.

Part III demonstrates how to create an actual newsletter and a small part of a real catalog—two advanced uses of PageMaker. Here, you will learn and use the more advanced features of PageMaker.

In Chapter 7, "Preparing a Newsletter," you will build a complete newsletter, containing three and four columns per page, one of the most popular uses of PageMaker. You will bring graphics and text in from several packages, including WriteNow and WordPerfect, and will place them in the publication. Chapter 7 uses the Autoflow and style sheet features as well as the new story editing features in PageMaker 4. In Chapter 8, "Building a Catalog," you will import text from Microsoft Word and graphics from Aldus FreeHand and use a scanner. You will use several advanced functions and will learn how to lay out pages efficiently.

EQUIPMENT AND SOFTWARE YOU WILL NEED

You can use any model Macintosh computer with Page-Maker 4 and this book. Your computer must have at least 1 MB of memory, although 2 MB is recommended. You must have a hard disk drive with at least 5 MB of free space. You need only one floppy drive.

You should have a printer to see your finished products. To produce the output quality shown in this book, you need a laser printer. It is assumed that you have an Apple LaserWriter IINT, although many other laser printers on the market can certainly be substituted. Dot matrix printers lack the quality of laser printers and are not recommended for use with PageMaker.

Regarding software, you must have System version 6.03 or above and Finder version 6.1 or above. And, of course, you need PageMaker. With version 4 of PageMaker you can do everything in the book, and with version 3 you can do most of the exercises.

This book was written on a Macintosh IICX with an extended keyboard and an Apple LaserWriter IINT printer. The screen illustrations were produced with an Apple color monitor in two-color mode. If you are using a different screen, your displays may differ slightly from the screen images shown in the book. Using a different model Macintosh should not affect how you use the book. Other keyboard models are discussed and taken into account in the instructions.

TYPOGRAPHICAL CONVENTIONS USED IN THIS BOOK

PageMaker 4 for the Macintosh Made Easy employs several typographical conventions that make it easier to use. These are as follows: **Bold type** is used for the text you are instructed to enter from the keyboard. Keys from the keyboard are presented in small capital letters; for example, RETURN and COMMAND. A plus sign (+) between keys means that you should press the keys simultaneously. A comma (,) indicates a separate keypress. For example COMMAND + SHIFT + M, RETURN means that you should press COMMAND and SHIFT and M, and then press RETURN separately.

To the extent that it is practical, the typographical and naming conventions used in the PageMaker manuals have been followed. Most importantly, terms such as "click," "drag," "choose," and "select" are used as they are in the PageMaker manuals.

ABOUT THE AUTHOR

Martin S. Matthews is a partner in Matthews Technology, a firm providing consulting, training, and seminars on computer topics to large and small firms nationwide. He assists companies and individuals in selecting and installing computer systems, advises in the design and development of software, and conducts training sessions and seminars. Martin combines expertise in computing with solid business experience. He has been president and vice president as well as systems designer and software developer for a variety of companies. Martin has more than 30 years of computer experience. *PageMaker 4 for the Macintosh Made Easy* is a result of a fourteen-year association with many different aspects of the printing and publishing industries. Martin Matthews and his wife Carole Boggs Matthews have authored twelve other computer books, including *Apple-Works Made Easy, Using PageMaker for the PC, AppleWorks:*

The Pocket Reference, WordStar Professional: The Complete Reference, Using WordStar Professional, Using 1-2-3 Release 3, Microsoft Works for the PC Made Easy, and *Q & A Made Easy.*

ADDITIONAL HELP FROM OSBORNE/McGRAW-HILL

Osborne/McGraw-Hill provides top-quality books for computer users at every level of computing experience. To help you build your skills, we suggest that you look for the books in the following Osborne series that best address your needs.

The "Teach Yourself" Series is perfect for people who have never used a computer before or who want to gain confidence in using program basics. These books provide a simple, slow-paced introduction to the fundamental uses of popular software packages and programming languages. The "Mastery Skills Check" format ensures your understanding concepts thoroughly before you progress to new material. Plenty of examples and exercises (with answers at the back of the book) are used throughout the text.

The "Made Easy" Series is also for beginners or users who may need a refresher on the new features of an upgraded product. These in-depth introductions guide users step-by-step from the program basics to intermediate-level usage. Plenty of "hands-on" exercises and examples are used in every chapter.

The "Using" Series presents fast-paced guides that cover beginning concepts quickly and move on to intermediate-level techniques and some advanced topics. These books are written for users already familiar with computers and software who want to get up to speed fast with a certain product.

The "Advanced" Series assumes that the reader is a user who has reached at least an intermediate skill level and is ready to learn more sophisticated techniques and refinements.

"The Complete Reference" Series provides handy desktop references for popular software and programming languages that list every command, feature, and function of the product along with brief but detailed descriptions of how they are used. Books are fully indexed and often include tear-out command cards. "The Complete Reference" series is ideal for both beginners and pros.

"The Pocket Reference" Series is a pocket-sized, shorter version of "The Complete Reference" Series. It provides the essential commands, features, and functions of software and programming languages for users of every level who need a quick reminder.

The "Secrets, Solutions, Shortcuts" Series is written for beginning users who are already somewhat familiar with the software and for experienced users at intermediate and advanced levels. This series provides clever tips, points out shortcuts for using the software to greater advantage, and indicates traps to avoid.

Osborne/McGraw-Hill also publishes many fine books that are not included in the series described here. If you have questions about which Osborne books are right for you, ask the salesperson at your local book or computer store, or call us toll-free at 1-800-262-4729.

OTHER OSBORNE/McGRAW-HILL BOOKS OF INTEREST TO YOU

We hope that *PageMaker 4 for the Macintosh Made Easy* will assist you in mastering this version of PageMaker, and will also pique your interest in learning more about other ways to better use your computer.

If you're interested in expanding your skills so you can be even more computer-efficient, be sure to take advantage of Osborne/McGraw-Hill's large selection of top-quality computer books that cover all varieties of popular hardware, software, programming languages, and operating systems. While we cannot list every title here that may relate to the Macintosh and to your special computing needs, here are just a few related books that complement *PageMaker 4 for the Macintosh Made Easy*.

For an excellent introduction to Excel for the Macintosh, look for *Excel Made Easy for the Macintosh* by Edward Jones. This step-by-step guide shows you how to design, build, edit, and print working spreadsheets, create charts, and work with databases. It covers versions 1.5 and 2.2.

HyperCard: The Complete Reference by Stephen L. Michel offers something for every Macintosh user. Newcomers will enjoy a tutorial section, while experienced users will benefit from a complete discussion of the facets of HyperTalk, HyperCard's scripting language. Learn all aspects of HyperCard, from installation to creating stacks.

If you're looking for the best way to get started in telecommunications or to get more out of the on-line services available today, see *Dvorak's Guide to PC*

Telecommunications. This book/disk package, written by the internationally recognized computer columnist John C. Dvorak with programming wiz Nick Anis, shows you how to instantly plug into the world of electronic databases, bulletin boards, and on-line services. The package includes an easy-to-read comprehensive guide plus two diskettes loaded with oustanding free software and is of value to computer users at every skill level.

DISK ORDER FORM
Save Time and Effort — Increase Accuracy

The word processing graphics files used to build the publications in this book, as well as the finished publications, are available on disks. While the disks are not required to build the publications, using them will save you the time and effort of entering text and creating graphics and will eliminate the possibility of introducing errors. The files are available on 800KB 3 1/2″ floppy disks for the Apple Macintosh.

Be sure that your input is accurate, save time, and explore PageMaker now by purchasing these disks,

To order, complete the following form and return it to Matthews Technology with your payment. Please allow up to four weeks for delivery.

TO: Matthews Technology
P.O. Box 967
Freeland, WA 98249

Please send me the disk set for *PageMaker 4 for the Macintosh Made Easy.* My check for $29.95 in U.S. funds and drawn on a U.S. bank is enclosed. (Washington state residents, add 7.8% sales tax for a total of $32.29.)

SEND TO:

Name: _____

Company: _____

Street: _____

City: _____ State: ____ ZIP: _____

Phone: _____

RETURN POLICY: Returns are accepted only if a disk is defective. In that case, return the disk within 15 days and you will be sent a replacement disk immediately.

Osborne/McGraw-Hill assumes NO responsibility for this offer. This is solely an offer of Matthews Technology and not of Osborne/McGraw-Hill.

WHY THIS BOOK IS FOR YOU

If you have recently purchased PageMaker or are contemplating doing so, *PageMaker 4 for the Macintosh Made Easy* was written for you. With it you will learn how to use PageMaker to create professional-quality documents, whether you are new to PageMaker or want to improve your skills.

The exercises and examples in this book are actual business forms and publications that illustrate realistic and comprehensive uses of PageMaker. The book is not a tutorial as much as it is a step-by-step guide to creating the examples presented. As you create the examples, you will learn the scope of capabilities available in PageMaker. The book offers ample explanation and visual representation of exactly what is occurring as you create these examples.

You will learn how to bring text and graphics into Page-Maker from many other programs, such as Microsoft Word, Aldus FreeHand, and Microsoft Excel. You can select the chapter that explains how to bring in the text or graphics from your particular word processor or graphics program and then adapt those instructions for use with your software in every other chapter. For example, Chapter 5 uses Microsoft Word, Chapter 6, MacWrite II, and Chapter 7,

WriteNow and WordPerfect. If you use WriteNow, scan the applicable pages of Chapter 7 to see which details you need to be aware of and use those in working with Chapter 5. In truth, working with the various packages is very similar from PageMaker's standpoint. The primary challenge is knowing what to do with the material once it is in Page-Maker.

LEARN MORE ABOUT SOFTWARE FOR THE MACINTOSH

Osborne/McGraw-Hill offers books on other word processing packages that you can use with PageMaker to maximize the power of this popular desktop publishing system.

Using WordPerfect for the Macintosh by Daniel J. Rosenbaum is a fast-paced, hands-on guide that leads you from fundamentals to intermediate techniques and even includes some advanced topics.

Microsoft Word Made Easy for the Macintosh Version 4.0, Third Edition by Paul Hoffman is a step-by-step introduction to using version 4.0 of Microsoft's popular word processor. If you have version 3.0 of this program, see Hoffman's *Microsoft Word Made Easy for the Macintosh, Version 3, Second Edition.*

Microsoft Word for the Macintosh: The Complete Reference by Michael A. Fischer, is a handy desktop encyclopedia of every MacWord command, feature, and function.

Using FullWrite by Greg Merriman introduces the basics of text processing with version 1.1 before moving onto intermediate applications with Ashton-Tate's document processing program.

THE PAGEMAKER ENVIRONMENT

Desktop Publishing and PageMaker
Using the Macintosh and Its Mouse
Getting Started with a Flyer

Part I, composed of Chapters 1, 2, and 3, introduces you to PageMaker and its environment. It is more a tutorial than the rest of the book so that all readers, regardless of prior experience with computers and PageMaker, are brought to a common level of understanding before the more advanced features of PageMaker are introduced.

Chapter 1, "Desktop Publishing and PageMaker," defines and explains some publishing terms and concepts necessary to create a document using desktop publishing. Chapter 2, "Using the Macintosh and Its Mouse," introduces you to the Macintosh on which PageMaker operates. In Chapter 3, "Getting Started with a Flyer," you use PageMaker to create an advertising flyer. PageMaker's basic menus and operating concepts are thoroughly explained with many illustrations of the screen.

If you are already familiar with the Macintosh and Page-Maker, simply scan Part I to review the terminology and concepts and become familiar with some of the changes in PageMaker 4, the latest release. If you are new to Page-Maker but are familiar with the Macintosh, spend more time with Part I because it is the foundation for the later chapters.

DESKTOP PUBLISHING AND PAGEMAKER

Planning
Design
Content Creation
Page Makeup
Printing

Desktop publishing is a most appropriate term for producing high-quality publications from desktop computers. When Paul Brainerd, president and founder of Aldus Corporation, coined the phrase, he envisioned an inexpensive desktop computer system that would perform most of the functions of expensive typesetting and layout. Desktop publishing is *page makeup* (typesetting and layout) at a moderate cost. It is the ability to do at your desk what you previously sent out to design, typesetting, and layout services or didn't have printed because of the high cost.

Two major advantages of desktop publishing are the reduced cost of producing quality publications and the ability to produce them in-house. The net result, in Brainerd's mind, is that the quality of business publications substantially improves.

Desktop publishing with PageMaker allows you to design a publication, add text, graphics, and *design elements* (lines, boxes, and so on), and then print it with a quality close to professional typesetting. PageMaker takes desktop publishing a step further by making the various functions relatively easy to learn and perform, thus allowing many more people to use it.

In producing a publication with PageMaker, you may use a laser printer for both typesetting and final printing, thereby completing the full publishing cycle on desktop equipment. Or, after completing the creation and page makeup with PageMaker, you can use a commercial typesetting machine or an imagesetter (which produces camera-ready text and graphics) and an offset printing press for the final steps. In both instances, you will be using desktop publishing for the critical creation and makeup functions. In the second case, for reasons of either quality or volume, you might chose to complete the process with traditional means. You will still save money and probably time, and will maintain greater control of the project.

Even though desktop publishing is easier and less expensive than traditional publishing, it still includes all the traditional steps. In that publishing involves the production of printed matter, it ranges from simple memos to letters, forms, reports, flyers, brochures, magazines, pamphlets, manuals, catalogs, directories, and complex, multivolume books. No matter how simple or complex the publication, it requires the same steps to produce. Obviously, the steps are more significant in some cases than in others.

The five steps are planning, design, content creation, page makeup, and printing. In the following paragraphs we'll look at each of these in detail.

PLANNING

Planning is concerned primarily with the content (in general terms), the schedule, and the budget. In planning, you determine what goes into a publication, who will perform the various tasks, how long each task will take, and how much the publication will cost. Planning a simple memo is easy: you have text on a single subject, you will write it yourself in a half hour, and the cost will be minimal. However, a monthly newsletter containing up to a dozen articles by different writers, with a number of illustrations and a fixed schedule and budget, can require substantial planning.

Planning a publication to be produced with PageMaker differs little from planning a publication to be produced with traditional techniques. In either case, the planning stage is very important. If, upon starting a publication, you pause to answer the questions of what, who, when, and how much, you will find the remaining publishing tasks much easier.

DESIGN

Once you have planned the content of a publication, you can determine how it will be displayed on the pages. Traditionally, this is the domain of the designer, whose objective is to produce a unique publication that is both attractive and easy to read. To achieve this, the designer considers all visual elements, from the overall appearance of the publication to the type size for subheadings. Elements to be considered include the size of the printed page, the number and size of columns, the typefaces and their sizes, the use and placement of design elements, and the style of titles, headings, subheadings, and captions.

Design can be broken down into a series of steps: establishing the design constraints, determining the master and regular page layouts, selecting the type, and determining the use of design elements. These steps are basically the same for both traditional and desktop publishing. Let's look at each.

Establishing Design Constraints

In the planning phase, you determined the budget and schedule constraints. Design constraints are of a physical nature, created primarily by the equipment used to produce the publication. For example, your typesetting machine or laser printer has a limited number of type styles and sizes. The printing press or laser printer used to print the publication is limited both in the size of paper it can handle and the area of the paper that can be printed upon (called the *image area*). To print a multipage publication, you may choose a large printing press on which several pages are printed together on a single large sheet. This sheet is then folded down to the individual page size and the folded edges trimmed off so that the pages can be turned. The size limitations of the folding and trimming machines determine the final page size (called the *trim size*). Finally, paper comes in predetermined sizes. If you design a publication larger than a standard size, you will have to print on the next larger size (probably more expensive) and then trim off the excess (also adding to the cost).

Your choice of desktop publishing hardware and software also influences your design options. In addition, if you use a laser printer for both typesetting and printing, you have one set of typeface, paper size, and image area constraints. If you use a commercial imagesetter and offset press, you have a second set of constraints. In any case, you must consider these requirements in your design.

Understanding the capabilities of your chosen production equipment is a mandatory first step in publication design. These constraints determine the parameters within which you design the publication. You will need to know these limits before you can proceed.

Determining the Master Page Layout

In designing a multipage publication, you want most, if not all, of the pages to reflect a common design. To do this with PageMaker, you design a *master page* (or pages) that contains the elements common to most pages. Among the common elements are page size, margins, number and size of columns, a layout grid of the margins and column edges, and the use of facing pages. Additionally, headers, footers, page number location, and common design elements, such as lines between columns, can be placed on the master page.

PAGE SIZE The first decision in designing a master page is the page size. The design constraints previously determined set the outer limits. Now, within those limits you

must determine the final page size. The standard 8.5 ×
11-inch letter size is often appropriate. However, paper size
does not necessarily constrain page size. You may want to
consider other sizes, depending on your publication and
how you will produce it. You may paste up several pieces to
create a single page (called *tiling*), or you may have several
pages on a single piece of paper. Both methods are shown
in Figure 1-1.

MARGINS   Once you know the page size, you can determine the image area. This is the area inside the margins of
a page in which you place the material to be printed. To
determine the image area, simply set the margins on the
four sides of the page—top, bottom, inside, and outside as
shown in Figure 1-2.

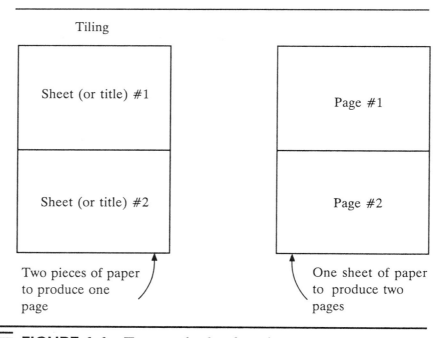

Tiling

Sheet (or title) #1

Sheet (or title) #2

Page #1

Page #2

Two pieces of paper
to produce one
page

One sheet of paper
to produce two
pages

FIGURE 1-1   Two methods of paging

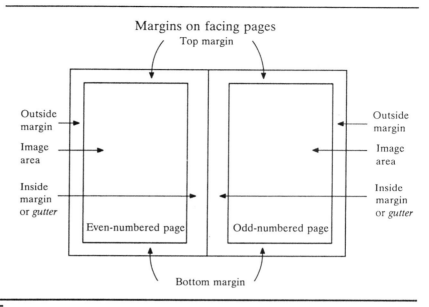

Margins on facing pages

Top margin

Outside margin

Image area

Inside margin or *gutter*

Even-numbered page

Outside margin

Image area

Inside margin or *gutter*

Odd-numbered page

Bottom margin

FIGURE 1-2   Locating the four margins

Again, the constraints of your equipment and software will influence your decision on margins. Other factors also play a part. For example, the type of page binding influences the inside margin or *gutter*. You can also use margins, such as a particularly large outside margin, as part of the distinctive style of the publication.

COLUMNS   Most newspapers, magazines, newsletters, and brochures, and even many books are designed with multiple columns per page because a narrower column is easier to read. In designing the master page, you determine the number and size of the columns that will appear on a page. PageMaker lets you create up to 20 columns per page; however, except for forms or special-purpose publications, you rarely will use more than three or four columns.

You also determine the amount of blank space between columns. A space of 1/4 inch or 6 millimeters is common, but there are no hard rules. Finally, you may have columns of equal or unequal size, depending on your needs and styling considerations. Figure 1-3 shows some examples.

LAYOUT GRID In building a master page, you automatically create a *layout grid*. This is a set of nonprinting dotted lines on the screen display of the page that will assist you in lining up text and graphics. The margins and column edges (referred to as *column guides* within PageMaker) form the foundation of the grid. In addition, you may add other

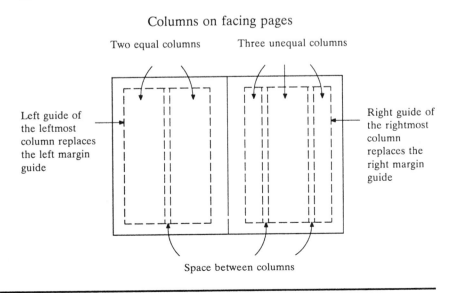

FIGURE 1-3 Columns and their components

nonprinting guides to assist in page makeup. For example, if you want all chapter heads to start on line 10, you can place a horizontal ruler guide there to remind you. Such a guide does not prevent you from placing text above line 10 on some pages.

FACING PAGES If you print on both sides of a page in a multipage publication, you will have facing pages — left and right pages beginning with pages 2 and 3. (See Figures 1-2 and 1-3.) You may want to create separate master pages in this situation to accommodate the differences between the left and right pages. For example, the left and right margins may need to be reversed because the inside margin, where the publication will be bound, is on the right side of the left page and the left side of the right page. Also a header, footer, or page number may be positioned toward the outside of each page, which is on opposite sides of facing pages.

Determining the Detail Page Layout

Once you've established the master page or pages, you lay out each regular page by customizing a master page layout. First, you make a mock-up of the publication by determining the length of the text and the size and number of photos or graphics. You create a *rough* of the publication by placing the text and graphics on each page as you want them. In PageMaker, you can use shading of various densities to represent text and graphics. You may create several roughs before settling on a final detailed layout. This final layout is called a *dummy* (or a *comp,* for comprehensive layout).

With PageMaker, you might want to use the actual text and graphics to create the roughs. Using the actual content is not much harder than placing shading, which is one advantage of desktop publishing.

Selecting Type

A major element in designing a publication is selecting the type to be used. You must consider not only the *typeface* or design of the type but also the *size, style* — whether it is light, roman (or medium), bold, or italic — and the spacing between letters (including *kerning*, which is removing space between certain letter pairs) and between lines (*leading*). Finally, you need to consider the alignment, or *justification,* of the type.

Whether you are doing traditional or desktop publishing, you must select a typeface, determine its size, style, spacing, and justification. The available typefaces depend upon the equipment you are using. You determine these when establishing the design constraints.

TYPEFACES You select a typeface because you like how it conveys your message to the reader. Your choice depends on the effects you want to achieve. Some typefaces are easier to read or more distinctive than others. Most designers believe that typefaces with small finishing strokes (called *serifs*) on the ends of the letters are easier to read in large blocks of text. A common example of such a face is Times. It and its derivatives are used in many newspapers, magazines, and books. A more modern typeface, without the extra strokes (called *sans serif*), can be very distinctive and clean looking. Sans serif typefaces, such as Helvetica, are commonly used in advertising and on business cards and stationery. The Apple LaserWriter, LaserWriter Plus, LaserWriter IINT, and LaserWriter IINTX all include Adobe Times and Adobe Helvetica typefaces. Figure 1-4 shows examples of these typefaces.

This is the Adobe Times typeface.
ADOBE TIMES adobe times
abcdefghijklmnopqrstuvwxyz
ABCDEFGHIJKLMNOPQRSTUVWXYZ
`1234567890-=[]\;',./~!@#$%^&*()_+{}|:"<>?

This is the Adobe Helvetica typeface
ADOBE HELVETICA adobe helvetica
abcdefghijklmnopqrstuvwxyz
ABCEDFGHIJKLMNOPQRSTUVWXYZ
`1234567890-=[]\;',./~!@#$%^&*()_+{}|:"<>?

FIGURE 1-4   Examples of Times and Helvetica typefaces

An individual publication should not have too many different typefaces. Three or four are normally considered the limit. This provides one face each for the text, titles, headings, and captions on charts or tables. Within a single typeface, you have the roman or medium weight, bold, and italic styles as well as varying sizes. Again, however, don't use too many sizes, or your publication will become hard to read. (The word *font* is frequently confused with the word typeface. A typeface is one particular design or face, independent of size or style; a font is a typeface of a given style, size, and orientation.)

TYPE SIZE Type size is measured in *points*. One point equals 1/72 inch. Points are measured from the top of the ascenders (the top of the letters "k" and "b," for example) to the bottom of the descenders (the bottom of the letters "p" and "y"). Using PageMaker 4 on the Macintosh with a PostScript printer, gives you access to type sizes from 4 to 650 points, in increments of 1/10 point. Normal text in books, newspapers, and newsletters ranges from 9 to 12 points, with titles and headlines in larger type, and some smaller "fine print." Selected examples of sizes from 6 to 72 points are shown in Figure 1-5.

HORIZONTAL SPACING The horizontal spacing of letters determines how long a line is. Line length is called the *column width* and is normally measured in either inches or *picas*. There are 6 picas to an inch and 12 points to a pica.

Horizontal spacing is a function of the size of individual letters and the spacing between them. Because almost all published material uses *proportionally spaced* typefaces (where a "w" takes more space than an "i"), letter size is the most important factor in spacing. Second, in addition to the normal spacing between words, extra space can be added between both letters and words to lengthen lines in order to align their right edges (*justifying* the lines). Space is often taken away between certain letter pairs to improve their appearance (called *kerning*). Kerning is a function of the typeface and case (upper or lower). For example, a lowercase "t" and "y" combination or an uppercase "A" and "W" combination can both be kerned to avoid awkward letter spacing that would otherwise be unattractive in certain typefaces. PageMaker includes a kerning table that automatically will kern problem pairs. In addition, Page-Maker allows manual kerning by which space can be added to or subtracted from any letter pair.

6-point type
8-point type
10-point type
12-point type
14-point type
18-point type
24-point type
36-point type
48-point type
60-point ty
72-point t

FIGURE 1-5 Selected examples of type sizes from 6 to 72 points

The extent of your concern with horizontal spacing depends on how you want your publication to read and look. Justifying your text (aligning it on both the left and right sides) may make it look better but it may not be easier to read. You can justify a line by adjusting the space only between words, or, to make the text look more professional, you can justify a line by adjusting the space between characters.

In PageMaker 4, several commands allow you to change the horizontal spacing of a line. First, if you are using a PostScript printer, you can adjust the width of a character from 1 to 250 percent of its normal (100 percent) width. This makes the character itself, not the space around it, wider or narrower as shown in Figure 1-6. Second, you can adjust the space between characters with six *tracking* settings, from very loose to very tight, as shown in Figure 1-7.

This is "Square" or 100% width of 24-point Times.

This is 70% width of 24-point Times.

This is 130% width of 24-point Times.

FIGURE 1-6   Character width

The tracking applied to this 12-point unjustified Times type is called "No Track."

The tracking applied to this 12-point unjustified Times type is called "Very Loose."

The tracking applied to this 12-point unjustified Times type is called "Loose."

The tracking applied to this 12-point unjustified Times type is called "Normal."

The tracking applied to this 12-point unjustified Times type is called "Tight."

The tracking applied to this 12-point unjustified Times type is called "Very Tight."

FIGURE 1-7 Tracking or spacing between characters

Third, PageMaker 4's new "Force justify" command can further change the horizontal spacing. (See the "Alignment" subsection that follows.)

Finally, you can adjust the range over which you are willing to let PageMaker automatically adjust the word and letter spacing when justifying or hyphenating a line. PageMaker automatically assigns its fonts a given (*default*) character and word spacing and uses its kerning table for the special spacing between certain pairs of characters. To justify a line or to provide for the grammatical hyphenation of a word, PageMaker may further adjust letter or word spacing. The limits within which it does this can be controlled. Word spacing can be set from 0 to 500 percent, 100 percent being the normal, default word spacing. Letter spacing can be set from -200 percent to 200 percent, 0 being the normal letter spacing.

VERTICAL SPACING The vertical spacing of lines of type is called *leading* (pronounced "ledding"). The term comes from the days of lead type when lead literally was added to the top and bottom of a line of type to adjust the spacing between lines. Today leading refers to the total height of a line from the top of the tallest characters in the line, to the top of the tallest characters in the line below. Leading, like type, is measured in points. Normally, leading is given in relation to the type size. For example, 10-point type with 11-point leading is described as 10/11 ("ten over eleven"). A 10/10 leading is really no leading; it is just the normal vertical spacing of a given font. As the leading increases, space is added between lines. For good readability of normal text, the leading should be one or two points greater than the type. PageMaker's "Auto" leading feature initially provides leading of 120 percent of the type size, such as 10/12 or 12/14. However, you can change the "Auto" leading percentage and manually specify leading in 1/10-point increments, including negative leading (such as 10/8), for special effects. Figure 1-8 shows examples of varying amounts of leading.

In PageMaker 4, you can choose the method of applying leading. There are two options: "Proportional" leading, with which proportional amounts of space are placed above the tallest ascender and below the lowest descender, and "Top of caps" leading, with which all of the space is placed

This is 10-point Times type with 10-point leading. It is called "10/10." Effectively this means that there is no leading.

This is 10-point Times type with 12-point leading. It is called "10/12." This is what PageMaker provides with its default "Auto" leading.

This is 10-point Times type with 14-point leading. It is called "10/14." The spread between the lines begins to look unattractive.

This is 10-point Times type with 8-point leading. It is called "10/8." This is "negative" leading, in which the lines begin to overlap.

FIGURE 1-8   Examples of 10/10, 10/12, 10/14, and 10/8 leading

below the lowest descender. This is demonstrated in Figure 1-9. Previous versions of PageMaker provided only proportional leading, which is also the traditional method of applying leading. "Top of caps" leading applies the same amount of space but does so in a way that is more easily measurable; there is a fixed point from which to measure — the top of capital letters.

ALIGNMENT   Text can be aligned on either the left or right margin, on both margins (*justified*), or in the center of the page (*centered*). Almost all text published in this country (except for titles, headings, and captions) is left-aligned.

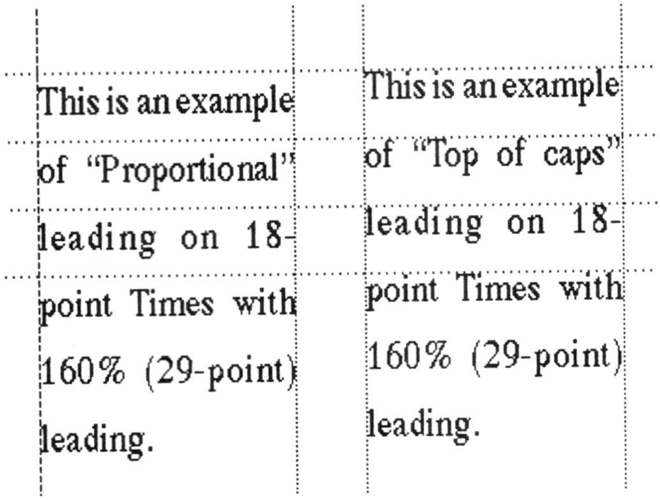

This is an example of "Proportional" leading on 18-point Times with 160% (29-point) leading.

This is an example of "Top of caps" leading on 18-point Times with 160% (29-point) leading.

FIGURE 1-9 "Proportional" vs. "Top of caps" leading

Because the Western eye is used to reading from left to right, left-aligned text is easier for us to read. Longer blocks of text prove easier to read when both the left and right margins are aligned. Right alignment and centering are used only in special circumstances, such as in titles and captions. PageMaker 4 has added the "Force justify" command to force the justification of the last line of a paragraph. Figure 1-10 shows examples of left-aligned, right-aligned, centered, justified, and force justified paragraphs.

Using Design Elements

The final step in the design process is to specify the use of design elements. These include the rules, boxes, rectangles,

This is an example of the normal letter
spacing and word spacing that PageMaker
uses with 12-point Times type that has been
left-aligned.

This is an example of the normal letter
spacing and word spacing that PageMaker
uses with 12-point Times type that has been
right-aligned.

This is an example of the normal letter
spacing and word spacing that PageMaker
uses with 12-point Times type that has been
centered.

This is an example of the normal letter spacing
and word spacing that PageMaker uses with
12-point Times type that has been justified.

This is an example of the normal letter spacing
and word spacing that PageMaker uses with
12-point Times type that has been force justi-
f   i   e   d

FIGURE 1-10 Types of alignment

and bullets that separate and emphasize the text. In traditional publishing, design elements are hand-drawn or
transferred from Zipatone (or dry transfer lettering) sheets
and are placed on the final, camera-ready copy. In desktop

publishing, and in PageMaker in particular, most of these elements are created with the computer on either the master or detailed page layouts.

Use design elements with caution. Lines, boxes, and bullets used appropriately are effective in enhancing the appearance and readability of a publication. Overuse or misuse, however, is distracting and can mar an otherwise good publication. The ease with which design elements are applied in the desktop publishing environment has sometimes led to their overuse.

CONTENT CREATION

The purpose of a publication is to disseminate the writing and graphics that make up its content. The planning and design work preceding content creation and the production steps following it only support the central functions of writing, drawing, and photographing the actual material. However, this book, which is about PageMaker, concerns primarily design and production. It addresses the creation phase only to the extent that text and graphics must somehow be brought into production. Therefore, the discussion of content creation is limited to considerations necessary for transferring text, graphics, and photos or other noncomputer-generated material, to the desktop publishing environment.

Generating Text

Almost all text to be published with PageMaker is first written on a word processor. The word processing files are then transferred to and used by PageMaker. But Page-Maker can also receive text directly from the keyboard. Let's look at both of these methods of generating text.

WORD PROCESSING PACKAGES There are considerable differences in how word processing packages code formatting information in their files. (Formatting information includes margins, indentations, carriage returns, tabs, and type specifications.) To be efficient, PageMaker must both read the files and pick up as much of the formatting information as possible. PageMaker does not handle all word processing packages, so check to see if yours produces files that PageMaker can use. As of this writing, Page-Maker 4 for the Macintosh can import text and preserve most of the formatting from Microsoft Word 1.05, 3, and 4, Microsoft Works 1 and 2, MacWrite II, WordPerfect for the Macintosh and WordPerfect 4.2, 5.0, and 5.1 for the PC, WriteNow, XyWrite III, and packages that can create either Rich Text Format (RTF) or DCA files. This list is constantly changing, so check the latest Aldus literature if your word processing package is not listed here. Page-Maker also supports ASCII (unformatted) text files.

To see how PageMaker interprets the formatting codes from your word processor, make a sample file in your word processor, using the formatting conventions you'll need. Do this before you begin to write. Then transfer the sample file to PageMaker to see how it handles the formatting conventions.

As you use the word processor, keep in mind the planned column width in PageMaker, as well as any unique characteristics you find in the sample file. You might use identical column widths in both the word processor and PageMaker to avoid problems. For example, a 1-inch indent in a 6-inch column might make sense in the word processor. However, a 1-inch indent in a 2-inch column would have to be decreased to look acceptable.

DIRECT ENTRY INTO PAGEMAKER For small amounts of text, such as captions, titles, and headings, direct keyboard entry into PageMaker is easier than using a word processor. This is especially convenient since you may not be aware of all the captions and other supporting text you'll need until you do the final page makeup. Using direct entry, you can place the text exactly where you want it, and PageMaker 4's new story editing features make direct text entry into PageMaker almost as easy as using a word processing program. On the other hand, with a word processor, captions, titles, and headings must be contained in several small files and placed individually or "cut" from a single file and then "pasted" in pieces around the publication.

Creating Graphics

In traditional publishing, figures or illustrations come from one of two sources: hand-drawn art and photographs. In both cases, they are produced separately from the text and must be pasted on during final page makeup. Desktop publishing still employs these two sources but can also use various forms of art (generically called *graphics*) from other sources. Art can be created with a computer and transferred directly to the desktop publication, and photographs and similar materials can be *scanned*—read by a machine that converts the image into computer-usable form—and imported as well.

Most graphics come into PageMaker in the size in which they were created. Once in PageMaker, they can be reduced or expanded to fit the space allocated. Drastically changing their size, however, affects the clarity of the final image. In PageMaker you can also *crop* (cut a side or sides from) a graphic to fit the allocated space. Although you cannot erase part of a graphic, you can cover it over or *mask* it with "Paper" colored shading. You can also use PageMaker's drawing tools to enhance the image.

A number of different types of Macintosh programs can be used to produce graphics within the computer. Page-Maker can directly read graphics disk files produced in four ways: *Paint-type* or bit-mapped graphics files, *draw-type* or object-oriented files, Encapsulated PostScript (EPS) files, and scanned images in the TIFF format. The following paragraphs will further describe each of these types of files.

PAINT-TYPE GRAPHICS Paint-type graphics create drawings with a series of dots, or *bits,* that are either turned on or off. On the screen, these bits, called *pixels,* are the smallest addressable unit. The number of pixels per square inch determines the clarity or *resolution* of what you see and depends on the type of display adapter and monitor that you have. On a laser printer, the quality of the final printed image varies with the number of dots per square inch that it prints. Most desktop laser printers currently print 300 dots per inch (*dpi*). Because of the difference in resolution between the screen (normally much less than 300 dpi) and printer, you probably will notice a difference in the clarity of the image.

Computer applications that generate paint-type graphics include DeskPaint, SuperPaint, and MacPaint. Use these applications for sketches and other freehand work that would traditionally be done by an artist or illustrator.

DRAW-TYPE GRAPHICS Draw-type graphics use drawing commands to create the image. One such command, for example, might be "draw a line between points A and B." Draw-type graphics are produced in the same way on both the screen and the printer. Consequently, the screen and printer images look very much alike.

Draw-type applications include Adobe Illustrator, Aldus Freehand, DeskDraw, and MacDraw. These applications are best used for precise, geometrical shapes, such as mechanical drawings and charts produced with a straight edge and compass, as well as many other forms of drawing.

ENCAPSULATED POSTSCRIPT (EPS) Encapsulated PostScript is a file format created by Adobe Systems that describes a graphic or text object using the PostScript language. Most graphics programs that can drive a PostScript printer also produce EPS files. EPS is really a special draw-type file format.

SCANNED IMAGES Scanned images are created by a scanner, which is a computer-peripheral device into or onto which an image is placed to produce the same image in the computer. Using a scanner, you can import images from drawings, as well as color or black-and-white photographs. The resolution of the image both on the screen and when printed depends on the capabilities of the scanner, your display card, and your printer. The scanned image is never as clear as the original photograph. Therefore, you may want to use scanned images only to create a dummy for sizing and placement and then have a commercial printer use the actual photo in the final printing. Higher resolution scanner files can be quite large, taking considerable disk space and slowing down printing. Consider using lower resolution files in scanning if the images are only for sizing a dummy.

Files produced by scanners must either use a Tag Image File Format (TIFF), a special format created for scanners, or be created through a compatible graphics application, such as DeskPaint or SuperPaint. Scanners that create files PageMaker can read include those produced by Apple, Canon, Datacopy, DEST, Hewlett-Packard, MicroTek, and Ricoh.

Linking Text and Graphics Files with PageMaker Files

Placing or importing a text or graphics file into a Page-Maker 4 publication automatically creates a link between the original text or graphics file and the PageMaker file on which you are working. This allows the PageMaker publication to reflect any changes made to the original document. It also requires that the original files remain accessible to the PageMaker file for as long as you want to maintain the link.

When you place a text file in a PageMaker publication, a complete copy of the text file is transferred to the Page-Maker file, and a link is automatically established with the original file. If the original file is changed, the PageMaker publication can automatically reflect the changes (with or without an alert that the change has taken place), or you can be notified that the original document has changed and then choose whether to include that change in the Page-Maker publication.

When you place a graphics file in a PageMaker publica-tion, you can choose whether to transfer the complete file to the publication. If you choose not to transfer the com-plete file, only a low resolution copy of the image is stored with the publication. This saves disk space and reduces PageMaker's processing time. On the other hand, if the PageMaker file cannot find the complete graphics file, you will not be able to print the graphics file at full resolution.

Files or parts of files that are pasted onto a PageMaker publication via the Clipboard from any file other than another PageMaker publication will not be linked to their original document. For files that are transferred from one PageMaker publication to another via the Clipboard, the original link, if any, will be transferred.

PAGE MAKEUP

Page makeup combines the traditional functions of typesetting and layout—the final two steps before printing. Typesetting is simply reproducing a manuscript with the correct fonts and spacing. Traditionally, the typeset manuscript is printed onto long sheets of photographic paper, called *galleys,* that are then cut and pasted onto finished pages; then photos and line drawings are added, followed by the design elements, headings, and page numbering. The layout process requires considerable skill and much patience—especially if major changes are introduced late in the process. With the advent of desktop publishing, this process is easier and requires less skill. Additionally, major changes can be handled with less effort.

Desktop publishing has also changed the order of the functions. Because the text is already in galley form when it comes from the word processor, in the first step of page makeup, you place the text and graphics onto the page layout. Then you select the desired type fonts (if this has not been done in the word processor). Finally, you adjust the layout and apply any remaining design elements.

Page makeup in a desktop publishing environment, then, has three subsidiary steps: placing text and graphics, font selection, and adding the finishing touches.

Placing Text and Graphics

At first you will probably spend most of your time in PageMaker placing text and graphics. How well you build the layout grid and create the text and graphics determines how easily the placement process goes. With experience, you can spend a greater proportion of your time planning and designing, rather than in this stage. Placing text and graphics, however, will always be a major part of desktop publishing, just as it is in traditional publishing.

In traditional publishing, you first pasteup text, leaving holes for the graphics. Then you pasteup the graphics. With desktop publishing, it is easier to first place and size the graphics and then to "flow" the text around them. We will be doing a fair amount of this in the chapters that follow. Therefore, we will delay discussing the methods and techniques for placing text and graphics until you can actually see the results as you build the publications.

Font Selection

Typesetting in traditional publishing requires retyping a manuscript into a typesetting machine. As the text is entered, the typesetter adds special commands to change fonts and type styles and to establish column widths and text indentation. Generally, the text is proofread both before and after it is typeset. With desktop publishing, the manuscript is typed only once into a word processor, so it needs to be proofread only once—before being transferred to PageMaker. Because in PageMaker column sizing is a part of page layout, it, too, isn't really a typesetting function in PageMaker. The only remaining typesetting task is to identify font changes—hence the change in terms to "font selection" for what is, in traditional publishing, all of typesetting.

Font selection is determining which typeface, size, and style to use and where. You may even be able to do this in your word processor. For example, with most word processors you can identify bold and italic styles. You should do as much formatting as you can in the word processor. You then will have less to do with the text in PageMaker, and the original word processing file will have most of the properties of the finished PageMaker publication.

POSTSCRIPT PageMaker on the Macintosh primarily works with PostScript-based printers and the fonts that are included with them. Most PostScript printers (including the Apple LaserWriter Plus, LaserWriter IINT, and Laser-Writer IINTX) include 11 typefaces and 35 typeface/style combinations. You often see these 35 typeface/style combinations referred to as 35 fonts, but as you read earlier, a font is a particular typeface and style as well as size and orientation. The 35 typeface/style combinations are comprised of eight typefaces (Avant Garde, Bookman, Courier, Helvetica, Helvetica-Narrow, New Century Schoolbook, Palatino, and Times) in four styles (medium or roman, bold, italic or *oblique,* and bold italic), and three typefaces (Symbol, Zapf Chancery, Zapf Dingbats) in one style each.

Three of the typefaces (Avant Garde, Helvetica, and Helvetica Narrow) are considered sans serif; the balance are serif designs.

All of the typeface/style combinations can be printed in any size from 4 to 650 points, in increments of 1/10th of a point. They can also be printed either vertically (portrait or "tall" orientation) or horizontally (landscape or "wide" orientation). There is, therefore, a very large number of fonts from which to choose when using most PostScript printers. In addition, you can utilize additional typefaces and styles stored on a disk connected either to your computer or to your printer. These are sometimes called soft fonts and can be transferred to the printer (*downloaded*) either manually or automatically. Adobe Systems, the creators of PostScript, offers many additional typefaces that can be downloaded, and a number of other firms, Bitstream in particular, offer many more. Soft fonts can take a lot of disk space, and downloading them at the time of printing can substantially add to your printing time. Appendix B, "Using Fonts and Laser Printers," explains more about these issues.

Adding the Finishing Touches

After you have placed the text and graphics and selected the type, you will need to make any corrections to the layout and add any final design elements. For example, you might want to emphasize your graphics with separating rules on the top and bottom.

This is the cleanup phase. You want to catch remaining errors, look for text or graphics improperly aligned, and, in general, correct any unsatisfactory aspect of the layout.

Look for pages that are "too busy," cluttered by too many design elements or different text treatments. The design should lead the reader's eye easily and effectively. If it doesn't do that, it isn't working.

Throughout the desktop publishing process, print your publication frequently to see how it looks. While you are adding the finishing touches, this becomes doubly important. You may have a WYSIWYG (what you see is what you get) screen image, but it is still almost impossible to visualize the final product without printing it several times.

PRINTING

Considering the amount of effort preceding it, printing is anticlimactic. If your final product is being produced on a laser printer, you simply choose the "Print. . ." command once more, perhaps increasing the number of copies. If you are printing the final product on a printing press, however, you must take the output of your laser printer or imagesetter to a printer and have it run off. In either case, there is little for you to do in the printing phase — it is the final step in creating your document. In desktop publishing, printing is important only in completing the publishing cycle.

The following chapters discuss each publishing step in greater depth as it relates to actually producing several publications. Before you get into the actual projects, let's briefly look at the Macintosh.

USING THE MACINTOSH AND ITS MOUSE

Introducing the Macintosh
The Macintosh Screen
Using the Mouse
Using Windows
Using the Scroll Bars
Using Menus

In this chapter, you will become acquainted with some of the essentials of the Apple Macintosh and you will learn to use and manipulate the mouse. You may never use all of the features and tools available on the Macintosh. By becoming familiar with some of them, however, you will begin to discover the additional capabilities that PageMaker has in the Macintosh environment.

This chapter is more a tutorial than the rest of the book. It proceeds more slowly in order to establish a common ground for using this book, the Macintosh, and PageMaker. If you are already familiar with using the Macintosh and the mouse, simply scan the chapter to verify that your use of a term or a procedure is the same as that used here.

INTRODUCING THE MACINTOSH

The Macintosh offers a standard environment for all of the programs or *applications* that run on it. This environment consists chiefly of a standard screen display or *visual interface,* which you use to communicate with Macintosh applications. Once you have learned to use the Macintosh interface, you'll find that working with PageMaker is very similar to working with various other applications. Page-Maker was originally designed, in fact, for the Apple Macintosh and takes full advantage of the Macintosh environment.

The Macintosh environment also provides a means of transferring information among applications, such as from MacWrite or DeskPaint to PageMaker. Through this feature, called the *Clipboard,* you can move graphics and text into PageMaker. (As you'll learn in Chapter 5, "Creating a Brochure," PageMaker offers various ways of transferring information with other applications.)

The quickest way to learn about the Macintosh and the mouse is to start using them. If you've not already done so, turn on your computer now, and let's get started.

If you have not already installed the System software on your Macintosh, refer to the Macintosh *Open Me First* portfolio and the *System Software User's Guide* for instructions. When you have completed the installation of the System software, and have all parts of your Macintosh connected and running, return here.

THE MACINTOSH SCREEN

When you turn on your computer, you'll notice that the first Macintosh screen that you see (Figure 2-1) has several standard features that will appear in most Macintosh screens. The top line, called the *menu bar,* contains the names of the menus that are currently available to you. Each *menu* provides a list of options from which you will choose, that tell the computer what to do next and how to do it. The set of menus displayed in the menu bar will vary, depending on the application you are currently using and what you are doing.

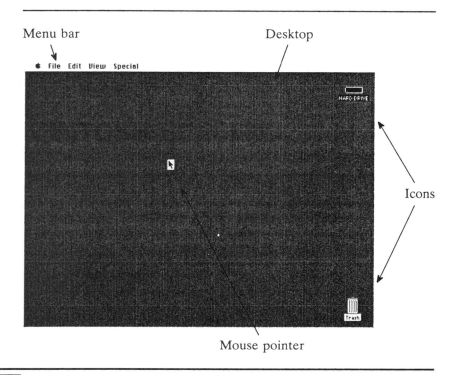

FIGURE 2-1   The Macintosh startup screen

The area below the menu bar is called the *desktop*. The item or items on which you are currently working, such as a letter, a drawing, or a PageMaker publication, will be displayed on the desktop.

On the right side of the desktop are two *icons,* small graphic representations of Macintosh Features. In Figure 2-1, the icons represent the startup disk drive and the trash can that you will use to dispose of files and folders. Your disk drive may be a *hard drive,* a sealed metal disk drive storing large amounts of information, or a *floppy drive,* which contains a removable, flexible plastic disk in a hard plastic case. PageMaker 4 must be installed on a hard drive. Finally, in the center of the screen is the *mouse pointer.* This shows you where the mouse is currently pointing.

USING THE MOUSE

You use the *mouse* to move the pointer on the screen. You can *select* an object by moving the mouse, pointing *on* an object—placing the mouse pointer on top of the object— and clicking the mouse button. Using the pointer in this way allows you to choose, for example, an option on a menu. While there are mice on the market with more than one button, all of the discussion in this book concerns the Macintosh mouse that has only one button. Practice moving the mouse as follows:

1. Place your hand on the mouse. The rectangular button should be under your fingers with the cord leading away from you.

2. Move the mouse across a flat surface, such as a table or desk, without pressing the button and watch the pointer

move on the screen. If you run out of room while moving the mouse, simply pick it up and place it where there is more room. Experiment with this now. Move the mouse to the edge of your work surface, then pick it up and place it in the middle of your surface, and move it again. Watch how the pointer continues from where the mouse was picked up.

Mousing Around

This book uses the following terminology to guide you in using the mouse:

Term	Action
Press	Hold down the mouse button
Release	Quit pressing the mouse button
Point on	Move the mouse until the tip of the pointer is on top of the item you want to select
Click	Quickly press and release the mouse button once
Double-click	Press and release the mouse button twice in rapid succession
Drag	Hold down the mouse button while you move the mouse (to move the highlight bar within a menu to the desired option, to move an object on the desktop, or to highlight contiguous text that you want to delete, move, or copy)

Select   Point on an item and press the mouse
                          button

Choose   Drag the pointer (and the correspond-
                          ing highlight bar) to a menu option and
                          release the mouse button

Practice using the mouse to perform some of the following actions:

1. *Point on* the Trash icon by moving the mouse (and the
   corresponding pointer) until the pointer is resting on it.

2. *Select* the Trash icon by *clicking*—quickly pressing and
   releasing the mouse button while pointing—on it. The
   Trash icon will become dark, indicating that it is selected.

3. *Drag* the Trash icon to the center of the screen by
   pointing on it and pressing and holding the mouse button while moving the mouse until the pointer and the
   icon move to the center of the screen, as shown in
   Figure 2-2.

4. *Drag* the Trash icon back to the lower right-hand corner.

5. *Click* on the HARD DRIVE icon. It will become dark,
   indicating that you have selected it, and the Trash icon
   will become light, indicating that you have deselected it.

6. *Double-click* (click twice in rapid succession) on the
   HARD DRIVE icon. A window will open to display the
   contents of the disk, as shown in Figure 2-3.

It sometimes takes a a couple of tries to get the rhythm
of double-clicking. A frequent problem is that people
double-click too slowly. In the Control Panel, discussed
later in this chapter, you can adjust the speed of double-
clicking.

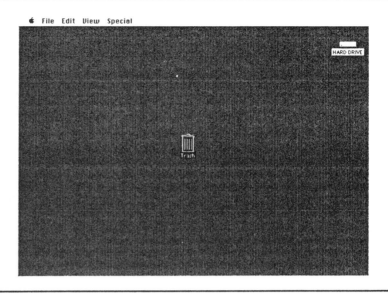

FIGURE 2-2   Trash icon moved to the center of the screen

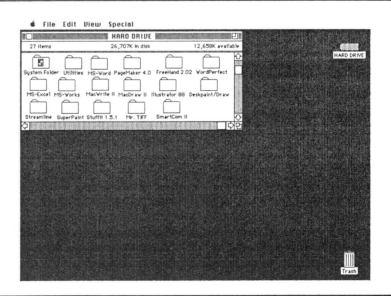

FIGURE 2-3   HARD DRIVE window opened

USING WINDOWS

A *window* is an area of the screen that you use for a specific purpose. It may momentarily display a piece of information, be your primary work space for several hours, or provide an interface (dialog box) through which you describe how you want something done.

To view the features of Macintosh windows:

1. Double-click on the Trash icon. A Trash window will open to display the contents of the trash. As shown in Figure 2-4, this window contains several features that are common to most windows.

At the top of the window is the *title bar*. In the center of the title bar is the name of the window, generally the same as the name of the icon from which it was opened. On the left end of the title bar is the *close box*. By clicking on the

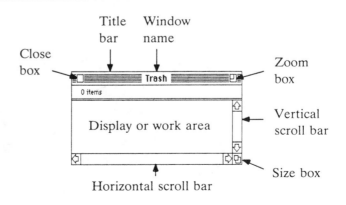

FIGURE 2-4 The Trash window

close box you can close the window. On the right end of the title bar is the *zoom box*. By clicking once on the zoom box you can enlarge or shrink the window. In the bottom right corner of the window is the *size box*. By dragging on the size box you can make the window any size you want. The bars above and to the left of the size box are the vertical and horizontal *scroll bars*. By using the scroll bars you can move or scroll the display area of the window.

Practice using some of the common window features now:

2. Click on the zoom box in the upper right corner. The window will expand to fill the majority of the screen.

3. Click on the zoom box again and the window will shrink to its original size.

4. Point anywhere on the title bar except in the close or zoom boxes. Press and hold the mouse button while moving the mouse away from you to move the window up to the middle of the screen. Release the mouse button. This is called *dragging the window.*

5. Point on the size box. Press and hold the mouse button while moving the mouse toward the lower right until the window fills the intervening space. Release the mouse button. This kind of dragging is called *sizing the window.*

6. Drag the size box back toward the upper left corner to make the window smaller.

7. Practice dragging the size box and sizing the window in many different sizes. Note that you can drag the size box up, down, left, and right as well as in any 45° diagonal direction. Be sure the window is fairly small when you have finished practicing.

8. Practice dragging the window around the screen by dragging on the title bar. Be sure the window partially overlaps your HARD DRIVE window when you have finished practicing.

9. Click anywhere on the HARD DRIVE window. Notice that the lines disappear from the title bar of the Trash window and appear in the title bar of the HARD DRIVE window. This means that the HARD DRIVE window has been selected and the Trash window deselected. When selected, the HARD DRIVE window also will overlap the Trash window.

10. Click anywhere on the Trash window. It will be selected, and the HARD DRIVE window will be deselected. Notice that the scroll bars also disappear from the HARD DRIVE window when it is deselected.

11. Click on the close box of the Trash window. The Trash window will close and will disappear into the Trash icon.

12. Double-click on the Trash icon to open the Trash window again. Notice how it returns in the exact size and at the same location on the screen that it occupied when you closed it.

13. Click on the close box to close the Trash window again.

USING THE SCROLL BARS

A Macintosh window is just that—an opening through which you can see something displayed. If what is displayed is very small, a small window will adequately display it all.

If what is displayed is very large, the largest window you can create (one that covers the entire screen) will not be large enough to display it all. In that case, you can horizontally or vertically move or *scroll* what the window contains.

Imagine that you are reading a billboard by looking through a stationary knothole close to the billboard. You must move the billboard from left to right to read a full line on it, and you must move the billboard from top to bottom to read all of the lines. The scroll bars perform the same function for a Macintosh window. The scroll bars move the *area being displayed* (not the window itself) up or down (vertically), or left or right (horizontally).

Each of the two scroll bars has three mechanisms for moving the area being displayed. First, there are the four *scroll arrows*. By clicking on one of the scroll arrows, you can move the display area in the direction of the arrow by a small increment. Second, there are the two square *scroll boxes*. By dragging a scroll box you can move the display area by a corresponding, proportional amount. Third, there are the scroll bars themselves. By clicking on the scroll bars (in areas other than the scroll arrows or scroll boxes), you can move the display area, in the direction corresponding to where you clicked, by a larger increment than you can move it with the scroll arrows.

Use the following instructions to practice using the scroll bars:

1. You can reduce the size of the HARD DRIVE window to that shown in Figure 2-5 by dragging on the size box.

2. Click on the down scroll arrow. Notice that the display area moves up, showing you the information below that previously shown. Notice, also, that the scroll box has moved down in the scroll bar.

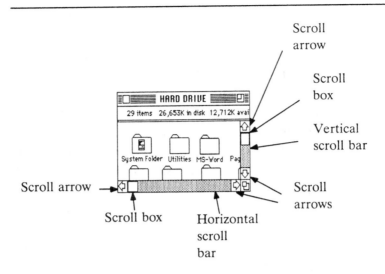

FIGURE 2-5   The HARD DRIVE window (sized small)

The position of the scroll box in the scroll bar represents the approximate position of the area displayed within the overall area. When the vertical scroll box is at the top of its scroll bar, you are looking at the top of the overall area. When the horizontal scroll box is at the left end of its scroll bar, you are looking at the left edge of the overall area. When both scroll boxes are in the middle of their scroll bars, you are looking at the middle of the overall area.

3. Click on the down scroll arrow several times until the scroll box is at the bottom of the vertical bar.

4. Click on the right scroll arrow several times until the scroll box is at the far right of the horizontal scroll bar.

5. Click on the up scroll bar, above the scroll box, until the scroll box is at the top of the vertical scroll bar.

6. Drag the horizontal scroll box a small amount toward the middle of the scroll bar. Note how this allows you to move the display area in very small increments.

The three scrolling mechanisms give you three levels of control. Clicking on the scroll bar moves the display area the furthest; dragging the scroll box can move the display area in the smallest and most precise increments; and clicking on the scroll arrows moves the display area a small to intermediate amount.

Manipulating windows—by selecting, dragging, opening, closing, zooming, sizing, and scrolling—is one of the two primary functions of the Macintosh environment. Practice these techniques until they are second nature. You will use them often. The second primary function of the Macintosh enviroment is the use of menus.

USING MENUS

Menus are the main path through which you give your Macintosh instructions. By making a choice on a menu, you give the computer a command. You will have access to different menus depending on what you are doing. You are currently at the System level, since you are not using an application such as PageMaker. Now you will take a look at the System menus and use one to create a new folder. There are five System menus: File, Edit, View, Special, and the Apple menu.

The File Menu

The File menu allows you to perform tasks related to files and the folders that contain them. A *folder* is a handy way

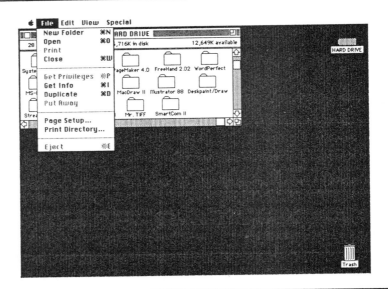

FIGURE 2-6 The File menu

of collecting and organizing *files,* in much the same way that paper file folders are used to gather together several documents or pieces of documents. Folders help you organize your work by giving you a single place to look for a file on a given subject. You can create new folders with the File menu. Use the following instructions to create a new folder to contain the files you will create in this book, if you have not already done so from Appendix A.

1. Select the File menu by first pointing on the word "File" in the menu bar.

2. Press and hold the mouse button. The File menu will open from the menu bar, as shown in Figure 2-6.

3. While still holding the mouse button to keep the File menu open, drag the highlight bar in the File menu until "New Folder" is highlighted, as shown here:

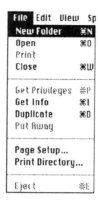

4. Release the mouse button. An "Empty Folder" will be created, as shown by the dark "Empty Folder" icon here:

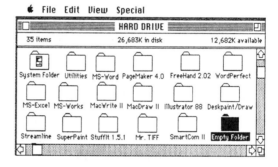

(If your HARD DRIVE window is too small, drag the size box until you can see the empty folder icon.)

By highlighting a menu option and releasing the mouse button, you have made a menu selection and have chosen whatever that option does. By selecting the "New Folder" option of the File menu, you have told the Macintosh to create a new folder for you.

 Making a menu selection in error is generally not catastrophic. If the action could be catastrophic, the Macintosh asks you if you are sure you want what you have selected. If you say no, the action will not occur.

On the File menu, some options are dark and others faint and hard to read. Only the dark options are currently available. The faint options are only available under certain circumstance. For example, the "Print" option is only available when a file that can be printed is selected.

In addition to creating new folders, the file menu also allows you to "Open" and "Close" files, folders, or icons. Choosing "Open" after having selected a file, folder, or icon is the same as double-clicking on it. As you have seen, when you open an icon or folder, you create a window with the same name as the icon or folder, and the contents of the icon or folder are displayed. When you open a file, the computer tries to *execute*—that is, display or run—the file. If the file contains a program like PageMaker, the program will be started and you use that application. If the file is a data file produced by a particular program, such as a Page-Maker *publication,* the associated program will be started and the data file then opened by the program. Choosing "Close" from the File menu has the same effect as clicking on the close button of a window.

Other File menu options allow you to "Print," and to "Get Info" about or "Duplicate" files and folders. Some menu options, such as "Page Setup. . ." and "Print Direc-tory. . .", have an ellipsis (. . .) following them. This means that when you select that menu option, a window called a *dialog box* will open. You then use that window to supply additional information, such as the number of copies to be printed, so that the option can be carried out. Only the first four File menu options are relevant to PageMaker. If you need further information about them, refer to the *System Software User's Guide* or the other Macintosh reference manuals.

The Edit Menu

The Edit menu provides the means of working with the Clipboard. The Clipboard is a holding place for text or graphics that you want to copy from one place to another, or that you want to remove ("Cut") from one location and put ("Paste") in another location. The "Copy," "Cut," and "Paste" options provide these functions. The Clipboard can hold only one piece of text or one graphic at a time. Therefore, if you try to place two pieces on the Clipboard, the first item will be replaced by the second. You can delete an item without affecting the contents of the Clipboard with the "Clear" option or the DELETE or BACKSPACE key.

The Edit menu also lets you look at the contents of the Clipboard, "Select All" of the items in a set—all the folders in the HARD DRIVE window, for example—and most importantly, to "Undo" the last operation you performed. Look at how some of the Edit menu options are used, and change the name of your new folder with these steps:

1. Open the Edit menu by pointing on the word "Edit" in the menu bar and pressing and holding the mouse button. The Edit menu will open, as shown here:

2. While still holding the mouse button, drag the highlight down to "Show Clipboard," then release the mouse button. The Clipboard window will open as shown in Figure 2-7.

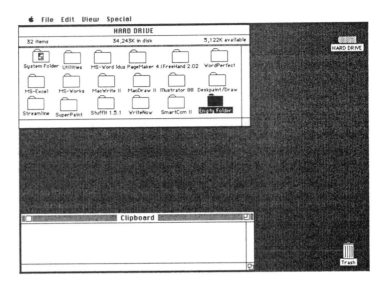

FIGURE 2-7 The Clipboard window

3. Click on the "Empty Folder" icon so it is again selected. It will become darker than the other folders.

4. Place the mouse pointer on the words "Empty Folder." Notice that the mouse pointer changes to an *I-beam* while it is in the text box. An I-beam is used to work with text and is conveniently shaped to fit between characters.

5. Select the Edit menu again and choose "Cut." The words "Empty Folder" will disappear from HARD DRIVE window and will appear on the Clipboard shown in Figure 2-8.

6. Select the Edit menu again, and choose "Paste." The words "Empty Folder" reappear under the icon in the HARD DRIVE window and are still on the Clipboard.

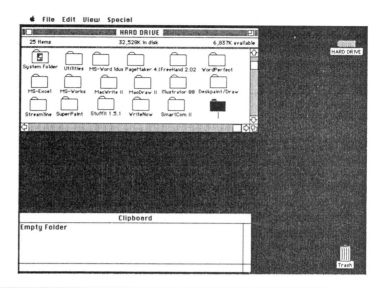

FIGURE 2-8 "Empty Folder" cut from new folder and placed on Clipboard

7. Select the Aldus "PageMaker 4.0" folder by clicking on it in the HARD DRIVE window. Select the Edit menu again and choose "Copy." The words "Aldus Page-Maker 4.0" will replace "Empty Folder" in the Clipboard and will remain in the text area of the Page-Maker folder.

8. Select the "Empty Folder" icon from the HARD DRIVE window again and, from the Edit menu, choose "Clear." The words "Empty Folder" will disappear from the folder and will not appear on the Clipboard.

9. From the Edit menu, choose "Undo." The words "Empty Folder" appear again below the icon in the HARD DRIVE window. (The "Undo" function works only if you want to undo the very last thing you did.)

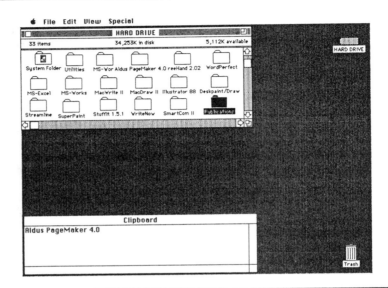

FIGURE 2-9   Folder renamed Publications

10. From the Edit menu, again choose "Clear."

    Notice that in the space below the "Empty Folder" icon, there is now a blinking vertical line. This is called the *insertion point*. The insertion point is where any characters you type will be placed.

11. Type **Publications** and see how the characters appear next to the insertion point in the space below the "Empty Folder" icon. Your screen should now look like that shown in Figure 2-9.

12. Select the Edit menu. Notice, as shown in the following menu, that the word "Undo" is now faint. You cannot undo the "Clear" comand because you have since performed an operation by typing the word "Publications."

13. Click on the Clipboard window to select it, and then, from the File menu, choose "Close." The Clipboard window will disappear.

Even though you can no longer see the Clipboard, it is still functioning. Text or graphics that you "Cut" or "Copy" will go to the Clipboard, and anything on the Clipboard can be transferred to the currently selected item by using the "Paste" option.

The View Menu

The View menu allows you to vary the way the contents of a folder are displayed. Open the View menu and look at the options.

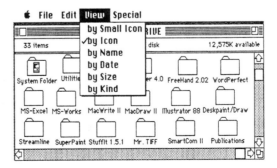

The default View menu options represent files and folders "by Icon," indicated by the check mark beside it. You have seen this in the previous figures throughout this chapter. There are two other methods of display. One of them, "by Small Icon," displays the icon and its name on the same line, as shown here:

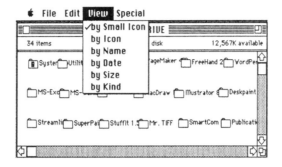

The other display alternative is to list contents in one of four sort orders: "by Name," as shown in Figure 2-10, "by

FIGURE 2-10   Content view sorted by name

Date," "by Size," and "by Kind." You may want to choose each of these views and look at them on your own. Each of the views serves a unique purpose, and you will probably find that eventually you will use them all.

The Special Menu

The Special menu provides several system-related options, as shown here:

The most important of the Special menu options is "Shut Down," which, as you probably know, turns off your Macintosh. Another important option in the Special menu is "Set Startup." Choose "Set Startup" now and look at its dialog box.

1. Select the Special menu and choose "Set Startup." This dialog box will open:

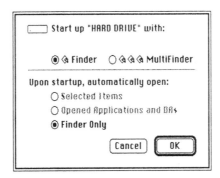

The primary purpose of the "Set Startup" option is to switch between the "Finder" and the "MultiFinder" options. The Finder and the MultiFinder are programs within the *Macintosh Operating System.* The Macintosh Operating System is a combination of programs that is standard with your Macintosh and provides the basic set of instructions that start and shut down your computer, move files to and from the disk drives, manage the desktop, load and close other applications, and move data between them, and many other functions. An operating system is the foundation set of programs without which nothing else would operate on your computer.

The Finder and MultiFinder are the components of the operating system that load other applications, control the switching between applications, and control the desktop. The primary difference between the Finder and the Multi-Finder is that with the Finder you can run only one application (such as PageMaker) at a time, while with the MultiFinder you can run several applications at a time. With the MultiFinder in use, the Macintosh Operating System is called a *multitasking operating system,* which means it can handle several tasks at the same time.

There are two reasons to run more than one application at a time. First, if you have some process that the computer can run by itself, such as printing or sorting a large file, you can run this process while performing other tasks that require your attention. The second reason for multitasking is to make it easier to switch often between two or more programs. In Chapter 6, "Generating an Annual Report," you will be transferring three tables and four charts from Excel to PageMaker, using the Clipboard. With the Finder, you must load and close both Excel and PageMaker (as well as their files) seven times to accomplish this transfer.

With the MultiFinder and both applications running, you only need to click first on one and then on the other applications window to switch back and forth — significantly less effort.

The penalty for MultiFinder is that it takes a lot of memory. To handle running both Excel and PageMaker in Chapter 6 you need 4 MB (roughly four million characters) of memory. But, with the cost of memory dropping rapidly, this is not a large penalty, and the feature is well worth the attendant cost.

If you have enough memory, turn on the MultiFinder. To do that:

2. Click on "MultiFinder" in the Startup dialog box.

3. Click on "OK" to close the dialog box.

When you change from the Finder to the MultiFinder, you must restart the system to effect the change. You could do this by choosing "Shut Down" from the Special menu and then pressing the POWER ON key. The Special menu also has an option called "Restart" for this very purpose.

4. Choose "Restart" from the Special menu.

Your computer will shut down and then automatically restart in the normal way. When the loading has completed, your screen will look as it did when you exited it except that the MultiFinder icon will appear in the upper right corner, as shown in Figure 2-11. When you have several applications running under MultiFinder, you can switch between them in three ways: by clicking on their respective windows, by clicking on the MultiFinder icon, or

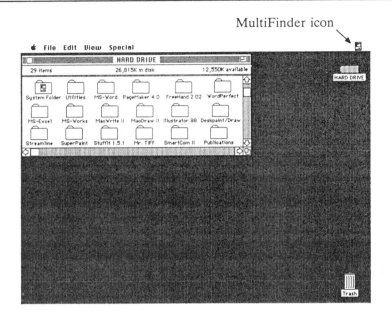

FIGURE 2-11 With MultiFinder active

by clicking on the application name shown in the Apple menu, which you will see in a moment. The MultiFinder is a significantly useful tool. Get to know it.

The other options in the Special menu are not pertinent to PageMaker and so are left to your own research.

The Apple Menu

The final menu in the Macintosh environment, the Apple menu, is far from the least significant. As you can see in Figure 2-12, the Apple menu, as it is displayed while Multi-Finder is active, displays all the applications currently running. You can choose a different application simply by dragging the highlight to it and releasing the mouse button.

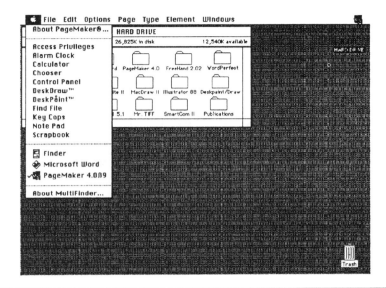

FIGURE 2-12 The Apple menu

The Apple menu also lists *desk accessories* (or *DAs*). Desk accessories are small applications that are available at any time, independent of what else you are running. Obvious desk accessories include the "Alarm Clock," "Calculator," and "Note Pad." Not so obvious and more important to PageMaker is the "Chooser." You use the Chooser to identify the printer you want to use and to connect to or disconnect from an AppleTalk network.

For PageMaker to print, you must first identify the printer you want to use with the Chooser. Do that now with the following instructions:

1. Select the Apple menu and choose "Chooser." The Chooser window will open.

In the list box on the left are the icons for the various devices for which programs have been installed on your computer. These programs are called *device drivers* and are necessary in order to use the device. The list box on the right is for a list of the physical devices connected to your computer. When you select a device driver, this box will display a list of devices from which you can select.

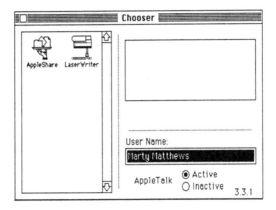

To make your selection, follow these steps:

2. Select (click on) the device driver that you want to use for printing, from the list on the left.

3. Select the actual device from the list on the right. If you are using LaserWriter IINT, your Chooser window will look like this:

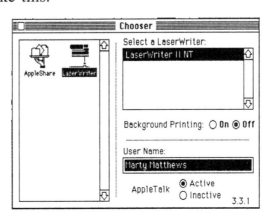

4. Click on the close box in the Chooser window to close the window and record your settings.

The other desktop accessories, especially the "Control Panel," can be very useful. In the "Control Panel," you can vary the double-click speed, the volume of the beep, the colors used on a color monitor, and many other defaults. Because they do not have a direct relationship to Page-Maker, they will not be explored here. You may want to explore them on your own.

You have just had a brief tour of the Macintosh. You should now understand enough of the environment in which PageMaker operates to get started with a project. In Chapter 3, you will use PageMaker to build the first solution.

GETTING STARTED WITH A FLYER

Planning and Designing the Flyer
Starting PageMaker
Creating the Layout
Entering the Text
Constructing the Border
Cleaning Up and Printing

In this chapter you will use PageMaker to create a flyer, the most basic of advertising pieces. This will give you an opportunity to review the basic functions of PageMaker before proceeding to more advanced features. The purpose of a flyer is to inform people about a subject as succinctly as possible. A flyer is rarely longer than one page, although it may be printed on both sides. The flyer you will create here is the one-page, single-sided publication shown in Figure 3-1.

There are many different ways to create a flyer, from writing it by hand to printing it in four colors. Here you will

CREATIVE
DESIGNS

Creative Designs specializes in the design, production, and promotion of all forms of printed material.

Creative Designs uses the latest in computer technology to design the initial layouts, typeset the necessary copy, and perform the final page composition. We then use the latest in four-color presses and bindery equipment to produce the highest quality publications obtainable. In addition, we have extensive direct mail marketing and fulfillment services available.

Creative Designs can assist you with any of the following:

- BOOKS
- MANUALS
- BROCHURES
- NEWSLETTERS
- BUSINESS PLANS
- ANNUAL REPORTS
- BUSINESS FORMS
- FLYERS
- POSTERS
- CATALOGS
- PAMPHLETS
- NEWSPAPERS
- PRESENTATIONS
- MAILING LABELS
- OR ANYTHING THAT CAN BE PRINTED

Call us at 1-800-555-5000 (nationwide) or stop in at our new plant at 1900 Westwind Avenue, Oceanside, WA 98999.

FIGURE 3-1 The printout of the finished flyer

produce a single-color flyer with a shaded rectangular border and a line across it. Also, you will use three fonts to produce the text (or *copy*).

PageMaker is an excellent tool for building a flyer because you can create the complete publication without using other applications. You can draw the rectangle, apply the shading, draw the line, and produce the copy in three fonts all within PageMaker. You could produce the copy in a word processor and then place that copy on the flyer using PageMaker; however, it is easier to produce a small amount of copy within PageMaker, especially because it saves having to switch between applications.

PLANNING AND DESIGNING THE FLYER

Because the flyer is fairly simple, planning it is also simple and straightforward. You will be able to produce the flyer in a couple of hours. Except for your time and the overhead associated with using the computer, your only direct cost is the printing. If you print multiple copies of the flyer on a laser printer, the cost will be five to seven cents per page, depending on how you amortize the printer. That is fairly expensive for larger volumes. If you want to print several thousand copies, you can take your laser-printed master page to a commercial printer and have it printed on an offset press for considerably less cost per page.

The design is not very complex either. Your design constraints are the limitations of the fonts and page sizes that are available with your printer (assumed here to be a LaserWriter IINT). These are not absolute limitations; however, for this flyer, the 8.5 × 11-inch page size and the fonts, available on a LaserWriter IINT, are adequate. Because you have a single page, you will not design a master page. The regular page design will include a shaded, rounded-corner rectangle and a page-wide horizontal line. The text, basic information about the capabilities and products of a hypothetical company, consists of a company name, a descriptive body, and a bulleted list of products. The company name will be 60-point Avant Garde-Demi Oblique (bold italic) with 66 points of *leading* (spacing between lines). The body text will be 12-point Palatino-Roman (medium weight), with PageMaker's automatic leading (12/14.5). The bulleted list of products will be 18-point Avant Garde-Demi (bold), again with automatic leading (18/21.5).

Once you have planned and designed the flyer, your primary remaining tasks are to create the text and make up the page. Before beginning the actual work on the flyer, however, we'll first start PageMaker and take a brief look at its menus and other facilities.

STARTING PAGEMAKER

When you've installed PageMaker, you will have a folder on your hard drive called Aldus PageMaker 4.0 that contains the PageMaker programs. If you followed the suggestions in Chapter 2, "Using the Macintosh and Its Mouse," you also will have created a folder called "Publications" to hold the publications produced using this book. The instructions in this and the remaining chapters assume that such a folder has been created.

 If you have not installed PageMaker, turn to Appendix A, "Installing and Starting PageMaker," and follow the instructions to complete the installation.

Use your normal method of starting your computer and starting PageMaker. (If needed, refer again to the discussion in Appendix A.) Now that you are in PageMaker, let's explore the menus before beginning on the flyer.

Exploring PageMaker's Menus

The initial PageMaker desktop screen, shown in Figure 3-2, uses the standard Macintosh format that you saw in Chapter 2. At the top of the screen is the menu bar with the Apple menu icon on the left and PageMaker's seven menu names to the right. Below the menu bar is the desktop,

FIGURE 3-2 The PageMaker desktop

where the publication window with the item that you are working on, is displayed.

The seven PageMaker menus allow you to direct Page-Maker to do what you want. The menus function as they do in other Macintosh applications. You select a menu by pointing on it with the mouse pointer, and then pressing the mouse button. You choose a menu option by holding the mouse button down, dragging the pointer until the menu option you want is highlighted, and then releasing the button. You can use shortcut keys to invoke some of the menu options, as you will learn later in this chapter.

In the following paragraphs, we'll discuss each of the menus and many of the shortcut keys. As you read, select the menu being discussed and view it on your own screen. Notice that some options appear in solid letters, while others are lighter or *dithered.* You can choose only the solid options. The lighter options are available only under certain circumstances (for example, "Save" can be chosen only if a publication is active in the window), and they will change from light to solid when you are able to use them. The individual options will be explained as they are used. Here they are simply introduced. (Appendix F, "Menu Options and Keyboard Commands," provides a detailed listing of each menu option and its corresponding shortcut key, as well as the many other keyboard commands available in PageMaker.)

FILE MENU The File menu contains the standard Macintosh options "New. . .," "Open. . .," "Close," and "Print. . ." to create a new publication, to open or close an existing one, or to print a publication. Note, however, that in PageMaker these commands refer to publications rather than folders. In addition, the PageMaker File menu includes "Save" to save publications, "Save as. . ." to name or rename a publication while saving it, "Revert" to load the last saved copy of the publication currently in the publication window, "Export..." to save a text file from a publication as a word processing file, "Place..." to pick up text or graphics created outside of PageMaker, "Links..." to reconnect or set options for the links joining a PageMaker publication with the text and graphic files that built it, "Book..." to group several publications into a book, "Page setup..." to establish primary page parameters such as size and margins, and "Quit" to both close a publication and exit PageMaker.

The "New...," "Open...," "Save," "Place...," "Links..." "Print...," and "Quit" options have shortcut keys, which are shown in the menu as the COMMAND key symbol and the characters N, O, S, D, =, P, or Q, respectively. To use these shortcut keys, press and hold the COMMAND key while simultaneously pressing an n, o, s, d, =, p, or q. In this book these commands are represented as COMMAND + N, COMMAND + O, COMMAND + S, COMMAND + D, COMMAND + =, COMMAND + P, and COMMAND + Q. (The plus sign means to continue holding the key on the left while pressing the key on the right.)

EDIT MENU The Edit menu has the standard Macintosh options "Cut," "Copy," "Paste," and "Clear" to remove, copy, move, and delete selected text or graphics. The short-cut keys for these options, COMMAND + X, C, V, or DELETE, are the same as they are in the Macintosh system. In addition, if you have an extended keyboard, the F2 can be used for "Cut," F3 for "Copy," and F4 for "Paste." To remove or to "Cut" a word, for example, select it with the mouse and then press COMMAND + X or F2. To move this item to a new location or to "Paste" it, select the insertion point as that location by clicking the mouse there, and pressing COMMAND + V or F4. To *copy* rather than *move* the item, choose "Copy," COMMAND + C or F3, instead of "Cut." Cut or copied items are automatically saved in an area of memory called the *Clipboard,* which allows them to be moved or copied onto either the current publication or another one. The "Clear" option, or the DELETE key (BACKSPACE on the Mac Plus and some third-party keyboards), lets you delete a selected item without putting it on the Clipboard. This preserves the current contents of the Clipboard, since a new item replaces the previous item; that is, the Clipboard holds only one item at a time.

The "Undo" option of the Edit menu is particularly useful. You can change your mind, canceling your most recent command, unless it deals with files, lines, or shading. If you have not selected or deselected an item or moved to another page since executing your last command, you can undo such actions as moving a block of text, cropping a graphic, or changing the page setup. You must usually choose "Undo" immediately after the command in order to correct it.

The "Select all" option allows you to select all the text and graphics in a publication window, or, if you are in a story, to select the entire story. "Find. . .," "Find next. . .," and "Change. . ." are used in the story editor to locate or replace text or formatting. "Spelling. . ." activates the spelling checker in the story editor, and "Show clipboard" displays the contents of the Clipboard. "Preferences. . ." lets you choose the unit of measure—inches, millimeters, picas, or ciceros and several other elements.

The "Edit story" option allows you to switch between layout and story views. The story view, new with Page-Maker 4, provides access to the story editor, which gives you greater speed and several word processing tools not available in the normal layout view.

```
 Edit  Options  P:
 Undo copy   ⌘Z

 Cut         ⌘H
 Copy        ⌘C
 Paste       ⌘U
 Clear
 Select all  ⌘A

 Find...      ⌘8
 Find next    ⌘,
 Change...    ⌘9
 Spelling...  ⌘L

 Show clipboard
 Preferences...

 Edit story   ⌘E
```

OPTIONS MENU   With the Options menu, shown in Figure 3-3, you can turn on or off several screen options, such as "Rulers" and "Guides." You can also add Column guides, lock the rulers' zero point ("Zero lock") or lock the guides ("Lock Guides"), and control the manner in which text flows across columns and pages ("Autoflow"). In addition, you can turn on or off a magnetic property of guides and rulers called "Snap to guides" and "Snap to rulers." Finally, from the Options menu you can create either a table of contents ("Create TOC") or an index ("Create index. . .") and add to or show the index ("Index entry. . ."

FIGURE 3-3   The Options menu

or "Show index. . ."). You'll use a number of these options later in this chapter where they'll be explained further.

PAGE MENU   The Page menu offers seven options for changing the page size in a window, from viewing a page that has been reduced to 25 percent of its original size, to viewing a full page, to viewing a part of a page that has been enlarged to 400 percent of its actual size. The Page menu also allows you to "Insert pages. . ." to and "Remove pages. . ." from a publication. With "Go to page. . ." or its shortcut key, COMMAND + G, you can bring up a particular page. Finally, this menu allows you to turn on or off the display of items from the master page ("Display master, items"), such as guides and headings, and to "Copy master guides" to a new page.

TYPE MENU   The Type menu, shown in Figure 3-4, allows you to select and change the typeface, size, and style of type. You control all aspects of type from this menu, including the leading, alignment, indents, tabs, hyphenation, and spacing. You will look at the Type menu in some depth later in this chapter.

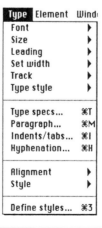

FIGURE 3-4   The Type menu

ELEMENT MENU The Element menu, shown in Figure 3-5, allows you to control the width and style of lines used alone or when drawing rectangles, circles, or ovals and to select the shade or pattern used to fill a rectangle or circle. Most of the options in the "Line" and "Fill" submenus are self-explanatory, with the following two exceptions: "None" and "Paper." The "None" option of the Line submenu is handy when, as in building the order form in Chapter 4, you may want to add shading without a visible border or rectangle. To do this, draw a rectangle with the "None" option, and then add shading. The "Paper" shading option of the Fill submenu creates an opaque absence of any shading that simply covers whatever is beneath it. You will see how this is used later in this chapter.

Additional options on the Element menu include "Bring to front" and "Send to back," which allow you to change the relative position of selected items, "Text rotation. . ." to rotate selected text in 90° increments, "Text wrap. . ." to control how text wraps around graphics, "Image con-

FIGURE 3-5 The Element menu

trol. . ." to control the contrast on scanned graphics,
"Rounded corners. . ." to change the degree of rounded
corners on rounded-corner rectangles, "Define colors. . ."
to define the colors to be applied to graphics and text, and
"Link info. . ." and "Link options. . ." for maintaining the
links established between a publication and the individual
text and graphic files used to create the publication.

WINDOWS MENU AND HELP The Windows menu is
the gateway to PageMaker's extensive on-line help system.
This system not only provides help on every command and
many topics, but also provides help on using "Help." Select
the Windows menu now, choose "Help. . .," and click on
"Using Help." Read the screen that appears and click on
the downward pointing arrow on screen to read the remaining screens. Note that at almost any time you can get
context-sensitive help—help that is related to whatever you
are doing—by simply pressing COMMAND + ?. Click on "Quit
Help" to leave "Help. . ." and return to the desktop.

The Windows menu also provides the means of turning
on and off several ancillary windows and other features.
These include the "Toolbox," "Scroll bar," "Style palette,"
and the "Color palette." You'll work at length with the
Toolbox later in this chapter.

You are now ready to begin constructing the flyer.

CREATING THE LAYOUT

The first step in building the flyer is to create the layout grid. This is a system of dotted lines that includes the margins and other guides that appear on your screen but do not print. These guides help you place text and graphics on a page. You begin the layout by creating a new publication and establishing the page setup. To create a new publication, select the File menu and choose "New" as shown here:

Establishing the Page Setup

When you request a new publication, PageMaker displays the Page setup dialog box shown in Figure 3-6.

The Page setup dialog box allows you to determine the page size and orientation (whether the text is horizontally oriented, "Wide," or vertically oriented "Tall"), the number of pages (and how they are numbered), whether the pages are double-sided or facing pages, and the margin

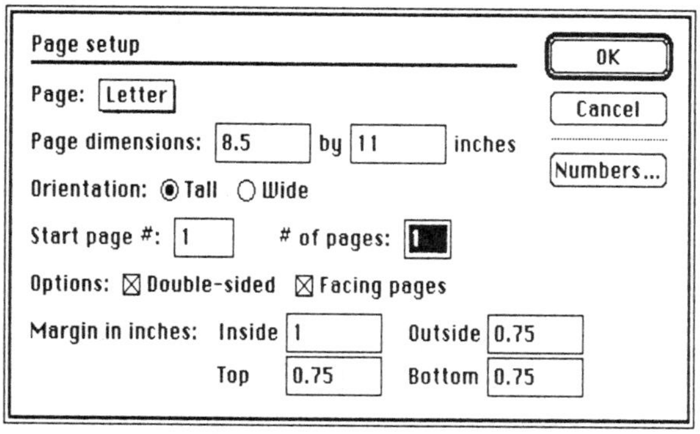

```
┌─────────────────────────────────────────────────────┐
│ Page setup                                  ┌──────┐ │
│                                             │  OK  │ │
│ Page: [Letter]                              └──────┘ │
│                                             ┌──────┐ │
│ Page dimensions: [8.5    ] by [11    ] inches│Cancel│ │
│                                             └──────┘ │
│ Orientation: ● Tall  ○ Wide                 ┌───────┐│
│                                             │Numbers…││
│ Start page #: [1   ]    # of pages: [■   ]  └───────┘│
│                                                      │
│ Options: ⊠ Double-sided  ⊠ Facing pages              │
│                                                      │
│ Margin in inches:  Inside [1   ]   Outside [0.75 ]   │
│                       Top [0.75]   Bottom  [0.75 ]   │
└─────────────────────────────────────────────────────┘
```

FIGURE 3-6   The initial Page setup dialog box

sizes. PageMaker will already have filled in the dialog box with the default values. You can recognize the defaults by the highlighted option buttons (black dots in circles), checked boxes, or the data in the text boxes such as the margin settings. For the flyer, you can accept all the defaults except the margin settings. You don't really want the double-sided option, which is the default, but the flyer only has one page, so it doesn't matter.

The margins you'll use for the flyer are 1 inch on the "Inside" and "Outside" and 1.25 inches on the "Top" and "Bottom." Because the inside margin is already 1 inch, you'll change only the other three. Follow these instructions to make those changes:

1. Point on and drag across the 0.75 in the "Outside" text box.

The 0.75 will become highlighted, and when you next enter a value, it will replace the highlighted contents.

2. Type **1** and press TAB.

The pointer will move to the "Top" text box, the top margin setting will be highlighted, and you can now change it.

3. Type **1.25** and press TAB to move to the "Bottom" text box.

4. Again type **1.25**. Your Page setup dialog box will now look like that shown in Figure 3-7.

5. Press RETURN or click on "OK" to complete the dialog box and return to the publication window.

Upon returning, you will see the outline of the flyer displayed in the center of the publication window, as shown in Figure 3-8. The margins that you just set are shown as a dotted rectangle within that outline. The flyer has been sized so that you can see the entire page within the window. Recall that the Page menu offers several alternative sizes for viewing the publication. The current setting, "Fit

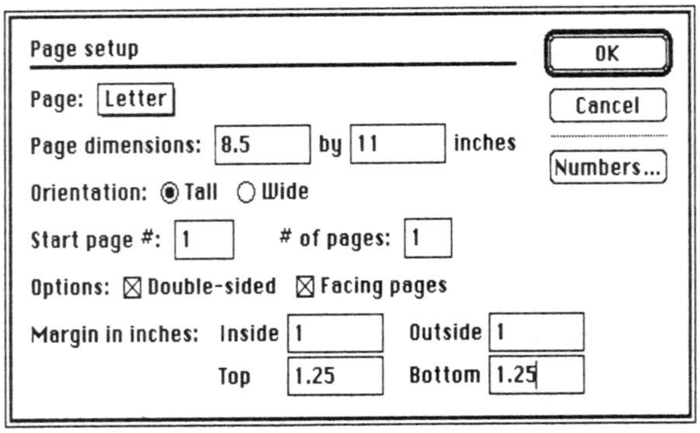

FIGURE 3-7   The final Page setup dialog box

Getting Started with a Flyer 81

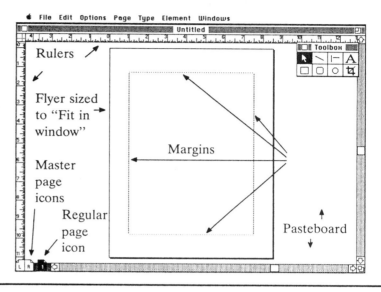

FIGURE 3-8 The flyer sized to "Fit in window"

in window," allows you to see the total page on the screen. The text in this view is very small, and most of it cannot be read; however, the page area displayed is large, allowing you to see the total page. On the other hand, with a "400% size" setting, the text is very large and the area very small, allowing you to see only a small portion of the page.

The area surrounding the flyer is called the *pasteboard.* You can use it as a temporary holding and work area by cutting and pasting or dragging items to and from the publication and the pasteboard. In the lower left corner are a series of icons representing the master and regular pages. The page icons with an "L" and an "R" represent left-facing and right-facing master pages. You won't be using the master pages in this application, of course, because the flyer contains only one page. The regular page icon, containing the numeral 1, is the current page in the publication window. You know that because the icon is highlighted. If you specified more pages in the Page setup dialog box, a numbered icon for each page would appear (up to the limit of the screen). To switch back and forth between pages, click on the appropriate page icon. Because there is only one page in the flyer, only one page icon appears.

In the upper right-hand corner of the publication window is another window, labeled "Toolbox," that contains eight tools. The most commonly used tool is the pointer (or arrow), which is highlighted in the upper left-hand box. It is used for pointing and selecting items both in the publication and on the menus. The capital "A" in the upper right-hand box represents the text tool. It is used for adding, deleting, and editing text. Below the text tool is the cropping tool, which is used to trim the sides of a graphic. The other four boxes are used to draw straight lines, perpendicular lines, rectangles, rounded-corner rectangles, and circles or ovals. Later in this and subsequent chapters we will further discuss the various tools.

The next step is to add and adjust the guides.

Adding Guides

PageMaker allows you to place nonprinting lines on the page to help you precisely align text and graphics. These lines, which are easily moved, are most useful when placed according to exact measurements, as on a ruler. Both vertical and horizontal rulers are, therefore, provided through the Options menu. They are turned on by default and should automatically display, as shown in Figure 3-8. Just in case, open the Options menu to see if there is a check mark beside "Rulers," as shown here. (Don't release your mouse button while pointing on the "Rulers" option or you will turn them off.)

The horizontal and vertical rulers are used to place not only guides, but text and graphics and design elements as well. The zero point on each ruler corresponds to the upper left-hand corner of the page. As you move the mouse, you will see a corresponding faint dotted line move in each of the rulers. Consequently, the rulers give you the precise measurement of where the pointer is on the page, regardless of where you move it in the window. When you change the image size, the rulers' dimensions will change accordingly. Experiment with the rulers until you are comfortable with them.

Using the rulers, you can see how the margins exactly fit the measurements set in the page setup of 1.25 inches on the top and bottom and 1 inch on each side.

COLUMN GUIDES   In addition to the margins, you may have columns for aligning text within the margins. Page-Maker assumes that the margins you established are the edges of your text and places a default set of *column guides* within the left and right margins, creating between them one column equal in size to the page width less the margins. In this case, however, the margins are the border around the text, and the actual text will be inside those margins. You use the column guides to specify where the actual text will appear. Therefore, you need to move the column guides. Do that now with the following instructions:

1. Point on the left margin guide, then press and hold the mouse button.

A double-headed arrow will appear, which allows you to move the column guide either left or right.

2. Drag the column guide to the right until the dashed line in the horizontal ruler line reaches 1.75, then release the mouse button.

3. Point on the right margin guide. Then press and hold the mouse button while dragging the column guide to the left until the line in the horizontal ruler reads 6.5." Finally, release the mouse button.

(These new column guides are not equidistant from the original margins because the shadow border requires a .25 -inch offset.)

RULER GUIDES Besides column guides, you can use other guide lines for various purposes. Because you create these lines from the rulers, they are called *ruler guides.* On the flyer, you'll want a ruler guide for the line between the company name and the body of the flyer. Add this ruler guide as follows:

1. Point on the top or horizontal ruler. Press and hold the mouse button until the double-headed arrow appears.

2. Drag a new ruler guide down until the dashed line in the left or vertical ruler reaches 3.25". Then release the mouse button.

When you have placed the column and ruler guides, your flyer will look like Figure 3-9.

The margin, column, and ruler guides constitute the initial layout grid for your flyer. You will add more guides later, but for now these will suffice. Let's add the text.

ENTERING THE TEXT

The text on the flyer consists of three segments: the company name, the body describing the company's capabilities, and a list of products. Each segment uses a different font and spacing, so each is entered separately. Let's start with the company name.

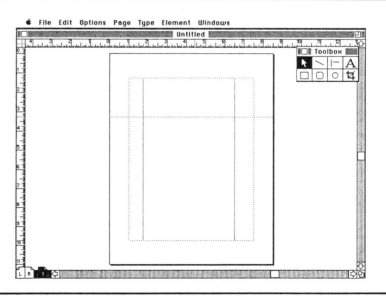

FIGURE 3-9   The flyer with three new guides

Building the Company Name

To enter text with PageMaker, you need the text tool from the Toolbox. You will also use the text tool when you're editing text. This tool allows you to select text in order to cut and paste and to change its typeface, size, or style. To select the text tool:

Point on the text tool (the capital A) in the Toolbox (see Figure 3-9) and click the mouse button.

The pointer becomes an I-beam when it is on the pasteboard or the publication. When you click the mouse button with the text tool active, the insertion point (a vertical line indicating where the text you type will be placed) moves under (or very close to) the I-beam icon.

SELECTING THE TYPE Because you want the company name to be larger and in bold type, you will change the type specifications. The type specifications control the typeface, the type size (points), the type style (bold, italic, and so on), the spacing between lines (leading), the letter positioning (subscript and superscript), and the case (lowercase and uppercase). To change the type specifications, follow these instructions:

1. Select the Type menu and choose "Type specs. . .," as shown in Figure 3-10. The Type specifications dialog box will open, as shown in Figure 3-11.

2. Point on the word "Times" in the "Font" option box, and press and hold the mouse button so that a list of typefaces appears.

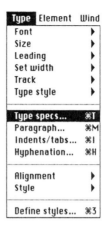

FIGURE 3-10 The Type menu with "Type specs..." selected

3. Drag the pointer up until it is pointing on "Avant Garde" (or the font you are using if not Avant Garde) as shown here:

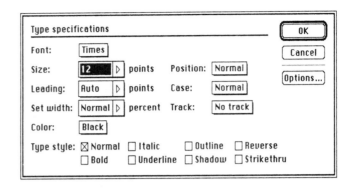

═══ **FIGURE 3-11**   The initial Type specifications dialog box

4. Release the mouse button.

   To make the company name larger, you will increase the size of the typeface from the standard 12 points to 60 points. The type size should already be highlighted, so all you need to do is type in the new size. (If your type size is not highlighted, click on the triangle next to the "12" in the "Size" text box.)

5. Type **60**. The number 60 will appear in the "Size" text box.

6. Press TAB to go to the "Leading" text box. The word "Auto" will be highlighted.

7. Type **66** to change the leading from automatic (which produces a leading of 72 points) to 66.

8. Click on the "Bold," "Italic," and "Shadow" "Type Style" check boxes to choose those style conventions. An "X" will appear in the boxes to indicate that they have been chosen.

9. Point on "Normal" in the "Case" option box. Press and hold the mouse button so that a list appears. Drag the pointer down until it is on "Small caps" and then release the mouse button.

Since you have left the default settings "Normal" for "Set width," "Black" for "Color," "Normal" for "Position," and "No track" for "Track," your dialog box should look like Figure 3-12.

10. Finally, click "OK" to accept the type specifications as they now stand and to return to the publication.

Now that you have established the type specifications, you can type the company name.

ENTERING THE COMPANY NAME Entering the company name is straightforward. You simply use the mouse to

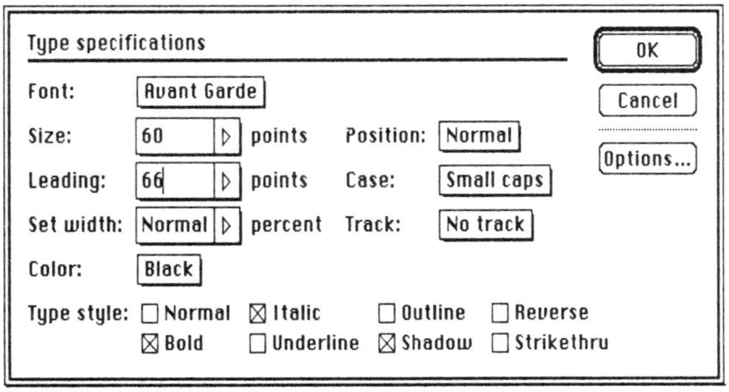

FIGURE 3-12 The final Type specifications dialog box for the company name

place the insertion point where you want to begin typing and then enter the text. Enter the company name as follows:

1. Position the I-beam pointer to the right of the left column guide and slightly below the top margin (about 2 inches on the vertical ruler—you will correct any alignment error later). Click the mouse button. A flashing vertical line will appear next to the left column guide representing the insertion point where the text will begin.

2. Type **Creative,** and press RETURN.

The word "Creative" appears on the flyer in bold italics, with small caps for the lowercase letters. (If you mistakenly entered "CREATIVE" in caps, all caps will be displayed instead of small caps.)
The next line must be right aligned in order to balance the two lines of the company name.

3. Now press COMMAND + SHIFT + R (press and hold both the COMMAND and SHIFT keys while pressing R) to right align the second line and then type **Designs**. Your flyer will look like Figure 3-13.

CENTERING THE COMPANY NAME You may notice that the company name is not exactly centered in its area. In our case, it is a little high. Yours may be the same, or too low, or too far to the left. This is because of a Page-Maker option that is normally very useful but prevents you from exactly centering the company name. This option, called "Snap to guides," makes all nonprinting guides (margins, column guides, and ruler guides) act like magnets. Whenever text or graphics or even the pointer nears a nonprinting guide, it is pulled to that guide.

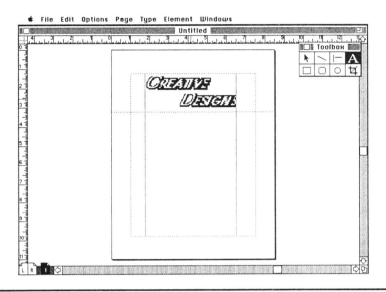

FIGURE 3-13   The flyer with the company name

To center the company name, select it with the pointer tool. Then turn off the "Snap to guides" option, and move the company name with the mouse until you are satisfied with its position. The instructions to do that are as follows:

1. Click on the pointer tool in the Toolbox.

2. Point on the word "Creative" and click the mouse button.

This selects the two lines of the company name and provides *handles*—horizontal lines with loops like window shades—on either side of the company name, as shown in Figure 3-14. With these handles the company name can be moved.

3. Select the Options menu and choose "Snap to guides" to turn them off, as shown in Figure 3-14.

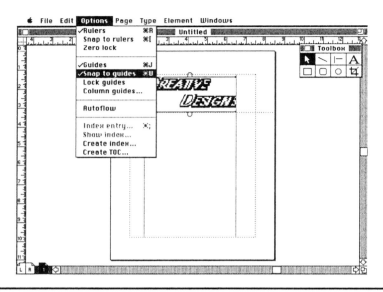

FIGURE 3-14 The flyer with company name and "Snap to guides" selected

Now the company name will not be pulled toward one of the guides, making it easier to move about.

4. Point somewhere in the middle of the company name. Then press and hold the mouse button until a four-headed arrow appears.

5. Hold the mouse button down and move the company name around until it is positioned the way you want it. Then release the mouse button. The final result should look something like Figure 3-15.

Don't be concerned that the final "s" in Designs overlaps the right column guide. It will correct itself when it is printed.

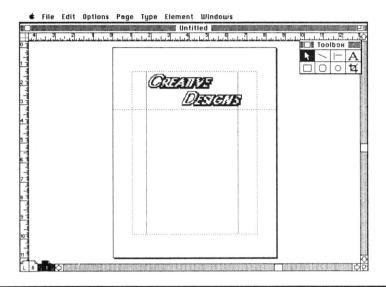

FIGURE 3-15   The flyer with the company name centered

Now you must restore "Snap to guides" so that you can use its magnetic capability to precisely place text and lines for the balance of the flyer.

6. Select the Options menu and choose "Snap to guides" to turn them back on.

PLACING A LINE   You want a line or rule, perpendicular to the margins, to separate the company name from the body of text, so you'll use the perpendicular-line tool to draw it from the left to the right margin. You will then look at the line width options in the Element menu to see if a different width would be better. To do this:

1. Click on the perpendicular-line tool (just to the left of the text tool) in the Toolbox. The pointer will change to a crossbar.

2. Point the crossbar at the intersection of the left margin (not the column guide) and the horizontal ruler guide that separates the company name from the body of the flyer.

3. Press and hold the mouse button while dragging the line across to the right margin, as shown in Figure 3-16. Do not release the button until you're satisfied with the position of the line.

If the line is not the way you want it, press DELETE to get rid of it and start over. Although you could use the pointer tool to click on the line and move it around the way you did the company name, the DELETE method is easier here.

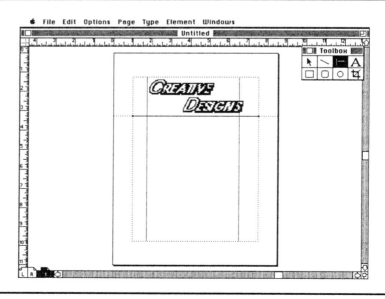

FIGURE 3-16 The flyer showing the horizontal line

The little boxes on the end of the line indicate that it is selected. If you click the mouse button, a new line will be started and the original will be deselected. Because you want to consider changing the width of the original line, it is important that it remain selected. To look at the line width:

4. Select the Element menu and drag the pointer until "Line" is highlighted and the Line submenu opens. Review the options, and without changing the selection, release the mouse button.

The 1-point line should already be selected as the default, as in Figure 3-17. This is a line width of 1/72 inch, which is acceptable for the flyer.

You now have done enough work to make it worthwhile to save your publication before continuing.

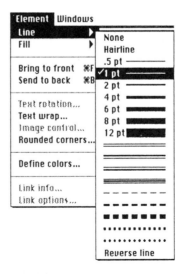

FIGURE 3-17 The Element menu and Lines submenu with a 1-point line selected

SAVING THE PUBLICATION Because you may require several hours, or even days, to construct a publication, you should save it periodically. Then, if you have a power outage or make a major mistake, you can quickly recover by retrieving the copy on disk. Let's save the flyer now.

1. Select the File menu and choose "Save as. . . ."

The Save as dialog box will open up as shown here:

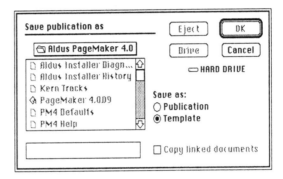

You can select a folder and filename, if you have created any, from the list box. Then select the name by clicking on it. Or you can simply type the name in the text box to avoid searching the list. Here you'll use both techniques. PageMaker lists the currently open folder name in the open folder box above the list box. If it is incorrect, drag on the open folder box until you are pointing to the correct one and click on it. Then type the filename in the text box. Here, you need to change the folder to Publications and then type the name of the publication—flyer.

If you are using a different folder name or want to change the publication name, you can make the necessary changes in the following commands.

The open folder box should currently show "Aldus Page-Maker 4.0." The PageMaker folder is on your hard drive on the same level as your system folder. If you followed the suggestions in Chapter 2, on this same level is a folder named "Publications," which you established to hold the results of what you produce in this book. You therefore want to store this flyer in that folder. To get to the Publications folder, you must move up to the hard drive level and then open Publications, as follows:

2. Drag on the open folder box until "HARD DRIVE" is highlighted and then release the mouse button.

3. Scroll the list box until "Publications" is visible and then double-click on it.

4. Type **flyer** in the file name text box, as shown here, and press RETURN or click on "OK" to save the file and close the dialog box.

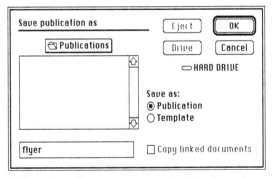

Your publication is now saved. Notice that the name "flyer" has appeared in the title bar.

INTERMISSION You may want to take a break now and continue at a later time. To close PageMaker, select the File menu and choose "Quit," as shown here:

Entering the Text Body

As you might imagine, entering the text body is also straightforward. After specifying the type and selecting the text tool, you simply type the desired text. You will go a step further and justify the text, but that is all there is to it.

CONTINUING   If you are returning from a break, reload PageMaker and open the flyer publication. To do that,

1. Reload PageMaker by double-clicking on the Aldus PageMaker 4.0 icon (or whatever your normal procedure is). The PageMaker desktop will appear.

2. Select the File menu and choose "Open. . . ." The "Open publication" box will appear.

3. Drag on the open folder box until "HARD DRIVE" is highlighted.

4. Double-click on "Publications."

5. Double-click on "flyer" in the list box, and it will be highlighted, as shown here:

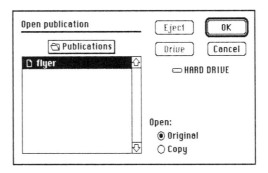

 As is true while saving the publication, if you are using a different folder scheme than the one described here, you will have to make the necessary changes to all of these instructions.

Your flyer will again appear in the PageMaker desktop on your screen.

GETTING READY   Until now you have used a publication size in which a full page fits on the screen. This helps in creating the layout grid and entering the company name, which is very large. The text body, however, is normal 12-point type and is not readable at the "Fit in window" size. Therefore, to enter the text body, you will enlarge the view you have of the page to full or "Actual size." Follow these steps:

1. Select the Page menu and choose "Actual size," as shown here:

Page	Type	Element
✓Fit in window		⌘W
25% size		⌘0
50% size		⌘5
75% size		⌘7
Actual size		**⌘1**
200% size		⌘2
400% size		⌘4
Go to page...		⌘G
Insert pages...		
Remove pages...		
✓Display master items		
Copy master guides		

The flyer will enlarge until a portion of it fills the pasteboard.

2. Use the vertical and horizontal scroll bars to center the flyer with the company name just below the ruler, as shown in Figure 3-18. (Click on the arrows at the ex-

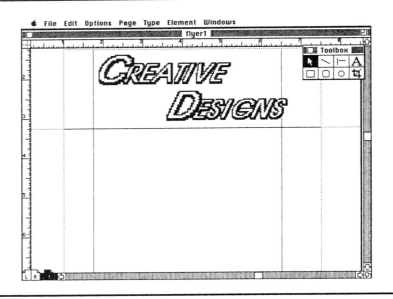

FIGURE 3-18   The flyer enlarged to actual size

tremes of the scroll bars to move the image in small increments, or drag the scroll boxes to move the image by larger amounts until the image is correctly placed.)

To enter the text, you must select the text tool and specify the type. The text will be entered in 12-point Palatino-Roman (medium weight.) You'll also want to use both uppercase and lowercase.

3. Click on the text tool.

4. Select the Type menu and choose "Type specs. . . ."

5. Drag the Font name option box until "Palatino" is highlighted.

6. If it's not already there, type **12** in the "Size" text box, press TAB, and type **Auto** in the "Leading" text box. Click in the "Normal" "Type style" check box, and then drag the "Case" option box until "Normal" is highlighted. Your Type specifications dialog box will look like the one shown in Figure 3-19.

7. Press RETURN or click "OK" to close the dialog box.

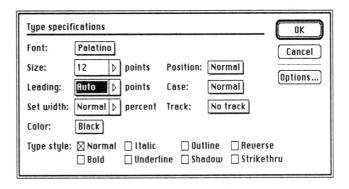

FIGURE 3-19 The Type specifications dialog box for the text body

TYPING THE TEXT BODY   You must place the insertion point where you want the text to begin. Be careful. If you improperly locate the insertion point, your text may not appear where you want it or may not appear at all. Also, as you type, you may notice that PageMaker is slow to display the results. Your text is there (assuming that the insertion point was correctly placed); pause, and you will see it appear. Follow these instructions to type the text body.

1. Position the I-beam pointer against the inside of the left column guide so that the dotted line in the vertical ruler is at 3.75 and then click the mouse button.

   The insertion point will appear in the text area against the column guide. If the insertion point is to the left of the column guide, move it by repositioning the pointer and clicking the mouse button again.

2. Type the following three paragraphs. (Press RETURN twice at the end of each paragraph.) When you are finished, your screen will look like Figure 3-20.

   Creative Designs specializes in the design, production, and promotion of all forms of printed material.

   Creative Designs uses the latest in computer technology to design the initial layouts, typeset the necessary copy, and perform the final page composition. We then use the latest in four-color presses and bindery equipment to produce the highest quality publications obtainable. In addition, we have extensive direct mail marketing and fulfillment services available.

   Creative Designs can help you with any of the following:

A fourth paragraph will be entered lower on the page to allow room for the product list. The fourth paragraph uses the same font and style as the first three. Again, be careful in positioning the insertion point.

3. Click on the vertical scroll bar below the scroll box to move the screen down until 8″ on the vertical ruler is approximately in the middle of your screen.

4. Click the pointer at 8.75″ on the inside of the left column guide. Then type the following:

   Call us at 1-800-555-5000 (nationwide) or stop in at our new plant at 1900 Westwind Avenue, Oceanside, WA 98999.

JUSTIFYING THE BODY   The paragraphs in Figure 3-20 look good, but for that final polished look, you'll want to

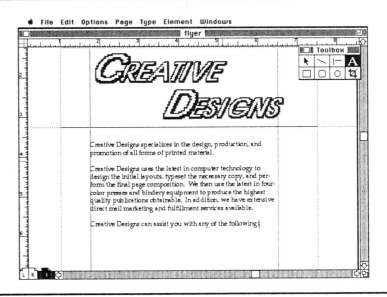

FIGURE 3-20   The first three paragraphs of the text body

justify them; that is, align them on the right as well as on the left. One of the beauties of PageMaker and laser printer technology is that justification looks almost as good as that done by a commercial typesetter. To justify, simply select the text and then choose the "Justify" option of the "Alignment" command. First you'll justify the first three paragraphs and then, separately, the fourth, as follows:

1. Click on the vertical scroll bar above the scroll box to move the screen up.

2. Place the pointer on the first letter of the first paragraph. Press and hold the mouse button.

3. Drag the pointer just below the third paragraph and release the mouse button. The first three paragraphs will be highlighted, as shown in Figure 3-21.

4. Select the Type menu, choose "Alignment," and then "Justify," as displayed in Figure 3-21.

5. If necessary, click below the scroll box in the vertical scroll bar to move back down to the fourth paragraph.

6. Position the pointer at the start of the fourth paragraph. Press and hold the mouse button while dragging down past the second line, then release the button.

7. Select the Type menu, choose "Alignment," and then "Justify." All four paragraphs will now be justified, as shown in Figure 3-22.

Listing the Products

Between the third and fourth paragraphs of the text body, you will list two columns of products. You could use tabs or spaces to indent and separate the two columns, but aligning

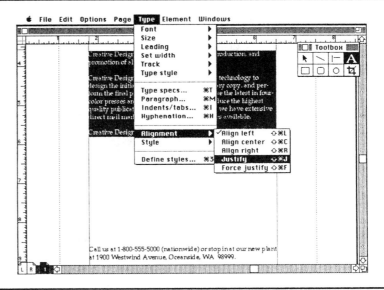

FIGURE 3-21 The three paragraphs and "Alignment" and "Justify" selected

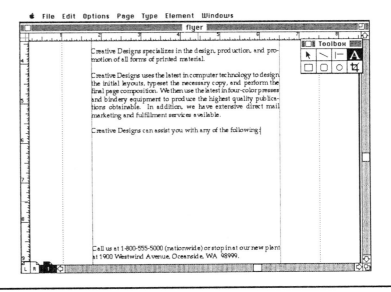

FIGURE 3-22 The effects of justification

the columns and keeping them that way may be difficult. Another solution is to establish two columns with Page-Maker's column guides. Let's do that now.

1. Select the Options menu and choose "Column guides. . .," as shown here:

The Column guides dialog box will open so that you can specify the number of columns and how much space to leave between them.

2. Type **2** in the "Number of columns" text box.

3. Press TAB to move to the "Space between columns" text box and type **.25**, as shown here:

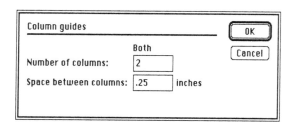

4. Then press RETURN to return to the publication.

Notice that there are two new column guides in the center of the flyer, but your original column guides have moved back under the margins. You must move them out again and position the center guides. To do that:

5. Click on the pointer tool in the Toolbox.

Next you'll move the column guides from under the margins. If you have not exactly centered the flyer on the screen, you may not be able to see one of the margins. If so, use the horizontal scroll bar to adjust the display until both margins are visible.

6. Point on the left-hand margin. Press and hold the mouse button while dragging the column guide to the 2″ mark. Then release the button.

7. Point on the right-hand margin. Press and hold the mouse button while dragging the column guide to the 6″ mark. Then release the button.

8. Point on the right center column guide and drag it to the 4 1/8″ mark on the horizontal ruler. Your screen should look like Figure 3-23. (Note that the left center column guide automatically moved to the 3 7/8″ mark because you have set a fixed space between columns.)

9. Now save your work by using the shortcut keys, COMMAND + S (press and hold COMMAND while pressing S).

TYPING THE LIST Now that the columns are in place, you can type in the list of products without worrying about the alignment. The font for the list will be 18-point Avant Garde-Demi (bold) small caps. You'll make these changes through the Type menu, as follows:

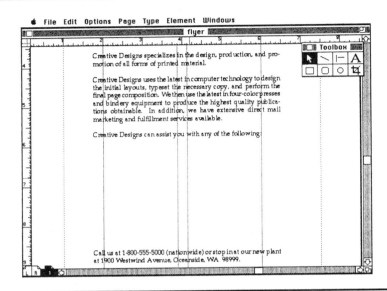

FIGURE 3-23 The final column guide positioning

1. Select the Type menu and choose "Type specs...." The Type specifications dialog box will open.

2. Drag the "Font" option box until "Avant Garde" is highlighted.

3. Type **18** in the "Size" text box and click on the "Bold" check box.

4. Drag on the "Case" text box until "Small caps" is highlighted. Your dialog box will then look like Figure 3-24.

5. Press RETURN to return to the publication. Before typing, you must move the insertion point again.

6. Click on the text tool.

7. Position the I-beam against the inside of the far left column guide and click the mouse button at 6.25″ on the vertical ruler.

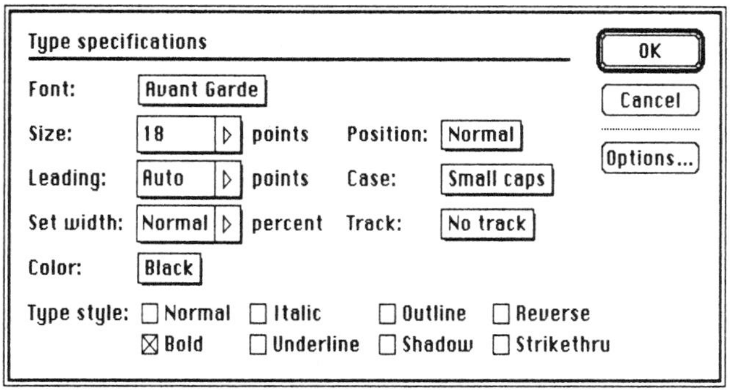

Type specifications _____ ☐ OK ☐

Font: [Avant Garde]   (Cancel)

Size: [18] ▷ points   Position: [Normal]   (Options...)

Leading: [Auto] ▷ points   Case: [Small caps]

Set width: [Normal] ▷ percent   Track: [No track]

Color: [Black]

Type style: ☐ Normal ☐ Italic   ☐ Outline ☐ Reverse
            ☒ Bold   ☐ Underline ☐ Shadow   ☐ Strikethru

FIGURE 3-24 The Type specifications dialog box for the product list

Each item on the list begins with a bullet. To produce a bullet, press OPTION + 8, simultaneously. After the bullet, type an *en-space,* a fixed-width space equal to one-half of the point size being used. The en-space is generated by pressing COMMAND + SHIFT + N, simultaneously. Press RETURN at the end of each line, and put an en-space between words except in the last line, where you should use normal spaces. Don't worry that the last line overlaps the fourth paragraph. That will be corrected.

8. Type the following list:

   • **Books**

   • **Manuals**

   • **Brochures**

   • **Newsletters**

   • **Business Plans**

   • **Annual Reports**

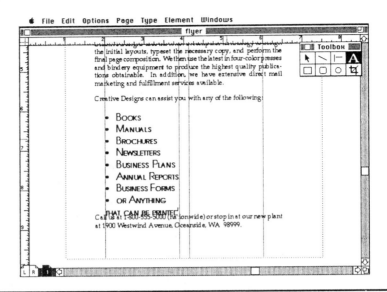

FIGURE 3-25   The left column completed

- **Business Forms**

- **or Anything that can be printed**

Your screen will look like the one shown in Figure 3-25.

9. Position the pointer against the inside of the left guide of the right column and click on 6.25″ then enter this list:

- **Flyers**

- **Posters**

- **Catalogs**

- **Pamphlets**

- **Newspapers**

Presentations
Mailing Labels

ADJUSTING THE LAST ITEM Because the "or Anything that can be printed" item in the first column takes two lines, it overlaps the fourth paragraph. To correct this, you will make it one line that spans both columns. To do that, you must "cut" the item from the list of products and "paste" it back. Then you will place a selection box around it and enlarge the selection box so that it is the same width as the sum of the two columns. Finally, you will center the item in the box at the bottom of the list. To make these adjustments, follow these instructions:

1. Drag down a horizontal ruler guide and place it against the bottom edge of the words "or Anything." You will use this to reposition the line of text when you paste it back.

2. Drag the I-beam across both lines of the "or Anything that can be printed" item in the left column to highlight it, as shown in Figure 3-26. Press COMMAND + X or F2 to cut it away from the rest of the column and press DELETE to move the insertion point up one line.

3. Click the I-beam against the inside of the far left column guide at 8 3/8″ on the vertical ruler.

4. Press COMMAND + V or F4 to paste the "or Anything" item back onto the flyer.

The "or Anything" item can now be expanded and centered.

5. Click on the pointer tool.

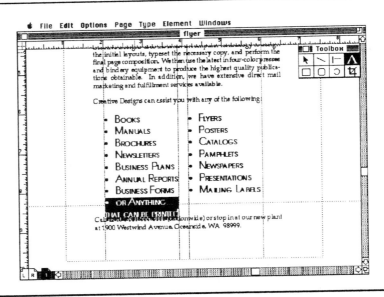

FIGURE 3-26   Both columns completed and the "or Anything" item selected

6. Click anywhere on the "or Anything" item.

A selection box will form around the text. Now you must enlarge the selection box to the width of the two columns—four inches. Notice that the lines above and below the text have small square boxes at each end. These are handles that you can use to change the width of the selection box.

7. Point on one of the right-hand handles of the selection box. Press and hold the mouse button while dragging the handle until it is on top of the rightmost column guide at 6″ on the horizontal ruler.

8. Point on the middle of the selection box and drag it up or down until it is just sitting on the horizontal ruler

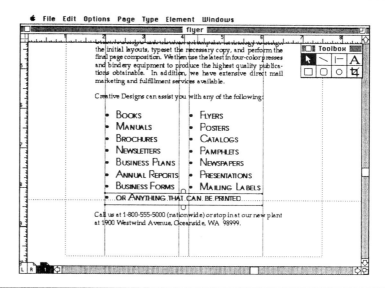

FIGURE 3-27 The selection box stretched across both columns

guide you originally placed under it. Your screen will look like that shown in Figure 3-27.

You have now stretched the selection box to fill both columns. When you center the item in the box, you will be finished with the text entry.

9. Click on the text tool.

10. Select the "or Anything" item by dragging across it.

11. Select the Type menu and then choose the "Alignment" and "Align center" options, as shown in Figure 3-28.

When you are finished, your screen should look like the one in Figure 3-29. This completes the entry of the text.

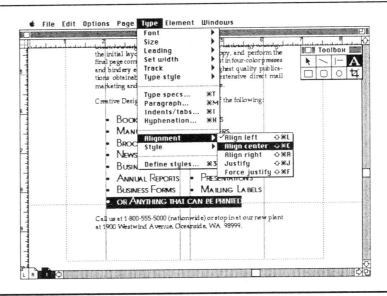

FIGURE 3-28 The Type menu with "Align center" and repositioned text selected

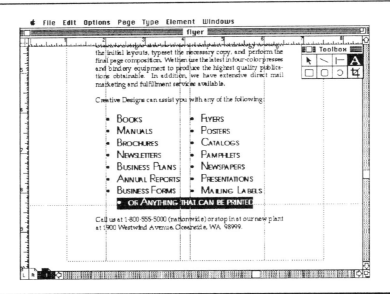

FIGURE 3-29 The final list of products

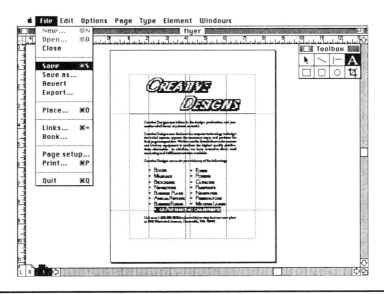

FIGURE 3-30 The full flyer with "Save" selected

Before proceeding, reduce the size of the flyer so that it again fits in the window, and then save it again.

12. Select the Page menu and choose "Fit in window."

13. Select the File menu and choose "Save." The screen will appear as in Figure 3-30.

This might be a good time to take another break. If you want to do that, use the earlier instructions for closing and reopening PageMaker and the flyer publication. Otherwise, continue and construct the border around the text.

CONSTRUCTING THE BORDER

The border around the text consists of two rounded-corner rectangles slightly offset from one another. A shadow effect is created by filling the area between the rectangles with black shading (see Figure 3-1). Although in PageMaker only complete rectangles or circles can be shaded, not a small portion of one as we want here, PageMaker makes each rectangle a layer and allows them to be "stacked" on top of one another. If the far right rectangle is shaded "Solid" and is on the bottom, and the other rectangle is shaded "Paper" and is stacked on top, you will get the effect you want. The text, which is another layer (actually a series of layers), must be on top of the stack to be readable.

Building the First Layer

PageMaker's "Snap to guides" (which cause the guides to act as magnets) are both a help and a hindrance in placing the rectangles. Two sides of each rectangle are on the margins, and the magnetic attraction will be beneficial. However, the other two sides are free of the margins but close enough to them for the magnetic attraction to interfere. To overcome this problem, you must carefully position the free end by using the rulers. Let's start with the leftmost rectangle—the one that will end up on top. It uses the top and left margins as guides and is .25 inch away from the bottom and right margins. The steps to create and place the first rectangle are as follows:

1. Select the rounded-corner tool (the second tool from the left in the bottom row). The pointer becomes a crossbar.

2. Place the crossbar on the intersection of the top and left margins. The crossbar will be attracted to the intersection and should stick there easily.

3. Press and hold the mouse button while dragging the pointer diagonally toward the opposite corner, the intersection of the bottom and right margins. A rectangle will begin forming.

4. Drag the pointer until the dotted line in the horizontal ruler reaches 7.25″ and the dotted line in the vertical ruler reads 9.5″. Then release the mouse button. Your flyer should look like the one shown in Figure 3-31.

PageMaker provides various degrees of rounded corners and shading. Therefore, to complete your first rectangle you must choose the type of rounded corner that you want and then apply the "Paper" shading. Because this rectangle is currently on top of the stack, once the shading is applied it will cover up the text layer beneath it. So you must move

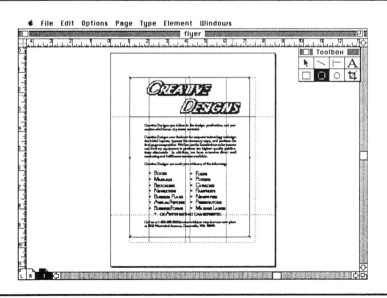

FIGURE 3-31 The flyer with the first rectangle selected

the shaded rectangle under the text on the stack, or "Send [it] to back." The following instructions explain how to perform those functions.

1. Select the Element menu and choose "Rounded corners. . .," as shown here:

The Rounded corners dialog box will open up, as shown here:

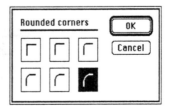

2. Click on the bottom right-hand option button for the most rounded of the corners and press RETURN or click on "OK."

3. Select the Element menu, choose "Fill," and then choose "Paper," as shown in Figure 3-32. The shaded rectangle will cover the text.

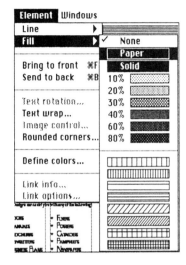

FIGURE 3-32 The Element menu with the "Fill" and "Paper" options selected

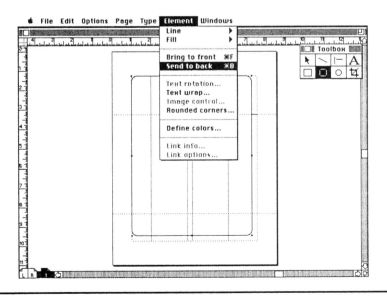

FIGURE 3-33 The shaded rectangle covering the text and "Send to back" selected

4. Select the Element menu and choose "Send to back," as shown in Figure 3-33. The text will reappear on top of the rectangle.

Building the Second Layer

The second layer is very similar to the first except that it is offset to the right and shaded black. The instructions to build it are as follows:

1. Place the crossbar pointer .25 inch in from the top and left margins. The dotted line in the horizontal ruler will be at 1.25", and the one in the vertical ruler will be at 1.5".

2. Press the mouse button and drag the pointer diagonally toward the opposite corner, to the intersection of the bottom and right margins. Then release the mouse button. Your flyer should look like that shown in Figure 3-34.

3. Select the Element menu and choose "Rounded corners. . . ."

4. Click on the bottom right-hand option button and press RETURN or click on "OK."

5. Select the Element menu, choose "Fill," and then "Solid." The text will again be covered up, as shown in Figure 3-35.

6. Select the Element menu and choose "Send to back." The text will reappear, and the shadow effect will be present. This is a good spot to save your handiwork.

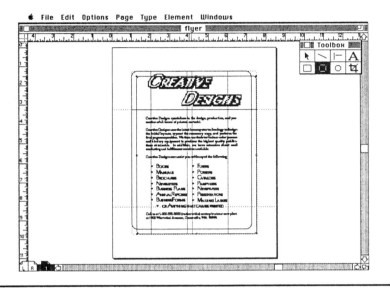

FIGURE 3-34 The flyer with the second rectangle selected

7. Select the File menu and choose "Save," as shown in Figure 3-36.

Except for cleaning up and printing, the flyer is now complete.

CLEANING UP AND PRINTING

The cleanup consists of scanning the flyer for mistakes or imperfections. To do this "under a magnifying glass," you'll first change the page size to 200 percent. Finally, you will print the publication and then save it one more time.

1. Select the Page menu and choose "200% size." Your screen should look like the one in Figure 3-37.

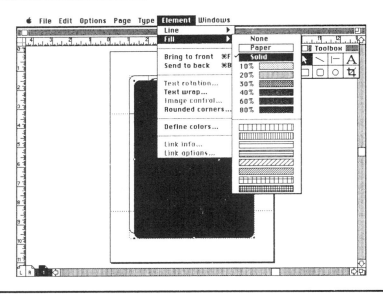

FIGURE 3-35 The second shaded rectangle covering the text and the Element menu with "Send to back" selected

2. Use the vertical and horizontal scroll bars to scan the flyer.

3. Return to the Page menu, choose "Fit in window," and click on the pointer tool.

4. Select the File menu and choose "Print. . . ." The Print dialog box will open up, as shown in Figure 3-38.

5. Accept all the defaults by clicking on "Print." Several message boxes will open up to tell you the status of the printing.

6. When the printing is complete (it may take a while), save the file one more time by pressing COMMAND + S.

7. Finally, end the session by selecting the File menu and choosing "Close" (see Figure 3-39).

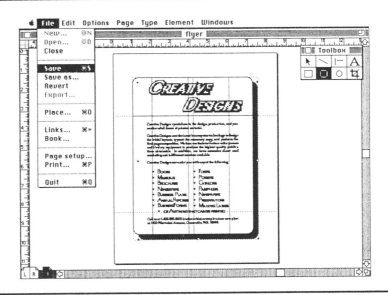

FIGURE 3-36 The completed flyer and the File menu with "Save" selected

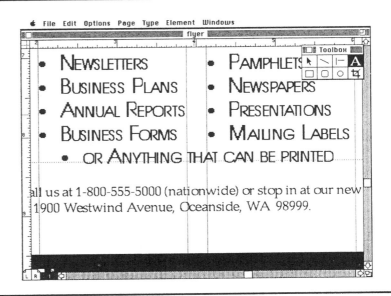

FIGURE 3-37 A part of the flyer at "200% size"

Print to: LaserWriter II NT

Copies: [1]   ☐ Collate   ☐ Reverse order

Page range: ● All ○ From [1] to [1]

Paper source: ● Paper tray ○ Manual feed

Scaling: [100] % ☐ Thumbnails, [16] per page

Book: ○ Print this pub only ○ Print entire book

Printer: [LaserWriter II NT]   Paper: [Letter]

Size: 8.5 X 11.0   inches   Tray: ● Select
Print area: 8.0 X 10.8   inches

[Print]
[Cancel]
[Options...]
[PostScript...]

FIGURE 3-38   The Print dialog box

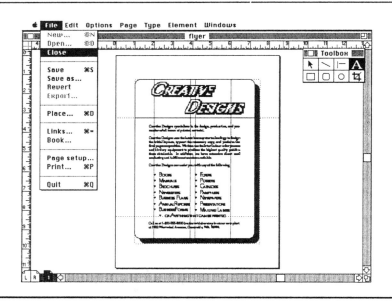

FIGURE 3-39   The File menu with "Close" selected

This chapter has covered a lot of ground. If some features and options remain unclear, don't worry about it. You'll have a chance to work with them in more detail in later chapters.

If you wish to leave PageMaker, select the File menu and choose "Quit." Otherwise, continue on to create an order form.

BASIC PAGEMAKER PUBLICATIONS

Making a Sales Order Form
Creating a Brochure
Generating an Annual Report

Part II illustrates three common uses of PageMaker: a business form, a sales brochure, and a formal financial report. In creating them you will use the capabilities of PageMaker, becoming increasingly familiar with how to use this desktop publishing tool. Having completed Part I, you'll find that Part II is faster, with less explanation of the commands and features that you already have discovered. When new techniques are introduced, however, the pace will slow down again—although not to the degree you experienced in Part I. From now on, you will find yourself moving through the applications as an experienced Page-Maker user.

Chapter 4 applies PageMaker to the task of creating a sales order form because that is similar to the custom-designed forms used by most organizations. Building this form serves as a model of how you can create other business forms using PageMaker. It uses PageMaker's line- and box-drawing tools, the multiple-column feature, and column shading to achieve a typeset look.

Chapter 5 demonstrates how to create a threefold, double-sided brochure—a commonly used format for professionally made brochures. You will use PageMaker's landscape orientation, place text from Microsoft Word, and place a drawing or graphic from Aldus FreeHand. Of course, you can use other word processing and graphics packages if you want.

Chapter 6 creates a set of formal financial statements, such as you might show to stockholders, a bank, or prospective investors. You will combine Excel spreadsheets and graphs with MacWrite II text to build these formal statements, although you could easily use other spreadsheet and word processing programs.

MAKING A SALES ORDER FORM

In this chapter, you will create the Sales Order form shown in Figure 4-1. In building the form you will incorporate several features that allow the Sales Order to look as if it came from a commercial printer. For example, the form uses several different type styles and sizes, varying line widths, and multiple columns (one, two, and six columns) to organize its contents. Two of the columns are shaded.

You can easily use these same techniques to create a variety of business forms. Once you have seen how easy it is

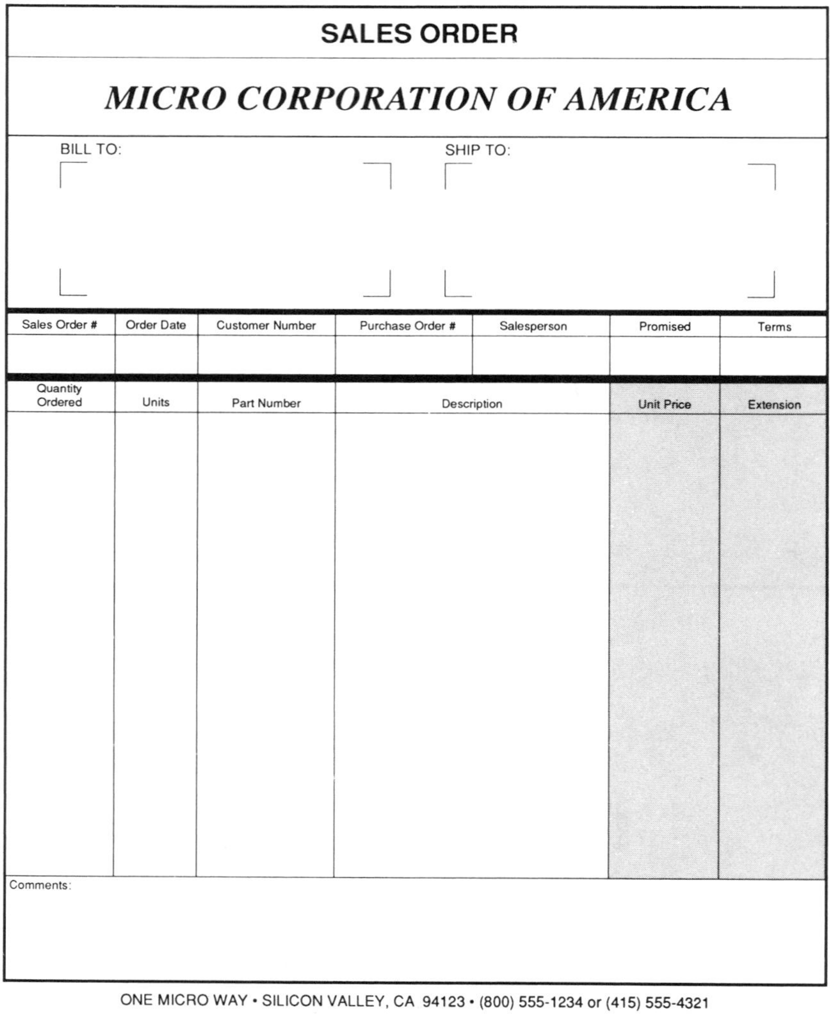

SALES ORDER						
MICRO CORPORATION OF AMERICA						

BILL TO:

SHIP TO:

Sales Order #	Order Date	Customer Number	Purchase Order #	Salesperson	Promised	Terms

Quantity Ordered	Units	Part Number	Description		Unit Price	Extension

Comments:

ONE MICRO WAY • SILICON VALLEY, CA 94123 • (800) 555-1234 or (415) 555-4321

FIGURE 4-1   The finished Sales Order form

to create this form, you'll want to create other forms with PageMaker. As you build this form, you may want to modify it to satisfy your specific needs. However, in order to follow the exact instructions, please delay your modifications until you have completed the chapter. Many of the instructions depend on precise measurements and character lengths.

PLANNING AND DESIGNING THE FORM

Your first step will be to plan and design the Sales Order form. This is where you decide what text labels and data you want on the form and how they are to be laid out on the page. To determine what labels and data you need on the form, you want to answer the questions: What information do I want to collect with the form? Who will use the form? How will it be used?

Information to Be Collected

In this case, we have answered these questions for you. The primary use of the Sales Order form is to record customer orders. The form will be used by salespersons to take down information from customers as they order. The order may come in by telephone or in person. After the Sales Order is completed, the contents will be entered into the computer, where other departments will use the information to fill the order and bill the customer.

The information will include the billing and shipping addresses for the accounts receivable and shipping departments. Critical information about the order will be collected, such as the sales order number, order date, customer number (assuming there is one), the customer's purchase order number, the name of the salesperson collecting the information, the date promised, and the terms of the order. Then the order will be itemized, and the quantity ordered (and in what units), the part number of the item, a description, the unit price quoted, and the extended price (unit price times quantity) will be listed. These last two items will not be filled in by the salesperson, so they are shaded on the form to remind them to leave that area blank. Finally, at the bottom there is an area for comments. With all this information, the order can be collected in a warehouse, shipped to the recipient, and then billed.

After the information is defined, it must be laid out on the page, then lines, fonts, and shading are added to it. The organization and design of the page will be as shown in Figure 4-1. Notice how the design features add interest and readability to the form.

Lines

One way to organize the parts of the form is to create different line widths. For example, imagine how the boxes in the middle of the form (containing Sales Order # and so on) might be lost without the heavier lines, which cause them to stand out. Also, because the horizontal lines gradually get heavier as you look down the page, your eye automatically attends to these important details rather than to the customer bill-to and ship-to information, which is already easy to see because of its location and spacing on the page.

Figure 4-2 shows the five line widths that are used. The line forming the border around the sales order will be 2 points wide; beneath the form title, .5 point; beneath the company name, 1 point; beneath the bill-to and ship-to information, 4 points; beneath the detail boxes, 6 points; the column dividers are .5 point; and beneath the columns, .5 point.

Fonts

Selecting different fonts (type styles and sizes) is another way for you to differentiate the areas of the form and enhance the appearance of the document.

The Sales Order form uses four fonts: the form title is 18-point Helvetica-Bold; the company name (which is to be emphasized), 24-point Times Bold-Italic; the return address and the bill to and ship to labels, 10-point Helvetica; and the rest of the text, 8-point Helvetica. Figure 4-3 shows these fonts.

Shading

Shading lends interest to the form, as you can see in Figure 4-3. The "Fill" option of the Element menu has several suboptions for shading an area. You can choose "Solid" or "Paper" shades as you did in Chapter 3, or you can choose a percentage of density to vary the darkness (or lightness) of the shaded area. Also, you can choose one of eight patterns for the background. In this chapter, you will use

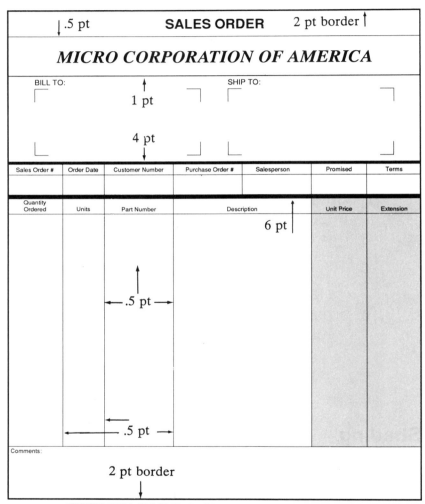

FIGURE 4-2 Line widths on Sales Order form

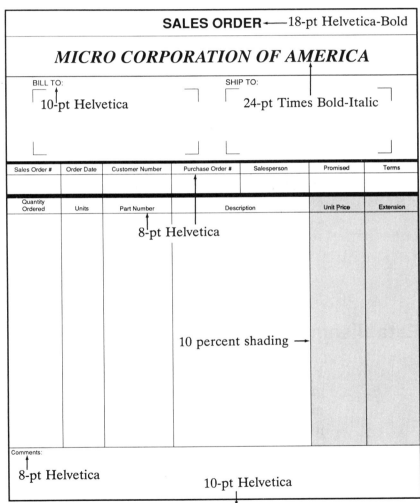

FIGURE 4-3 Fonts and shading on Sales Order form

10 percent shading, which is dark enough to be noticed, but light enough to show the Unit Price and Extension entries that will be filled in later.

Having completed the planning and design for the Sales Order form, you are now ready to begin building it.

SETTING DEFAULTS

Before getting started, turn on your computer and load PageMaker. As soon as you have done that, return here. If you have difficulties, return to Appendix A, "Installing and Starting PageMaker," and review the steps.

Your first step is to establish the document defaults.

Establishing Defaults

You want to set the defaults for the overall type of document and its size. You do this by filling in the Page setup dialog box. This allows you to specify the size of the page, its orientation, that is, vertical or horizontal ("Tall" or "Wide"), whether it is double-sided or has facing pages, the number of pages in the publication, and what margins you are using as the default.

To set the page specifications, follow these steps:

1. Choose "New. . ." from the File menu.

The Page setup dialog box will be displayed. Scan the box and note which options need to be changed. The "Page

dimensions" option is 8.5 x 11 inches, which is what you
want. The Orientation is "Tall" (vertical) also what you
want. However, the "Double-sided" and "Facing pages"
options are checked and the Sales Order form has only one
side. In addition, the margins are too wide for the Sales
Order format. Those options will be changed, as shown in
Figure 4-4.

2. Turn off the "Double-sided" option by clicking in the
   check box.

This also turns off the "Facing pages" option, because
you can't have facing pages without a double-sided page.

3. Drag across the "Left" margin number and type in **.5** to
   reset it, and then press TAB to advance the insertion
   point to the "Right" margin.

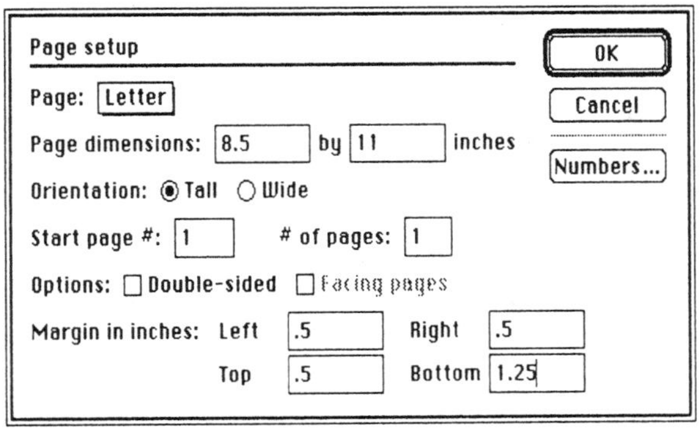

FIGURE 4-4 Page setup options for Sales Order form

4. Type in **.5** and then press TAB to advance the insertion point to the "Top" margin.

5. Type in **.5** and then press TAB to advance the insertion point to the "Bottom" margin.

6. Type in **1.25** and then press RETURN to complete the dialog box.

Your screen shows the page outline with the dotted margin guides within it, as shown in Figure 4-5.

In the upper right corner is the Toolbox, which you'll be using often. The pointer tool (the arrow) is currently selected, as indicated by the highlighted background.

Now that the page setup is completed, you can set the rest of your defaults.

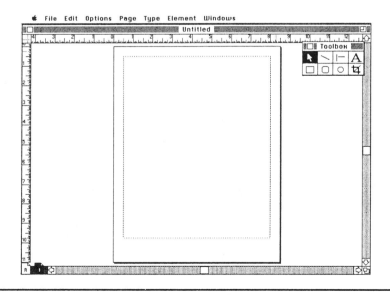

FIGURE 4-5   The initial page setup

Setting Up Ruler Guides

When rulers are turned on, as they are in Figure 4-5, they appear on the top (the horizontal ruler) and left side (the vertical ruler) of the screen. Within them are faint, dotted lines that move as the mouse pointer is moved. You can track the insertion point exactly by noting its position on the scale marks of the rulers. From the rulers you can drag *ruler guides,* the longer dotted lines used to further define the areas of the Sales Order form. By lining up the ruler guides to exact scale marks, you can precisely place text, lines, shading, and graphics.

If your rulers are not turned on, do so now.

1. Choose "Rulers" on the Options menu.

Setting Line Width Default

You will now set the line width default. You must set the default with the pointer tool or a drawing tool *before* drawing a line, box, or circle. Otherwise, you will not be setting the default but merely setting the size of the line you just drew. For example, if you first select a 2-point line width with the pointer tool and then draw a box with the square box tool, it will be 2 points. If you then draw a line using the perpendicular-line tool and, before deselecting it (by clicking the mouse elsewhere), change the line width to 1 point, the next line you draw will revert to 2 points by default.

Most line widths in the Sales Order form are .5 point wide. To make that your default:

1. Choose ".5 pt" on the Line option of the Element menu, as shown in Figure 4-6. The default line width is set for most of your lines.

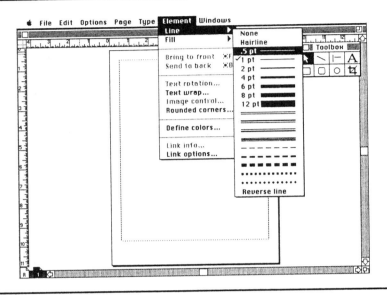

FIGURE 4-6   Setting line width default to ".5 pt"

Setting Type Specifications

Setting the defaults for the type specifications works the same way as the line defaults. The defaults are the type specifications you set either with the pointer tool or, prior to establishing the insertion point, with the text tool.

Setting the type specifications defaults defines the characteristics of the type most commonly used in the Sales Order form. You may recall from Figure 4-3 that the most common type is 8-point Helvetica. You will use a shortcut technique to get to the type specifications. Although you could choose the "Type specs..." option from the Type menu, now you will press two shortcut keys. To set the type specifications, follow these steps:

1. Press COMMAND+T (for "Type specs"). The Type specifications dialog box will be displayed.

2. Drag the "Font" option box until "Helvetica" is highlighted.

3. Type **8** in the "Size" text box to set the type size at 8 points.

4. Verify that "Type style," "Position," "Case," and "Set width" are all set for "Normal"; that "Auto" appears in the "Leading" text box; that "Color" is set to "Black"; and that "Track" is set to "No track."

5. When the dialog box is completed, as shown in Figure 4-7, click on "OK" or press RETURN to tell PageMaker that you are finished with the "Type specs."

The alignment is another aspect of the type for which you want to establish a default. Most of the text in the Sales Order form is centered.

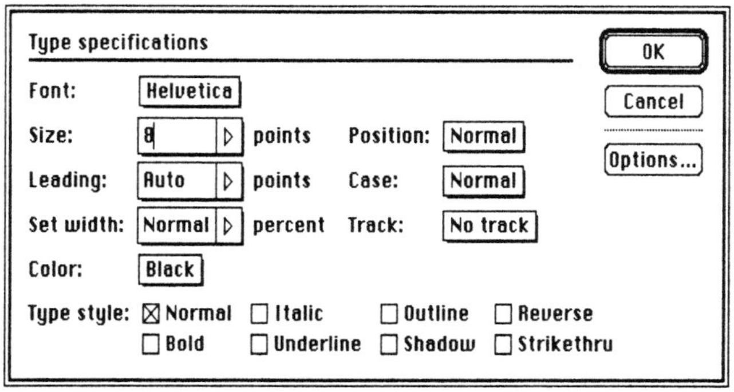

FIGURE 4-7 Type specifications for Sales Order defaults

6. Choose "Align Center" from the "Alignment" option submenu of the Type menu or use the shortcut key COMMAND+SHIFT+C.

Your type defaults are now set and you can begin drawing guide lines. You can change the type specifications for a particular entry (and preserve your document defaults) by setting an insertion point *before* changing the specifications for that entry.

ENTERING THE BORDER AND HORIZONTAL LINES

The Sales Order form uses many lines to define the various areas. You will enter these lines now. First, you will define the outline of the form. Then you will enter several ruler guides to help you determine where the actual lines are to be placed within the form.

From Chapter 3, "Getting Started with a Flyer," you'll recall the benefits of "Snap to guides." These give guide lines a magnetic property that attracts the pointer as it nears them and allows you to match up your pointer to an exact location. You'll find this feature useful here. However, you'll need to turn off the "Snap to guides" to perform another task later.

You create the border of the Sales Order form by placing a rectangle around the page, exactly where the margin guides are now located. To do this, you'll place the square-corner tool at the upper left-hand corner of the margins and then drag the expanding rectangle diagonally to the lower right-hand corner before releasing the mouse button.

If you find that the border is not where you want it, press the DELETE key while the border lines are still selected. (They are selected as long as the lines of the rectangle contain tiny boxes at the corners and midpoints.) If the border becomes deselected, select the pointer tool from the Toolbox, click it on the top or bottom border to select the rectangle again (the left and right sides will work if you first move the column guide from beneath the margin before clicking on them), and then continue.

Follow these steps to build the border line of the form, which is shown in Figure 4-8.

1. Select the square-corner tool (bottom left in Toolbox).

2. Place the crossbar icon that replaced the pointer so that it is exactly in the upper left corner of the margins.

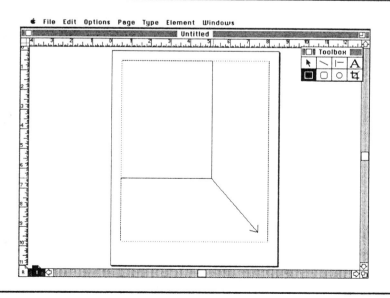

FIGURE 4-8 Building the border line

(Notice how the "Snap to guides" helps you by attracting the pointer to the margins.)

3. Drag the rectangle diagonally to the lower right-hand corner of the margins.

4. Release the mouse button when the rectangle exactly covers the margins.

While the box is still selected, you can specify the 2-point line width as shown in Figure 4-9.

5. Choose "2 pt" from the Line option of the Element menu.

Now you will place the ruler guides for the seven horizontal lines. These will help you exactly place the actual horizontal and vertical lines of the form.

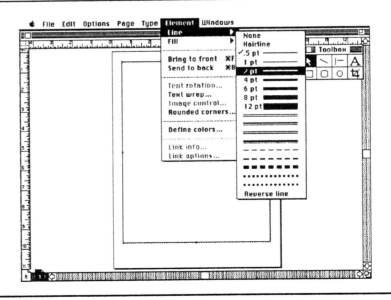

FIGURE 4-9   Line option from the Element menu set to "2 pt"

Notice that as you position the lines, the scale marks on the rulers become dimmer when the moving dotted line in the rulers is exactly over them. Similarly, the crossbar seems to disappear when it is exactly lined up over a ruler guide line.

You are currently looking at a "Fit in window" image on the screen. This lets you see the whole page on one screen, but you cannot see any particular part of it in much detail. For instance, look at the horizontal and vertical rulers. They are divided into sixteenths, and you will be placing some of the lines on the eighths scale marks. Since you cannot see them very clearly and may not be able to precisely place the guides on the marks, you can correct the positioning later in an "Actual size" screen image.

Follow these steps to place the ruler guides:

1. Select the pointer tool.

2. Press the mouse button on the horizontal (top) ruler and drag a ruler guide to 1 inch on the vertical ruler.

3. Drag a second ruler guide to 1 3/4 inches on the vertical ruler.

4. Drag a third ruler guide to 3 3/8 inches.

5. Drag a fourth ruler guide to 3 5/8 inches.

6. Drag a fifth ruler guide to 4 inches.

7. Drag a sixth ruler guide to 4 3/8 inches.

8. Drag a seventh ruler guide to 8 3/4 inches.

When you complete these steps, your screen will look like Figure 4-10. Now you will draw the actual horizontal lines on the form.

9. Select the perpendicular-line tool.

10. Place the crossbar on the intersection of the first horizontal ruler guide (at 1 inch on the vertical ruler) and the left margin. Press the mouse button and drag the crossbar to draw a line to the right margin guide. Make sure that the new line is exactly over the ruler guide before releasing the mouse button.

If the line has been incorrectly placed, press the DELETE key before it is deselected, that is, before you click the mouse button on a different line. (You can tell that it is selected because the ends of the lines have tiny boxes on them.) If it becomes deselected before you can delete it, you'll have to select the pointer tool, click on the incorrect line to select it (you may have to move the guide line up or down before the actual line, which lays on it, can be se-

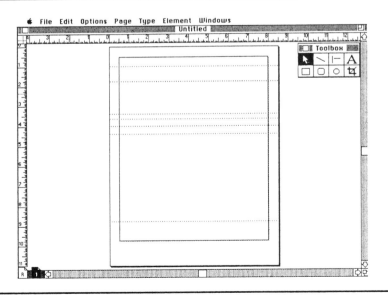

FIGURE 4-10 Horizontal ruler guides on the form

lected), press DELETE to delete the line, and then select the perpendicular-line tool once again before continuing.

Before the line is deselected, you should also check that the line width is correct. It should be the default .5 point.

11. Select the Line option of the Element menu and verify that ".5 pt" is checked.

12. In the same way that you did in step 10, draw the second horizontal line at 1 3/4 inches on the vertical ruler.

13. Choose "1 pt" from the Line option of the Element menu before the line is deselected.

14. Draw the third horizontal line at 3 3/8 inches.

15. While the line is selected, choose "4 pt" from the Line option.

16. Draw the fourth horizontal line at 3 5/8 inches.

17. While the line is selected, verify that ".5 pt" is checked on the Line option.

18. Draw the fifth horizontal line at 4 inches.

19. Choose "6 pt" on the Line option.

20. Draw the sixth horizontal line at 4 3/8 inches.

21. Verify that ".5 pt" is checked on the Line option.

22. Draw the seventh horizontal line at 8 3/4 inches.

23. Verify that ".5 pt" is checked on the Line option.

24. Select the Options menu and choose "Guides" to turn off the ruler guides to allow you to look at the lines you have drawn.

Your screen should look like Figure 4-11.

You have successfully entered all the horizontal lines for the Sales Order form. Continue even if you can tell that some of the lines need adjusting. You will adjust them later. Now you will enter the actual text.

ENTERING NONCOLUMNAR TEXT

In Figure 4-1 you can see that four areas of the Sales Order form may be considered to be one column wide: the areas containing the title of the form, the company name, the "Comments" area, and the address line at the bottom of the page.

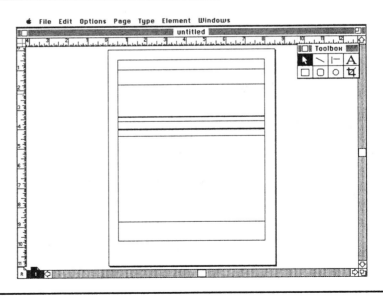

FIGURE 4-11   The form with all horizontal lines

It is important to enter the single-column text before placing the column guides. Otherwise, PageMaker will try to keep the text all within the current column, causing text (such as the company name) to wrap around on several lines. So, first proceed with the single-column text, then the two-column text, and so on.

First you'll enter the form title.

Form Title

The title of the form is, "Sales Order." This will be placed in the top area of the form. As you recall from the design discussion, the type will be 18-point Helvetica.

The current default of "Snap to guides," which causes the guide lines to act as magnets as the pointer gets close to them, is usually helpful because the magnetic property helps you line up the pointer with the guide. But for entering text, it will hinder you by causing the centering to be off. One of your first tasks will be to disable the "Snap to guides."

Follow these steps to enter it:

1. Choose "Guides" in the Options menu to turn them back on and the "Snap to guides" option in the Options menu, causing them to be disabled (no check mark beside it).

2. Select the text tool (the one marked "A").

At this point you'll change to "Actual size" so that you can more accurately enter the text. Although you could choose the "Actual size" option from the Page menu, you will use a shortcut method of varying the screen image size by pressing COMMAND+1.

When you expand the screen image to "Actual size," the view that you see will depend on what was highlighted or selected when you gave the command. The object highlighted or selected will become the center of the screen. So selecting what you want to see ahead of time saves you from having to position the screen with the scroll bars in "Actual size." Here you want to position the screen so you can see the top two bands of the form.

3. Click the I-beam in the middle of the third band at 4 inches on the horizontal ruler and 2 1/2 inches on the vertical ruler.

4. Select the "Actual size" screen image by pressing COMMAND+1.

Your screen should look like Figure 4-12. If it does not, adjust it by using the scroll bars.

Now you will enter the text. The title will be centered between the right and left margins because you have used that for the default alignment. However, you also want it to be centered between the top margin and the first horizontal line. To do this, you must click the pointer in the position where you want the letters to be—as close to the middle of the band as possible. You can do a final adjustment later.

5. Click in the top band of the page, close to the middle horizontally, and at 3/4 inches on the vertical ruler.

6. Press COMMAND+T for "Type specs."

7. Type **18** for "Size" and click on "Bold" in the Type specifications dialog box, as shown in Figure 4-13. The "Font" should still be set to the default, "Helvetica."

8. Click on "OK" or press RETURN to complete the dialog box.

9. Press the CAPS LOCK key. (It isn't necessary to change the default "Case" from "Normal" in the Type specifications dialog box, when you simply want the standard upper- or lowercase.)

10. Type **SALES ORDER**.

You'll see that the title, centered as the default specifies, is now on the page.

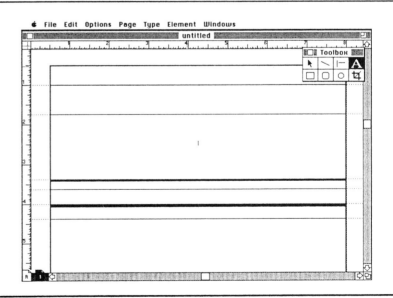

FIGURE 4-12 "Actual size" screen image before entering title

```
┌──────────────────────────────────────────────────────────┐
│  Type specifications _____ ╭──────╮ │
│                                                  │  OK  │ │
│  Font:      │Helvetica│                          ╰──────╯ │
│                                                  ┌──────┐ │
│  Size:      │18│  ▷│ points   Position: │Normal│ │Cancel│ │
│                                                  └──────┘ │
│  Leading:   │Auto│ ▷│ points   Case:    │Normal│ ┌────────┐│
│                                                  │Options…││
│  Set width: │Normal│▷│ percent  Track:  │No track│└────────┘│
│                                                           │
│  Color:     │Black│                                       │
│                                                           │
│  Type style: ☐ Normal  ☐ Italic    ☐ Outline  ☐ Reverse  │
│              ☒ Bold    ☐ Underline ☐ Shadow   ☐ Strikethru│
└──────────────────────────────────────────────────────────┘
```

FIGURE 4-13   The Type specifications dialog box for the form title

Name of Company

The company name is entered in the band below the form title. Recall from the design discussion that the name is in 24-point Times, centered, and Bold-Italic.
Follow these steps to enter it:

1. Click in the band below the form title, at 1 3/8 inches on the vertical ruler and 4 1/4 inches on the horizontal ruler.

2. Press COMMAND+T for "Type specs."

3. Choose "Times," "Bold," and "Italic." Enter **18** for "Size" and then verify that "Position" and "Case" are "Normal," that "Leading" is "Auto," and click on "OK."

4. Type **MICRO CORPORATION OF AMERICA.**

The page will now contain the company name centered in Times Bold-Italic with the type specifications set forth in your design. Your screen should look like Figure 4-14.

You'll now skip to the bottom of the page and enter the company address.

Address of Company

The company address will be entered on the last band of the page, just below the bottom margin. It will be 10-point Helvetica in "Normal" style.

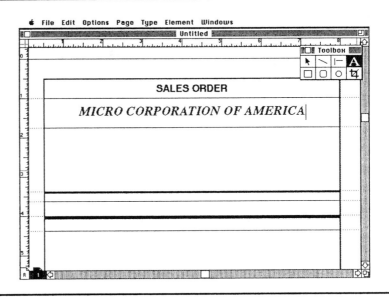

══ **FIGURE 4-14** The completed title and company name

Between the street and city, and between the ZIP and the phone numbers, you will enter a bullet. In PageMaker, this is done by pressing OPTION+8 simultaneously. (The 8 should be typed on the regular keyboard, not the numeric keypad.) You will also place a space on either side of the bullet.

Follow these steps to enter and edit the address:

1. Verify that the text tool is selected.

2. Adjust the screen by dragging the vertical scroll box two-thirds of the way down the bar so that you can see the last two lines of the form, as shown in Figure 4-15.

3. Place the I-beam in the last band of the page, between the bottom margin guide and the edge of the page. Place the I-beam so that the top part rests anywhere horizon-

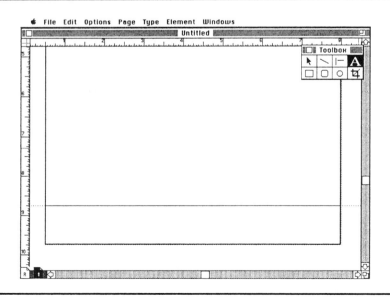

FIGURE 4-15   The last two lines of the form

tally on the bottom margin guide. Click the mouse button. The insertion point will appear between 4 and 5 inches on the horizontal ruler.

4. Press COMMAND+T for "Type specs," type **10** for "Size" and verify that the font is set to "Helvetica," "Leading" to "Auto," and "Type style," "Position," and "Case" to "Normal" in the Type specifications dialog box. Click on "OK."

5. Type **ONE MICRO WAY**. Press OPTION+8 to insert a bullet. Type **SILICON VALLEY, CA 94123**. Press OPTION+8 to insert another bullet. Type **(800) 555-1234 or (415) 555-4321**. Figure 4-16 shows the result.

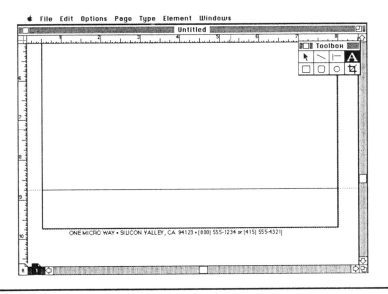

FIGURE 4-16 The address at the bottom

Sometimes, when text is below the bottom margin as in this case, it does not get properly centered. Check that next.

6. Select the pointer tool.

7. Click in the middle of the address text so that it becomes selected, as shown in Figure 4-17.

A selection box (two lines, one above and one below the text) will appear. The lines have handles on them and tiny boxes on each end of the lines that can be used to move the text. When they are moved, the lines become a solid box.

8. Stretch the text by dragging one of the tiny boxes on the left end of the lines until it is under the left margin, at 1/2 inch on the horizontal ruler.

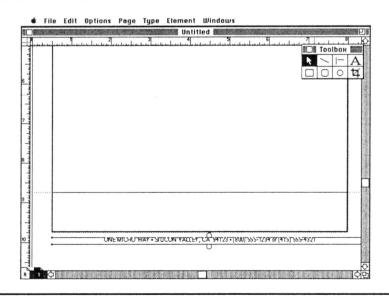

FIGURE 4-17   The address with a selection box around it.

9. Adjust your screen by clicking on the horizontal scroll bar between the scroll box and the right scroll arrow.

10. Then stretch the text toward the right margin by dragging one of the tiny boxes on the right end until the selection box is under the right margin, at 8 inches, as shown in Figure 4-18.

The lines and handles will disappear when you select something else. For now, click the pointer in the pasteboard to see the text without the selection box.

You'll now enter the last of the single-column text — the "Comments:".

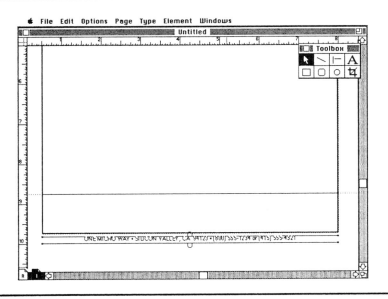

FIGURE 4-18 The address selection box extended to the right margin

Comments Area

The "Comments" area is entered similarly in the band of the page just above the bottom margin, as shown in Figure 4-19. The type specifications are 8-point Helvetica. However, the word "Comments:" is not centered; it is left-aligned with an en-space separating it from the border.

Follow these steps to enter it:

1. Use the horizontal scroll bar to position the screen so that the left margin is visible, as seen in Figure 4-19.

2. Select the text tool.

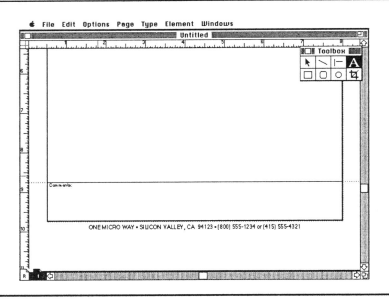

FIGURE 4-19 The "Comments:" area in the bottom band

3. Click the I-beam in the band just above the bottom margin, at 8 7/8 inches on the vertical ruler and 5/8 inch on the horizontal ruler. The insertion point will jump to the center, but you will fix that next.

4. Press COMMAND+SHIFT+L to left-align the text.

5. Press COMMAND+T for "Type specs."

6. Verify that the default type specifications are set to "Helvetica," "8" for "Size," and "Normal" Type style, "Position," and "Case." Then click on "OK."

7. Press CAPS LOCK to release it.

8. Press COMMAND+SHIFT+N to insert an en-space and type **Comments:**

The text will be left-aligned and should look like Figure 4-19. If it is not placed exactly as you want it, you will be able to correct it soon.

9. To look at the overall form, press COMMAND+W. The "Fit in window" view will appear.

Although you cannot see the printing, you can see the positioning of the text within the bands. You may now want to correct some of the positioning of the text.

Correcting the Text Positioning

If you look closely at the positioning of the form title and the company name, you may discover that the text is not centered, either vertically or horizontally, exactly as you want it. For instance, it may be too close to an upper or lower line. Correct this as you did the address by selecting the text with the pointer tool, producing a selection box with the handles around the text. You move the text by pressing the mouse button until a four-headed arrow appears and then you can drag the text block into position.

You will use the shortcut method of switching your screen image from "Fit in window" to "Actual size" and back. Recall that to do this you first select an object near the center of what you want to be displayed and then press COMMAND+1.

If the form title is not centered correctly, follow these steps to correct it:

1. Select the pointer tool.

2. Click on the company name and then press COMMAND+1.

3. Arrange the screen with the scroll bars so that the form title is easily visible.

4. Click on the form title so that a selection box appears around it.

5. Drag the selection box around until it is centered as you want it.

If the company name is not centered between the lines, follow a similar procedure to correct it. Check the comments and address as well.

When you are satisfied with your form, you need to restore the "Snap to guides" and screen size, as follows:

6. Click the mouse button in the pasteboard to clear the selected text (to get rid of the lines and handles).

7. Choose "Snap to guides" in the Options menu. A check mark will appear next to the option.

8. Press COMMAND+W to return to the "Fit in window" screen image.

You can now enter the vertical lines and fill in the labels of the form. But first, you must save your work.

SAVING YOUR WORK

Now is a good time to save your Sales Order form. Remember that "Publications" is our name for the folder used to store the publications created here. If you have used a different name, alter the following instructions accordingly.

To save your file with the shortcut technique, follow these steps:

1. Press COMMAND+S for save.

2. When the Save as dialog box is displayed, type **order** in the text box, as shown here:

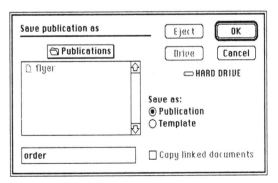

3. When you are satisfied with the name, press RETURN.

Now you are ready to enter the "BILL TO:/SHIP TO:" area of the form.

ENTERING THE BILL TO:/ SHIP TO: AREA

In Figure 4-1 you can see that the BILL TO:/SHIP TO: area can be visualized as two columns. And establishing two columns turns out to be the easiest way to create this area.

After setting up the two columns, you will again place several ruler guides to define precisely where to put the corner brackets surrounding each address area.

Setting Up Two Columns

It is easy to set up columns with PageMaker. You simply specify the number of columns and the spacing between them in the dialog box displayed when you select the "Column guides..." option in the Options menu. Once the column guides are placed on the page, you arrange them as you want and then draw the corner brackets.

Follow these steps to set up two columns:

1. Choose the "Column guides..." option on the Options menu.

You will be shown the Column guides dialog box. It asks the number of columns to be set up and the spacing between them. Specify two columns with .5 inch, as shown here:

2. Type **2** and press TAB.

3. Type **.5** and press RETURN.

```
┌──────────────────────────────────────────────────┐
│  Column guides                          ┌────────┐│
│                                         │   OK   ││
│                                         └────────┘│
│                                          ┌────────┐│
│  Number of columns:       ┌──────┐       │ Cancel ││
│                           │ 2    │       └────────┘│
│  Space between columns:   ┌──────┐                 │
│                           │ .5   │                 │
│                           └──────┘                 │
└──────────────────────────────────────────────────┘
```

You'll see two column guides in the center of the page. These are the innermost delimiters of the two columns and are separated by the .5 inch that you specified. The left and right margins hide the outer column guides. Next you will bring in the outer column guides so that the columns are narrower.

4. Select the Option menu and make sure that "Snap to rulers" is turned on (checked).

5. Press and hold the mouse button on the left margin to select the column guide there.

6. With the Double arrow icon, drag the column guide right to 1 inch on the horizontal ruler.

7. Drag the right column guide left to 7 1/2 inches on the horizontal ruler.

You have just created the two column delimiters, as shown in Figure 4-20, and will now set up additional ruler guides to help place the corner brackets and text.

Entering Ruler Guides

You will now set up four horizontal ruler guides and four vertical ones. They will be used when you draw the corner brackets.

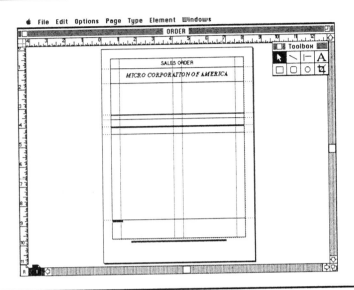

FIGURE 4-20 Column guides for two columns

As you drag the ruler guides from the two rulers onto the form, you'll know when you have placed them exactly on a mark because the dotted line in the ruler disappears when it is exactly over one of the scale marks.

To place the horizontal ruler guides, follow these steps:

1. Press on the horizontal (top) ruler and drag a horizontal ruler guide down to 3 1/4 inches on the vertical ruler.

2. Drag a horizontal ruler guide to 3 inches on the vertical ruler.

3. Drag a horizontal ruler guide to 2 1/4 inches.

4. Drag a horizontal ruler guide to 2 inches.

Your page will look like the one shown in Figure 4-21. Now you will add the vertical ruler guides.

5. Press on the vertical ruler and drag a vertical ruler guide right until it reaches 7 1/4 inches on the horizontal ruler.

6. Drag another vertical ruler guide to 4 3/4 inches on the horizontal ruler.

7. Drag a vertical ruler guide to 3 3/4 inches.

8. Drag a vertical ruler guide to 1 1/4 inches.

Your finished screen will look like the one shown in Figure 4-22.

You'll need to make sure the guide lines are precisely lined up, or the corner brackets will be off, and it will be apparent. To do this, you'll return the screen to "Actual

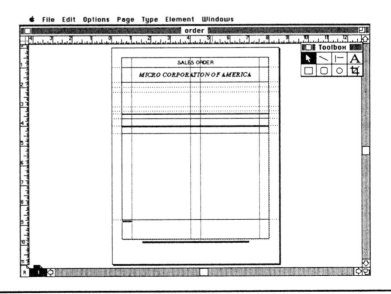

FIGURE 4-21 Horizontal guides on columns for the BILL TO:/SHIP TO: brackets

size" and then adjust the lines so that they are exactly on the ruler scale marks.

9. Select the company name as the item to center on and press COMMAND+1.

10. Adjust your screen image with the scroll bars until your screen looks like the one shown in Figure 4-23.

11. Adjust the ruler and column guides so that they are exactly at 2, 2 1/4, 3, and 3 1/4 inches on the vertical ruler; and at 1, 1 1/4, 3 3/4, 4, 4 1/2, 4 3/4, 7 1/4, and 7 1/2 inches on the horizontal ruler.

Once your guide lines are precisely set up, the boxes formed by the lines will be perfectly square.

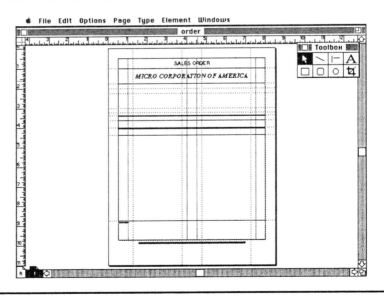

FIGURE 4-22 The completed vertical and horizontal guides for brackets

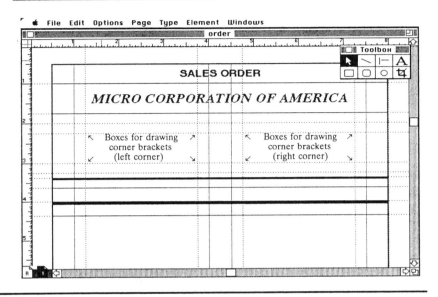

FIGURE 4-23 "Actual size" screen showing BILL TO:/SHIP TO: area

Notice in Figure 4-23 that in each column there are four small corner boxes formed by the guide lines. Two sides of each box are used to form the corner brackets; for example, on the top left box, the top and left sides of the box will be used for drawing the corner brackets. You can be comfortable that the corner brackets will be correctly drawn when the boxes are perfectly square.

Drawing BILL TO:/SHIP TO: Corner Brackets

You will first draw the corner brackets for the left column by drawing two lines in each of the four boxes in the left column, as shown in Figure 4-23. You will use the perpendicular-line tool for drawing. In choosing the tool you want, you'll use a shortcut (by pressing SHIFT+F3) if you have an extended keyboard. You'll also double-check that the default is correctly set for a .5 point line.

To draw the lines, follow these steps:

1. Select the Line option of the Element menu and verify that the ".5 pt" option is checked. If it is not, drag the highlight bar to it and release the mouse button.

2. Press SHIFT+F3, or click in the Toolbox to get the perpendicular-line tool.

You'll see the pointer become a crossbar. During the following steps, use Figures 4-23 and 4-24 to assure yourself that you are drawing the lines in the appropriate locations.

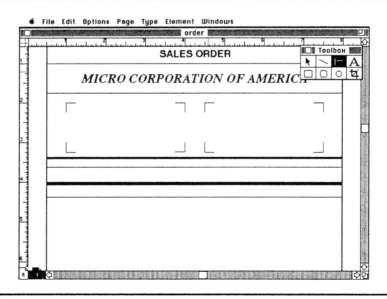

FIGURE 4-24 The screen showing eight corner brackets

3. Place the crossbar in the upper left corner of the top left box at 1 inch on the horizontal ruler, and 2 inches on the vertical ruler. Draw a 1/4-inch horizontal line along the top of the box to form the top of the corner bracket.

4. Again place the crossbar in the upper left corner of the top left box and draw a 1/4-inch vertical line down to the bottom of the box, along the left guide line.

5. Place the crossbar on the lower left corner of the bottom box at 1 inch on the horizontal ruler, and 3 1/4 inches on the vertical ruler. Draw a 1/4-inch vertical line to the top of the box.

6. Again, place the crossbar on the lower left corner of the bottom box and draw a horizontal line across to the right side of the box.

7. Draw similar lines to form corner brackets on the upper right box of the left column, beginning at 4 inches on the horizontal ruler and 2 inches on the vertical ruler.

8. Draw the corner bracket on the lower right box of the left column.

9. Draw the four corner brackets in the right column in the same way.

Turn off your "Guides" from the Options menu and your screen will look like the one shown in Figure 4-24 when you're done. Be sure to turn your "Guides" back on.

Typing Text

Once you have drawn the corner brackets, you can type in the text. Because the default for alignment is still "Centered," you'll change it so that the text will be left-aligned.

You'll use the shortcut method to do this. You will also verify and choose the type specifications for 10-point Helvetica.

To enter the text, follow these steps:

1. Press SHIFT+F4, or click in the Toolbox, to get the text tool.

2. Place the I-beam above the upper left corner bracket in the left column so that the top crossbar of the icon disappears into the line above it at 1 3/4 inch on the vertical ruler; then click the mouse button.

3. Press COMMAND+SHIFT+L to left-align the text (the insertion point will relocate).

4. Press COMMAND+T for "Type specs," type in **10** in the "Size" text box, and verify that the other defaults have not changed in the Type specifications dialog box; then click on "OK."

5. Press the CAPS LOCK key to turn on capital letters.

6. Type **BILL TO:**.

7. Move the I-beam to the right column above the upper left corner bracket so that the top crossbar of the icon disappears in the line above it at 1 3/4 inches on the vertical ruler, then click.

8. Press COMMAND+SHIFT+L to left-align the text.

9. Press COMMAND+T for "Type specs," type **10** in the "Size" text box, and verify that the other defaults have not changed in the Type specifications dialog box; then click on "OK."

10. Type **SHIP TO:**.

Your screen will look like the one shown in Figure 4-25.

Before you continue, you should clean up the page by removing some of the ruler guides. You can identify which lines are the ruler guides because the lines contain wider spaced dots, or are a different color on color screens, than the column guides. Also, the ruler guides span from the top of the page to the bottom; the column guides fall between the top and bottom margins. Be careful not to accidentally move one of the other lines.

To remove the guides, follow these steps:

11. Press COMMAND+W for "Fit in window."

12. Select the pointer tool by pressing SHIFT+F1 or by clicking on it in the Toolbox.

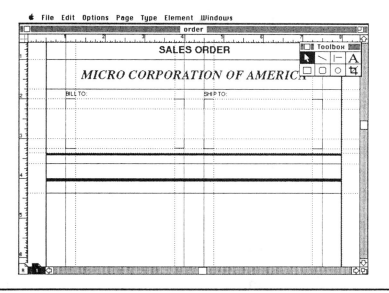

FIGURE 4-25 The completed BILL TO:/SHIP TO: area

13. Drag both the horizontal and vertical guide lines (the ones that run to the edges of the page) to the pasteboard before releasing the mouse button.

When you are finished, your page will look like the one shown in Figure 4-26.

You can now complete the Sales Order form by filling in the order detail area of the form.

BUILDING THE DETAIL AREA OF THE FORM

The order details consist of two areas of information: a column area and a detail area. The column area is made up

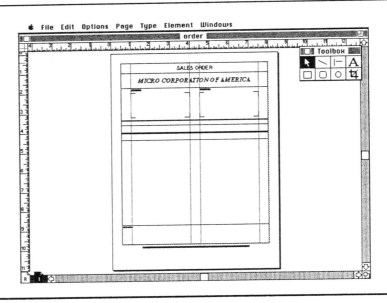

FIGURE 4-26 The form after the ruler guides have been removed

of six columns, each with a label box immediately above it. Above the column labels is the detail area. It contains a row of seven detail boxes, each having its own label box, as shown in Figure 4-1.

To define the order details, you will first set up the six column guides with no spaces separating them. Then you will draw the actual lines. Finally, you will fill in the text and fill two of the columns with shading.

Setting Up Guide Lines for Six Columns

Again, your first task is to set up and then arrange the column guides for the lines. Then you can use them to draw the actual lines.

To draw the column guides, follow these steps:

1. Verify that you are working with the pointer tool. If not, press SHIFT+F1 or click on it in the Toolbox.

2. Choose "Column guides. . ." from the Options menu.

3. When prompted by the dialog box, type **6** for "Number of columns," press TAB, and type **0** for "Space between columns," as shown here:

```
┌──────────────────────────────────────────────────┐
│ Column guides ──────────────────────    ( OK )    │
│                                          (Cancel) │
│                                                    │
│  Number of columns:        [6    ]                 │
│  Space between columns:    [0    ]                 │
│                                                    │
└──────────────────────────────────────────────────┘
```

4. Press RETURN to complete the dialog box. (PageMaker will insert column guides on the page at 1 3/4, 3, 4 1/4, 5 1/2, and 6 3/4 inches on the horizontal ruler.)

Because you need to be able to see the page with greater accuracy in order to place the guide lines, you will switch the screen to "Actual size." You want to be able to see the middle of the page.

5. Press COMMAND+1 to return the screen view to "Actual size."

Now you will arrange the column guides in the appropriate locations by dragging them to specific locations on the horizontal ruler.

6. Drag the far left column guide from 1 3/4 to 1 1/2 inches on the horizontal ruler.

7. Drag the next column guide from 3 to 2 1/4 inches.

8. Drag the third column guide from 4 1/4 to 3 1/2 inches.

9. Drag the fourth column guide from 5 1/2 to 6 inches.

10. Drag the fifth column guide from 6 3/4 to 7 inches. (You may want to turn off or move your Toolbox to see the far right vertical rule. To turn it off, click on the close box in the upper left corner. Turn it back on by choosing "Toolbox" from the windows menu. To move it, drag on the "Toolbox" title bar.)

Your page will look like the one shown in Figure 4-27.

11. Press COMMAND+W to return to "Fit in window" view.

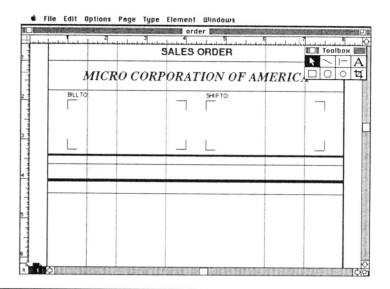

FIGURE 4-27   The form showing six adjusted column guides

Now you will draw the actual lines.

Drawing the Column Lines

As shown in Figure 4-28, the lines that you will draw extend vertically from the horizontal line at 3 3/8 inches to the line at 8 3/4 inches. The end result will be to define the order columns, including both the initial detail area and the six columns below it. Both the detail boxes and the columns have label areas, as shown in Figure 4-28.

To draw the lines, follow these steps:

1. Press SHIFT+F3 or click on the perpendicular-line tool in the Toolbox.

2. Place the crossbar on the top of the leftmost column guide, at 1 1/2 inches on the horizontal ruler and 3 3/8 inches on the vertical ruler, until the crossbar seems to disappear.

3. Drag the line down to 8 3/4 inches on the vertical ruler before releasing the mouse button.

4. Verify that the line size is correct by selecting the Line option in the Element menu and seeing whether the ".5 pt" option is checked. If not, choose that option.

5. Draw four other vertical lines for the four remaining column guides in the same way.

Notice that above the "Description" label is an extra line separating the "Purchase Order #" column from the "Salesperson" column. Draw that line now.

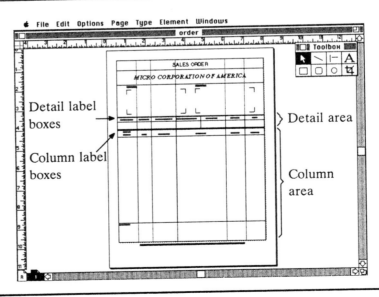

═══ **FIGURE 4-28** The screen showing label areas for boxes and columns

6. Draw a vertical line from the intersection of 3 3/8 inches on the vertical ruler and 4 3/4 inches on the horizontal ruler to 4 inches on the vertical ruler.

Your page will look like the one shown in Figure 4-29.

7. Save your work by pressing COMMAND+S.

Now you can begin entering the text.

Entering the Detail Box Labels

As shown in Figure 4-28, you've established two areas with the horizontal and vertical lines: a detail area containing label boxes and detail boxes, and six columns, each with label boxes. You will first fill in the labels in the detail area.

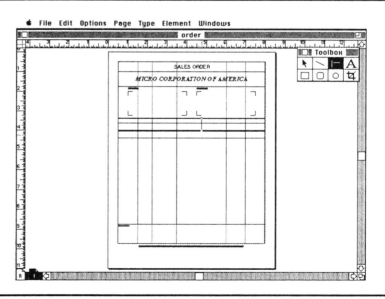

FIGURE 4-29   The form with last short vertical line selected

To place the text, you'll have to work in the "Actual size" mode. You'll notice that it is not easy to exactly center text in the boxes. You'll want to place the insertion point in the same place in each label area. Use the cross-bars at the top and bottom of the I-beam to locate the vertical insertion point. Otherwise, your text may be centered between the right and left sides but not between the top and bottom sides of the boxes. If some of them are off-center, it will be obvious.

To enter the text, follow these steps:

1. Press COMMAND+1 to get the "Actual size" view of the page. If necessary, use the horizontal scroll bar to adjust the view.

The view should show the detail area in the middle of the screen, with the left margin slightly visible, as shown in Figure 4-30.

2. Press SHIFT+F4 or choose the text tool from the Toolbox.

3. Turn off the CAPS LOCK. (You needn't make changes in the Type specifications dialog box because you want the defaults.)

4. Place the I-beam in the label area of the upper left detail area so that the crossbar on the bottom of the icon disappears in the bottom line of the box; then click the mouse button.

5. Type in **Sales Order #**.

Your screen will look like the one shown in Figure 4-31. Continue with the rest of the labels:

6. Place the I-beam in the next label box to the right, positioning it as before, and click the mouse button.

7. Type in **Order Date**.

8. Move to the third detail label box, place the I-beam, click, and type **Customer Number**.

9. In the fourth label box, place and click the I-beam as you did earlier. Then press COMMAND+SHIFT+L to left-align the label, type two em-spaces (a fixed width space equal to the full type size) by pressing COMMAND+SHIFT+M twice, type **Purchase Order #**, press TAB, and type **Salesperson**.

10. Type **Promised** in the sixth label box.

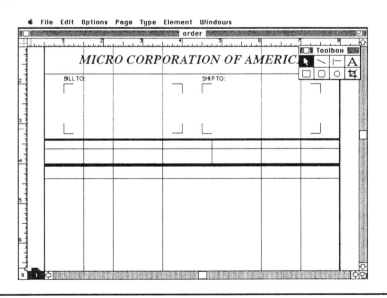

FIGURE 4-30 The "Actual size" view of the detail boxes

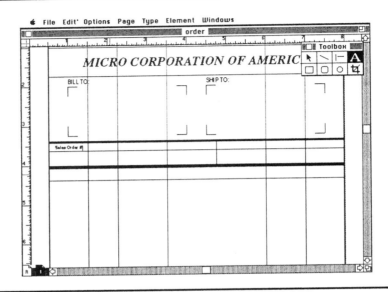

FIGURE 4-31   The first detail label filled in

11. Type **Terms** in the seventh box.

    Your screen will look like the one shown in Figure 4-32.
    If some of your text is not centered between the upper
    and lower lines, you must adjust it by using the same
    technique that you used earlier to adjust the form title and
    company name. You can follow these quick steps if neces-
    sary to adjust any of the label text.

12. Drag down a horizontal ruler guide and place it just
    under the items you believe are correctly centered.

13. Select the pointer tool by pressing SHIFT+F1 or clicking
    on it.

14. Click on the uncentered text.

15. When you can see the text inside the selection box, press the mouse button until the pointer becomes a four-headed arrow, and then drag the text up or down until the selected text is just sitting on the ruler guide.

You will enter the column titles in a similar manner.

Entering the Column Labels

The label box for the first column contains two lines of text; the rest of the columns, only one. Consequently, the positioning of the I-beam within the first label box differs. Otherwise, the task is very similar to that of filling in the detail label boxes.

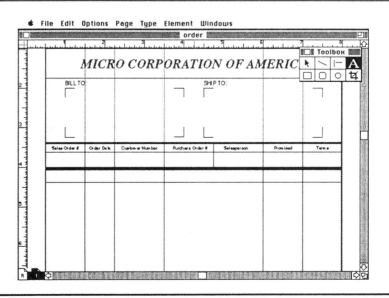

═══ **FIGURE 4-32**   The form showing detail labels filled in

To enter the column labels, follow these steps:

1. If necessary, adjust your screen with the horizontal scroll bar to position the window so that the left margin is just visible.

2. Press SHIFT+F4 or select the text tool from the Toolbox.

3. Place the I-beam in the first label box above the left column so that the top of the I-beam rests in the middle of the upper line at 4 3/16 inches on the vertical ruler; then click.

4. Type **Quantity** and press RETURN.

5. Type **Ordered**.

6. Place the I-beam in the second label box so that the bottom of the I-beam disappears into the bottom line, click, and type **Units**.

7. In the same way, type **Part Number** in the third box.

8. Type **Description** in the fourth box.

9. Type **Unit Price** in the fifth box.

10. Type **Extension** in the sixth label box.

Your screen will look like the one shown in Figure 4-33. Again, you may have to center some of the text. If you need to do this, use the technique that you used for adjusting the detail labels to move the text to where you want it.

11. Press COMMAND+W to return the screen to the "Fit in window" image. Your screen should look like Figure 4-28.

Your final step is to supply the shading in the last two columns.

Shading Two Columns

The fifth and sixth columns will be given 10 percent shading so that the sales staff leaves them blank. To shade an area, you must have a rectangle or circle to contain the shading; using the line tool to draw a rectangle with intersecting lines won't do. It must be a rectangle or an oval

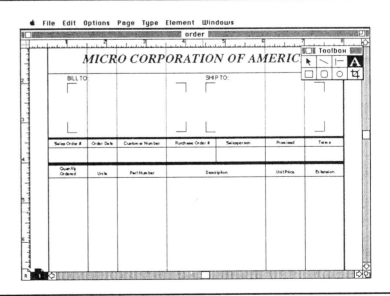

FIGURE 4-33   The form after all labels are entered

made with a rectangle or oval tool. Then you simply tell PageMaker to fill in the area with the shading of your choice. Because the columns are already defined by lines of their own, you will draw an invisible rectangle (one without lines) to hold the shading.

As you will recall from the flyer example in Chapter 3, PageMaker builds documents in layers. When you first draw the rectangle, it will be on top of the stack of layers, which won't be a problem because its sides are invisible and it is empty. However, as soon as you fill in shading, the shaded rectangle will cover up the text and column lines beneath it. You therefore must place the shaded rectangle on the bottom of the stack, which allows the text and column lines to show up.

To add the shading, follow these steps:

1. Press SHIFT+F1, or click in the Toolbox, for the pointer tool.

2. Choose "None" in the Line option of the Element window to draw a rectangle without visible lines.

3. Select the square-corner tool from the Toolbox by pressing SHIFT+F5.

4. Position the crossbar on the upper left corner of the "Unit Price" label box at 6 inches on the horizontal ruler and 4 inches on the vertical ruler.

When the crossbar icon is correctly positioned, the intersection beneath it will disappear. Similarly, as you draw the rectangle, the original lines will disappear when the invisible rectangle lines are directly over them.

5. Drag the rectangle diagonally to the lower right corner of the "Extension" column, at 8 inches on the horizontal

ruler and 8 3/4 inches on the vertical ruler, before releasing the mouse button.

Before deselecting the box, select the shading.

6. Choose "10%" from the Fill option of the Element menu.

The columns are filled in with the shading, and everything under it has been covered up, as shown in Figure 4-34. You'll now send the top layer, the shaded rectangle, to the bottom of the stack, or to the back.

7. Choose "Send to back" from the Element menu.

The Sales Order form is now complete. Save your work.

8. Press COMMAND+S for save.

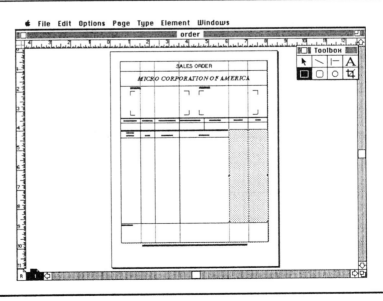

FIGURE 4-34 Right two columns shaded before "Send to back"

The final product now appears on your screen. You may want to look at the whole Sales Order form in "Actual size" or even at "200%" and make any necessary adjustments.

PRINTING THE SALES ORDER FORM

Your Sales Order form is now ready to be printed.

1. Press COMMAND+P to print.

2. When the Printer dialog box is presented, verify that it is acceptable, and when your printer is ready, click on "Print."

Check that your Sales Order form is similar to that shown in Figure 4-1. If not, correct, save, and reprint it.

This concludes the building of the Sales Order form. You can use the techniques presented in this chapter to produce many forms for your own company or business. In addition, you can add graphics or a company logo if you want, as you'll see in the next chapter.

Chapter 5, "Creating a Brochure," demonstrates how to build a threefold, double-sided brochure.

chapter **5**

CREATING A BROCHURE

Brochures come in many forms. The one that you will build in this chapter is a single sheet of 8.5 × 11-inch paper, printed on both sides and folded into thirds, as shown in Figure 5-1. It is the standard form of brochure used for direct mail solicitation. Its purpose is to provide information about a company's capabilities—in this case, a firm engaged in desktop publishing.

You create the brochure with a combination of text entered in both PageMaker and Microsoft Word to take advantage of the capabilities of each. It is easier to enter

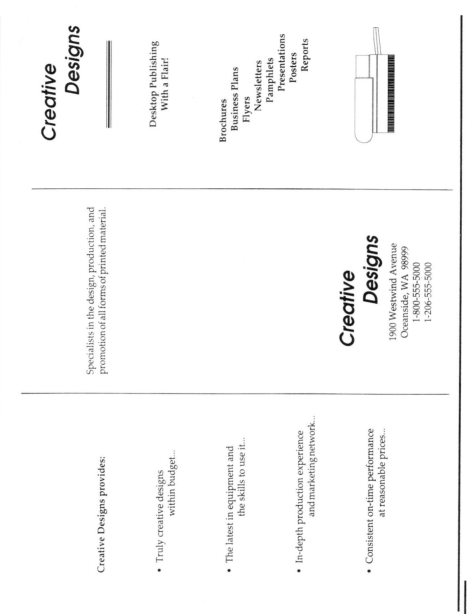

FIGURE 5-1 The printout of finished brochure with graphics (page 1)

What can we do for you?

- Save Money...
  We have highly efficient equipment and the skills necessary to produce the best quality products at the lowest prices — benefits we pass on to you.

- Eliminate Hassle...
  We are designers, managers, and skilled craftsmen who help you plan, design, produce, and promote your printed products. We understand the intricacies of typesetting, printing, bindery, and direct mail solicitation. We oversee the project from beginning to completion.

- Create Effective Publications...
  A truly effective publication - one that accomplishes its purposes - is the only kind we produce: sales brochures that sell; training manuals that teach; and newsletters that inform. An effective publication is a sound investment.

How are our services used?

- Finding Answers...
  What is the purpose of the publication? What is the audience? What copy, graphics, and photos are to be used? What size and shape is desired? What length is it? What color is appropriate?

- Setting Budgets and Schedules...
  How much do you want to spend and when do you want the work completed? How can we help you stretch your dollars, giving you the best publication in the time you have to produce it?

- Planning and Design...
  Based on your specifications, we create a design and a production plan to meet your needs.

- Production and Promotion...
  We use the latest equipment and specialized talents and skills to produce and promote your publication.

Who uses our services?

Big and small companies, public and private agencies, including architects, aerospace companies, banks, bakeries, contractors, CPA firms, doctors, hospitals, libraries, local governments, schools, universities, and wineries.

We will provide you a specific list of our customers in your industry if you request it.

We welcome all projects where quality, attention to detail, and creativity are of concern.

For outstanding results, let us assist you with your next project.

FIGURE 5-1 The printout of finished brochure with graphics (page 2)

small amounts of text requiring special formatting or placement in PageMaker. However, it is easier to enter and edit larger blocks of text in a word processor, especially when indenting frequently. You will enter the company name, product list, and address directly into PageMaker because they are short, use unique fonts, and are independently located on the brochure. And you will enter the balance of the brochure in Microsoft Word, where you can easily indent, check the spelling, and perform other editing.

If you use a word processor other than Microsoft Word (and it is supported by PageMaker), use it instead. Read through the Word instructions and duplicate them in your word processor. Also check the index for the pages (if any) on which we discuss your word processor and scan them to see if any specific instructions are needed to use your word processor with PageMaker for a project like this brochure.

In addition to the text, this brochure will include a horizontal line element, vertical lines that serve as text separators, and a graphic from Aldus FreeHand. This allows you to combine all of the major elements of a PageMaker publication: both internally and externally created text and graphic elements.

PLANNING AND DESIGNING THE BROCHURE

Planning the brochure is reasonably simple. You may want to have a marketing or public relations person create the copy (or the first draft of it), but the brochure can easily be a one-person project. If you plan on printing a large quantity (over a hundred copies), you will produce a set of originals on your laser printer and then take them to a commercial printer for the final product. During the planning, you should also consider the mailing costs and procedures for distributing the brochures.

The design begins with a single 8.5 × 11-inch, standard, letter-size piece of paper. You will use both sides of the paper, considering each side a page. Each page will be divided into three columns with a 1/2-inch margin on all edges. When the paper is folded, the columns become panels.

Three fonts are used in creating the brochure: the title (the company name) is set in 24-point Avant Garde Demi-Oblique (bold-italic) type; the rest of the right column on the first page uses 14-point Palatino Bold; and the balance of the brochure uses 12-point Palatino Roman with headings in bold. You may wish or need to use other typefaces, sizes, or styles to correspond with those you have available. The fonts used here are those available on the Apple LaserWriter IINT, which we use as the model throughout this book. There are many printer and font vendors that you may also use. (See Appendix B, "Using Fonts and Laser Printers," for a discussion of these.)

The graphic on the cover is created with Aldus Free-Hand. It is a quick sketch of the Apple LaserWriter II. If you do not have FreeHand, you can use any other drawing package you have available. As with the word processor, look at the instructions we give for FreeHand, and then consult the index to see if we discuss your drawing package. While you can use a paint program, the result will be different. If you don't wish to do a drawing you can use any appropriate clip art (or "click art") you have.

The vertical lines or rules between columns are hairlines, the smallest line width available in PageMaker. Therefore, except for possible font or graphic substitutions, the brochure design is unaffected by system constraints.

Before bringing up PageMaker to create the brochure, you'll look at creating the text and graphics with Microsoft Word and Aldus FreeHand. If you do not want to enter the text and graphics files used to build the PageMaker publications in this book, you can buy a disk containing those files, as well as files containing the finished publications. See the order form contained in this book.

CREATING THE TEXT AND GRAPHICS

Because the primary focus of this book is PageMaker, the following discussion will only briefly examine what you do in Microsoft Word and Aldus FreeHand to create the text and graphics for this brochure. Notice particularly the constraints that PageMaker places on files imported from these applications. If you are using a different word processor or drawing application, you'll want to look at the chapter that discusses how those applications are used, in addition to reading the material below.

Entering the Text With Microsoft Word

Text brought into PageMaker from Microsoft Word 4 retains almost all of the formatting and style settings chosen in Word. You will therefore set the spacing, indents, tabs, font, font size, and font style all within Word. When you transfer the document over to PageMaker, all of this information will accompany it. As you will see in Chapter 7, "Preparing a Newsletter," you can also establish styles by using Word's style sheet and transferring them to Page-Maker with the text. For now, however, you will not use a style sheet.

SETTING UP MICROSOFT WORD   It is important that the format settings are correctly set in Microsoft Word because you'll see their effects in PageMaker. Start Word now, open a new document, and make these settings:

1. Set tabs at .5 and 1 inch.

2. Turn on justification.

3. Turn on "Show ¶" (COMMAND + Y) to allow you to count the returns between the paragraphs that you will be entering.

4. Set the font to 12-point Palatino.

5. Set document margins at 1 inch for the top and bottom, 3 inches for the left, and 2.1 inches for the right margin.

These margin settings are calculated roughly to produce text that is the same width as the columns into which you will be placing text in PageMaker. These settings can only be arrived at through trial and error. Your PageMaker columns will be about 2.7 inches wide. Because of kerning and other character spacing in PageMaker, its 2.7-inch column translates to about 3.4-inch columns in Microsoft Word. Therefore, the 3-inch left margin and 2.1-inch right margin were chosen to give a 3.4-inch column with an 8.5-inch page.

TEXT ENTRY   The actual text entry is straightforward. Simply follow the text, spacing, and style annotations shown in Figure 5-2. Enter the same number of hard returns and tabs, and apply the bold style where shown (on the headings). The paragraphs are indented .5 inch, and the bullet character is character number 165, which is entered by pressing COMMAND + OPTION + Q and typing **165**. If you are

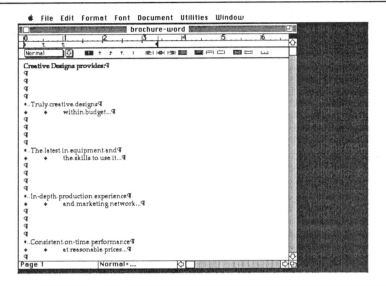

FIGURE 5-2 Text entered in Microsoft Word
(part 1 of 5)

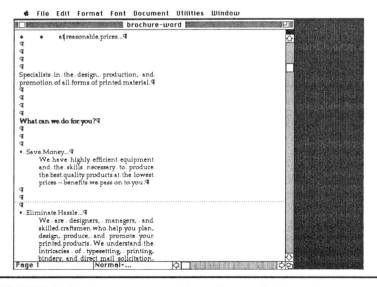

FIGURE 5-2 Text entered in Microsoft Word
(part 2 of 5)

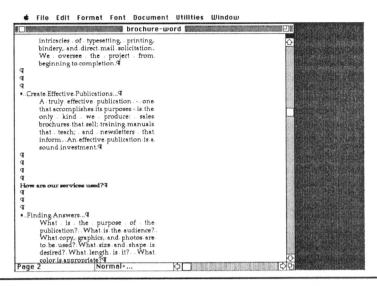

FIGURE 5-2 Text entered in Microsoft Word (part 3 of 5)

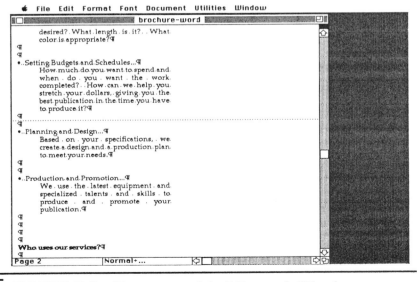

FIGURE 5-2 Text entered in Microsoft Word (part 4 of 5)

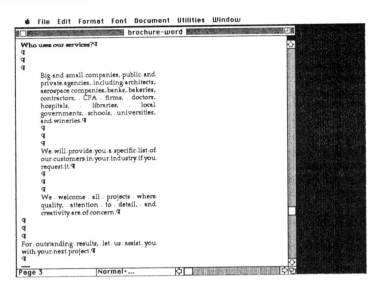

FIGURE 5-2 Text entered in Microsoft Word
(part 5 of 5)

using different copy on your brochure, make a reasonable guess as to spacing and style in Microsoft Word and then make any necessary corrections in PageMaker. Keep in mind that the indents and character spacing in Figure 5-2 are tailored to this particular copy. With different copy, you may want to redesign.

When you have finished entering the copy, save it in your Publications folder with the filename brochure-word. Then you may want to print the file.

 If your printout is not exactly centered on the page it could be because of the margin settings.

Creating a Graphic With Aldus FreeHand

Creating the graphic in Aldus FreeHand is less demanding than entering the text in Microsoft Word because, for the purposes of this exercise, all you want to do is place a single graphic in a PageMaker publication. Unlike text, you needn't format the graphic. You may want to take the time to create the drawing shown here, or you may want to substitute something else.

Import or create whatever graphic you want to use now. When you have finished, you should have a drawing on your screen. The one used here is shown in Figure 5-3. Save the drawing as you normally would. Then, "Export" the drawing in one of three formats: Encapsulated Post-Script (EPS), QuickDraw (PICT) or Tag Image File Format (TIFF). If the drawing or graphic that you are using is not in one of these three formats, then you must convert it to one of these formats by, for example, using the "Export" command in Aldus FreeHand. Place the exported file in your Publications folder.

SETTING UP THE BROCHURE

You greatly simplify the remaining tasks when you correctly lay out the brochure and set the defaults appropriately before entering text or graphics. In addition, the setup phase helps you place the imported text correctly. The importance of this phase cannot be overemphasized.

Establishing the Layout

The layout is governed by two dialog boxes: the Page setup dialog box, and the Column guides dialog box. Both of

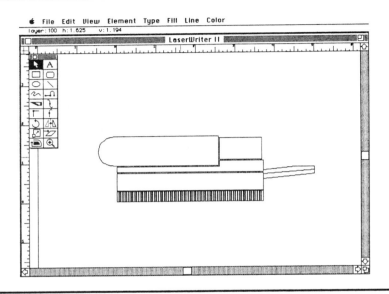

FIGURE 5-3   Graphic of LaserWriter II created with
Aldus FreeHand

these must be set for the brochure to be produced properly. For example, you must select "Wide" Orientation in
the Page setup dialog box to rotate the page on the screen
and to have it print properly. "Wide" Orientation (also
called landscape orientation) indicates that the 11-inch
edge of an 8.5 × 11-inch piece of paper is horizontal.
"Tall" Orientation (also called portrait orientation), indicates that the ll-inch edge is vertical.

PAGE SETUP   The first step is to create a new publication and do the page setup. In addition to setting the
"Wide" Orientation of the page on the screen, you will
reset the margins and turn off the "Double-sided" option.
Even though the brochure is double sided, both sides have
the same layout (margins, columns, and guides). This
means you can save time by defining the layout on one

master page and applying it to both pages. If you left "Double-sided" turned on (an "X" in the check box), PageMaker would assume that the two sides are different and would have two master pages, which defeats your purpose. Use the following instructions to define the page setup:

1. Choose "New" from the File menu.

2. Click on the "Wide" Orientation option button.

3. Drag across the "1" in the "# of pages" text box and type **2**.

4. Click on the "Double-sided" check box to turn it off.

5. Drag across the "1" in the "Left" margin text box.

6. Type **.5** and press TAB to move to the "Right" margin text box.

7. Type **.5** and press TAB to move to the "Top" margin text box.

8. Type **.5** and press TAB to move to the "Bottom" margin text box.

9. Type **.5** for the "Bottom" margin.

When you have finished, your dialog box should look like the one shown in Figure 5-4.

10. Click on "OK" to create the new publication.

COLUMN GUIDES The brochure has three columns of text on each page. The space between the columns varies. The easiest way to handle this is to set up five columns on each page, with two of the columns serving as variable

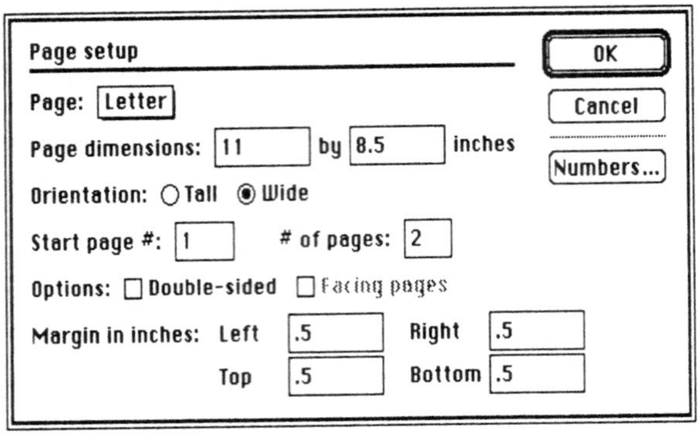

```
┌─────────────────────────────────────────────────────────┐
│  Page setup                              ┌──────────┐     │
│                                          │    OK    │     │
│  Page: [Letter]                          └──────────┘     │
│                                          ┌──────────┐     │
│  Page dimensions: [11    ] by [8.5    ] inches │ Cancel │ │
│                                          └──────────┘     │
│  Orientation: ○ Tall  ● Wide             ┌──────────┐     │
│                                          │Numbers...│     │
│  Start page #: [1    ]  # of pages: [2  ]└──────────┘     │
│                                                           │
│  Options: ☐ Double-sided  ☐ Facing pages                  │
│                                                           │
│  Margin in inches: Left  [.5    ]  Right  [.5    ]        │
│                     Top  [.5    ]  Bottom [.5    ]        │
└─────────────────────────────────────────────────────────┘
```

FIGURE 5-4   The Page setup dialog box

space between the text columns. In this way, you can handle the varying widths without trying to move the column guides as you are flowing text. The instructions to establish the columns and set their default widths follow. First, though, you need to set the unit of measure to be used on the rulers.

1. Choose "Preferences" from the Edit menu.

2. Drag on the "Measurement system" option box until "Inches decimal" is highlighted.

   You'll find that it is easier to work with the decimal scale than fractions when you are placing precise column and ruler guides.

3. Drag on the "Vertical ruler" option box until "Inches decimal" is highlighted.

4. Click on "OK" to close the Preferences dialog box, which should now look like this:

```
┌──────────────────────────────────────────────────────┐
│ Preferences                                  ┌────────┐│
│                                              │   OK   ││
│ Layout view:                                 └────────┘│
│                                              ┌────────┐ │
│    Measurement system:  [Inches decimal]     │ Cancel │ │
│                                              └────────┘ │
│    Vertical ruler:      [Inches decimal] [      ] points│
│                                                        │
│    Greek text below:    [6        ] pixels             │
│                                                        │
│    Guides:      Detailed graphics:   Show layout problems:│
│    ⦿ Front      ○ Gray out          ☐ Loose/tight lines │
│    ○ Back       ⦿ Normal            ☐ "Keeps" violations│
│                 ○ High resolution                      │
│                                                        │
│    Story view:                                         │
│    Size: [12  ] [▷] points  Font: [Times]              │
└──────────────────────────────────────────────────────┘
```

5. Click on the master page icon (the page icon with an "R" in it on the bottom left of the screen).

6. Choose "Column guides" from the Options menu to access the Column guides dialog box.

7. Type **5** for the "Number of columns."

The space between columns does not matter because you have established additional columns for that purpose. Therefore, to remove confusion, you will set the space between the columns to zero.

8. Press TAB to move to the "Space between columns" text box and type **0**. The Column guides dialog box should now look like this:

```
┌──────────────────────────────────────────────┐
│ Column guides                       ┌────────┐│
│                                     │   OK   ││
│                                     └────────┘│
│                                     ┌────────┐ │
│                                     │ Cancel │ │
│                                     └────────┘ │
│ Number of columns:        [5      ]           │
│ Space between columns:    [0      ]           │
│                                                │
└──────────────────────────────────────────────┘
```

9. Press RETURN to return to the publication.

RULER GUIDES Next, you'll place two vertical ruler guides to divide the page into three equal panels. Since you will be moving the column guides, these rulers will serve as fixed points of reference to visually check on how the layout is coming. Later you'll draw a hairline rule down these guides. You may find it difficult to achieve the placement of the ruler and column guides at the exact positions suggested. Come as close as you can in the current "Fit in window" view. Later, when you are in "Actual size" view, you can refine the position and become more precise.

1. Drag a vertical ruler guide to 7.33 inches on the horizontal ruler.

2. Drag a vertical ruler guide to 3.67 inches on the horizontal ruler.

ADJUSTING PAGE 1 Once the master set of columns and guides is positioned, you can go to each page and adjust the column widths for that page.

1. Click on the page 1 icon on the bottom left of the screen to bring page 1 up on the screen. Notice that the columns and two vertical ruler guides have been copied over from the master page.

2. Drag the leftmost column guide (between columns 1 and 2 as shown in Figure 5-5), from 2.5 to 3.3 inches on the horizontal ruler.

3. Drag the rightmost column guide (between columns 4 and 5) from 8.5 to 8.15 inches on the horizontal ruler.

4. Drag the column guide under the right margin at 10.5 inches to 10.2 inches on the horizontal ruler.

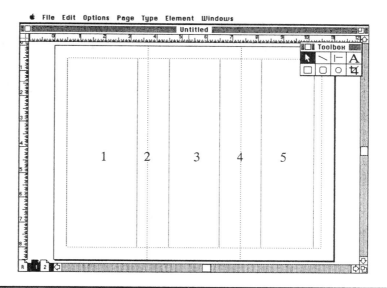

===== **FIGURE 5-5**   Column layout of page 1

This completes the layout of the first page. If you would like to be very accurate, expand the image to "Actual size" and adjust the lines exactly to the dimensions just given. Before expanding, position the mouse pointer in the top third of the middle column. Then press and hold COMMAND + OPTION while clicking the mouse button. The image will expand to "Actual size" and will be centered where you placed the pointer. This allows you to see the middle column and ruler guides. When you are done, return to the "Fit in window" view by pressing and holding COMMAND + OPTION while clicking the mouse button again.

ADJUSTING PAGE 2   Next, adjust the columns on page 2 with these instructions:

1. Click on the page 2 icon to activate that page.

2. Drag the leftmost column guide (between columns 1 and 2) from 2.5 to 3.25 inches on the horizontal ruler.

3. Drag the next column guide (between columns 2 and 3) from 4.5 to 4.1 inches.

4. Drag the next column guide (between columns 3 and 4) from 6.5 to 6.9 inches.

5. Drag the rightmost column guide (between columns 4 and 5) from 8.5 to 7.8 inches.

Your second page should now look like the one shown in Figure 5-6. Again, if you wish more precision, expand your view to "Actual size" and adjust the placement of the guides. Return to the "Fit in window" view when you are finished.

6. Click on the page 1 icon to return to that page.

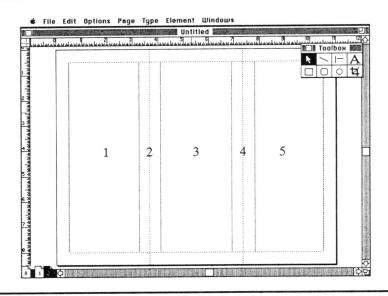

FIGURE 5-6 Column layout of page 2

Setting the Defaults

As a general rule, you should set all the defaults before starting work on a publication. This gives you a known starting place for all related functions, including text entry and drawing.

In earlier steps you set the page defaults, chose the decimal inch preference, and established the number of columns. The only defaults remaining to be set are the type and line specifications and the type of justification. Use the following instructions to set the remaining defaults.

1. If necessary, turn the Toolbox back on by choosing it in the Windows menu. Then verify that the pointer tool is selected.

2. Press COMMAND + T to open the Type specifications dialog box.

3. Drag on the "Font" option box until "Palatino" is highlighted.

4. Confirm that the "Size" text box reads "12," that leading is "Auto," and that "Set width," "Type style," "Position," and "Case" are all set to "Normal."

Your Type specifications dialog box should look like the one shown in Figure 5-7.

5. Click on "OK" or press RETURN to complete the Type specifications dialog box.

6. Press COMMAND + SHIFT + J to set "Justify" as the default alignment.

7. Choose "Hairline" from the Line option of the Element menu as the default line width.

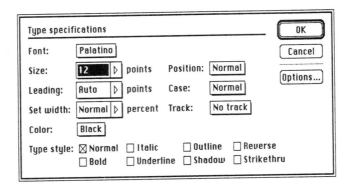

FIGURE 5-7 The Type specifications dialog box with default settings

This completes the setting of the defaults. Now go to the right column and enter the cover of the brochure.

CREATING THE COVER

The first page of the brochure contains three columns. When it is folded, the right column becomes the cover, the middle column becomes the back, and the left column becomes the inside flap—the first panel seen when the brochure is opened. The cover contains the company name at the top, a short line segment under the name, a slogan in the middle, and a list of products below the slogan. Finally, a graphic will be placed at the bottom of the cover.

Each item on the cover—name, line segment, slogan, and product list—requires unique treatment and will therefore be discussed separately in the paragraphs that follow.

Entering the Company Name

The company name consists of the words "Creative Designs." You'll enter these words on separate lines using 24-point Avant Garde Demi-Oblique (bold-italic) type. (If you don't have this specific font, use 24-point Helvetica bold italic or the next closest font that you have available. The italics sets apart the company name from the rest of the brochure.)

The design objective is to center the words "Creative Designs" between the fold and the edge of the page. To do this, you will left-align the first word against a column guide .8 inch from the fold and right-align the second word against a column guide .8 inch from the edge of the page. You have already set the column guides appropriately, so you need only align the words. You'll use the "Actual size" view to perform these tasks. Use the following instructions to enter the company name and align it:

1. Position the mouse pointer at 8.5 inches on the horizontal ruler and 1.7 inches on the vertical ruler.

2. Press and hold COMMAND + OPTION while clicking the mouse button to expand the view to "Actual size."

The view should be centered on the point where you placed the mouse pointer. Note the precision with which you can control the view.

3. Select the text tool from the Toolbox.

4. Click to the right of the left column guide in the right column at 1.15 inches on the vertical ruler to position the insertion point.

5. Press COMMAND + T to open the Type specifications dialog box.

6. Drag on the "Font" option box until "Avant Garde" is highlighted, and then type **24** in the "Size" text box, and click on both "Bold" and "Italic" "Type style" check boxes, as shown in Figure 5-8.

7. Press RETURN to return to the publication.

8. Press COMMAND + SHIFT + L to select left alignment.

9. Type **Creative** and press RETURN.

10. Press COMMAND + SHIFT + R to select right alignment.

11. Type **Designs** and press RETURN.

The company name should appear as shown in Figure 5-9. Next you will place the short line segment under the name.

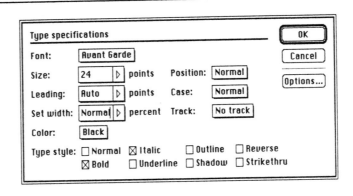

FIGURE 5-8 The Type specifications dialog box with the company name settings

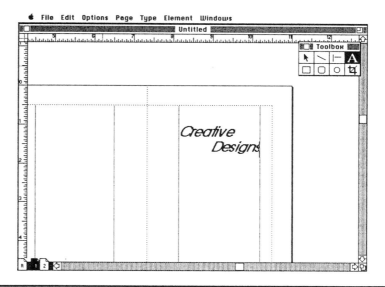

══ **FIGURE 5-9**   "Actual size" view showing the company name properly aligned

Drawing a Line

The line segment under the name is a design element; an artistic touch to separate and emphasize the name. First you will place one horizontal and two vertical ruler guides to establish where the actual line will be drawn. After you draw the line, you will select the kind of line it will be from the Line option of the Element menu. The instructions for drawing the line are as follows:

1. Select the perpendicular-line tool from the Toolbox.

2. Drag down a horizontal ruler guide and place it at 2.15 inches on the vertical ruler.

3. Drag over two vertical ruler guides. Place one at 9.95 inches and the other at 8.4 inches.

4. Draw a horizontal line from 8.4 to 9.95 along the ruler guide you placed at 2.15 inches on the vertical ruler (see Figure 5-10).

5. While the line is still selected, pull down the Element menu and choose from the Line option submenu, the triple line (as shown in Figure 5-10).

If the line segment is deselected before you choose the line style from the Line option, you will need to reselect it. Reselecting a line takes several steps. First you must select the pointer tool. Then you must temporarily move the horizontal ruler guide so that the actual line can be selected. Once the line is selected, you can choose the line

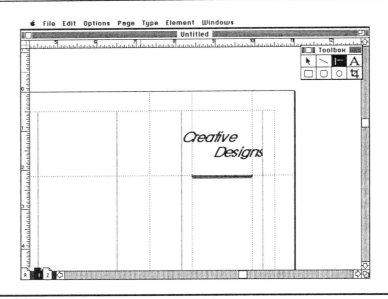

FIGURE 5-10   Triple line segment under the company name

specification. Finally, you must restore the ruler guide and the default line width. The steps to do that are as follows:

 Follow alternate steps 6 through 12 *only* if your line was deselected before getting to the line menu.

6. Select the pointer tool.

7. In the right margin, point on the horizontal ruler guide you placed at 2.15 inches and drag it up to .25 inch in the top margin.

8. Click on the line segment to select it.

9. Choose the triple line option shown in Figure 5-10 from the Line option of the Element menu.

Because you have now changed the default line type, you must restore the hairline as the default. You also need to restore the horizontal ruler guide to 2.15 inches.

10. Click the pointer outside of the publication to deselect the line segment.

11. Choose "Hairline" from the Line option of the Element menu.

12. Drag the horizontal ruler guide, which you temporarily placed at .25 inch, back down to 2.15 inches.

Whether or not you used the alternate steps, you should now get rid of the vertical ruler guides so that they won't interfere with entering the remaining text on the cover. Use these steps:

13. Select the pointer tool (if it isn't already selected).

14. Drag the vertical ruler guide at 8.4 inches off the right edge of the publication.

15. Drag the vertical ruler guide at 9.95 inches off the right edge of the publication.

Entering the Remaining Cover Text

The remaining text on the cover consists of a two-line slogan and a list of eight products. You will place the insertion point before entering the text and reset the type specifications. In order to place the product list, you'll set a series of tab stops. Use these instructions to carry out those tasks and enter the remaining text:

1. Select the text tool.

2. Click to the right of the left column guide in the right column at 3 inches on the vertical ruler to place the insertion point.

3. Press COMMAND + T to open the Type specifications dialog box.

4. Type **14** in the "Size" text box and click on "Bold" in the Type Style check box, as shown in Figure 5-11.

5. Press RETURN or click on "OK" to close the dialog box.

6. Press COMMAND + SHIFT + C to center the text.

7. Type **Desktop Publishing** and press RETURN.

8. Type **With a Flair!** and press RETURN.

9. Press RETURN four times to provide a separation between the slogan and the product list.

10. Press COMMAND + SHIFT + L to left-align the products.

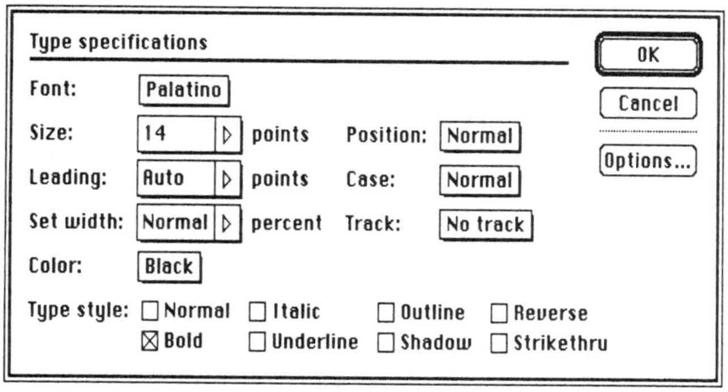

```
┌─────────────────────────────────────────────────────────────┐
│  Type specifications                              ┌─────────┐ │
│                                                   │   OK    │ │
│  Font:      │Palatino│                            └─────────┘ │
│                                                   ┌─────────┐ │
│  Size:      │14    ▷│  points   Position: │Normal│ │ Cancel  │ │
│                                                   └─────────┘ │
│  Leading:   │Auto  ▷│  points   Case:     │Normal│ ┌─────────┐│
│                                                   │Options...││
│  Set width: │Normal▷│  percent  Track:  │No track│ └─────────┘│
│                                                              │
│  Color:     │Black│                                          │
│                                                              │
│  Type style: ☐Normal  ☐Italic     ☐Outline  ☐Reverse        │
│              ☒Bold    ☐Underline  ☐Shadow   ☐Strikethru     │
└─────────────────────────────────────────────────────────────┘
```

FIGURE 5-11 The Type specifications dialog box for the bottom of the cover

The list of products is to be stairstepped across the page. There are several ways to do this, but the easiest way is to use tabs. Because the normal tab spacing at every half inch is too wide for this list, you must reset the tabs with the Indents/tabs dialog box. Setting the tab stops is a two-step process when you need accuracy, as you do here. Place the pointer on the tab ruler close to where you think you want to add a tab stop and press and hold the mouse button. Then move the tab left and right while watching a text box containing the exact tab setting. When that setting is correct, release the mouse button. Follow these steps:

11. Press COMMAND + I to open the Indents/tabs dialog box.

12. Press and hold the mouse button at .2 inch on the tab ruler to create a new tab stop (which is displayed as a bent arrow icon). Look at the "Position" text box above the tab ruler. Drag the tab icon left and right until the text box reads exactly .2. Then release the mouse button.

13. Repeat step 12 to place a new tab stop at .35 on the tab ruler.

14. Drag the existing tab stop at .5 right to .55.

15. Place new tab stops at .70 and .90.

16. Drag the existing tab at 1.0 right to 1.05.

17. Place a new tab stop at 1.25.

The reason for the uneven tab stops (.15 and .20 between tabs) is that all tabs at .20 would be too wide to fit in the space available, all at .15 too narrow, and you can't set tabs in between. Your "Indents/tabs" dialog box should look like this:

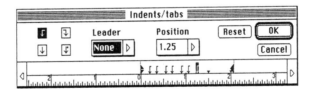

18. Click on "OK" to return to the publication.

19. Use the vertical scroll bar to adjust the screen image so that it extends from about 1 to about 6.5 on the vertical ruler.

20. Type the list of products shown below (omitting the commas). After each product, press RETURN. Before typing in the second product, press TAB; before the third product, press TAB twice; and so on for the remaining products. The last item, Reports, will have seven tabs. The product list is:

Brochures, Business Plans, Flyers, Newsletters, Pamphlets, Presentations, Posters, Reports

Figure 5-12 shows what the slogan and product list should look like at "Actual size" when they are properly entered. Figure 5-13 shows the same thing with "Fit in window" view.

21. Press and hold COMMAND + OPTION while clicking the mouse button to go to the "Fit in window" view.

22. Press COMMAND + S to save the brochure. The Save dialog box should appear.

23. Type **brochure** in the filename text box, as shown here, and press RETURN.

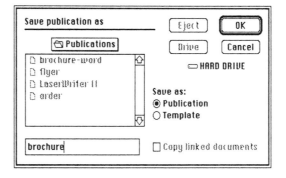

You are now ready to construct the middle column.

CONSTRUCTING THE MIDDLE COLUMN

You build the middle column in two separate phases. First, you will construct the lower part of the middle column. The lower portion consists of the company name, copied from the cover, followed by the address and phone numbers, which you will enter. Later, you will add a block of text written in Microsoft Word to the upper part of the column.

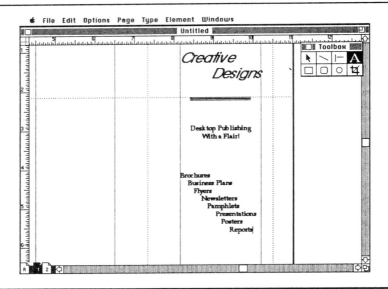

FIGURE 5-12 Page 1 of brochure in "Actual size"

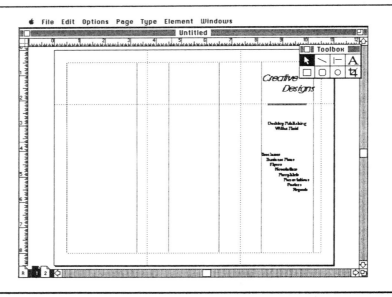

FIGURE 5-13 Page 1 of brochure in "Fit in window"

Copying the Company Name

The company name in the middle column is the same size and style as the company name on the cover. The simplest thing to do, then, is to use PageMaker's "Copy" command to copy the name from the cover to the middle column. When you use the "Copy" command on the Edit menu or the COMMAND + C or F3 keys, what you have selected will be copied to the Clipboard. Then, by using the "Paste" command from the Edit menu or the COMMAND + V or F4 keys, the information on the Clipboard will be copied to the center of the screen. The instructions to do that are as follows:

1. Select the pointer tool.

2. Drag a horizontal ruler guide down to 6.8 inches on the vertical ruler.

3. Click in the middle of the company name on the cover to select it.

4. Press COMMAND + C or F3 to copy the company name onto the Clipboard.

5. Move the mouse pointer to 5.5 inches on the horizontal ruler and 6.5 inches on the vertical ruler.

6. Press and hold COMMAND + OPTION while clicking the mouse button to expand the view to "Actual size."

7. Press COMMAND + V or F4 to insert the company name in the middle of the screen.

8. Drag the company name so that the bottom of the word "Designs" is just sitting on the horizontal ruler guide that you placed at 6.8 inches and the left text selection boxes are on the left column guide.

9. Place the pointer on one of the right text selection boxes and drag it to the right margin.

Figure 5-14 shows the company name set in the middle column.

Adding the Address and Phone Numbers

The final step in creating the lower middle column is entering the company's address and phone numbers. These are centered below the company name and use the default 12-point regular type. The instructions to do this are as follows:

1. Select the text tool.

2. Click the text tool to the right of the left column guide of the middle column at 7.1 inches on the vertical ruler.

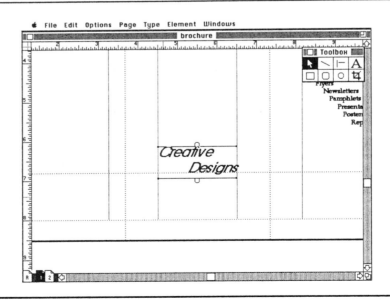

FIGURE 5-14   The company name in the middle column

3. Press COMMAND + SHIFT + C to center the address and phone numbers.

4. Press COMMAND + T and check that the default type specifications have not changed from "Palatino," "12" points, "Auto" Leading, and "Normal" type style. Press RETURN.

5. Type the following address and phone numbers, pressing RETURN after each line, and type two spaces between the state and the ZIP code):

   1900 Westwind Avenue
   Oceanside, WA 98999
   1-800-555-5000
   1-206-555-5000

When you have entered the address and phone numbers, your screen should look like the one shown in Figure 5-15. You must now adjust the column guides on the middle column so that it can accept the block of text from Microsoft Word that you will be placing there.

6. Press and hold COMMAND + OPTION while clicking the mouse button for a "Fit in window" view.

7. Select the pointer tool.

8. Drag the left column guide of the middle column (between columns 2 and 3) from 4.5 to 4 inches on the horizontal ruler.

9. Drag the right column guide of the other middle column (between columns 3 and 4) from 6.5 to 7 inches on the horizontal ruler.

10. Press COMMAND + S to save the brochure.

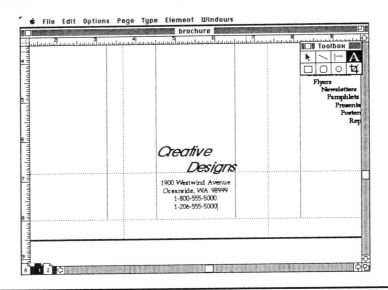

FIGURE 5-15   The middle column with company name and address

You have now completed all of the direct entry work, and your screen should look like the one in Figure 5-16. This would be a good time to take a break. If you leave PageMaker, remember to check all your defaults when you return. When you are ready to resume, you will place the text you created in Microsoft Word.

PLACING TEXT ON THE FIRST PAGE

Placing text is easy. You simply identify the file containing the text and the upper left-hand corner of the column in which you want to place it. PageMaker then *flows* the text into that column until it reaches the bottom margin, other

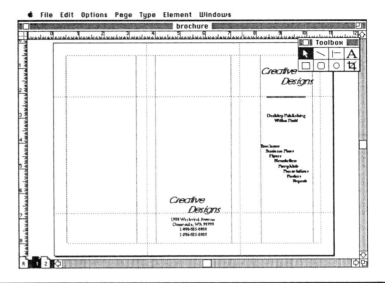

FIGURE 5-16 Page 1 with middle and right columns
filled in

text, or a graphic. If there is more text than the original
column can hold, you can flow the excess into as many
additional columns as necessary to complete the article or
whatever it is you are placing.

In this brochure you will initially place the text in the
left column of the first page. Then you will place a block of
text in the middle column and place the remainder on the
second page. In Chapter 7, "Preparing a Newsletter," you
will see how to flow multiple columns of text automatically
with PageMaker's "Autoflow" feature.

Placing Text in the Left Column

Your first step is to identify the name of the file containing
the text to be placed. The Publications folder that is speci-

fied in the instructions below, is a sample name. Yours may differ. If it does, you'll need to change the instructions accordingly. Use the shortcut key, COMMAND + D, for the "Place" command. "Place" retrieves files created by other programs for you to place in the current publication. When PageMaker has retrieved a text file, the pointer changes to a text icon (*not* a text tool) that looks like this:

After the text icon appears, PageMaker will flow text into the column in which you click the mouse button. Before placing the text, you can still use the pointer to choose commands, scroll the window, and change pages even though it has become a text icon. The pointer will again become the familiar arrow icon when you move it to the menu bar, the horizontal or vertical scroll bar, or to the page icons. The primary function here, however, is to place text in columns. The steps to identify the file and place the text in the left column are as follows:

1. Press COMMAND + D to open the Place dialog box.

2. Double-click on "brochure-word" in the Files list box, if it is shown. Otherwise, drag the open folder box to highlight "HARD DRIVE." Then select the Publications folder and finally double-click on the "brochure-word" file, as shown here:

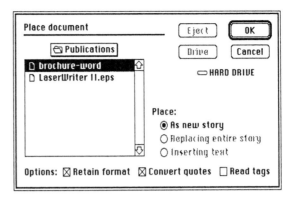

3. Move the text icon to the left column guide of the left column at 2 inches on the vertical ruler. This is just above the horizontal ruler guide you placed at 2.15 inches.

4. Click the mouse button.

Text flows into and fills the left column from the point where you clicked the mouse button. Your screen should look like the one shown in Figure 5-17. On the top and bottom of the text is a selection box with text handles — lines on either ends of the column of text with tiny boxes on their ends and a loop in the center like a window shade. The top loop is empty and the bottom loop has a downward pointing triangle in it. The empty loop means that this is the beginning of the article. The triangle means that there is more text than could be placed in the left column. If you had placed all of the text in the column, an empty loop would appear at the bottom.

The text handles work in several ways. If you click on the triangle in the bottom loop, your pointer will once again turn into a text icon, and you can flow the remaining text into another column by clicking in that column. If you press and hold the mouse button while pointing at either the top or bottom loop, the text handles work like window

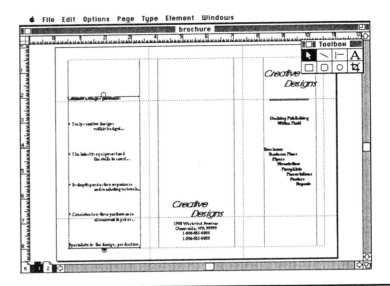

FIGURE 5-17 Page 1 showing the text placed in the left column

shades, moving up or down, showing or hiding text as they go. Finally, you can point on any of the four tiny boxes on the ends of the handles and drag the text inside or beyond the original column boundaries. In that case, PageMaker will reflow the text to fit the new line length. Here, you will use the window shade principle to define exactly how much text is to remain in the left column.

5. Point on the triangle in the loop of the lower handle, press and hold the mouse button, and drag the handle up until you have only the title line at the top and four two-line pairs beneath it.

6. Release the mouse button.

7. If the third paragraph, beginning "In-depth Production. . ." does not fit on two lines and is forced over to a third line, drag to the right a small amount on one of the small boxes on the right. The third item should snap back to two lines.

The left column is complete. You are now ready to work on the middle column.

Flowing Text into the Middle Column

For the middle column, you will pick up the remaining text to be placed by clicking on the bottom loop of the text handle in the left column, again turning the pointer into a text icon. Then, by clicking near the top of the middle column, you'll flow the text down that column. Notice that it stops when it reaches the company name. Finally, using the window shade effect, you'll "roll up" the text, leaving only the single block of text that you want in the middle column. The instructions to do this are as follows:

1. Click on the triangle in the bottom loop in the left column. The pointer will become a text icon.

2. Move the text icon to the left column guide of the middle column at 1.5 inches on the vertical ruler and click.

Text should flow down the column, stopping just above the company name.

3. Drag the lower loop up until only a two-line paragraph remains.

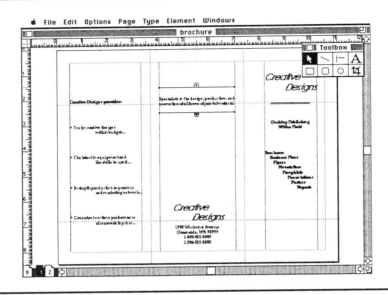

≡≡≡ **FIGURE 5-18** Complete text of page 1

This completes the first page. Your page should look like the one shown in Figure 5-18. Let's save the brochure and then continue with page 2.

4. Press COMMAND + S to save the brochure.

BUILDING PAGE 2

The second page is the inside of the brochure. As you fold back the cover (the right column of page 1) and then the inside flap (the left column of page 1), you will see the second page in its entirety. It consists of the remaining text that you created in Microsoft Word. You simply flow it in, column by column. When you are done, you will look at each column to make sure that it is aligned with the others.

Flowing Text onto Page 2

Flow the text, column by column from the left, filling each column until the bottom loop of the selection box in the right column is empty. Use the following instructions to do that:

1. Click in the middle of the paragraph at the top of the middle column of page 1 to reselect it (since saving the publication deselected it).

2. Click on the lower loop in the text handle of that paragraph to again display a text icon.

3. Click on the page 2 icon.

4. Place the text icon on the left column guide of the left column and on the top margin of the page.

5. Click the mouse button.

Text should flow in to fill the column as shown in Figure 5-19. There should be a bold heading and three paragraphs. Not all of the third paragraph will be visible until the text is adjusted. This column of text, as a whole, needs to be moved up and then the text handle pulled down so that the last paragraph can be completely seen. Had you originally placed the text icon above the top margin so that the text would all fit in the column, the column guides that you set up for the left column would not be in effect because they do not extend above the top margin. Instead, PageMaker would use some arbitrary lines as the default column guides.

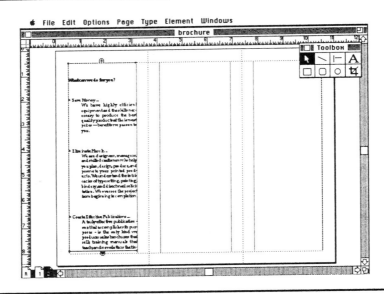

FIGURE 5-19   Page 2 with the left column as it is initially flowed

6. Press and hold the mouse button in the middle of the left column until you see a four-headed arrow. Then drag the text up until the dotted line in the vertical ruler, showing where the upper handle is, reads .3 inch.

7. Pull down the bottom handle until the rest of the third paragraph is visible.

In pulling down the bottom handle and displaying the third paragraph, the indent on either the last or second to the last line may be temporarily removed. If that happens, drag the handle up above the third paragraph (but not into the second paragraph), release the mouse button, and then drag the handle down again. The third paragraph should then be correct and fully visible. (See Figure 5-20.)

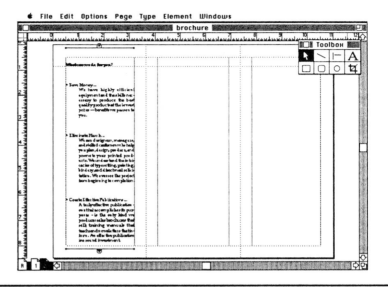

FIGURE 5-20   Page 2 with the text in the left column
adjusted

8. Click on the loop in the bottom handle of the left column, changing the pointer to a text icon.

9. Place the text icon against the left column guide and the top margin in the middle column, and click the mouse button.

10. Click on the loop at the bottom of the middle column.

11. Place the text icon in the left corner under the top margin in the right column, and click.

This completes placing text on page 2, as shown in Figure 5-21. You'll now want to align the three columns horizontally.

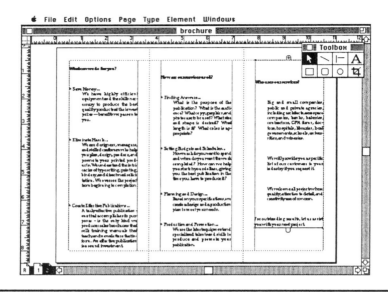

FIGURE 5-21 Page 2 completely filled in with text

Adjusting the Alignment

The three columns are probably not aligned because of the variable amount of space you picked up at the end of each column. In Word, you placed four lines of blank space between the material that forms each column. When you pick up the remainder at the bottom of each column, some of the four lines may remain with the previous column and some may move to the new column. It is impossible to tell how much is in either column. To cure that, you'll individually align the columns now, as follows:

1. Drag down a horizontal ruler guide to .85 inch on the vertical ruler.

This horizontal ruler guide should now be just under each of the three headings. Assuming that it isn't, continue on.

2. Press and hold the mouse button in the middle of the left column of text until the four-headed arrow appears. Then drag the text up or down until the heading is just sitting on the horizontal ruler guide.

3. Similarly adjust the middle and right columns.

4. Place the pointer at 5.5 inches on the horizontal ruler and 2 on the vertical ruler, press and hold COMMAND + OPTION while clicking the mouse button to go to the "Actual size" view.

Figure 5-22 shows the middle of the second page at "Actual size." Now, at "Actual size," see if the alignment is

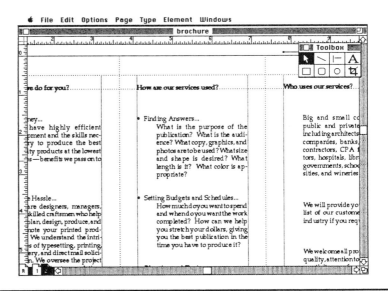

FIGURE 5-22 Middle of page 2 at "Actual size"

correct. If it is, go on to the cleanup phase. Otherwise, use the procedure described in step 2 to adjust the alignment.

Cleaning Up

Examine both sides of the brochure to see if the text is properly aligned for a "balanced" and attractive look. If something is awry, click on it with the pointer tool and, while holding down the mouse button, position the offending text in a better location. When you are finished, save and print the brochure. The instructions that follow assume that the text in the left column of the first page is a little low. If that is not the case in your brochure, substitute for the left column of the first page, the section you want to correct in your brochure in the following instructions:

1. Click on the page 1 icon.

2. If necessary, press and hold COMMAND + OPTION while clicking the mouse button to go to the "Fit in window" view.

3. To position the left column on the screen at "Actual size," place the pointer at 2.5 inches on the vertical ruler and 3.5 inches on the horizontal ruler; then press and hold COMMAND + OPTION while clicking the mouse button.

4. Drag the text in the left column up until the heading is just sitting on the horizontal ruler guide placed at 2.15 inches.

When you are satisfied that the left and middle columns of the first page are properly aligned (they should look like those shown in Figure 5-23) continue on to save and print the brochure.

5. Press COMMAND + S to save the file.

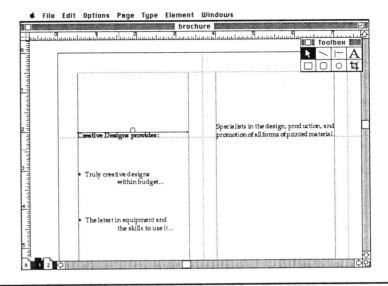

═══ **FIGURE 5-23** Page 1 showing the left column realignment

6. Press COMMAND + P to bring up the Print dialog box.

7. After readying your printer and making any necessary changes to the Print dialog box, press RETURN to start printing.

Your printed brochure should look like the one shown in Figure 5-24.

ADDING OPTIONS

The options consist of placing some vertical rules between columns and placing a graphic on the cover. Your sense may be that these will add clutter to the brochure, or you

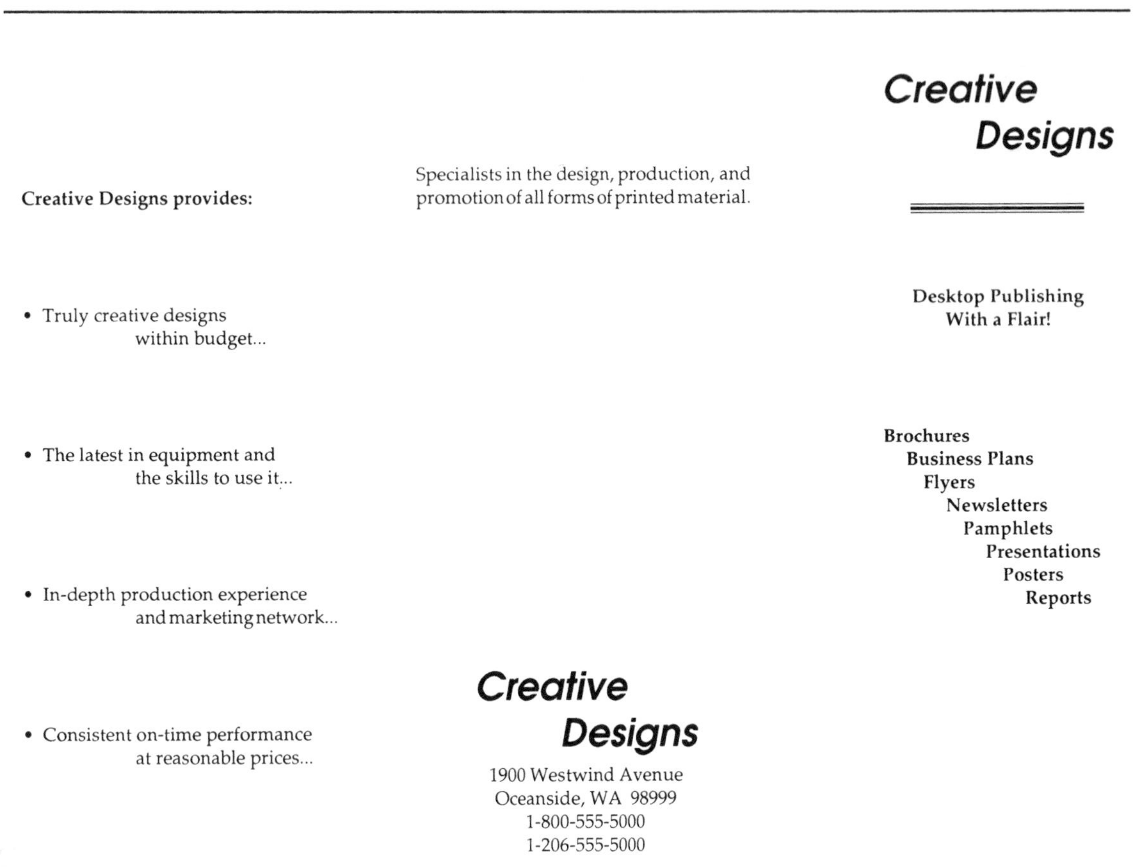

Creative
Designs

Desktop Publishing
With a Flair!

Brochures
Business Plans
Flyers
Newsletters
Pamphlets
Presentations
Posters
Reports

Specialists in the design, production, and
promotion of all forms of printed material.

Creative Designs provides:

• Truly creative designs
within budget...

• The latest in equipment and
the skills to use it...

• In-depth production experience
and marketing network...

• Consistent on-time performance
at reasonable prices...

Creative
Designs

1900 Westwind Avenue
Oceanside, WA 98999
1-800-555-5000
1-206-555-5000

FIGURE 5-24   Printed brochure without the graphics (page 1)

What can we do for you?

- Save Money...
  We have highly efficient equipment and the skills necessary to produce the best quality products at the lowest prices—benefits we pass on to you.

- Eliminate Hassle...
  We are designers, managers, and skilled craftsmen who help you plan, design, produce, and promote your printed products. We understand the intricacies of typesetting, printing, bindery, and direct mail solicitation. We oversee the project from beginning to completion.

- Create Effective Publications...
  A truly effective publication - one that accomplishes its purposes - is the only kind we produce: sales brochures that sell; training manuals that teach; and newsletters that inform. An effective publication is a sound investment.

How are our services used?

- Finding Answers...
  What is the purpose of the publication? What is the audience? What copy, graphics, and photos are to be used? What size and shape is desired? What length is it? What color is appropriate?

- Setting Budgets and Schedules...
  How much do you want to spend and when do you want the work completed? How can we help you stretch your dollars, giving you the best publication in the time you have to produce it?

- Planning and Design...
  Based on your specifications, we create a design and a production plan to meet your needs.

- Production and Promotion...
  We use the latest equipment and specialized talents and skills to produce and promote your publication.

Who uses our services?

Big and small companies, public and private agencies, including architects, aerospace companies, banks, bakeries, contractors, CPA firms, doctors, hospitals, libraries, local governments, schools, universities, and wineries.

We will provide you a specific list of our customers in your industry if you request it.

We welcome all projects where quality, attention to detail, and creativity are of concern.

For outstanding results, let us assist you with your next project.

═══ **FIGURE 5-24** Printed brochure without the graphics (page 2)

may have other design objections. So, at your discretion, carry on.

Placing Vertical Rules

The vertical rules or lines are drawn on the vertical ruler guides that mark the points where the brochure will be folded. The rules serve two purposes: first, they assist in folding the brochure; second, when the brochure is opened, they help to visually separate the three columns. The instructions to draw the rules are as follows:

1. Press and hold COMMAND + OPTION while clicking the mouse button to go to the "Fit in window" view.

2. Select the perpendicular-line tool.

3. Draw a line along the vertical ruler guide at 3.67 inches on the horizontal ruler, from the top margin at .5 inch to the bottom margin at 8 inches.

4. Select the Line option of the Element menu and check that "Hairline" is still the chosen default.

5. As in step 3, draw a line along the vertical ruler guide at 7.33 inches on the horizontal ruler.

6. Click on the page 2 icon to go the second page.

7. If necessary, press and hold COMMAND + OPTION while clicking the mouse button to return to the "Fit in window" view.

8. Draw two lines along the vertical ruler guides at 3.67 and 7.33 inches on the horizontal ruler.

9. Select the Options menu and choose "Guides" to turn them off and allow you to see the lines you just drew.

Figure 5-25 shows the second page with vertical rules.

10. Select the Options menu and choose "Guides" to turn them back on again.

Placing a Graphic

To give some visual identification to the brochure, you will add an outline drawing of an Apple LaserWriter II printer to the cover. As discussed earlier in this chapter, this drawing (graphic) was created in Aldus FreeHand. At this point, we need only retrieve the file and place it on the cover.

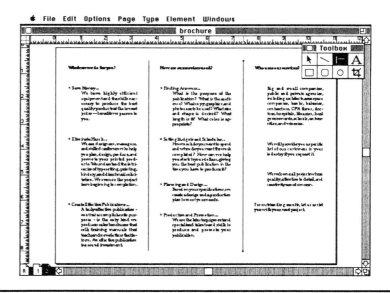

FIGURE 5-25   Page 2 showing the vertical lines

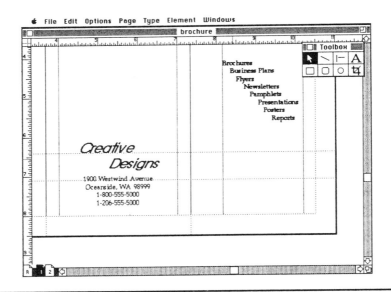

FIGURE 5-26 Lower right-hand corner of the cover with guides

The instructions to place the graphic are as follows:

1. Select the pointer tool.

2. Click on the page 1 icon to return there.

3. Place the pointer at 6.5 inches on the vertical ruler and 7.5 inches on the horizontal ruler. Press and hold COMMAND + OPTION while clicking the mouse button to go to "Actual size."

4. Drag the horizontal ruler guide that was placed earlier at 6.8 inches, up to 6.4 inches on the vertical ruler.

5. Drag a new horizontal ruler guide down to 7.1 on the vertical ruler.

The space between the two horizontal ruler guides in the right column (shown in Figure 5-26) is where the graphic will be placed.

6. Press COMMAND + D to open the Place dialog box.

7. Double-click on the filename in the list box of the graphic that you want to use as LaserWriterII.eps is shown here:

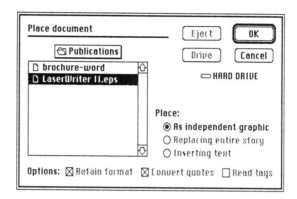

8. Place the eps, draw, or TIFF icon (depending on the type of graphic you are placing) in the corner of the left column guide of the right column and the horizontal ruler guide at 6.4 inches, then drag it diagonally to the right margin and the horizontal ruler guide at 7.1 inches.

As you can see in Figure 5-27, the graphic fits nicely in the spot set aside for it. Yours may do the same, or it may come in the wrong size or in the wrong position as a result of a positioning error. You can correct either condition.

If the position is incorrect, simply point in the middle of the graphic and drag it in the direction necessary for proper positioning. If the size is wrong, point on one of the tiny corner size boxes and drag the box diagonally either to expand or to contract the graphic to fit your requirements.

Figure 5-28 shows the final first page in the "Fit in window" view. This completes the brochure. All that remains is to save and print it.

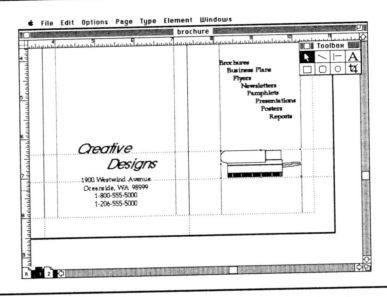

FIGURE 5-27 Lower part of the cover showing the graphic

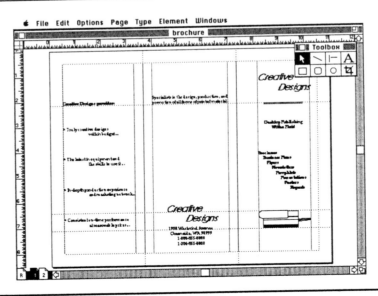

FIGURE 5-28 Final page 1 with graphic in the "Fit in window" view

9. Press and hold COMMAND + OPTION while clicking the mouse button to go to the "Fit in window" view.

10. Press COMMAND + S to save the brochure.

11. Press COMMAND + P to open up the Print dialog box. Make any necessary changes, ready your printer, and press RETURN to start printing.

12. If you want to leave PageMaker at this point, press COMMAND + Q.

Your final printed result should look like that shown in Figure 5-1—a professional quality brochure.

In Chapter 6, "Generating an Annual Report," you will generate a set of financial statements of equal quality.

chapter **6**

GENERATING AN
ANNUAL REPORT

The annual report discussed in this chapter is suitable for many organizations interested in communicating their financial performance and corporate progress to their shareholders or backers. It contains a formal set of financial reports, several charts on the financial position over the past several years, and a narrative discussion of the company's performance over the past year and prospects for the new year. For the purposes of the example, the normal annual report of 15 to 20 pages has been truncated to 6 pages. (The finished 6 pages are shown in Figure 6-1a

Micro Corporation of America
1990 Annual Report

Profile

Micro Corporation of America is observing its eleventh anniversary as a company providing microcomputer systems and related services worldwide. Incorporated in 1979, the company has been publicly owned since 1986.

MCA corporate headquarters is in Silicon Valley, California, the heartland of America's computer technology. The company's 487 employees serve clients from five regional offices in New York, Atlanta, Dallas, Chicago, and Los Angeles, plus two international offices in London, England, and Tokyo, Japan.

The company is organized into three operating groups.

MCA Systems is a leading supplier of microcomputer systems to large and medium sized businesses, which it also provides with other services and products.

MCA Government Systems serves local, state, and federal government agencies, developing state-of-the-art computer software and designing and integrating computer systems.

MCA Systems Services provides systems engineering and technical assistance, scientific support services, and training programs to a wide variety of clients.

MCA stock is traded over the counter, under the ticker symbol of MICA.

The company is an equal opportunity employer, M/F/H/V.

FIGURE 6-1a The finished annual report (page 1)

Micro Corporation of America

FINANCIAL HIGHLIGHTS
(In thousands except per share & employees)

Years ended June 30	1990	1989	1988
FOR THE YEAR:			
Revenue	$54,725	$40,840	$29,594
Net Income	$5,851	$4,366	$3,164
Net Income per Share	$1.68	$1.25	$1.11
Average Shares Outstanding	3,485	3,485	2,854
NET MARGIN	10.7%	10.7%	10.7%
AT YEAR END:			
Total Assets	$31,548	$23,543	$17,060
Total Plant & Equipment	$12,253	$9,144	$6,626
Total Equity	$22,189	$16,339	$11,216
Number of Employees	487	363	263
RETURN ON EQUITY	26.4%	26.7%	28.2%

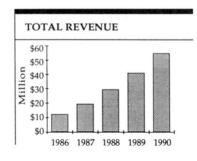

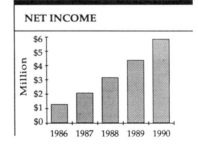

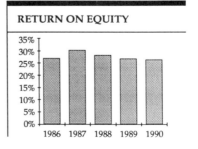

2

FIGURE 6-1b The finished annual report (page 2)

Micro Corporation of America

To our shareholders:

Micro Corporation of America achieved record earnings for the fifth consecutive year in fiscal 1990, its eleventh year in business.

Net income for the year ended June 30, 1990 totaled $5,850,000, or $1.68 per share, representing a 34 percent increase from the prior year's record $4,366,000, or $1.25 per share. Fiscal 1990 revenue was $54,725,000, a 34 percent increase from $40,840,000 a year earlier.

Shareholders' equity increased 36 percent to $22,189,000, while the rate of return on average shareholder equity was an outstanding 26.4 percent. Bookings rose substantially, resulting in a 46 percent increase in the backlog, to $78,374,000.

We have continuously strengthened the company's balance sheet in the five years since fiscal 1986. Shareholders' equity has increased by over 400 percent, yet the return on equity has remained a very healthy 26 percent.

All Segments Growing

Continued success by MCA Systems, largest of the company's three operating groups, in obtaining large computer systems integration contracts should increase revenue profitably.

MCA Government Systems has identified large new segments of the markets they serve that offer potential for producing substantial additional revenue and earnings.

MCA Systems Services sees a growth opportunity in developing and marketing its capabilities for fabricating complex microcomputer software. The group also plans major efforts to market its technical support skills. Both of these efforts are aimed at contract opportunities developing in fiscal 1991.

New Director, Management Promotions

At the shareholders' meeting in October 1989, George E. Maynard, the retired chairman of Maynard Associates, Inc., was elected a director of the company, succeeding William J. Shallcross, who did not stand for reelection.

Roberto A. Martinez, president of MCA Systems Services since 1988, was elected a senior vice president of the company, and James R. Harrington, vice president-finance and chief financial officer since 1987, was named executive vice president and chief financial officer.

Looking Ahead to 1991

The company has the key ingredients for success in the markets into which it is moving, and I am optimistic about its future.

I expect fiscal 1991 to be an even better year than fiscal 1990. New products and services will be coming to market in addition to new contracts that will offer a firm foundation for growth in the new year. The men and women of Micro Corporation of America are committed to the long-term growth and success of the company.

Jennifer E. Evans
Chairman and President

3

FIGURE 6-1c The finished annual report (page 3)

Micro Corporation of America

CONSOLIDATED STATEMENT OF OPERATIONS
(In thousands except per share data)

Years ended June 30	1990	1989	1988
REVENUE			
Net Sales	$54,725	$40,840	$29,594
COST OF SALES			
Cost of Goods Sold	14,776	11,027	7,990
Direct Costs	1,256	937	679
Total Cost of Sales	16,032	11,964	8,670
GROSS INCOME	$38,693	$28,876	$20,924
INDIRECT OPERATING COSTS			
Salaries & Wages	13,930	10,395	7,533
Payroll Taxes	1,811	1,351	979
	1,478	1,103	799
Total Labor Expense	17,218	12,850	9,311
Advertising	3,095	2,310	1,674
Depreciation	1,935	1,444	1,046
Leases & Rentals	2,902	2,166	1,569
Taxes	1,548	1,155	837
Miscellaneous	1,161	866	628
Total Nonlabor Expense	10,641	7,941	5,754
Total Indirect Expense	27,859	20,790	15,065
NET OPERATING INCOME	$10,834	$8,085	$5,859
Other Income (Expense)	(2,476)	(1,848)	(1,339)
NET INCOME BEFORE TAXES	8,358	6,237	4,520
Provision for Income Taxes	2,507	1,871	1,356
NET INCOME	$5,851	$4,366	$3,164
NET INCOME PER SHARE	$1.68	$1.25	$1.11
AVERAGE SHARES OUTSTANDING	3,485	3,485	2,854

4

FIGURE 6-1d The finished annual report (page 4)

Micro Corporation of America

CONSOLIDATED STATEMENT OF CONDITION
(In thousands)

Years ended June 30	1990	1989	1988
ASSETS			
Current Assets			
Cash and Equivalents	1,286	960	695
Net Accounts Receivable	7,483	5,584	4,047
Inventory	9,737	7,266	5,266
Total Current Assets	$18,506	$13,810	$10,008
Plant and Equipment			
Leasehold Improvements	5,678	4,237	3,071
Furniture & Equipment	10,897	8,132	5,893
Subtotal at Cost	16,575	12,369	8,963
Less Accum. Depreciation	(4,322)	(3,225)	(2,337)
Net Plant & Equipment	$12,253	$9,144	$6,626
Other Assets	789	589	427
TOTAL ASSETS	$31,548	$23,543	$17,060
LIABILITIES			
Current Liabilities			
Accounts Payable	3,683	2,749	1,992
Current Portion of Notes	487	363	263
Taxes Payable	2,378	1,775	1,286
Total Current Liabilities	$6,548	$4,887	$3,541
Net Long Term Notes	2,811	2,318	2,304
TOTAL LIABILITIES	$9,359	$7,204	$5,845
EQUITY			
Common Stock	697	697	571
Paid-in Capital	3,485	3,485	2,854
Retained Earnings	18,007	12,157	7,791
TOTAL EQUITY	$22,189	$16,339	$11,216
TOTAL LIABILITIES & EQUITY	$31,548	$23,543	$17,060

5

FIGURE 6-1e   The finished annual report (page 5)

Micro Corporation of America

One Micro Way
Silicon Valley, CA 94123
(800) 555-1234 or
(415) 555-4321

FIGURE 6-1f The finished annual report (page 6)

through f.) In addition to these 6 pages, an annual report would normally include a table explaining changes in financial position, a set of notes on the financial statements, and a description and photographs of the company.

In this chapter, you will combine the three primary ingredients of an annual report—tables of financial data, charts of financial data, and narrative—with a simple but attractive design. You will create the tables and charts with Microsoft Excel and will write the narrative in MacWrite II. As in previous chapters, you may, of course, use other products that serve the same functions. You will use Page-Maker's master pages to create a master design for all but the first page. Then you will place the tables, charts, and narrative information on the regular pages (the actual pages of the report), align and adjust them, and add some titles and lines. The result is a professional-looking annual report.

If you use a word processor other than MacWrite II, read through the MacWrite II instructions and then adjust them in your word processor. If you use a spreadsheet program other than Microsoft Excel for the tabular data, you may need to place tabs manually before each number (a very laborious job). Of course, you can use a word processor, either in column mode or with tabs, for the tabular data. As long as PageMaker will import the word processor's files with the tabs or columns intact, this method will work. Test a sample before doing the entire set of tables. The limitations of using a word processor are encountered in entering the data and performing the arithmetic for which a spreadsheet is generally much easier.

For the charts, you can use DeltaGraph, Cricket Graph, or similar products in place of Excel. The instructions here apply to Excel. For the other products, you will have to do your own research.

PLANNING AND DESIGNING THE ANNUAL REPORT

In previous chapters, planning and design have been almost trivial, but both take on real significance here. The quality of your publication and the ease with which you produce it will depend on how well you have done the planning and design.

Preparing the Plan

Planning the publication of an annual report can be a sizable task. It involves coordinating the efforts of several people to create the narrative, tables, and charts, all requiring top management approval. The report must be produced on a fixed schedule that puts it in the hands of shareholders just before the annual meeting.

Begin planning by identifying the components of the report, who will produce them, and who must approve them. Then develop a schedule by first determining the date by which the report must be in the hands of shareholders. Backing off from that date, plot all activities to determine when each event must occur, based on how long each will take. In scheduling the publication of an annual report, you should be aware of all time-consuming steps, leave plenty of time for review and approval, and have all contributors committed to achieving the schedule.

Planning the budget is largely a matter of how fancy you want the report to be. On the low end, you can simply reproduce what comes off your laser printer and have an attractive and low-cost annual report. At the other extreme, you can incorporate a number of four-color photographs, print the report on special paper, and bind it in a glossy cover. Whichever way you choose, the budgeting is a significant aspect of planning.

Creating the Design

Designing the annual report requires four steps: determining the format and general content, identifying the constraints, designing the master page layout, and designing any custom aspects of the regular pages. Although the last two steps are more obviously design-related, they must be built on the foundation of the first two.

Annual reports are usually produced on 8.5 × 11-inch pages—a good format for production on a laser printer. These pages are printed double-sided and have facing pages. The annual report you will build in this chapter uses this standard format.

The *content* of your annual report—the number and length of narrative articles, the number of photographs, the number of tables and graphs—is the primary constraint around which you must build a design. It is, of course, difficult to get this information early. Without it, though, you can only guess at the detail design (which is often what is done).

Other than the size and content, the constraints boil down to special requirements for color, typefaces, types of paper, and any special effects, such as cutting a patterned hole in a page. Annual reports are meant to reflect the pride that owners and managers have in an organization. As a result, they can be very elaborate and present a real challenge to the designer.

DESIGNING THE MASTER PAGES PageMaker's master page feature is very useful because it allows you to design a pair of facing pages that can be used as the basis for a number of regular pages. In the design presented here, three elements can be placed on the master pages and then repeated automatically on the regular pages. These are a 6-point line at the top of both pages, the company name just under the line, and the page number at the bottom of the page.

If this feature doesn't sound like much of an advantage, remember that each of these three elements will appear on all 6 pages (or 15 to 20 pages in a real-world annual report), identically placed and spaced on each page. Further, should you want to change any of the elements, you need only change the master page(s) to make a change throughout the entire publication.

As with all PageMaker pages, you create the master pages by manipulating the image area within which the master design elements are placed. You create this area by setting the margins and column guides. For this annual report, the image area will be formed by a single column with 1/2-inch top, bottom, and outside margins. The inside margin will be 2 inches, partly for binding purposes and partly as a design element. With the master design elements, this image area provides the master layout for the annual report.

DESIGNING THE REGULAR PAGES Your primary design task on the regular pages is to determine how to place the report's content within the master layout, so that you have an easily readable and attractive publication. The content can be divided into three classes: tables, charts, and narrative. Each of these must be separately designed into the annual report and yet must be consistent, or at least harmonious, with the rest of the publication.

One way to provide consistency among different components of a publication is to standardize a typeface and type size. For this annual report, you will use Palatino throughout: the company name and headings of the narrative will be 14-point bold; the body of both the tables and narrative will be 12-point Roman (medium weight); and the headings on the tables and charts will be 12-point bold.

This selection assumes that you are using a LaserWriter IINT, which includes the typeface and sizes mentioned. If that is not the case, use the fonts you have that are closest to these. For example, you can use Times throughout. Of course, you will have to adjust the spacing. See Appendix B, "Using Fonts and Laser Printers" for more about fonts.

The second technique for getting a consistent look among the different components is to standardize the types or thickness of the lines you use. On the master page, a 6-point line was specified to be the heading on each page. This line is also used as a heading for the four charts. Similarly, a 1-point line is used as the secondary header line on all tables and charts. Finally, a hairline is used on the tables to separate item categories.

A third technique, a consistent column width for tables and narrative, is also used to give the annual report a harmonious look. For the opening material, which should be easy to read, the single 6-inch column is very effective for both the tables and the narrative. For the notes and detail material in the back of the report, you would probably specify narrower columns.

The result of the design is a clean-looking, and easy-to-read annual report. It also is not difficult to produce with PageMaker, MacWrite II, and Excel. Let's start out by looking at the components of MacWrite II and Excel.

DEVELOPING THE TABLES, CHARTS, AND NARRATIVE

This discussion of developing the components in Excel and MacWrite II will be brief and primarily limited to the constraints that PageMaker places on files brought over from these applications. If you are using different applications to create the material, you will still find it worthwhile to read this material because of the general instructions it contains on creating the components of the annual report.

Writing the Narrative with MacWrite II

The narrative in the annual report consists of two segments: the "Profile" on the cover and the letter to the shareholders on page 3. You could build these as either one or two files. Because both segments use a common typeface, size, and column width, you will combine them in one file and thereby gain a small savings in keystrokes.

Text created with MacWrite II and placed by Page-Maker can transmit to PageMaker all of its major formatting characteristics. These include typeface, type style and size, all sorts of tabs, indents, and line spacing. This means that all of the formatting you need for the narrative in the annual report can be applied in MacWrite II and transmitted to PageMaker.

SETTING DEFAULTS The default settings that you must set in MacWrite are straightforward. Select "Show Ruler" from the Format menu, drag a left-aligned tab to the .5 inch mark, and then click on the justified text icon. Then choose "Palatino" from the Font menu, and make sure that "12" is selected on the Size menu and "Plain Text" is selected on the Style menu. Finally, from the Format menu open the Paragraph dialog box and type **14 pt** as the Line Spacing. These defaults will serve to format the majority of the narrative—the body of the text. The individual headings will be changed to bold and 14-point type as they are entered.

ENTERING TEXT Load MacWrite II on your word processor now, and set the defaults outlined in the previous paragraph. Then type the narrative itself.

As you can see in Figure 6-2a, the heading "Profile" is the first word you type. You want to make this bold and 14-point. To preserve the defaults, type **Profile**, press RETURN, highlight the word, and change its style to "Bold" and

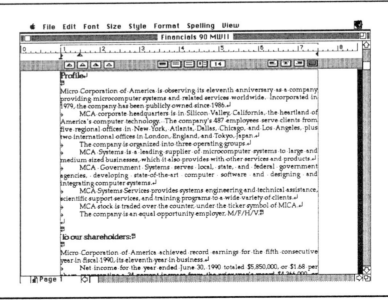

FIGURE 6-2a The text to be entered with MacWrite II (screen 1)

its size to 14. Then use the DOWN ARROW key to move to the next line, press RETURN again, and begin typing the narrative. By individually adjusting each of the headings in this manner, you can preserve the default body text type specifications.

Other than the headings, entering the narrative is routine word processing. Simply type the paragraphs shown in Figures 6-2a-c or Figures 6-1a and 6-1c. Before the second and subsequent paragraphs of each section, press TAB to indent. At the end of the document and before the chairman's name and title, press RETURN three times to add three blank lines.

When you are finished entering the narrative, save the file in the Publications folder with the filename Financials 90 MWII. You may wish to print the document using MacWrite. The results will look very similar to the final product produced by PageMaker.

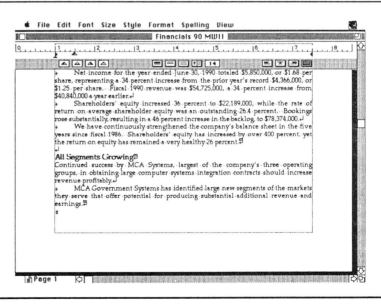

FIGURE 6-2b   The text to be entered with MacWrite II (screen 2)

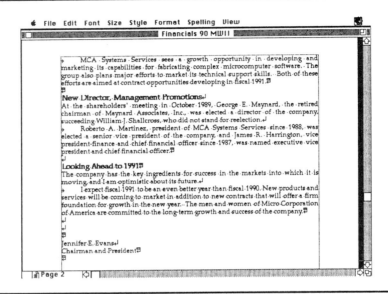

FIGURE 6-2c The text to be entered with MacWrite II (screen 3)

Producing the Tables and Charts With Excel

A major benefit of Excel is that you can produce both the tables and charts in the same package. With this integration, you can be assured that the charts will reflect the numbers in the tables. Such a capability is valuable in an annual report.

BUILDING THE TABLES Both the tables and the charts are transferred from Excel to PageMaker using the Macintosh Clipboard. This method transfers most of what you want. All of the tabular content is transferred and, most importantly, a tab is inserted between each column. Furthermore, in PageMaker you can define either decimal-aligned or right-aligned tabs where you want them and can therefore recover the tabular structure. PageMaker's limit of 40 tabs should give you more than enough columns for most purposes.

All text formatting established in Excel—such as typefaces, type styles, and type sizes—will be lost when brought into PageMaker, so there is no point in taking time in Excel to do that, as you did in MacWrite. Text imposed into PageMaker via the Clipboard, however, assumes the default type specifications set in PageMaker. Therefore, if you set the default type specifications before bringing in the tabular data, it can be formatted the way you want it. In this case, set the PageMaker Type specification dialog box defaults to 12-point Palatino-Roman.

There are three tables in the annual report: the Financial Highlights table, which summarizes information from the other two tables, is shown in Figure 6-3; the Consolidated Statement of Operations (income statement) is

	A	B	C	D
53	FINANCIAL HIGHLIGHTS			
54	(In thousands except per share & employees)			
55				
56	Years ended June 30	1990	1989	1988
57				
58	FOR THE YEAR:			
59	Revenue	$54,725	$40,840	$29,594
60	Net Income	$5,851	$4,366	$3,164
61	Net Income per Share	$1.68	$1.25	$1.11
62	Average Shares Outstanding	3,485	3,485	2,854
63				
64	NET MARGIN	10.7%	10.7%	10.7%
65				
66	AT YEAR END:			
67	Total Assets	$31,548	$23,543	$17,060
68	Total Plant & Equipment	$12,253	$9,144	$6,626
69	Total Equity	$22,189	$16,339	$11,216
70	Number of Employees	487	363	263
71				
72	RETURN ON EQUITY	26.4%	26.7%	28.2%

FIGURE 6-3 Financial Highlights table as it looks in Excel

shown in Figure 6-4; and the Consolidated Statement of Condition (balance sheet) is shown in Figure 6-5. Because the first table draws information from the other two, it is worthwhile to build a single spreadsheet containing all three tables and all four charts.

All three tables are built with four columns. The left-most column, for the descriptions, is 30 characters wide. The other columns, for the *numbers,* are each 10 characters wide (Excel's "Standard Width"). Excel's "General alignment" is also used so that titles and line descriptions are left-aligned, while the numbers are right-aligned.

Most of the numbers are formatted with a comma format and no decimal places represented by Excel as #, ## Ø. Therefore, the default format should be set to that. In the income statement and balance sheet, summary lines are formatted as currency, again with no decimal places. The net income per share is formatted as currency with two decimal places, and the two percentage lines in the Financial Highlights are formatted as percentages with one decimal place.

Detail lines in the tables are indented three spaces at the first level, six spaces at the second level, and nine spaces at the third level (simulating tab stops every three characters). Don't let this confuse you. On the Excel screen, and when these tables are brought over to Page-Maker, the indents are equal to roughly one, two, and three characters.

The income statement is placed in the range A1 through D43. The balance sheet is placed in the range H1 through K43, and the Financial Highlights table is placed in the range A53 through D72.

Using Figures 6-3, 6-4, and 6-5, and the previous notes, build the Excel worksheet containing the three tables. When you have finished building the worksheet, save it in

	A	B	C	D
1	CONSOLIDATED STATEMENT OF OPERATIONS			
2	(In thousands except per share data)			
3				
4	Years ended June 30	1990	1989	1988
5				
6	REVENUE			
7	Net Sales	$54,725	$40,840	$29,594
8				
9	COST OF SALES			
10	Cost of Goods Sold	14,776	11,027	7,990
11	Direct Costs	1,256	937	679
12	Total Cost of Sales	16,032	11,964	8,670
13				
14	GROSS INCOME	$38,693	$28,876	$20,924
15				
16	INDIRECT OPERATING COSTS			
17	Salaries & Wages	13,930	10,395	7,533
18	Payroll Taxes	1,811	1,351	979
19		1,478	1,103	799
20	Total Labor Expense	17,218	12,850	9,311
21				
22	Advertising	3,095	2,310	1,674
23	Depreciation	1,935	1,444	1,046
24	Leases & Rentals	2,902	2,166	1,569
25	Taxes	1,548	1,155	837
26	Miscellaneous	1,161	866	628
27	Total Nonlabor Expense	10,641	7,941	5,754
28				
29	Total Indirect Expense	27,859	20,790	15,065
30				
31	NET OPERATING INCOME	$10,834	$8,085	$5,859
32				
33	Other Income (Expense)	(2,476)	(1,848)	(1,339)
34				
35	NET INCOME BEFORE TAXES	8,358	6,237	4,520
36				
37	Provision for Income Taxes	2,507	1,871	1,356
38				
39	NET INCOME	$5,851	$4,366	$3,164
40				
41	NET INCOME PER SHARE	$1.68	$1.25	$1.11
42				
43	AVERAGE SHARES OUTSTANDING	3,485	3,485	2,854

FIGURE 6-4 Statement of Operations as it looks in Excel

	H	I	J	K
1	CONSOLIDATED STATEMENT OF CONDITION			
2	(In thousands)			
3				
4	Years ended June 30	1990	1989	1988
5				
6	ASSETS			
7	Current Assets			
8	Cash and Equivalents	1,286	960	695
9	Net Accounts Receivable	7,483	5,584	4,047
10	Inventory	9,737	7,266	5,266
11	Total Current Assets	$18,506	$13,810	$10,008
12				
13	Plant and Equipment			
14	Leasehold Improvements	5,678	4,237	3,071
15	Furniture & Equipment	10,897	8,132	5,893
16	Subtotal at Cost	16,575	12,369	8,963
17	Less Accum. Depreciation	(4,322)	(3,225)	(2,337)
18	Net Plant & Equipment	$12,253	$9,144	$6,626
19				
20	Other Assets	789	589	427
21				
22	TOTAL ASSETS	$31,548	$23,543	$17,060
23				
24	LIABILITIES			
25	Current Liabilities			
26	Accounts Payable	3,683	2,749	1,992
27	Current Portion of Notes	487	363	263
28	Taxes Payable	2,378	1,775	1,286
29	Total Current Liabilities	$6,548	$4,887	$3,541
30				
31	Net Long Term Notes	2,811	2,318	2,304
32				
33	TOTAL LIABILITIES	$9,359	$7,204	$5,845
34				
35	EQUITY			
36	Common Stock	697	697	571
37	Paid-in Capital	3,485	3,485	2,854
38				
39	Retained Earnings	18,007	12,157	7,791
40				
41	TOTAL EQUITY	$22,189	$16,339	$11,216
42				
43	TOTAL LIABILITIES & EQUITY	$31,548	$23,543	$17,060

FIGURE 6-5 Statement of Condition as it looks in Excel

the Publications folder with the name Financials 90 Excel. Now you can use the information in the tables to build the charts.

BUILDING THE CHARTS When charts are brought into PageMaker, they are brought in as a graphic, with all accompanying text. Since the quality of such text is considerably inferior to text produced in PageMaker, you will omit text from the charts in Excel and will add it in Pagemaker.

The four charts, shown in Figure 6-6, are produced from data in the Financial Highlights table, except that the order of years is reversed and two previous years are added. Figure 6-7 shows the revised data used for the charts.

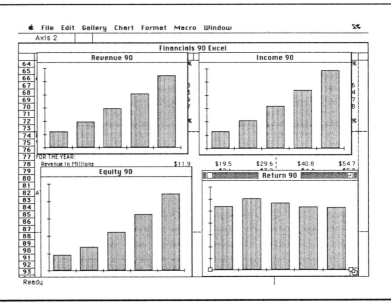

FIGURE 6-6 The four charts produced by Excel

	A	B	C	D	E	F
74	CHART DATA					
75	Years ended June 30	1986	1987	1988	1989	1990
76						
77	FOR THE YEAR:					
78	Revenue in Millions	$11.9	$19.5	$29.6	$40.8	$54.7
79	Net Income in Millions	$1.3	$2.1	$3.2	$4.4	$5.9
80	Net Income per Share	$0.89	$1.10	$1.11	$1.25	$1.68
81						
82	AT YEAR END:					
83	Total Assets in Millions	$6.9	$11.2	$17.1	$23.5	$31.5
84	Total Equity in Millions	$4.7	$6.9	$11.2	$16.3	$22.2
85	Number of Employees	108	173	263	363	487
86						
87	RETURN ON EQUITY	27.0%	30.2%	28.2%	26.7%	26.4%

FIGURE 6-7   The data from which the charts are produced

Note that most of the numbers have been divided by 1,000 and rounded to the nearest decimal to produce figures in millions. This produces more meaningful summary figures for charting.

Create a table such as the one shown in Figure 6-7, and then follow these steps to produce the charts shown in Figure 6-6.

1. Highlight the amounts to be charted—for example, the revenue totals in the cell range B78 through F78—and create a new chart by selecting "New..." from the File menu and clicking on "chart."

2. Select one of the columns on the chart, choose "Patterns..." from the Excel Format menu, select the fourth pattern displayed, click on "Apply to All," and click on "OK."

3. Select the vertical axis, choose "Patterns..." from the Excel Format menu again, click on "None" in the "Tick Labels" option box, and click on "OK."

4. Select the horizontal axis, choose "Patterns. . ." from the Format menu, click on "None" in the "Tick Labels" option box, and click on "OK" again.

5. Save the chart in the Publications folder under the name Revenue 90.

6. Repeat steps 1 through 5 for the remaining three charts using the ranges B79 through F79 for Income; B84 through F84 for Equity; and B87 through F87 for Return. Then save these charts in the Publication folder as Income 90, Equity 90, and Return 90.

With the tables, charts, and narrative prepared, you can load PageMaker and begin the production of the annual report.

USING MULTIFINDER

To build the annual report in the following sections, you will be using the Clipboard to transfer seven documents (the three tables and four charts) between Excel and Page-Maker. Using the Finder component of the Macintosh operating system, you must open and close Excel, the Financials 90 document, PageMaker, and the annual report seven times to accomplish this task. Using MultiFinder, if you have enough memory (about 4 MB), both programs and their respective documents can be opened at the same time. Then to switch between the two programs, you need only click on the appropriate window.

If you are not already using MultiFinder and have enough memory, change to MultiFinder now before beginning the construction of the annual report. Choose "Set Startup. . ." from the Special menu, click on "MultiFinder,"

click on "OK," and then choose "Restart." Then open
Excel, open Financials 90 Excel, and open PageMaker.

DEFINING THE LAYOUT

Because the annual report is a six-page publication, creating a good working layout is more significant than it was in
earlier chapters. Much of the weight of this falls on the
master pages, where the master layout is established. Also,
however, the defaults now affect more of your work and so
are more important.

Setting the Defaults

Setting the defaults upon starting a new publication should
be second nature to you by now. The pattern of going
through the Page setup and Type specifications dialog
boxes is virtually the same as in previous chapters. However, the annual report has only a single column on most
pages, so there is no need to bring up the Column guides
dialog box unless you have changed the startup default.
You'll start with the Page setup.

PAGE SETUP   The Page setup dialog box needs a little
attention. You must be sure that the "Double-sided" and
"Facing pages" check boxes are checked and that the number of pages and margins are set. Do that with the
following instructions:

1. Choose "New" from the File menu.

2. Click on the "Tall" option button to turn it on, if it is not already on.

3. Drag across the "1" in the "# of pages" text box and type **6**.

4. Click on the "Double-sided" and "Facing pages" check boxes, if they are not already checked.

5. Drag across the "1" in the "Inside" margin text box.

6. Type **2** for the "Inside" margin and press TAB.

7. Type **.5** for the "Outside" margin and press TAB.

8. Type **.5** for the "Top" margin and press TAB.

9. Type **.5** for the "Bottom" margin.

Your dialog box should look like the one shown in Figure 6-8.

10. Click on "OK" to close the dialog box.

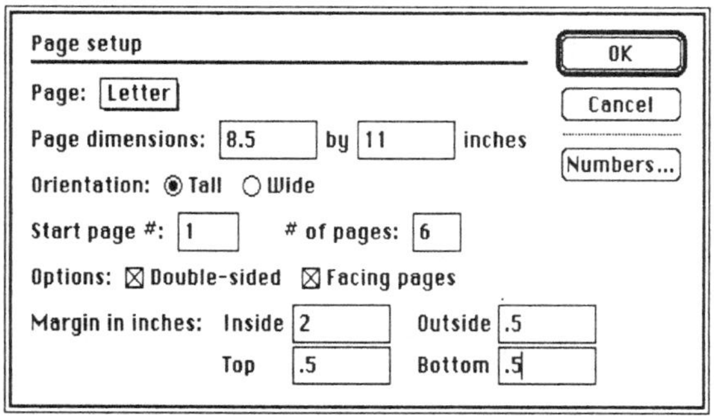

FIGURE 6-8 The Page setup dialog box

OTHER DEFAULTS The other defaults consist of the type specifications, the use of rulers and their unit of measure, the default line width, the type alignment, and turning off the Toolbox. You may want to make some of these permanent defaults, not just defaults for a given publication. If so, you must set them *before* opening a new publication. Should you want to do that now, choose "Close pub" from the File menu, carry out the following instructions, and then go back and redo the page setup. Otherwise, just follow these instructions:

1. If your rulers are not already on, choose "Rulers" from the Options menu.

2. Choose "Preferences. . ." from the Edit menu.

3. Drag both the "Measurement system" and the "Vertical ruler" option boxes until "Inches decimal" is highlighted, and then click on "OK" to close the Preferences dialog box.

4. If you have an extended keyboard, choose "Toolbox" from the Windows menu to turn it off.

5. Choose "Type specs. . ." from the Type menu.

6. Drag the "Font" option box until "Palatino" is highlighted.

7. Type **14** in the "Size" text box.

8. Make sure "Auto" leading is selected.

9. Click on the "Bold" check box to turn it on.

Your Type specifications dialog box should look like the one shown in Figure 6-9. Throughout the annual report, you will change the type specifications frequently, both for a particular use and as a default.

10. Click on "OK" to close the Type specifications dialog box.

11. Choose "Align left" from the Alignment option of the Type menu to turn it on.

12. Choose "6 pt" from the Lines option of the Element menu to set it as the line width default.

Like the type specifications, the line width default will change several times while you build the annual report. The defaults you just set represent the initial settings that you need to at least construct the master pages.

Constructing the Master Pages

As you saw in the design, each master page contains a heavy 6-point line at the top, the company name just under the line, and a page number in the lower outside corner. You will see how to produce these elements in the following paragraphs.

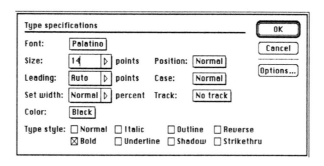

FIGURE 6-9 The initial Type specifications dialog box

In the instructions that follow, you'll often be using specific ruler coordinates, such as "5 inches on the horizontal ruler." This will be abbreviated as "5H." When both vertical and horizontal ruler coordinates are needed, they will be noted as "5H/3V."

When two pages are displayed on the screen, notice on the horizontal ruler that the zero point is between the two pages on the screen. From that point, the ruler's scales go in both directions. So there are two of each scale marks; for example, two 1-inch marks, one for each page. We will tell you which ruler mark to use (the left or right) by noting it in front of the coordinates, for example, "right 5H/3V."

DRAWING THE LINES   The heavy line at the top of each page is the common design element that ties the annual report together. It is a very simple but important technique. Draw it with the following instructions:

1. Click on one of the master page icons (L or R) to bring them on the screen.

2. Press SHIFT-F3 or click in the Toolbox to select the perpendicular-line tool.

3. Draw a line along the top margin of the left page, from left 8H to left 2H.

4. Draw a line along the top margin of the right page, from right 2H to right 8H.

The 6-point line is considerably wider than the top margin guide. As a result, the line can sit above the guide or hang below it. In this case, you want the line to hang below the guide.

ENTERING THE NAME The second element on the master pages is the company name immediately below the line you just drew. You will enter the name on the left page, copy it to the Clipboard, and then insert it on the right page. The instructions for this are as follows:

1. Drag down a horizontal ruler guide to .8V.

2. Place the pointer at left 6.5H and 1V.

3. Press and hold COMMAND+OPTION while clicking the mouse button to expand the view to "Actual size."

4. Press SHIFT+F4 or click in the Toolbox to select the text tool.

5. Position the I-beam with the small middle crossbar sitting on the horizontal ruler guide at .8V to the right of the left margin and click the mouse button.

6. Type **Micro Corporation of America.**

   Your screen should look like that shown in Figure 6-10.

7. Drag across the company name to select it.

8. Press COMMAND+C or F3 to copy the company name to the Clipboard.

9. Use the horizontal scroll bar to move the screen to the right until right 2.5H appears in the middle of your screen.

10. Position the I-beam with the small middle crossbar sitting on the horizontal ruler guide at .8V to the right of the left margin on the right page and click the mouse button.

11. Press COMMAND+V or F4 to paste the company name back onto the publication.

When you press COMMAND+V or F4, you should see a second copy of the company name appear at the top of the right page.

12. Drag across the company name on the right page to highlight the name.

13. Press COMMAND+SHIFT+R to right-align it.

The company name should be properly aligned on the right master page as shown in Figure 6-11.

ADDING THE PAGE NUMBER PageMaker can automatically number the pages of a document. If you place a

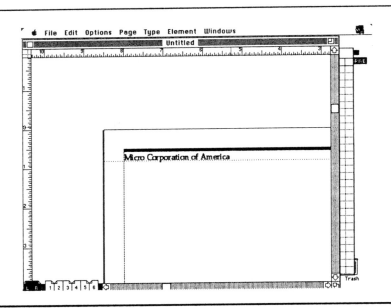

FIGURE 6-10 The left master page with the line and name in place

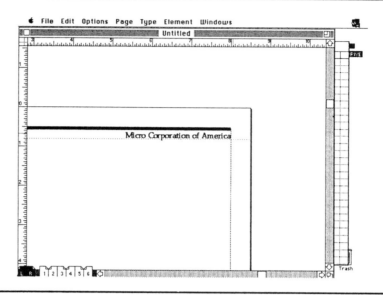

══════ **FIGURE 6-11**   The right master page with the company
name properly aligned

COMMAND+OPTION+P, on the master pages where you want
the page number to appear, PageMaker will insert the
numbers on the regular pages. Use the following instructions to do that:

1. Press and hold COMMAND+OPTION while clicking the
   mouse button to go to "Fit in window" view.

2. Place the pointer at left 6.5H/9.5V.

3. Press and hold COMMAND+OPTION while clicking the
   mouse button to expand the view to "Actual size."

4. Place the small middle crossbar of the I-beam on the
   bottom margin at 10.5V, to the right of the left margin,
   and click the mouse button.

5. Press COMMAND+T to open the Type specifications dialog
   box.

6. Type **10** in the "Size" text box, click on "Normal" for the Type style, and click on "OK" to close the dialog box.

7. Press COMMAND+OPTION+P to place the page number placeholder on the master page.

The letters "LM" (for "Left Master") should appear in the lower left corner of your left master page, as shown in Figure 6-12.

8. Drag across the page number to select it.

9. Press COMMAND+C or F3 to copy the page number to the Clipboard.

10. Use the bottom horizontal scroll bar to shift the screen to the right until right 4.5H is in the middle of your screen.

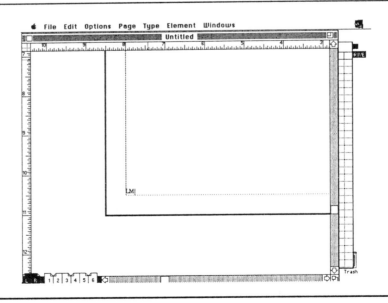

FIGURE 6-12   The lower left master page with the page number placeholder

11. Position the I-beam with the small middle crossbar sitting on the bottom margin at 10.5V to the right of the left margin on the right page and click the mouse button.

12. Press COMMAND+V or F4 to paste a copy of the page number placeholder back on the publication. This time the page number's placeholder should be "RM" for "Right Master."

13. Drag across the page number on the right page to highlight it.

14. Press COMMAND+SHIFT+R to right-align the page number on the right page as shown in Figure 6-13.

15. Press and hold COMMAND+OPTION while clicking the mouse button to go to "Fit in window" view.

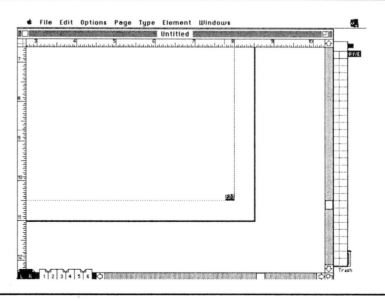

FIGURE 6-13 The lower right master page with the page number placeholder

16. Press COMMAND+S to open the Save dialog box.

17. Drag the Open folder list box to get first the HARD DRIVE and then the Publications folder, type **Financials 90** for the filename, and press RETURN to complete saving the file.

BUILDING THE TITLE PAGE

Now that the master pages are complete, you can begin building the regular pages. Because the first page is the title page, you will construct it differently than the others. To do that you must get rid of all the master page items. You will then use the same design elements from the master pages — the company name and the 6-point line — but in different positions, to create the title. Once the title is complete, you will place the first segment of the narrative, the company profile, on the bottom of the title page.

Creating the Title

The title consists of the company name on top, the words "1990 Annual Report" in the middle, and the default 6-point line on the bottom. All three items are placed about a third of the way down the page.

COPYING THE NAME To ensure that the company name is the same, copy it to the Clipboard before leaving the master pages. Then go to the first page, get rid of the master page items, and recopy the company name onto that page. The instructions to do that are as follows:

1. Still using the text tool, drag across the company name on the right master page.

2. Press COMMAND+C or F3 to make a copy on the Clipboard.

3. Click on the page 1 icon to go to that page. Note that right master page items are displayed.

4. Choose "Display master items" from the Page menu, as shown in Figure 6-14, to turn off the master items on page 1.

5. Drag a horizontal ruler guide down to 3V.

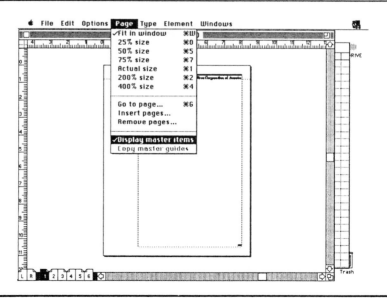

═══ **FIGURE 6-14**   The Page menu with "Display master items" highlighted

6. Position the I-beam with the small middle crossbar sitting on the horizontal ruler guide at 3V to the right of the left margin and click the mouse button.

7. Press COMMAND+V or F4 to copy the company name onto the first page as shown in Figure 6-15.

ADDING THE SECOND TITLE LINE The second line of the title is placed immediately below the company name and is set in the default 14-point, bold, Palatino font. The instructions for adding the second line are as follows:

1. Drag a horizontal ruler guide down to 3.3V.

2. Place the pointer at right 6.5H/4V.

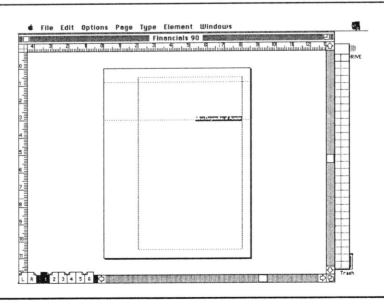

FIGURE 6-15 Page 1 with the company name on the horizontal ruler guide

3. Press and hold COMMAND+OPTION while clicking the mouse button to expand the view to "Actual size."

4. Place the middle crossbar of the I-beam on the horizontal ruler guide and click the mouse button.

5. Press COMMAND+R for right alignment.

6. Type 1990 **Annual Report**.

If your second line is not (for some reason) in 14-point, bold Palatino, as shown in Figure 6-16, highlight the line and change the type specifications.

DRAWING THE LINE   Our standard 6-point line is placed below the two title lines. The following instructions assume that the 6-point line is still the default.

1. Press and hold COMMAND+OPTION while clicking the mouse button to go to "Fit in window" view.

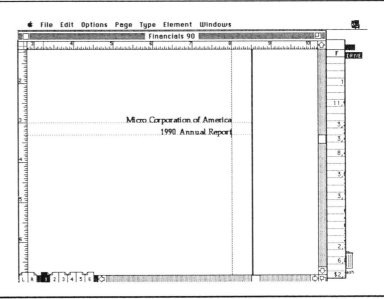

══ **FIGURE 6-16**   Page 1 with the two title lines

2. Press SHIFT+F1 or click in the Toolbox to select the pointer.

3. Drag the horizontal ruler guide from 0.8 to 4V.

4. Press SHIFT+F3 to select the perpendicular-line tool.

5. Draw a line across the horizontal ruler guide at 4V from the left to the right margin (letting it hang below the guide).

Placing the Narrative

The narrative that you wrote in MacWrite II had two main segments: a company profile and a letter to the shareholders. The text file containing both segments is placed on the first page. Then the text handle is pulled up until only the first segment remains. That segment is then checked, any necessary corrections made, and the first page is complete. The instructions to do this are as follows:

1. Press SHIFT+F1 or click in the Toolbox to select the pointer.

2. Press COMMAND+T to open the Type specifications dialog box.

3. Type **12** in the "Size" text box, click on "Normal" type style, and then click on "OK."

4. Drag the horizontal ruler guide at 4 down to 6V.

5. Press COMMAND+D to open the Place dialog box.

6. Open the Publications folder, select the Financials 90 MWII file, and click on "OK."

7. Click the text icon on the horizontal ruler guide and the left margin.

If you have not made any changes in the narrative, your page should look like that shown in Figure 6-17. The short line at the very bottom of the page is the "To our shareholders:" line from the second segment of the narrative. You need to drag the lower text handle above this line. When you have done that, your page should look like the one shown in Figure 6-18. You can then check this first segment.

8. Drag the lower loop of the text handle up until it is above the bottom line, as shown in Figure 6-18.

9. Press SHIFT+F4 or click in the Toolbox to select the text tool.

10. Drag the text tool across the word "Profile." Press COMMAND+T to open the Type specifications dialog box.

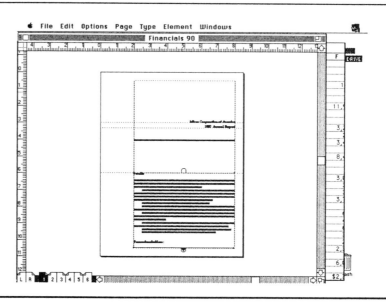

FIGURE 6-17 Page 1 with the text as initially placed

Check the settings against the formatting you established in MacWrite—Palatino, 14-point size, 14-point
leading, and bold (line spacing in MacWrite). If any is not
correct, fix it, and then click on "OK."

11. Next drag across the remainder of the text displayed on
    the first page. Again press COMMAND+T to open and
    check the type specifications. This text should be 12-
    point Palatino with 14-point leading and normal style.
    Make any necessary corrections and click on "OK."

Your completed first page should look like Figure 6-19
when it is printed. Now let's pick up the remainder of the
narrative and flow it onto the third page.

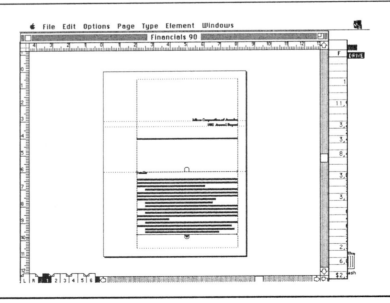

FIGURE 6-18   Page 1 with the text adjusted

Micro Corporation of America
1990 Annual Report

Profile

Micro Corporation of America is observing its eleventh anniversary as a company providing microcomputer systems and related services worldwide. Incorporated in 1979, the company has been publicly owned since 1986.

MCA corporate headquarters is in Silicon Valley, California, the heartland of America's computer technology. The company's 487 employees serve clients from five regional offices in New York, Atlanta, Dallas, Chicago, and Los Angeles, plus two international offices in London, England, and Tokyo, Japan.

The company is organized into three operating groups.

MCA Systems is a leading supplier of microcomputer systems to large and medium sized businesses, which it also provides with other services and products.

MCA Government Systems serves local, state, and federal government agencies, developing state-of-the-art computer software and designing and integrating computer systems.

MCA Systems Services provides systems engineering and technical assistance, scientific support services, and training programs to a wide variety of clients.

MCA stock is traded over the counter, under the ticker symbol of MICA.

The company is an equal opportunity employer, M/F/H/V.

FIGURE 6-19 The completed first page as it looks printed

FORMING THE LETTER TO THE SHAREHOLDERS

The third page is entirely taken up with the letter to the shareholders, the second segment of the narrative. This letter is flowed onto the page, and then aligned in rapid order.

Flowing the Text

Before leaving page 1, pick up the text from the lower text handle, turn the pages, and flow the remaining narrative onto page 3. The instructions to do this are as follows:

1. Press SHIFT+F1 or click in the Toolbox to select the pointer.

2. Click on the text to select it. The text handles will appear.

3. Click on the lower loop of the text handle. The text icon should appear.

4. Click on the icon for pages 2 and 3.

5. Place the text icon on the top and left margins (above the company name and the line) of page 3 and click to flow the text down the page.

6. Drag the bottom text handle down to the bottom of the page until the bottom loop is blank, as shown in Figure 6-20.

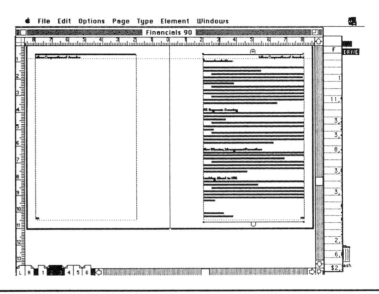

FIGURE 6-20   Page 3 with the text as it is initially placed

Aligning the Text

As shown in Figure 6-20, the letter is squeezed on the page. You can get the room you need by reducing the leading in the last five lines on the page (three blank lines plus the chairman's name and title). Finally, you will drag the entire letter down so that the chairman's title is resting on the bottom margin. Do that with these steps:

1. Press SHIFT+F4 or click in the Toolbox to select the text tool.

2. Drag across the last five lines of the letter, as shown in Figure 6-21.

3. Press COMMAND+T to open the Type specifications dialog box.

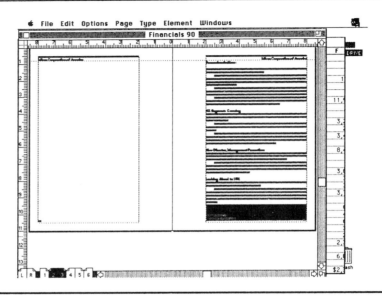

FIGURE 6-21   Page 3 with the last five lines highlighted

4. Drag across the 14 in the "Leading" text box and type
12. Your dialog box should look like the one shown in
Figure 6-22.

5. Press RETURN or click on "OK" to close the dialog box.

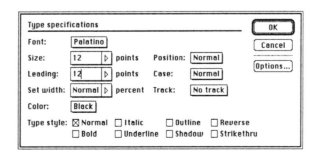

FIGURE 6-22   Type specifications dialog box set to
12-point leading

6. Press SHIFT+F1 or click in the Toolbox to select the pointer.

7. Drag the horizontal ruler guide from .8V down to 1.2V.

8. Click on the letter to select it. Text handles should appear on either end of the letter.

9. Drag the letter down, keeping it in the margins, until the first line is just below the horizontal ruler guide at 1.2V and the last line is sitting on the bottom margin. Your page 3 should look approximately like the one shown in Figure 6-23.

You may need to go to "Actual size" to determine that the first line is below the horizontal ruler guide. If the text still does not fit between the ruler guides, use the text

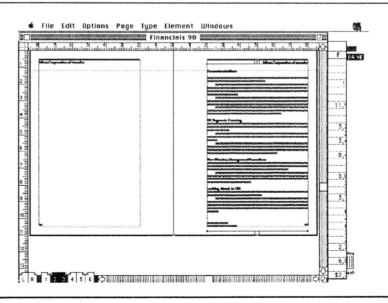

FIGURE 6-23 Page 3 with the text in its final position

tool to highlight the last line of the last full paragraph (containing the one word "company") through the chairperson's name and change the leading to 11.5.

10. Press COMMAND+S to save the annual report.

The letter on page 3 exactly fits the page with the small correction in the leading at the bottom, as shown in Figure 6-24. Actually the original letter was longer, so text was removed until the fit was close, and then the leading was adjusted as the final tweak. Had you wanted to include more text, you could have reduced the leading in the rest of the letter. If you *do* change the leading, remember to change it on a paragraph-by-paragraph basis. If you select the entire letter and change the leading, you will also change the leading of the three paragraph headings, making them hard to read.

With all of the narrative pages completed, you can now turn to the tables and charts, beginning with the Financial Highlights table and the charts that go on page 2.

ASSEMBLING THE FINANCIAL HIGHLIGHTS AND CHARTS

The second page is assembled from a combination of the Financial Highlights table and the four charts. The table is placed at the top of the page, and the four charts are arranged at the bottom. In addition, a number of lines are added to the page to separate and enhance the components.

Micro Corporation of America

To our shareholders:

Micro Corporation of America achieved record earnings for the fifth consecutive year in fiscal 1990, its eleventh year in business.

Net income for the year ended June 30, 1990 totaled $5,850,000, or $1.68 per share, representing a 34 percent increase from the prior year's record $4,366,000, or $1.25 per share. Fiscal 1990 revenue was $54,725,000, a 34 percent increase from $40,840,000 a year earlier.

Shareholders' equity increased 36 percent to $22,189,000, while the rate of return on average shareholder equity was an outstanding 26.4 percent. Bookings rose substantially, resulting in a 46 percent increase in the backlog, to $78,374,000.

We have continuously strengthened the company's balance sheet in the five years since fiscal 1986. Shareholders' equity has increased by over 400 percent, yet the return on equity has remained a very healthy 26 percent.

All Segments Growing

Continued success by MCA Systems, largest of the company's three operating groups, in obtaining large computer systems integration contracts should increase revenue profitably.

MCA Government Systems has identified large new segments of the markets they serve that offer potential for producing substantial additional revenue and earnings.

MCA Systems Services sees a growth opportunity in developing and marketing its capabilities for fabricating complex microcomputer software. The group also plans major efforts to market its technical support skills. Both of these efforts are aimed at contract opportunities developing in fiscal 1991.

New Director, Management Promotions

At the shareholders' meeting in October 1989, George E. Maynard, the retired chairman of Maynard Associates, Inc., was elected a director of the company, succeeding William J. Shallcross, who did not stand for reelection.

Roberto A. Martinez, president of MCA Systems Services since 1988, was elected a senior vice president of the company, and James R. Harrington, vice president-finance and chief financial officer since 1987, was named executive vice president and chief financial officer.

Looking Ahead to 1991

The company has the key ingredients for success in the markets into which it is moving, and I am optimistic about its future.

I expect fiscal 1991 to be an even better year than fiscal 1990. New products and services will be coming to market in addition to new contracts that will offer a firm foundation for growth in the new year. The men and women of Micro Corporation of America are committed to the long-term growth and success of the company.

Jennifer E. Evans
Chairman and President

3

FIGURE 6-24 The finished page 3 as it looks printed

Bringing in the Table

The Financial Highlights table is placed on the second page from the Macintosh Clipboard. To do this, you will leave PageMaker, activate (or open if you are not using Multi-Finder) Excel, highlight the range you want to transfer, copy it to the Clipboard, activate PageMaker, and place the text on page 2. You will then adjust the tabs, change the style of the heading, and finally draw a line under the dates at the top of the table to set them off.

TRANSFERRING THE TABLE Your first task is to transfer the table from Excel. To do that, use the following instructions:

1. If you are using MultiFinder, and Excel has been opened, click on a part of the spreadsheet window that is showing or click on the icon in the upper right corner until the Excel icon appears. If you are not using Multi-Finder, quit PageMaker, load Excel, and open the Financials 90 Excel spreadsheet.

2. In Excel, with the Financials 90 spreadsheet on the screen, highlight the Financial Highlights in the range A53 through D72.

3. Press COMMAND+C, F3, or choose Copy from the Edit menu to copy the Financial Highlights to the Clipboard.

4. With the MultiFinder, reactivate PageMaker by either clicking on a part of the PageMaker window, or clicking on the icon in the upper right corner. With Finder, quit Excel, reload PageMaker, and open the Financials 90 worksheet.

You should be looking at pages 2 and 3 of the annual report.

5. Press COMMAND+V or F4 to paste the Excel range into the PageMaker publication. The range should appear in the upper middle portion of the screen.

6. Drag the table to page 2, placing the upper left corner on the left margin and the horizontal ruler guide at 1.2V.

The table should fit on the page without any column separation, as shown in Figure 6-25.

ADJUSTING TABS   The columns, as they transfer across from Excel do not look very good. It is easy, though, to use PageMaker's Indents/tabs dialog box to fix that situation.

In PageMaker, you can use four different types of tabs: normal left-aligned tabs, center tabs, right-aligned tabs, and decimal tabs. For the financial tables in the annual report,

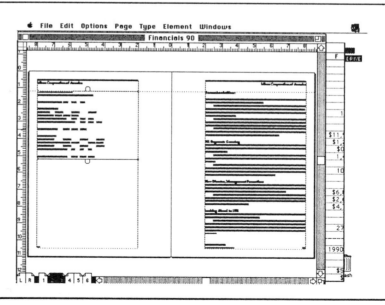

FIGURE 6-25   Initial placement of Financial Highlights table

you want to use either right-aligned tabs or decimal tabs. In either case, you can adjust individual lines. With right-aligned tabs you will have nice straight columns, as in Excel itself, with one exception: negative numbers in parentheses will not line up. Using decimal tabs just for the lines with negative numbers will adjust this. Better yet, if the entire table is formatted with decimal tabs, the negative numbers are properly aligned, and the dollars per share and percentage figures protrude to the right, indicating that these numbers differ from the others. Although you can also adjust the lines that stick out, in the annual report you'll use decimal tabs without adjustment. Do that now with the following instructions:

1. Press SHIFT+F4 or click in the Toolbox to select the text tool.

2. Drag across the entire table on page 2 to highlight it.

3. Press COMMAND+1 to go to actual size.

4. Press COMMAND+I to open the Indents/tabs dialog box.

5. Click on the decimal tab button, the lower right of the four tab buttons.

6. Click the leftmost tab stop at 3.75 inches on the tab ruler.

7. Click the center tab stop at 4.75 inches.

8. Click the rightmost tab stop at 5.75 inches. Your dialog box should look like the one shown in Figure 6-26.

9. Click on "OK" to close the dialog box.

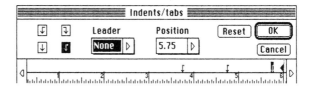

FIGURE 6-26   The completed Indents/tabs dialog box

CHANGING THE HEADING   The table, as it comes in from the Clipboard, picks up the default type specifications from PageMaker. This is what you want except for the heading. That you want to change to Palatino Bold. Do so with the following instructions:

1. Drag across the heading, "FINANCIAL HIGH-LIGHTS."

2. Press COMMAND+T to open the Type specifications dialog box.

3. Click on the "Bold" check box, and click on "OK."

DRAWING THE LINE   To finish the Financial Highlights table, you will place a line under the years to set them apart. Do that now with the following instructions:

1. Drag a horizontal ruler guide down to 2V (it should be immediately under the row that begins "Years ended June 30").

2. Press SHIFT-F3 or click in the Toolbox to select the perpendicular-line tool.

3. Draw a line across the horizontal ruler guide at 2V from the left to the right margin.

4. Before deselecting the line, choose the "1 pt" line from the Line option of the Element menu. Your screen should look like Figure 6-27.

5. Press COMMAND+W to return to "Fit in window" view.

6. Press COMMAND+S to save the publication.

Adding the Charts

The charts are built in three stages: first, a layout grid is constructed, and a number of lines are drawn; second, the Excel charts are placed and aligned on the grid; and third,

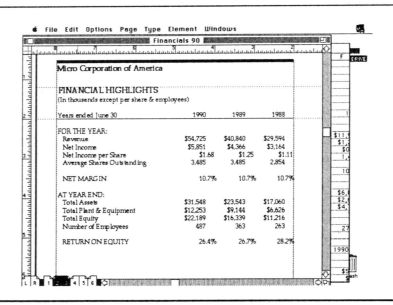

FIGURE 6-27 The Financial Highlights table with the line in place

the titles are added to each chart. Each stage will be discussed in the paragraphs that follow.

DRAWING THE LINES To set the charts apart and give them a weight equal to the other components of the annual report, you will draw a set of lines around them. To draw these lines accurately and to place the graphs accurately, you need to add an extensive network of horizontal and vertical ruler guides as well as dividing the page into two columns. Once this layout is complete, the lines can be drawn. The instructions to build the grid and draw the lines are as follows:

1. Press SHIFT+F1 or click in the Toolbox to select the pointer.

2. Choose "Column guides . . ." from the Options menu.

The Column guides dialog box that is displayed has a "Set left and right pages separately" check box. Because you have already finished page 3, the easiest solution is to give both pages the same setting; that is, to leave the check box empty. If, for some reason, your dialog box comes up with the box checked, simply click on the box to turn it off. You will get columns on page 3 as well as on page 2, but that doesn't matter. The column guides on page 3 won't affect the text that is already on the page.

3. Type **2** in the "Number of columns" text box, press TAB, type **.4** in the "Space between columns" text box, and press RETURN.

4. Drag down six horizontal ruler guides to 5.5, 6, 7.5, 8, 8.5, and 10 on the vertical ruler.

5. Drag over four vertical ruler guides to 7.5, 5.5, 4.3, and 2.3 on the left horizontal ruler.

When you have completed the layout grid for the charts, your screen should look like the one shown in Figure 6-28.

6. Press SHIFT-F3 or click in the Toolbox to select the perpendicular-line tool. Select the Options menu and make sure that both "Snap to rulers" and "Snap to guides" are on (checked).

7. Draw a line along the horizontal ruler guide at 5.5V from left 8H to left 5.2H.

8. Before deselecting the line you just drew, look at the Line option of the Element menu and make sure that the 6-point line is still chosen. If it isn't, click on it for the selected line; then switch to the pointer tool and

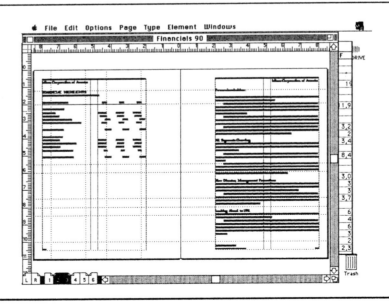

FIGURE 6-28 The layout grid for the charts on page 2

again choose the 6-point line to reset the default. Switch back to the perpendicular-line tool.

9. Draw a line along the horizontal ruler guide at 5.5V from left 4.8H to left 2H.

10. Draw two lines along the horizontal ruler guide at 8V, one from left 8H to left 5.2H, and the second from left 4.8H to left 2H.

11. Press SHIFT-F1 or click in the Toolbox to select the pointer.

12. Choose the "1 pt" line in the Line option of the Element menu.

13. Press SHIFT+F3 or click in the Toolbox to select the perpendicular-line tool again.

14. Draw two lines along the horizontal ruler guide at 6V, one from left 8H to left 5.2H, and the second from 4.8H to left 2H.

15. Draw two lines along the horizontal ruler guide at 8.5V, one from left 8H to left 5.2H, and the second from left 4.8H to left 2H.

16. Draw two lines along the vertical ruler guide at left 8H, one from 5.5V to 7.7V, and the second from 8V to 10.2V.

17. Draw two lines along the vertical ruler guide at left 4.8H, one from 5.5V to 7.7V, and the second from 8V to 10.2V.

18. Select the Options menu and choose "Guides" to turn them off so you can better see the lines you just drew. Figure 6-29 shows the results.

19. When you have finished admiring your work, again choose "Guides" from the Options menu to turn them back on.

20. Press COMMAND+S to save the publication.

This might be a good time to take a break. If you leave PageMaker, remember to check the defaults and reset them as necessary when you return.

ADDING THE CHARTS   The charts are brought in via the Clipboard from Excel. They will appear in the middle of the PageMaker screen in their original size. You will need to first place their upper left corner and then size them to the required dimensions. The points at which you place and then size the charts are not always on ruler guides (although the resulting charts will be). Therefore, you must

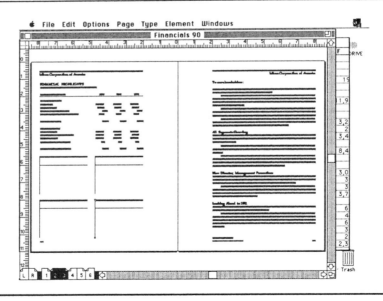

FIGURE 6-29   The completed lines for the charts on page 2 with "Guides" off

turn off the "Snap to guides" option. (Leave "Snap to rulers" on.) To place and size the charts, use the following instructions:

1. Press SHIFT+F1 or click in the Toolbox to select the pointer.

2. Place the pointer at left 5H/8V.

3. Press and hold COMMAND+OPTION while clicking the mouse button to expand the view to "Actual size."

4. Press COMMAND+U to turn off the "Snap to guides" option.

5. Activate Excel in the method appropriate for your system.

6. Open the Revenue 90 chart from the Publications folder.

7. Choose "Select Chart" from the Chart menu and press COMMAND+C or F3 to copy the chart to the Clipboard.

8. Activate PageMaker and press COMMAND+V or F4 to paste the chart on the annual report.

9. Place the upper left corner of the chart at left 7.6H/6V.

10. Drag the lower right corner to left 5.4H/7.6V.

As you are dragging the lower right corner, a box appears, as shown in Figure 6-30, that shows you the dimensions that the chart will occupy. When you release the mouse button, you will see that the actual chart is smaller and should sit on the horizontal ruler guide at 7.5 and be against the vertical ruler guide at 5.5, as shown in Figure 6-31. (The box that appears in Figure 6-30 is where the selection handles will appear.)

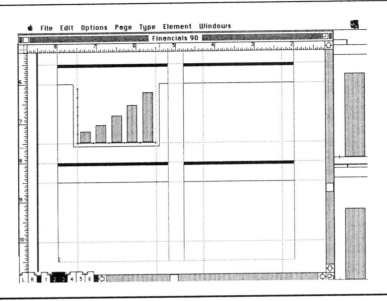

FIGURE 6-30   The placement of the Revenue chart
before the mouse button is released

11. If the Revenue chart is not sitting on the horizontal
    ruler guide at 7.5V or is not against the vertical ruler
    guide at 5.5H, drag it into position.

12. Activate Excel, open the Income 90 chart, choose
    "Select Chart" from the Chart menu, and press
    COMMAND+C or F3 to copy the chart to the Clipboard.

13. Activate PageMaker and press COMMAND+V or F4 to
    paste the chart onto the annual report.

14. Place the upper left corner at left 4.4H/6V.

15. Drag the lower right corner to left 2.2H/7.6V.

16. If the Income chart is not sitting on the horizontal ruler
    guide at 7.5V or is not against the vertical ruler guide
    at 2.3H, drag it into position.

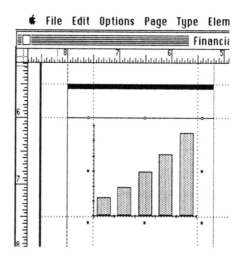

═══════ **FIGURE 6-31**   The final placement of the Revenue chart after the mouse button is released

17. Activate Excel, open the Equity 90 chart, choose "Select Chart" from the Chart menu, and press COMMAND+C or F3 to copy the chart to the Clipboard.

18. Activate PageMaker and press COMMAND+V or F4 to paste the chart onto the annual report.

19. Place the upper left corner at 7.6H/8.5V and drag the lower right corner to 5.4H/10.1V.

20. Adjust the placement of the Equity chart as necessary.

21. Activate Excel, open the Return 90 chart, choose "Select Chart" from the Chart menu, and press COMMAND+C or F3 to copy the chart to the Clipboard.

22. Activate PageMaker and press COMMAND+V or F4 to paste the chart onto the annual report.

23. Place the upper left corner at 4.4H/8.5V and drag the lower right corner to 2.2H/10.1V.

24. Adjust the placement of the Return chart as necessary.

25. Press COMMAND+S to save the annual report.

Figure 6-32 shows the four charts as they should look after placement.

ADDING THE TITLES Your final task in building the charts is to add titles to each one. There are four title elements on each chart: a main title above the chart, a horizontal axis with year titles, a vertical axis with scale titles, and, on three of the charts, a second vertical axis

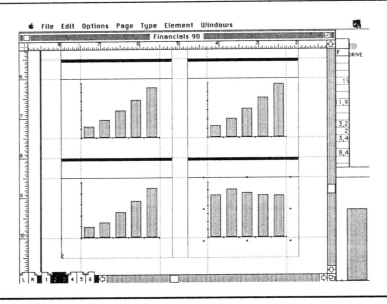

FIGURE 6-32 The four charts in position after placement

with the title "Millions." Start with the main title above the chart, using these instructions:

1. Press COMMAND+T to open the Type specifications dialog box.

2. Click on "Bold" for the "Type Style."

3. Click on "OK" to close the Type specifications dialog box.

4. Press SHIFT+F4 or click in the Toolbox to select the text tool.

5. Press CAPS LOCK to turn it on.

6. Click the text tool at left 7.9H/8.35V.

7. Type an em-space (COMMAND+SHIFT+M and type **SHAREHOLDERS' EQUITY**.

8. Click at 4.7H/8.35V, enter an em-space, and type **RETURN ON EQUITY**.

9. Click at 7.9H/5.85V, enter an em-space, and type **TOTAL REVENUE**.

10. Click at 4.7H/5.85V, enter an em-space, and type **NET INCOME**.

Your screen should look like Figure 6-33.

Horizontal Axis Titles   Next, add the years to the bottom of each chart with these instructions:

1. Press COMMAND+T to open the Type specifications dialog box.

2. Type **10** in the "Size" text box, click "Normal" for the Type style, and click on "OK" to close the dialog box.

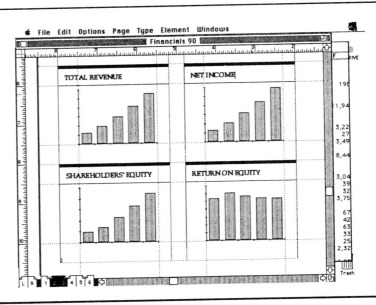

FIGURE 6-33 Primary titles on the charts

3. Click the text tool to the right of the left margin at 8H/7.7V.

4. Press TAB, type **1986**, press TAB, type **1987**, press TAB, type **1988**, press TAB, type **1989**, press TAB, and type **1990**.

5. Press COMMAND+I to open the Indents/tabs dialog box.

6. Click on the centering tab button in the lower left corner. Then enter new tabs by clicking at .7, 1.1, 1.5, 1.9, and 2.3 inches on the tab ruler. Click on "OK" to close the dialog box.

The row of years will jump into alignment under each of the columns as shown here:

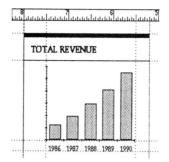

7. With the text tool, drag over the row of years to select them all (being sure you highlight from the left margin through 1990).

8. Press COMMAND+C or F3 to copy the years to the Clipboard.

9. Click the text tool inside the left margin of the right column at 5.2H/7.7V and press COMMAND+V or F4 to paste the row of years under the Net Income chart.

10. Click the text tool inside the left margin of the left column at 8H/10.2V and press COMMAND+V or F4 to paste the set of years under the Equity chart.

11. Click the text tool inside the left margin of the right column at 5.2H/10.2V and press COMMAND+V or F4 to paste the set of years under the Return chart.

Vertical Axis Tables   Next add the scale and annotation to the vertical axes.

1. Click the text tool inside the left margin of the left column at 8H/6.2V.

2. Type **$60**, press RETURN, type **$50**, press RETURN, type **$40**, press RETURN, type **$30**, press RETURN, type **$20**, press RETURN, type **$10**, press RETURN, press COMMAND+SHIFT+N (for an en-space), and type **$0**.

3. Drag the text tool down the column of numbers, highlighting them all. Press COMMAND+T to open the Type specifications dialog box, drag across "Auto" in the leading text box, type **16**, and press RETURN.

4. Press SHIFT+F1 or click in the Toolbox to select the pointer.

5. Click on the numbers you just entered to select them and drag one of the right-hand selection boxes to 7.7H to place the numbers in the Total Revenue chart. Then drag the whole column to the right so the right edge of the selection box is at 7.5H as shown here:

6. While the column of numbers is still selected, press COMMAND+C or F3 to copy it. Then immediately press COMMAND+V or F4 to paste the column of numbers on the annual report.

7. Drag the new copy of the column of numbers (which is on top of the original column of numbers) over to the Net Income chart.

8. Paste two more copies of the vertical scale onto the publication and drag one to the Equity chart and the other to the Return chart.

9. Press SHIFT+F4 or click in the Toolbox to select the text tool.

10. Edit the column of numbers in the Net Income chart so it reads $6, $5, $4, $3, $2, $1, and $0 (remember to remove the en-space on $0).

11. Edit the column of numbers in the Equity chart so it reads $25, $20, $15, $10, $5, and $0 (add an en-space before $5) and change the leading to 19-point.

12. Edit the column of numbers in the Return chart so it reads 35%, 30%, 25%, 20%, 15%, 10%, 5%, and 0% (add an en-space before 5%), and decrease the leading to 14-point.

Second Vertical Axis Titles   Finally, add and rotate the second vertical label.

1. With the text tool, click at 7.9H/7.9V, and type **Million**.

2. Drag over the word "Million," and from the Type menu, choose "130%" as the "Set width" option, and choose "Very loose" as the "Track" option. Then press COMMAND+SHIFT+C to center the word.

3. Press SHIFT+F1 or click in the Toolbox to select the pointer. Click on the word "Million" and drag one of the right-hand text handles to 7.5H.

4. From the Element menu, choose "Text rotation...", select the second rotational step, 90 degrees to the right, as shown here, and click on "OK."

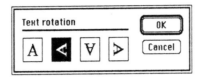

5. With the pointer, drag the rotated word "Million" so it spans from 6V to 7.5V at roughly 7.85H on the Total Revenue chart.

6. When the word "Million" is in place, press COMMAND+C or F3 to copy it.

7. Press COMMAND+V or F4 to paste a copy of the word back onto the publication and drag that copy to a similar position on the Net Income chart.

8. Press COMMAND+V or F4 to paste a second copy of the word "Million" back onto the publication and drag that copy to a position on the Equity chart, similar to the position on the Revenue chart.

9. Press COMMAND+S to save the annual report.

Figure 6-34 shows the completed titles on each of the four charts, and Figure 6-35 shows page 2 as it looks printed.

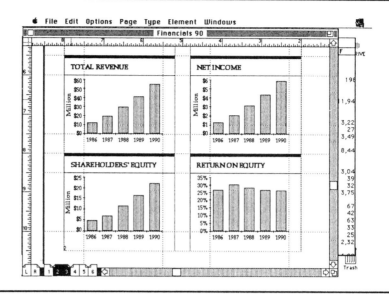

═══════ **FIGURE 6-34** Completed titles on the charts

ADDING THE FINANCIAL STATEMENTS

You will place the Consolidated Statement of Operations (income statement) on page 4 and the Consolidated Statement of Condition (balance sheet) on page 5. You will handle them exactly as you did the Financial Highlights table: you will place the table, set the tab stops, make the heading bold, and add the lines.

Placing the Tables

Retrieving text files should be almost routine by now. Let's do it twice more with the following instructions:

Micro Corporation of America

FINANCIAL HIGHLIGHTS
(In thousands except per share & employees)

Years ended June 30	1990	1989	1988
FOR THE YEAR:			
Revenue	$54,725	$40,840	$29,594
Net Income	$5,851	$4,366	$3,164
Net Income per Share	$1.68	$1.25	$1.11
Average Shares Outstanding	3,485	3,485	2,854
NET MARGIN	10.7%	10.7%	10.7%
AT YEAR END:			
Total Assets	$31,548	$23,543	$17,060
Total Plant & Equipment	$12,253	$9,144	$6,626
Total Equity	$22,189	$16,339	$11,216
Number of Employees	487	363	263
RETURN ON EQUITY	26.4%	26.7%	28.2%

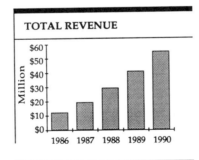

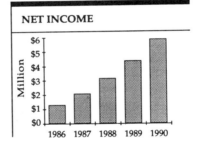

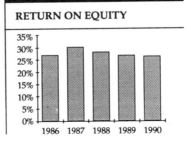

2

FIGURE 6-35 Page 2 as it looks printed

1. Press COMMAND+T to open the Type specifications dialog box.

2. Type **12** in the "Size" text box and verify that "Auto" appears in the "Leading" text box and that "Normal" is checked as the "Type style."

3. Click on "OK" to close the Type specifications dialog box.

4. Click on the icon for pages 4 and 5 to change pages.

5. Drag horizontal ruler guides down to 1.2V and 9.8V.

6. Activate Excel, select or highlight the range A1 through D43, and press COMMAND+C or F3 to copy the table to the Clipboard.

7. Activate PageMaker and press COMMAND+V or F4 to paste the Consolidated Statement of Operations on the annual report.

8. Drag the table to page 4 between the two horizontal ruler guides you just placed there.

9. Activate Excel, select or highlight the range H1 through K43, and press COMMAND+C or F3 to copy the table to the Clipboard.

10. Activate PageMaker and press COMMAND+V or F4 to paste the Consolidated Statement of Condition on the annual report.

11. Drag the table to page 5 between the two horizontal ruler guides you placed there earlier.

12. Adjust the tables on both pages 4 and 5 so that the top line is just under the horizontal ruler guide at 1.2V and

the bottom line is just above 9.8V, as shown in Figure 6-36.

CHANGING THE HEADING AND TABS The changes that need to be made to the tables on pages 4 and 5 are the same as the changes you made to the Financial Highlights table on page 2. Highlight the table, move the tabs, and make the heading bold. Use the following instructions to do that:

1. Press SHIFT+F4 or click in the Toolbox to select the text tool.

2. Drag across the entire table on page 4 to highlight it and press COMMAND+1 to go to "Actual size" view.

3. Press COMMAND+I to open the Indents/tab dialog box.

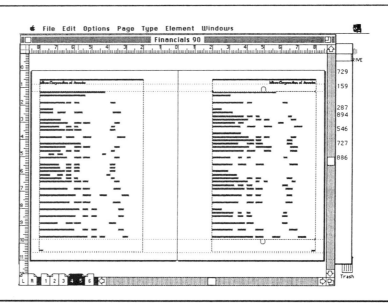

FIGURE 6-36 Tables properly aligned on pages 4 and 5

4. Click on the decimal tab button and drag three tab stops to 3.75, 4.75, and 5.75 on the tab ruler. Your dialog box should look like the one shown in Figure 6-37.

5. Click on "OK" to close the dialog box.

6. Press the UP ARROW key to go to the top of the table. If there is a blank line (because of extra tabs) between the first and second line, delete it.

7. Drag across only the heading (the top line of the table) on page 4 and press COMMAND+SHIFT+B to make it bold.

8. Drag across the entire table on page 5 to highlight it.

9. Press COMMAND+I, click on the decimal tab button, drag the three tab stops to 3.75, 4.75, and 5.75 on the tab ruler and click on "OK."

10. Press the UP ARROW key to go to the top of the table. If there is a blank line between the first and second lines, delete it.

11. Drag across the heading (the top line of the table) and press COMMAND+SHIFT+B to make it bold.

12. Press COMMAND+W to change to "Fit in window" view.

When you have completed these steps, your pages 4 and 5 should look like those shown in Figure 6-38.

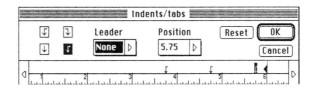

FIGURE 6-37   The completed Indents/tabs dialog box

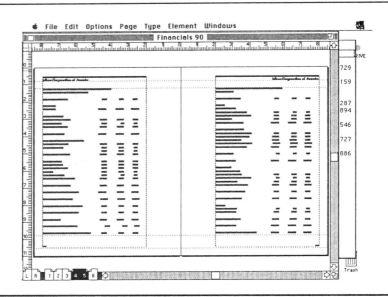

═══════ **FIGURE 6-38** The financial statements with the tabs
adjusted and columns aligned

DRAWING LINES Your final task to complete the tables
on pages 4 and 5 is to add a series of lines on each of them
to emphasize or separate various segments. Like the Financial Highlights table, both of these will have a 1-point line
under the dates. In addition, though, a number of hairlines
will be added to the table itself. Add these lines by using
the following instructions:

1. Press COMMAND+U to turn the "Snap to guides" option
   back on.

2. Press SHIFT+F3 or click in the Toolbox to select the
   perpendicular-line tool.

3. Drag a horizontal ruler guide down to 2V.

4. Draw a line across the table on page 4 on the horizontal
   ruler guide at 2V from 8H to 2H.

5. Select the Line option of the Element menu and confirm that "1 pt" is chosen; if not, choose it now for this and for the next line.

6. Draw a similar line across the table on page 5 on the horizontal ruler guide at 2V from 2H to 8H.

7. Press SHIFT+F1 or click in the Toolbox to select the pointer.

8. Choose "Hairline" from the Line option of the Element menu.

9. Press SHIFT+F3 or click in the Toolbox to select the perpendicular-line tool.

10. Place the pointer at left 5H/4V, press and hold COMMAND+OPTION while clicking the mouse button for "Actual size."

11. Drag down a horizontal ruler guide and draw a line across the Consolidated Statement of Operations (page 4) for each of the following six points on the vertical ruler: 2.65, 4.05, 7.45, 9.05, 9.85, and the existing ruler guide at 9.80. Use the scroll bar as necessary.

Note that the last two lines produce a double line at the bottom of the Statement of Operations, as shown in Figure 6-39.

12. Press COMMAND+W to return to "Fit in window" view.

13. Place the pointer at right 5H/4V, press and hold COMMAND+OPTION while clicking the mouse button for "Actual size."

14. Drag down a horizontal ruler guide and draw a line across the Consolidated Statement of Condition (page 5) for each of the following seven points on the vertical

ruler: 3.45, 5.60, 5.65, 7.95, 9.45, 9.80, and 9.85. Use the scroll bar as necessary.

15. Press COMMAND+W to return to "Fit in window" view.

16. Press CTRL+S to save the publication.

Figure 6-40 shows all of the lines on pages 4 and 5 as they look on the screen with the guides turned off. Figures 6-41 and 6-42 show how the Statement of Operations and Statement of Condition look as they are printed.

FINISHING THE BACK COVER

The back cover of the annual report, page 6, has only the company's address and phone number in addition to the

Payroll Taxes	1,811	1,351	979	519
	1,478	1,103	799	1,429
Total Labor Expense	17,218	12,850	9,311	
				729
Advertising	3,095	2,310	1,674	
Depreciation	1,935	1,444	1,046	2,159
Leases & Rentals	2,902	2,166	1,569	
Taxes	1,548	1,155	837	
Miscellaneous	1,161	866	628	287
Total Nonlabor Expense	10,641	7,941	5,754	1,894
Total Indirect Expense	27,859	20,790	15,065	2,546
NET OPERATING INCOME	$10,834	$8,085	$5,859	4,727
Other Income (Expense)	(2,476)	(1,848)	(1,339)	6,886
NET INCOME BEFORE TAXES	8,358	6,237	4,520	
Provision for Income Taxes	2,507	1,871	1,356	
NET INCOME	$5,851	$4,366	$3,164	
NET INCOME PER SHARE	$1.68	$1.25	$1.11	
AVERAGE SHARES OUTSTANDING	3,485	3,485	2,854	

FIGURE 6-39 The lines at the bottom of the Statement of Operations

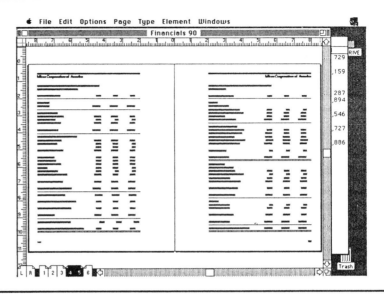

FIGURE 6-40   Pages 4 and 5 with the lines completed and "Guides" off

items from the master page. Use the following instructions to finish that page and the annual report:

1. Press SHIFT+F1 or click in the Toolbox to select the pointer.

2. Click on the page 6 icon to turn the page.

3. Press COMMAND+T to open the Type specifications dialog box.

4. Type **14** in the "Size" text box and click on "Bold" for the "Type style."

5. Click on "OK" to close the Type specifications dialog box.

6. Place the pointer at left 5H/2V, press and hold COMMAND+OPTION while clicking the mouse button for "Actual size."

Micro Corporation of America

CONSOLIDATED STATEMENT OF OPERATIONS
(In thousands except per share data)

Years ended June 30	1990	1989	1988
REVENUE			
Net Sales	$54,725	$40,840	$29,594
COST OF SALES			
Cost of Goods Sold	14,776	11,027	7,990
Direct Costs	1,256	937	679
Total Cost of Sales	16,032	11,964	8,670
GROSS INCOME	$38,693	$28,876	$20,924
INDIRECT OPERATING COSTS			
Salaries & Wages	13,930	10,395	7,533
Payroll Taxes	1,811	1,351	979
	1,478	1,103	799
Total Labor Expense	17,218	12,850	9,311
Advertising	3,095	2,310	1,674
Depreciation	1,935	1,444	1,046
Leases & Rentals	2,902	2,166	1,569
Taxes	1,548	1,155	837
Miscellaneous	1,161	866	628
Total Nonlabor Expense	10,641	7,941	5,754
Total Indirect Expense	27,859	20,790	15,065
NET OPERATING INCOME	$10,834	$8,085	$5,859
Other Income (Expense)	(2,476)	(1,848)	(1,339)
NET INCOME BEFORE TAXES	8,358	6,237	4,520
Provision for Income Taxes	2,507	1,871	1,356
NET INCOME	$5,851	$4,366	$3,164
NET INCOME PER SHARE	$1.68	$1.25	$1.11
AVERAGE SHARES OUTSTANDING	3,485	3,485	2,854

4

FIGURE 6-41 Finished Statement of Operations as it looks printed

Micro Corporation of America

CONSOLIDATED STATEMENT OF CONDITION
(In thousands)

Years ended June 30	1990	1989	1988
ASSETS			
Current Assets			
Cash and Equivalents	1,286	960	695
Net Accounts Receivable	7,483	5,584	4,047
Inventory	9,737	7,266	5,266
Total Current Assets	$18,506	$13,810	$10,008
Plant and Equipment			
Leasehold Improvements	5,678	4,237	3,071
Furniture & Equipment	10,897	8,132	5,893
Subtotal at Cost	16,575	12,369	8,963
Less Accum. Depreciation	(4,322)	(3,225)	(2,337)
Net Plant & Equipment	$12,253	$9,144	$6,626
Other Assets	789	589	427
TOTAL ASSETS	$31,548	$23,543	$17,060
LIABILITIES			
Current Liabilities			
Accounts Payable	3,683	2,749	1,992
Current Portion of Notes	487	363	263
Taxes Payable	2,378	1,775	1,286
Total Current Liabilities	$6,548	$4,887	$3,541
Net Long Term Notes	2,811	2,318	2,304
TOTAL LIABILITIES	$9,359	$7,204	$5,845
EQUITY			
Common Stock	697	697	571
Paid-in Capital	3,485	3,485	2,854
Retained Earnings	18,007	12,157	7,791
TOTAL EQUITY	$22,189	$16,339	$11,216
TOTAL LIABILITIES & EQUITY	$31,548	$23,543	$17,060

5

FIGURE 6-42 Finished Statement of Condition as it looks printed

7. Press SHIFT+F4 or click in the Toolbox to select the text tool.

8. Click at 1.5V to the right of the left margin to place the insertion point.

9. Type the following lines, pressing RETURN at the end of each line.

One Micro Way
Silicon Valley, CA 94123
(800) 555-1234 or
(415) 555-4321

When you are done, page 6 should look like Figure 6-43 on the screen and like Figure 6-44 when it is printed.

10. Press COMMAND+S to save the publication.

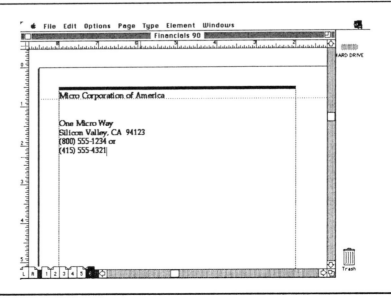

FIGURE 6-43 The completed last page on screen

Micro Corporation of America

One Micro Way
Silicon Valley, CA 94123
(800) 555-1234 or
(415) 555-4321

FIGURE 6-44 The completed last page as it looks printed

11. Press COMMAND+P to open the Print dialog box. Make any necessary changes and press RETURN to print the annual report.

12. Choose "Quit" from the File menu to leave Page-Maker.

The finished annual report is a very attractive piece. The newsletter in Chapter 7 is even nicer!

ADVANCED PAGEMAKER SOLUTIONS

Preparing a Newsletter
Building a Catalog

P art III focuses on two publications to demonstrate PageMaker's more advanced functions. These two publications are a newsletter in Chapter 7 and a catalog in Chapter 8. Because you are now familiar with the basics of PageMaker, the pace quickens. Less emphasis is placed on explaining the features and more is on using them to create an application.

One of the primary uses of PageMaker has been to create newsletters. Consequently, no PageMaker book is complete without exploring this application in detail. The newsletter in Chapter 7 is modeled after an actual one that is produced with PageMaker. It demonstrates how to create a multipage newsletter with three or four columns per page, using graphics and text from multiple sources. In

Chapter 7 you will use the master layout pages in conjunction with custom pages to produce a dummy publication — the base from which all issues of the newsletter are created. In many ways this is the most important chapter in the book: upon completing this chapter, you will be well versed in the essentials of using PageMaker to produce complex publications.

In Chapter 8 you will produce three pages of a catalog. Like the newsletter in Chapter 7, the catalog is modeled after an actual one that is created with PageMaker. This chapter demonstrates how to produce a multipage, two-column product catalog using the master page layout as a standard.

PREPARING A NEWSLETTER

Planning and Designing the Newsletter
Creating Text and Graphics for the Newsletter
Setting Defaults
Important Techniques Used in This Chapter
Setting Up a Dummy Publication
Constructing a Specific Issue of the Newsletter
Using the Story Editing Features

I n this chapter, you'll find that creating newsletters is a task well-suited to PageMaker. You will create a four-page newsletter that uses graphics, multiple fonts, multiple columns, varying line widths, automatic and customized leading, and other techniques to make attractive and readable copy.

An actual newsletter is used as the example in this chapter. *The Orator* is a quarterly published for the Churchill Club by Opinion Movers of Palo Alto, California. *The Orator* is created on the Macintosh with PageMaker.

The names of most individuals and companies on the original newsletter have been changed, except for public figures and the editor, Rich Karlgaard, who has generously given ideas and advice for this chapter.

The newsletter articles are written by several individuals: the newsletter's regular staff and two contributing authors. For the purposes of this example, assume that the articles written by the staff were produced with Microsoft Word. One contributing author used WriteNow as the word processor; the other, WordPerfect. Part of your task in this chapter is to take text from these three word processors and integrate them into one newsletter.

The newsletter contains two graphics. When publishing the actual newsletter, the Opinion Movers staff creates a placeholder for the graphics in the newsletter and then gives the actual graphics to a commercial printer to place and print. In this chapter, you will create placeholders for both graphics. Then you will create a computer file of the first graphic with a scanner and place it in the placeholder using PageMaker. You will not create the second graphic.

You needn't use all three word processors or the scanner. Simply read the explanation, noting the particulars about the text, and then use your own word processor (if it is supported by PageMaker). For the graphics, you can substitute clip art if you want experience in placing and working with graphics. Or you can simply read the details, and provide the space for the graphics to see how working text around the graphics is handled within PageMaker. A disk that contains both the text and the graphic is available from the author; you can order it by using the form in this book.

PLANNING AND DESIGNING THE NEWSLETTER

As with all publications, planning and design are critical to the successful creation of a newsletter.

Planning the Newsletter

The planning stage for a newsletter may be extensive because the publisher may be coordinating the efforts of many individuals. Bringing all factors together against a deadline, and within budget, may be a challenge.

Essentially, the planning task consists of four steps:

1. Identifying what materials—graphics, articles, and artwork—are needed in the newsletter.

2. Identifying who will be responsible for each item.

3. Determining when each item must be submitted to be included in the newsletter.

4. Determining what the cost elements are and what the newsletter will cost.

You must do the planning in detail. For example, you must both identify what articles are needed and estimate, with reasonable accuracy, how many words the text should be. If you need 500 words and get 1,000, you're in as much trouble as if you only received 100 words. You must plan for contingencies in any case. If a writer breaks her leg the day before a deadline, you must be able to wing it; that is, have plans to cover such an event, such as other writers or filler articles.

The Orator contains text from four sources: standard text that is included in all the newsletters, such as the masthead; articles prepared for this particular issue by *The Orator* staff; a short article from one contributing author; and a longer article by a second contributing author. Figure 7-1 shows the four pages.

The length of each article is closely planned and monitored by the staff to fit in the available space in the four-page newsletter. The planning closely ties in with the design of the newsletter.

Designing the Newsletter

A primary design consideration is to evaluate the newsletter for standard formatting, graphics, and text; that is, to determine which parts of the newsletter are the same from issue to issue. By isolating these standard parts and saving them separately, you can save yourself many hours of repetitive work.

One of the overall objectives of this chapter is to produce a dummy publication containing all recurring formatting, graphics, and text, and then use that to create an issue of *The Orator*. To do this requires that you examine the makeup and layout of each page of the newsletter.

THE ORATOR
Volume 4, Issue 4—November 1989

SOUTH AFRICA'S BUTHELEZI TO ADDRESS CHURCHILL CLUB ON DECEMBER 4TH

The Churchill Club will sponsor its eighth and final event of 1989 on Thursday, December 4th, at the Santa Clara Marriott. The guest: Gatsha Buthelezi, Chief Minister of the Kwa-Zulu homeland in South Africa. The event starts at 6 P.M.

CHURCHILL CLUB

Chief Gatsha Buthelezi claims the support of South Africa's six million Zulus, the nation's largest ethnic group. Despite his moderate voice (or perhaps because of it), this makes him a powerful voice in this turmoiled region. Tom Lodge, a political-science professor at the University of Witswatersrand, says, "It is a dangerous situation to leave Buthelezi out of the equation." Chief Buthelezi himself asserts, "There can't be a successful negotiation without me."

Chief Buthelezi comes across to many white South Africans as comfortably moderate. To them, he embodies the hope for the future. He speaks about whites' fears without fanning them. He says he doesn't want to overthrow white South Africa's values and aspirations. Rather, he says, he wants blacks to be able to share them.

A more serious difference is between Chief Buthelezi and the African National Congress, the broadly based antiapartheid organization that has recently espoused violence. The ANC (and its leader, the jailed Nelson Mandela) quietly supported Buthelezi in the 1970s, recognizing his ability to mobilize people from the rural areas. But in the 1980s the ANC became impatient with Buthelezi's pleas for peaceful change. The group now espouses violence as a necessary catalyst for change in South Africa.

The Orator is published quarterly by The Churchill Club. Subscriptions are guaranteed free of charge to all corporate and individual members. Printing of The Orator is donated by Pandick Press, San Francisco.

Editor: Richard Karlgaard
Historian: Michael Perkins
Cartoonist: Kurt Peterson

Ennui and the brush-Winston as the artist

Broadly speaking, human beings may be divided into three classes: those who are toiled to death, those who are worried to death, and those who are bored to death.

Churchill himself, of course, was by no means immune to these afflictions about which he wrote. But what was he to do about it?

Churchill typically sought surcease in a number of activities, including reading, fencing, swimming, riding, hunting, flying, polo, horse racing, gardening, and brick-laying. He was also a collector of butterflies and tropical fish and had a number of pets.

Further, Churchill was something of the big kid indulging in everything from toy trains, tin soldiers, and erector sets to

> "The tired parts of the mind can be rested and strengthened, not merely by rest, but by using other parts"

building sandcastles and snow-men.

The common denominator in all this activity was change. As Churchill himself writes,

Continued on page 2

FIGURE 7-1 Page 1 of the newsletter (1 of 4)

Change is the master key. A man can wear out a particular part of his mind by continually using it and tiring it. The tired parts of the mind can be rested and strengthened, not merely by rest, but by using other parts. It is only when new cells are called into activity, when new stars become lords of the ascendant, that relief, repose, refreshment are afforded.

At age 40 Churchill found himself out of political office for the first time in fifteen years and he needed to discover a new way to creatively fill up the hours.

Exercise, travel, solitude, light socializing, even golf (which he likened to chasing a pill around a cow pasture) did not suffice. It was then, with a friend's encouragement, that he took up painting.

Intensity, Relish and Audacity
Painting at once provided Churchill an opportunity to use his hands as well as a different part of his brain. The "muse of painting" had come to his rescue.

The nonprofit Churchill Club provides a nonpartisan forum for public discourse on timely issues, particularly those in which business and politics converge. The Club is named after Winston Churchill, whose character and career personify the democratic values of open discourse, diversity and freedom. Accordingly, Club membership is without regard to sex, lifestyle, legitimacy, sobriety, race, color, creed, physical or mental disposition, or origin.

When Churchill took up the brush, he did it with the same intensity, relish, and audacity as everything he undertook, and he was not discouraged by the results. Painting also proved to be the perfect diversion. In Painting as a Pastime he writes,

I know nothing which, without exhausting the body, more entirely absorbs the mind. Whatever the worries of the hour or the threats of the future, once the picture has begun to flow along, there is no room for them in the mental screen. They pass out into shadow and darkness. All one's mental light, such as it is, becomes concentrated on the task. Time stands respectfully aside.

Churchill chose to devote his painting to landscapes and still lifes in an impressionist style. His brilliant colors became a type of trademark: "I cannot pretend to be impartial about the colours," he wrote. "I rejoice with the brilliant ones and am genuinely sorry for the poor browns."

In search of beautiful scenes, Churchill took his easel with him wherever he traveled including the Middle East and North America. On a trip to Scotland he wrote to his wife, "In the afternoon I went out and painted a beautiful river in the afternoon light with crimson and golden hills in the background."

From the Riviera he writes of a villa that he painted "all in shimmering sunshine and violet shades."

Antidote to Melancholy and Ennui
In the end, painting was to

There is something about a martini —a tingle remarkably pleasant

Thus began poet Ogden Nash in *A Drink with Something in It.*

The perfect dry martini contains gin, vermouth, and a twist of lemon. It must be very cold, but not contain ice or water, so keep your gin in the freezer and vermouth in the refrigerator. The especially discriminating may use Tanqueray gin and Noilly extra dry vermouth.

Polish a martini glass and put it in the freezer along with your jigger and stirring rod. The glass should be large, but light, with a feathered rim and a long stem to keep the martini cold. With a sharp knife, cut a generous twist from a ripe, fresh lemon. Be careful to separate the yellow peel from the white pulp, as the peel contains the lemon oil and the pulp would impart a bitter flavor to the martini.

Take the glass from the freezer. Twist the lemon peel to release its oil. Rub the oily surface around the inside of the glass and along its rim, then drop the twist in the glass. Take the gin from the freezer (or Stolichnaya vodka if you feel diffident about gin) and measure two jiggers into the glass. Take the vermouth from the refrigerator and measure a third of a jigger into the glass. Stir vigorously, but do not shake. Remove to a pleasant setting and enjoy.

by "Christopher Russell"

MY EARLY LIFE

prove one of the chief antidotes to Winston's sometime melancholy and ennui. It also served to deepen Churchill's powers of observation, so much that he had come to see that "the whole world is open with all its treasures, even the simplest objects have their beauty."

Like the poet and artist William Blake, Churchill had learned not only to see with, but through the eye.

*Contributed by
Michael Perkins
Club Historian*

It took me three tries to pass into Sandhurst. There were five subjects, of which Mathematics, Latin and English were obligatory, and I chose in addition French and Chemistry. In this hand I held only a pair of Kings--English and chemistry. Nothing less than three would open the jackpot. I had to find another useful card.

W.S. CHURCHILL

FIGURE 7-1 Page 2 of the newsletter (2 of 4)

Members Only

GOVERNOR DEUKMEJIAN INTRODUCES CHILDREN'S INITIATIVE AT 10-9-89 MEETING

Governor George Deukmejian proposed a $5 million program to bolster statewide child care and medical services at a joint meeting of the Churchill Club and Commonwealth Club on October 9, 1989.

Before 500 people at the San Jose Hyatt, the governor outlined a seven-point "children's initiative" that included a call for expanded drug abuse prevention programs and a crackdown on parents who evade payment of child support.

He also promised to hire more senior citizens to work in child care centers and offered to write legislation providing incentives for drug companies to produce vaccines for childhood diseases.

The Churchill Club thanks the Commonwealth Club for co-sponsoring this fine event.

COMING DECEMBER 4TH

"IMMIGRATION OUT OF CONTROL," COLORADO'S LAMM TELLS CLUB

Warning that the United States is at a crossroads, Colorado Governor Richard Lamm called for stronger border control measures during an address to the Churchill Club on October 16, 1989.

"The creativity and capital of this country, for all its genius, cannot keep pace with the demands put on it if we have to solve not only our own unemployment rate, but that of Mexico, Guatemala, and El Salvador," said the four-term governor.

CLUB MEMBERS IN THE NEWS

Board member Bill Reichert is now vp/marketing at The Learning Company, a Menlo Park-based educational software firm. Reichert's alma mater, New Venture Consultants, is the newest corporate member of the Club...John Sewell, former vice president and general manager of Kodak's largest division, joined the board of Redlake Corporation, a Morgan Hill company that manufactures and sells photo-instrumentation equipment. Redlake is also a Club corporate member...Bob Hansens of Business Solutions Consultants is forming the Silicon Valley Entrepreneur's Club. First meeting is scheduled for January 24th at the San Jose Hyatt. Call Bob at (408) 458-1303 for more information...Club chairman Tony Perkins has returned to Silicon Valley Bank as vice president of SVB's technology group. Also new with SVB are Club members Henry Kellog and Eric Jones.

T.J. Rodgers confirmed for late January

Semiconductor entrepreneur T.J. Rodgers will address the Churchill Club in late January.

Founder and CEO of Cypress Semiconductor, Rodgers has engineered one of Silicon Valley's brightest stories of late. Cypress went public last summer at a valuation of $270 million.

Invitations to a *Night with T.J. Rodgers* will be mailed in early January.

CLUB INFORMATION

Membership
Ken Bailey
Silver City Bank
(415) 555-1234

Speaker Information
Julia Conner
Pacific Research Capital
(415) 555-4321

Media Relations
Susan Casper
Ocean Products
(408) 555-9876

Former H&Q president Tom Volpe on February 19th

Tom Volpe, founder of Volpe Covington, a new investment banking firm that includes Arthur Rock and Warren Hellman as major investors, will address the Churchill Club on Thursday, February 19th.

Volpe has had a meteoric career in investment banking. After taking his AB and MBA from Harvard —with a one-year stopover at the London School of Economics—he began his career with White, Weld & Company, later moving to Blyth, Eastman, Dillon.

At age 30 Volpe joined Hambrecht & Quist as a general partner and opened the investment banking firm's New York Office. In 1984 he became president and CEO of H&Q.

Invitations to *A Night with Tom Volpe* will be mailed to all Club members in early January.

Pandick California, Inc.

The **Financial Printer**

(415) 543-4433

Offices in

San Francisco • Los Angeles • Newport Beach

FIGURE 7-1 Page 3 of the newsletter (3 of 4)

Board of Directors

Chairman
Co-Founder
Anthony DeVoe
Silver City Bank

Director of Marketing
Co-Founder
Richard Karlgaard
Opinion Movers

Director of Finance
Edward Hecht
PX, Inc.

Director of Speakers
Susan Casper
Ocean Products

Director of Membership
Ken Bailey
Silver City Bank

Director of Operations
Edward Osborne
Reiley Aerospace

Director, Scholarship Committee
William Shelly
Nordic Distributors

Club Historian
Michael Rains
South Port Cold Storage

Corporate Secretaries
Frederick Shelly
Scott Katz
Shelly, Katz, & Greenlee

Tom Cook
Cook Corporation

Barry Burton
Standard Computer

Marjorie Walters
South American Importers

Diane Graves

Robert Lusk
Graves, Lusk, Meadows, & Thomas

Timothy Lamson
Lamson Associates

James North, Jr.
Technology Consultants, Inc.

Stephen Petosa
RotoGraphic Corporation

Alex Lange
Pacific Imports

Grant Strom
Strom Computer

Peter Dayton
Creative Designs

Doug Hendrix
Strom Computer

Steve Masion
Pacific Southern

Michael Boggs
New Toy Corporation

Cordell Tucker
Tucker Steel Pipe

Michael Jones
Smith and Jones

Senior Advisory Board

Roger Weiss
President and CEO
Silver City Bank

Ed Adams
U.S. Congressman

Norm Browning
U.S. Congressman

Judy Carlson
President
Carlson Associates

Robert Wohlers
Chairman
New Toy Corporation

Robert Freeland, Jr.
President
Robert Freeland Associates

Larry Meadows
Partner
Graves, Lusk, Meadows, & Thomas

Samuel Robinson
General Partner
Robinson Venture Partners

William Dunn
Chairman
Leader Corporation

Joe Parsons
Managing Partner
Springtime Capital

Richard Van Waters
President
Vanguard Trucking

James Johnston
President and CEO
Northern Metal Fabricators

Robert Dyer
Vice President
Pacific Imports

Consuelo Martinez
Director
Center for Better Learning

Lorayne Easton
Political Consultant

Ryland Keeney
Managing Partner
Thomas and Keeney

George Maynard
President & CEO
Micro Corporation of America

Rob Younger
Editor
Silver City Evening News

Walter A. McIntyre
Professor of Political Science
Northern University

Corporate Members

ABC Corporation
American Consultants
Arrow Brothers
Art Treasures
Avery Products
Barringer, Easter, & McGrath
Bayside Interiors
Berg Equipment
Bergman Communications
Central Area Bank
Commercial Bank
Dick Shepard & Co.
Doolittle, Peters, & Curfman
Edwards and Rogers
EG Enterprises
Electronic Instruments
Everett Anchor & Chain
First East/West Bank
Formal Technology
Foster Homes, Inc.
Frank Reiley & Co.
Frankel and Associates
Graves, Lusk, Meadows, & Thomas
Gregory Dunn Ventures
Gunderson, Dimple, & Eagen
Hamlin National
KRGT Silver City
KSAB Bayside
KTZZ Silver City
Leader Corporation
Management Services
McKee Engineering
Micro Corporation of America
Network Ventures
New Technology Consultants
New Toy Corporation
Northern Ventures Partners
Opinion Movers
Pacific Construction
Pacific Press
Pacific Research Capital
Pacific Systems Corp.
Pacific Technology Review
Pauley Furniture
Personal Technology
Peterson Bailey Co.
Philips Manufacturing
Plaza, Hawkins, & Grant
Plum Warehouse
Plywood Fabricators
Quantum Research
Que Technology
Reiley Aerospace
Richards Hotels
Ricker & Ricker
Sierra Partners
Silver City Bank
Silver City Entrepreneurs Club
Silver City Evening News
Silver City Journal
Small Properties
Smith and Jones
South American Imports
Tanqueray and Noily
Thomas Insurance
Travel Partners
Tyler, Funk, & Bailey
Warehouse Furniture
Western Bank
Western Taxi
Williams, Anderson Associates

FIGURE 7-1   Page 4 of the newsletter (4 of 4)

If you examine the four pages in Figure 7-1, you will see some common design elements in each. Lines, fonts, and shading all play important design roles.

LINES Lines are frequently used to create highlights and points of interest, as well as to define areas of the newsletter. Most of the lines are hairline width and are used to define margins, columns, and boxes for short inserts. Other lines are wider, marking the heads of columns, separating categories of information, or emphasizing certain articles. In the actual *Orator,* the staff creates wider lines by drawing boxes and filling them with black shading. Then the commercial printer applies colors and shades to the lines. However, in this chapter you will create most of the wider lines by drawing actual lines rather than boxes, making them 6 and 12 points wide, in contrast to the hairline width of many of the lines. Some of the wider lines contain text. You'll create those by drawing boxes, filling them with shading, and then using *reverse type,* white letters on a black background, to create the text.

FONTS The text you will be entering in this chapter uses two typefaces and 14 fonts. The Times typeface is used for most of the text, and Helvetica is used in a few instances. The title of the newsletter is 48 points; the headlines, 16 points; the text, some of which is italic, 6, 8, and 12 points.

SHADING Shading is used in several ways. First, it is used as a background for headlines of some smaller inserts. Second, it provides the background in the placeholders for the graphics. Third, for articles that span two columns, a box is drawn and filled with "paper" shading to cover the column dividers. Page 3 of the newsletter contains examples of all three types of shading.

LEADING In order to fit some of the text within the given space, you will vary the leading (the spacing between the lines). PageMaker assumes 120 percent leading in its "Auto" leading option. If you are using 10-point type, the automatic leading will be 12 points, or 10/12. In two cases, you will make this smaller to squeeze the text together slightly. Although you could also make the font size smaller, here you will vary the leading.

ADVERTISEMENT One advertisement, for the printer who donates the printing for the newsletter, is included in *The Orator*. Because the ad spans two columns, you will create a box around the column guides and rules and fill the box with "paper" to hide the dividing guides and rules. Then you will type the text for the ad in PageMaker, varying the font sizes and style as you type. The advertisement is a standard part of the newsletter and will be included in the dummy publication.

GRAPHICS There are two graphics: a standard club logo of Winston Churchill that occurs in every publication and a sketch or cartoon that varies with each issue. You will scan the Churchill graphic, creating a computer-readable file that is then placed in the dummy publication. After doing this once, you will not have to repeat it with each issue.

You will create a placeholder for the second graphic and assume that you give the illustration to the commercial printer to size and print. With an actual newsletter, you would probably produce the two graphics in the same way so that the effect would be consistent.

If you don't have access to a scanner, you can substitute clip art for the Churchill graphic. That will allow you to experiment with placing the graphic and flowing text around it, even though it isn't exactly right for the publication.

LAYOUT The layout for the newsletter will be measured in picas and points, which is the most accurate method for what you're doing. Picas and points are the standard units of measurement in the U. S. printing industry. There are about 6 picas per inch and 12 points per pica. Figure 7-2 shows the standard page layout with the primary measurements. You will use 3 picas for the outside and inside margins, 2.5 picas for the top margin, 4 picas for the bottom margin, and 3/4 pica (9 points) to separate the columns. The standard page will have four columns, although the first page has three.

CREATING TEXT AND GRAPHICS FOR THE NEWSLETTER

Next you will create the text and graphics for the newsletter. The text is created outside of PageMaker with word processors that can interface with PageMaker. The Churchill graphic will be produced by a scanner, which must be able to produce a file containing a computer image that is compatible with PageMaker. The second graphic will be pasted on the newsletter before it is printed by a commercial printer, so you needn't concern yourself with it here.

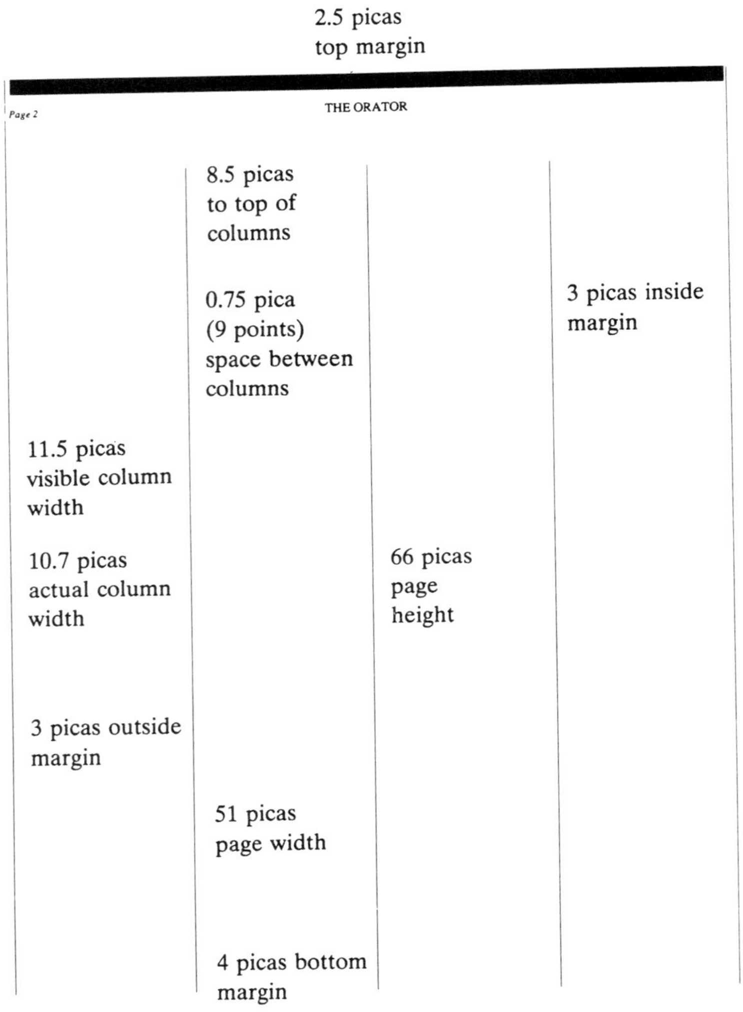

2.5 picas
top margin

Page 2   THE ORATOR

8.5 picas
to top of
columns

0.75 pica   3 picas inside
(9 points)   margin
space between
columns

11.5 picas
visible column
width

10.7 picas   66 picas
actual column   page
width   height

3 picas outside
margin

51 picas
page width

4 picas bottom
margin

FIGURE 7-2   Standard layout used in *The Orator*

Creating Text with the Word Processors

Three word processors are used to create the text that will be integrated into the newsletter. You may not want to use all three, or you may have a different word processor that you normally use. In that case, create the text files with your own word processor. The word processor used most for this newsletter is Microsoft Word.

CREATING FILES WITH MICROSOFT WORD Assume here that the staff of *The Orator* writes all their text using Microsoft Word as the word processor. This package was selected because it can transmit a full complement of type-faces, sizes, and styles to PageMaker. The newsletter makes considerable use of all three.

Two files will be built with Microsoft Word. One contains four items of standard text that appear in all issues of the newsletter. The other contains six specific articles that will appear only in this one issue. You would normally create several files for this many articles.

Figure 7-3 contains the standard text that you will enter with Microsoft Word. It is the longest file and will take some time to enter. Be patient, because you'll learn much about composing with PageMaker while using a file of this size.

CREATING STYLE SHEETS WITH MICROSOFT WORD In Microsoft Word you can use style sheets to specify the fonts and other style elements you want. For the first-file, you'll be using a style sheet that you will create just for this newsletter. It will have a separate style for each change in font. You can quickly apply these styles as you type and know that you have a consistent application of style. Both Microsoft Word and PageMaker will use the style sheet to

The Orator is published quarterly by The Churchill Club. Subscriptions are guaranteed free of charge to all corporate and individual members. Printing of The Orator is donated by Pandick Press, San Francisco.

2 returns

Editor: Richard Karlgaard
Historian: Michael Perkins
Cartoonist: Kurt Peterson

10-point
Times
italics
style (BI)

2 returns

The nonprofit Churchill Club provides a nonpartisan forum for public discourse on timely issues, particularly those in which business and politics converge. The Club is named after Winston Churchill, whose character and career personify the democratic values of open discourse, diversity and freedom. Accordingly, Club membership is without regard to sex, lifestyle, legitimacy, sobriety, race, color, creed, physical or mental disposition, or origin.

2 returns

CLUB INFORMATION

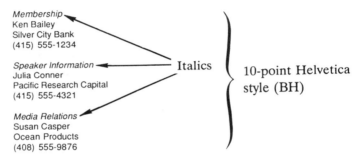

Membership
Ken Bailey
Silver City Bank
(415) 555-1234

Speaker Information
Julia Conner
Pacific Research Capital
(415) 555-4321

Media Relations
Susan Casper
Ocean Products
(408) 555-9876

Italics

10-point Helvetica
style (BH)

2 returns

Board of Directors ◄─── 16-point Times bold style (HL)

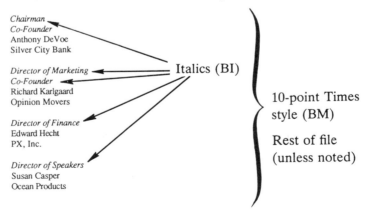

Chairman
Co-Founder
Anthony DeVoe
Silver City Bank

Director of Marketing
Co-Founder
Richard Karlgaard
Opinion Movers

Director of Finance
Edward Hecht
PX, Inc.

Director of Speakers
Susan Casper
Ocean Products

Italics (BI)

10-point Times
style (BM)

Rest of file
(unless noted)

FIGURE 7-3 Masthead-Word file created with Microsoft Word (1 of 3)

Director of Membership
Ken Bailey
Silver City Bank

Director of Operations
Edward Osborne
Reiley Aerospace

Director, Scholarship Committee ◄── Italics
William Shelly
Nordic Distributors

Club Historian
Michael Rains
South Port Cold Storage

Corporate Secretaries
Frederick Shelly
Scott Katz
Shelly, Katz, & Greenlee

2 returns

Tom Cook
Cook Corporation

Barry Burton
Standard Computer

Marjorie Walters
South American Importers

Diane Graves
Robert Lusk
Graves, Lusk, Meadows, & Thomas

Timothy Lamson
Lamson Associates

James North, Jr.
Technology Consultants, Inc.

Stephen Petosa
RotoGraphic Corporation

Alex Lange
Pacific Imports

Grant Strom
Strom Computer

Peter Dayton
Creative Designs

Doug Hendrix
Strom Computer

Steve Masion
Pacific Southern

Michael Boggs
New Toy Corporation

Cordell Tucker
Tucker Steel Pipe

Michael Jones
Smith and Jones   16-point

2 returns   Times bold (HL)

Senior Advisory Board

Roger Weiss
President and CEO
Silver City Bank

Ed Adams
U.S. Congressman

Norm Browning
U.S. Congressman

Judy Carlson
President
Carlson Associates

Robert Wohlers
Chairman
New Toy Corporation

Robert Freeland, Jr.
President
Robert Freeland Associates

Larry Meadows
Partner
Graves, Lusk, Meadows, & Thomas

Samuel Robinson
General Partner
Robinson Venture Partners

William Dunn
Chairman
Leader Corporation

Joe Parsons

FIGURE 7-3   Masthead-Word file created with Microsoft Word (2 of 3)

Managing Partner
Springtime Capital

Richard Van Waters
President
Vanguard Trucking

James Johnston
President and CEO
Northern Metal Fabricators

Robert Dyer
Vice President
Pacific Imports

Consuelo Martinez
Director
Center for Better Learning

Lorayne Easton
Political Consultant

Ryland Keeney
Managing Partner
Thomas and Keeney

George Maynard
President & CEO
Micro Corporation of America

Rob Younger
Editor
Silver City Evening News

Walter A. McIntyre
Professor of Political Science
Northern University

2 returns   16-points Times bold (HL)

Corporate Members ◀

ABC Corporation
American Consultants
Arrow Brothers
Art Treasures
Avery Products
Barringer, Easter, & McGrath
Bayside Interiors
Berg Equipment
Bergman Communications
Central Area Bank
Commercial Bank
Dick Shepard & Co.
Doolittle, Peters, & Curfman
Edwards and Rogers
EG Enterprises
Electronic Instruments
Everett Anchor & Chain
First East/West Bank
Formal Technology
Foster Homes, Inc.
Frank Reiley & Co.
Frankel and Associates

6-points Times
style (BS)
Rest of page

Graves, Lusk, Meadows, & Thomas
Gregory Dunn Ventures
Gunderson, Dimple, & Eagen
Hamlin National
KRGT Silver City
KSAB Bayside
KTZZ Silver City
Leader Corporation
Management Services
McKee Engineering
Micro Corporation of America
Network Ventures
New Technology Consultants
New Toy Corporation
Northern Ventures Partners
Opinion Movers
Pacific Construction
Pacific Press
Pacific Research Capital
Pacific Systems Corp.
Pacific Technology Review ◀——— Italics
Pauley Furniture
Personal Technology
Peterson Bailey Co.
Philips Manufacturing
Platis, Hawkins, & Grant
Plum Warehouse
Plywood Fabricators
Quantum Research
Que Technology
Reiley Aerospace
Richards Hotels
Ricker & Ricker
Sierra Partners
Silver City Bank
Silver City Entrepreneurs Club
Silver City Evening News ◀——— Italics
Silver City Journal ◀
Small Properties
Smith and Jones
South American Imports
Tanqueray and Noilly
Thomas Insurance
Travel Partners
Tyler, Funk, & Bailey
Warehouse Furniture
Western Bank
Western Taxi
Williams, Anderson Associates

FIGURE 7-3   Masthead-Word file created with Microsoft Word (3 of 3)

format the text properly. To change a style in either Microsoft Word or PageMaker, you simply change the style sheet, and all of the text that uses that style will instantly change.

You will be creating six styles on a style sheet for this newsletter, as shown in Figure 7-4. These are used to change typeface between Times and Helvetica, or size to 6, 10, 12, or 16 points, or to apply the italic style. Load Microsoft Word and follow these steps to build a style sheet:

1. Choose "Show Ruler" from the Format menu to turn it on.

2. Choose "Define Styles. . ." from the Format menu. The Define styles dialog box will open.

3. Type **BM,Body Medium**, drag across "Normal" in the "Based on" text box and press DELETE; choose "Times"

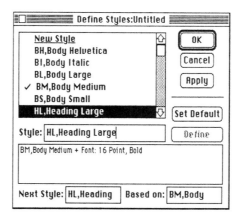

FIGURE 7-4 Microsoft Word style sheet for the newsletter

and "10" points from the Font menu, click on "Define," and click on "OK."

Steps 2 and 3 produce the first style—Body Medium, or BM, as shown in the bottom left corner of the ruler. In addition to being 10-point Times Roman as you have set it, BM also assumes the defaults flush left and Auto leading. This style was defined first because it is the standard upon which you will base all other styles. In other words, all of the other styles will be the Body Medium style with some modification. For example, BS, Body Small, is 6-point Body Medium—flush left, 6-point Times Roman with Auto leading, and BI, Body Italic is italicized Body Medium—flush left, 10-point Times Italic with Auto leading.

Basing a set of styles on a single style is a very useful capability. It means that you can change the base style and all of its derivatives simultaneously. For example, all but one of the styles used in the newsletter are the Times typeface. If you wanted to change all occurrences of Times to Palatino, all you would need to do is change Body Medium style to Palatino and all of the derivative styles would change except those that had a different typeface already. Continue on and define the rest of the styles.

4. Choose "Define Styles. . ." again from the Format menu or press COMMAND + T. When the Define styles dialog box opens, notice that the "Based on" text box now reads "BM,Body," indicating that the style you are about to define is based on the BM style.

5. Type **BL,Body Large**, choose 12 points from the Font menu, and click on "Define." Body Large will be defined with the same specifications as Body Medium but at 12 points instead of 10.

6. Click on "New Style," type **BS,Body Small**, choose "Character" from the Format menu, type **6**, click on "OK," and click on "Define."

7. Repeat step 6 for **BI,Body Italic**, which is defined as Body Medium with italic; **BH,Body Helvetica**, which is Body Medium with Helvetica; and **HL,Heading Large**, which is Body Medium with bold 16-point type.

8. When you have entered all of the styles, as shown in Figure 7-4, click on "OK" to close the Define styles dialog box.

APPLYING STYLE SHEETS WITH MICROSOFT WORD

Use Figure 7-3 to type the first file. Input each column independently, using the styles indicated. The file itself will be one continuous column. Use a single line between sections and paragraphs unless directed otherwise. For example, "2 returns" means to press RETURN twice.

Follow these steps to enter the text:

1. Drag the style option box in the lower left corner of the ruler until "BI,Body Italic" is selected. Then, type the first three paragraphs in Figure 7-3.

2. Press COMMAND + SHIFT + S, type **bh**, and press RETURN to select the BH,Body Helvetica style. Then type the "Club Information" shown in Figure 7-3. After typing the first line of each section — for example, "Membership" — and before pressing RETURN, press and hold COMMAND while clicking anywhere in the line to select it and then press COMMAND + SHIFT + I to make the line italic.

3. Choose "Styles. . ." from the Format menu, click on "HL,Heading Large" to apply it and type **Board of Directors**.

4. Type the remaining text applying the HL, BM, BI, and BS styles as indicated. Use any of the three techniques demonstrated to apply the styles. Apply italic where indicated by using the COMMAND + SHIFT + I procedure in step 2.

5. When you have entered the text, save the file in the Publications folder with the name Masthead-Word. (This assumes that you are using the Publications folder. If you are using a different folder for the PageMaker files created in this book, change the folder name accordingly.)

The second file produced with Microsoft Word contains the six articles that will appear in this single issue. Figure 7-5 shows these articles. Follow these steps to enter the text:

6. Open a new document, choose "Define Styles. . ." from the Format menu, choose "Open. . ." from the File menu, select "Masthead-Word," and press RETURN. The Masthead-Word style sheet will be transferred to the new document. Click on "OK" or press RETURN to close the Define styles dialog box.

7. Type the articles, applying the various styles as described in the discussion of the Masthead-Word document. (In the four instances where the year "1986" appears, enter it just as you see it in Figure 7-5. You will correct it to 1989 by using the story editing features at the end of this chapter.)

8. When you have completed typing the new document, save it in the Publications folder with the name Vol4Issue4-Word.

SOUTH AFRICA'S BUTHELEZI TO ADDRESS ⎫ 16-point Times
CHURCHILL CLUB ON DECEMBER 4TH ⎬ bold(HL)

12-point Times (BL) —

The Churchill Club will sponsor its eighth and final event of 1986 on Thursday, December 4th, at the Santa Clara Marriott. The guest: Gatsha Buthelezi, Chief Minister of the Kwa-Zulu homeland in South Africa. The event starts at 6 P.M.

Chief Gatsha Buthelezi claims the support of South Africa's six million Zulus, the nation's largest ethnic group. Despite his moderate voice (or perhaps because of it), this makes him a powerful voice in this turmoiled region. Tom Lodge, a political-science professor at the University of Witswatersrand, says, "It is a dangerous situation to leave Buthelezi out of the equation." Chief Buthelezi himself asserts, "There can't be a successful negotiation without me."

Chief Buthelezi comes across to many white South Africans as comfortingly moderate. To them, he embodies the hope for the future. He speaks about whites' fears without fanning them. He says he doesn't want to overthrow white South Africa's values and aspirations. Rather, he says, he wants blacks to be able to share them.

A more serious difference is between Chief Buthelezi and the African National Congress, the broadly based antiapartheid organization that has recently espoused violence. The ANC (and its leader, the jailed Nelson Mandela) quietly supported Buthelezi in the 1970s, recognizing his ability to mobilize people from the rural areas. But in the 1980s the ANC became impatient with Buthelezi's pleas for peaceful change. The group now espouses violence as a necessary catalyst for change in South Africa.

2 returns

Members Only ◄——— 16-points Times bold (HL)

GOVERNOR DEUKMEJIAN INTRODUCES CHILDREN'S INITIATIVE AT 10-9-86 MEETING ——

10-point Times (BM) —

Governor George Deukmejian proposed a $5 million program to bolster statewide child care and medical services at a joint meeting of the Churchill Club and Commonwealth Club on October 9, 1986.

Before 500 people at the San Jose Hyatt, the governor outlined a seven-point "children's initiative" that included a call for expanded drug abuse prevention programs and a crackdown on parents who evade payment of child support.

He also promised to hire more senior citizens to work in child care centers and offered to write legislation providing incentives for drug companies to produce vaccines for childhood diseases.

The Churchill Club thanks the Commonwealth Club for co-sponsoring this fine event.

2 returns

"IMMIGRATION OUT OF CONTROL," COLORADO'S LAMM TELLS CLUB ◄——— Italic

Warning that the United States is at a crossroads, Colorado Governor Richard Lamm called for stronger border control measures during an address to the Churchill Club on October 16, 1986.

"The creativity and capital of this country, for all its genius, cannot keep pace with the demands put on it if we have to solve not only our own unemployment rate, but that of Mexico, Guatemala, and El Salvador," said the four-term governor.

2 returns

FIGURE 7-5 Vol4Issue4-Word file created with Microsoft Word (1 of 2)

CLUB MEMBERS IN THE NEWS   Italic

Board member Bill Reichert is now vp/marketing at The Learning Company, a Menlo Park-based educational software firm. Reichert's alma mater, New Venture Consultants, is the newest corporate member of the Club...John Sewell, former vice president and general manager of Kodak's largest division, joined the board of Redlake Corporation, a Morgan Hill company that manufactures and sells photo-instrumentation equipment. Redlake is also a Club corporate member...Bob Hansens of Business Solutions Consultants is forming the Silicon Valley Entrepreneur's Club. First meeting is scheduled for January 24th at the San Jose Hyatt. Call Bob at (408) 458-1303 for more information...Club chairman Tony Perkins has returned to Silicon Valley Bank as vice president of SVB's technology group. Also new with SVB are Club members Henry Kellog and Eric Jones.

2 returns

T.J. Rodgers confirmed for late January   16-point Times bold

Semiconductor entrepreneur T.J. Rodgers will address the Churchill Club in late January.   10-point
        Founder and CEO of Cypress Semiconductor, Rodgers has engineered one of Silicon Valley's   Times
brightest stories of late. Cypress went public last summer at a valuation of $270 million.
        Invitations to a *Night with T.J. Rodgers* will be mailed in early January.   (BM)

2 returns

Former H&Q president Tom Volpe on February 19th   16-point Times bold

Tom Volpe, founder of Volpe Covington, a new investment banking firm that includes Arthur Rock and Warren Hellman as major investors, will address the Churchill Club on Thursday, February 19th.
        Volpe has had a meteoric career in investment banking. After taking his AB and MBA from Harvard --with a one-year stopover at the London School of Economics--he began his career with White, Weld & Company, later moving to Blyth, Eastman, Dillon.
        At age 30 Volpe joined Hambrecht & Quist as a general partner and opened the investment banking firm's New York Office. In 1984 he became president and CEO of H&Q.
        Invitations to *A Night with Tom Volpe* will be mailed to all Club members in early January.

FIGURE 7-5   Vol4Issue4-Word file created with Microsoft Word (2 of 2)

9. Then type the rest of the articles, setting the type for the titles as noted in Figure 7-5.

You'll create the next file with WriteNow.

CREATING A FILE WITH WRITENOW   One contributing author, Christopher Russell (a pen name), uses WriteNow as his word processor. The WriteNow file is very short, as shown in Figure 7-6.

Within this article you will use three different typefaces: 16-point Times bold for the headline, 10-point Times-Roman for the text, and 10-point Times italic for the byline. With WriteNow 2.0 or 2.2 you can easily apply all of these-styles, and then transfer them to PageMaker. Start WriteNow (or your word processing program) and type the short article, adding the formatting as shown in Figure 7-6.

There is something about a martini --a tingle remarkably pleasant   16-point Times bold

Thus began poet Ogden Nash in *A Drink with Something in It.*   Italics

The perfect dry martini contains gin, vermouth, and a twist of lemon. It must be very cold, but not contain ice or water, so keep your gin in the freezer and vermouth in the refrigerator. The especially discriminating may use Tanqueray gin and Noilly extra dry vermouth.

    Polish a martini glass and put it in the freezer along with your jigger and stirring rod. The glass should be large, but light, with a feathered rim and a long stem to keep the martini cold. With a sharp knife, cut a generous twist from a ripe, fresh lemon. Be careful to separate the yellow peel from the white pulp, as the peel contains the lemon oil and the pulp would impart a bitter flavor to the martini.   10-point Times

    Take the glass from the freezer. Twist the lemon peel to release its oil. Rub the oily surface around the inside of the glass and along its rim, then drop the twist in the glass. Take the gin from the freezer (or Stolichnaya vodka if you feel diffident about gin) and measure two jiggers into the glass. Take the vermouth from the refrigerator and measure a third of a jigger into the glass. Stir vigorously, but do not shake. Remove to a pleasant setting and enjoy.

Italic   *by "Christopher Russell"*

FIGURE 7-6   Martini-WN file created with WriteNow

When you are done, save the file in the Publications folder with the name Martini-WN.

The last file will be entered with WordPerfect.

CREATING A FILE WITH WORDPERFECT   The second contributing author, Michael Perkins, uses WordPerfect. His article is one in an ongoing series about Winston Churchill, so the file is appropriately named Churchill.WP. The text is primarily 10-point Times-Roman, as shown in Figure 7-7, and the headline is 16-point Times bold. The Churchill quotes are in italics.

The majority of the formatting that you apply in Word-Perfect can be transferred to PageMaker. This includes typefaces, sizes, styles, and importantly, tabs, indents, and margins. Because in WordPerfect the margins are transferred to PageMaker, if you don't want the margins to appear in your PageMaker publication, you must set them at a nominal value, such as .01. (Left and right margins are not really a problem with Microsoft Word, because Page-Maker ignores them.) Therefore, type the Churchill articles now, applying the formatting shown in Figure 7-7, but with left and right margins of .01. When you are done, save the file in the Publications folder with the name Churchill-WP.

You now have the four text files ready to be integrated into PageMaker. This is a good time to take a break. When you return, you'll create the graphics for the newsletter.

Using Graphics Within the Newsletter

You have several options for using graphics within Page-Maker. You can create a graphic with one of the painting or drawing programs, such as DeskPaint or Adobe Illustrator. You can create a graphic file by scanning a photo or

Ennui and the brush-Winston as the artist

16-point
Times bold

Broadly speaking, human beings may be divided into three classes: those who are toiled to death, those who are worried to death, and those who are bored to death. Italic

Churchill himself, of course, was by no means immune to these afflictions about which he wrote. But what was he to do about it?

Churchill typically sought surcease in a number of activities, including reading, fencing, swimming, riding, hunting, flying, polo, horse racing, gardening, and brick-laying. He was also a collector of butterflies and tropical fish and had a number of pets.

Further, Churchill was something of the big kid indulging in everything from toy trains, tin soldiers, and erector sets to building sandcastles and snowmen.

The common denominator in all this activity was change. As Churchill himself writes,

Change is the master key. A man can wear out a particular part of his mind by continually using it and tiring it. The tired parts of the mind can be rested and strengthened, not merely by rest, but by using other parts. It is only when new cells are called into activity, when new stars become lords of the ascendant, that relief, repose, refreshment are afforded. Italic

At age 40 Churchill found himself out of political office for the first time in fifteen years and he needed to discover a new way to creatively fill up the hours.

Exercise, travel, solitude, light socializing, even golf (which he likened to chasing a pill around a cow pasture) did not suffice. It was then, with a friend's encouragement, that he took up painting.

Intensity, Relish and Audacity Italic

Painting at once provided Churchill an opportunity to use his hands as well as a different part of his brain. The "muse of painting" had come to his rescue.

When Churchill took up the brush, he did it with the same intensity, relish, and audacity as everything he undertook, and he was not discouraged by the results. Painting also proved to be the perfect diversion. In Painting as a Pastime he writes,

I know nothing which, without exhausting the body, more entirely absorbs the mind. Whatever the worries of the hour or the threats of the future, once the picture has begun to flow along, there is no room for them in the mental screen. They pass out into shadow and darkness. All one's mental light, such as it is, becomes concentrated on the task. Time stands respectfully aside.

Churchill chose to devote his painting to landscapes and still lifes in an impressionist style. His brilliant colors became a type of trademark: "I cannot pretend to be impartial about the colours," he wrote. "I rejoice with the brilliant ones and am genuinely sorry for the poor browns."

In search of beautiful scenes, Churchill took his easel with him wherever he traveled including the Middle East and North America. On a trip to Scotland he wrote to his wife, "In the afternoon I went out and painted a beautiful river in the afternoon light with crimson and golden hills in the background."

From the Riviera he writes of a villa that he painted "all in shimmering sunshine and violet shades."

10-
point
Times

▬▬▬ **FIGURE 7-7** Churchill-WP file created with WordPerfect (1 of 2)

Antidote to Melancholy and Ennui   Italic

In the end, painting was to prove one of the chief antidotes to Winston's sometime melancholy and ennui. It also served to deepen Churchill's powers of observation, so much that he had come to see that "the whole world is open with all its treasures, even the simplest objects have their beauty."
Like the poet and artist William Blake, Churchill had learned not only to see with, but through the eye.

10-point
Times

Contributed by
Michael Perkins   Italic
Club Historian

2 returns

MY EARLY LIFE

2 returns

It took me three tries to pass into Sandhurst. There were five subjects, of which Mathematics, Latin and English were obligatory, and I chose in addition French and Chemistry. In this hand I held only a pair of Kings--English and chemistry. Nothing less than three would open the jackpot. I had to find another useful card.

2 returns

W.S. CHURCHILL

FIGURE 7-7   Churchill-WP file created with WordPerfect (2 of 2)

line drawing with a scanner. Or you can take the graphic to a commercial printer and have the printer incorporate it into the newsletter before it is printed.

Opinion Movers lets the commercial printer handle the graphics for *The Orator*. Figure 7-8 shows a copy of the camera-ready artwork of Winston Churchill that is submitted to the printer along with the newsletter master copy.

If you have a scanner, the Churchill drawing in Figure 7-8 is reproduced in Appendix C and can be removed for use here. If you don't have a scanner but wish to try placing a graphic, substitute a clip art graphic for the actual graphic in this book. For example, you might use one of the drawings in T/Maker's Clickart Collection. If you don't want to handle the graphics right now, simply follow the

FIGURE 7-8 Churchill.TIF art for scanning

instructions for building the newsletter, including saving a spot for the graphics. You will still have the experience of working around the graphics, which is valuable in itself.

SCANNING GRAPHICS FOR PAGEMAKER If you have a scanner and want to produce the newsletter with a scanned drawing, follow these instructions:

1. Remove Appendix C from the book.

2. Start your scanner and load its driver software.

3. Scan the logo.

4. Crop the resulting screen image so that only the logo is left.

5. Save the file in the Publications folder with the name Churchill.TIF.

Now that you have created the text and graphics, you can begin to build the newsletter. The first thing you'll do is set the defaults within PageMaker.

SETTING DEFAULTS

Some of the defaults set will become permanent within your PageMaker system and will be present when you start PageMaker (unless you change them again), while others will be set for the current publication only. The timing of default selection determines the extent to which they are permanent. You will change many of these as you create individual parts of the newsletter, but the overall defaults will govern many aspects of the tasks you'll be doing.

Startup Defaults

When you set defaults with no publications on the desktop and before opening or initiating a publication, the defaults become permanent to the PageMaker system. This means that they will be present each time you start PageMaker.

In the following paragraphs you will set your preferences for measurement to be the startup defaults—not necessarily because you want them to be PageMaker system defaults but because they affect the page setup, which is normally your first step in creating a new publication. For example, before you set up the margins, you want to specify what scale will be used—inches, centimeters, or picas.

If you are using PageMaker, close any active publication so that you have no publications open for the next few steps.

SETTING PAGE PREFERENCES In this newsletter, you'll be using picas and points for the scale on the rulers. Set the default in this way:

1. Choose "Preferences. . ." from the Edit menu.

2. Drag on the "Measurement system" option box until "Picas" is selected.

3. Drag on the "Vertical ruler" option box until "Picas" is selected and click on "OK" to close the dialog box.

Once you have established the startup defaults, you will establish the publication defaults.

Publication Defaults

The publication defaults are effective for the current publication only. They are set after a publication has been initiated within PageMaker. In this case, your first step is to create a new publication and establish the page setup options.

ESTABLISHING MARGINS The margins for the newsletter are extremely important. With multiple columns, each additional character of space matters when you are trying to fit text within the given area. In addition, if you make your margins too small, the outer edges of your text may not print. (Printers have an outer limit beyond which they will not print.) You will set the inside and outside margins to 3 picas, the top margin to 2.5 picas, and the bottom margin to 4 picas.

To set the margin specifications, follow these steps:

1. Choose "New. . ." from the File menu.

2. Verify that the options set in the Page setup box are "Letter;" 51 by 66 picas; "Tall;" "Double-sided;" and "Facing pages."

3. If not already highlighted, drag across the "# of pages" option and type **4**.

4. Drag across the "Inside" margins and then set it and the "Outside" margin at 3 picas, the "Top" margin at 2.5, and the "Bottom" margin at 4, as shown in Figure 7-9. Use TAB to go from field to the other.

5. Press RETURN to complete the dialog box.

Your screen should show the page outline with the dotted margin guides within it.

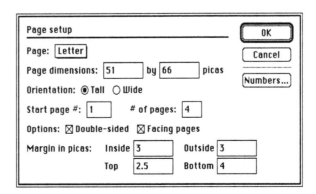

FIGURE 7-9   Page setup dialog box

SETTING LINE WIDTHS Most of the lines within the newsletter are hairline width. Set that as the publication default.

Choose "Line" from the Element menu and select "Hairline."

ESTABLISHING TYPE SPECIFICATIONS The first file to place within the newsletter is the Microsoft Word Masthead-Word file. Most of its text is 10-point Times, normal style. You'll set the default type specifications to be consistent:

1. Press COMMAND + T for the Type specifications dialog box.

2. Type **10** as the "size" and verify that "Times" and "Normal" Style, Position, and Case, and "Auto" leading are set.

3. When finished, click on "OK" to complete the dialog box.

Another default that you want to establish is the text alignment. Most of the text in the newsletter is left-aligned.

4. Verify that "Align left" has been selected in the "Alignment" option of the Type menu.

Your type defaults are now set.

SETTING UP OTHER OPTIONS You'll use the rulers in two ways while building the newsletter. First, when switching from the "Fit in window" view to the "Actual size" view, you'll place the pointer before making the switch so that you can control the image you get. Second, you'll be placing different forms of text (articles, headings, and titles) that must be located in specific spots. The horizontal and vertical ruler guides, which you will pull from the rulers, are essential for that task.

In addition, you'll want access on the screen to the horizontal and vertical scroll bars, the magnetic properties of the "Snap to guides" option and, at least at first, the Toolbox. You'll use the shortcut keys to access the Toolbox for most of the chapter. Also, the "Guides" option will let you see the nonprinted margin, column, and ruler guides on the screen.

To set up the rulers and other options, use the following instructions:

> Verify that "Rulers," "Snap to rulers," "Guides," and "Snap to guides" are checked on the Options menu. If any are not, choose them now. Also, verify that the Toolbox is displayed. If it isn't, turn it on from the Windows menu.

You'll see the horizontal ruler across the top of the page and the vertical ruler on the left side of the page, as well as the Toolbox. The ruler should be in picas and show that the page is 66 picas long by 51 picas wide.

To access the maximum working area, drag the right edge of the publication Window over the icon area to the right edge of the screen, so that the publication Window fills the screen if it didn't to start with.

IMPORTANT TECHNIQUES USED IN THIS CHAPTER

Throughout the chapter you will repeatedly use techniques for working with text and graphics. These techniques will not be explained each time they are used; rather, they will be described here. If you need to review a technique, you can scan this section of the chapter to refresh your memory.

Switching Between "Actual size" and "Fit in window"

In order to place the text, graphics, and lines exactly, you'll have to switch between "Actual size" and "Fit in window" many times. You'll find that this is an extremely efficient way to place and then verify lines, text, and graphics. There are two steps. First, when you are in "Fit in window" view and want the "Actual size" view, position your pointer on what you want to appear in the middle of the screen and then press and hold COMMAND + OPTION while clicking the mouse button. To help you place the pointer, you will often be given the horizontal and vertical ruler coordinates like this: 6H/2.5V, which should be read "6 picas on the horizontal ruler and 2.5 picas on the vertical ruler." Second, when you are in "Actual size" and want a "Fit in window" view, press and hold the COMMAND + OPTION while clicking the mouse button.

 For the remainder of this chapter and in Chapter 8, the phrase "press and hold COMMAND + OPTION while clicking the mouse button" will be abbreviated to "COMMAND + OPTION + click." COMMAND + OPTION + click acts as a switch between the two views.

Try it out now for a quick test:

1. Place your pointer at 6H/6V and COMMAND + OPTION + click for an "Actual size" view.

2. Return to the "Fit in window" view with another COMMAND + OPTION + click.

 You can also return to "Fit in window" by pressing COMMAND + W. Since the precision placement is not needed when returning to "Fit in window," as it is when going to

"Actual size," pressing COMMAND + W is often the preferred approach. For the rest of the book, only the statement "return to 'Fit in window' view" will be used, and you can decide whether to use COMMAND + OPTION + click or to press COMMAND + W.

Concepts of Layers

With PageMaker, you build publications in layers. For instance, entered text is one layer. When you place a graphic on top of the text, that becomes a second layer. If you build a box or draw a line, you will add another layer. You can see the top layer and, if it is transparent, you can see what lies beneath it. You manipulate what appears by filling boxes with shading and by sending the layers either to the front or the back of the layer stack. For example, if you type text and then draw a box around it without a fill pattern or screen, you can still see the text because the box is empty. However, if you fill it with shading, you will not be able to see the text until you send the box to the back of the stack. Then the text will be on top and the shaded box will appear in the background.

The Toolbox Tools

The Toolbox contains four tools that you will need—the pointer tool, the text tool, the perpendicular-line tool, and the square-corner tool. You will switch from one to another to perform various tasks. Although you'll start with the Toolbox, you'll soon want to remove its image from the screen so that you can see all of the horizontal ruler. After you remove it, if you have an extended keyboard, you'll use shortcut keys to access the tools — for example, SHIFT + F1 for the pointer. You'll be reminded at the time which keys to use though you'll soon memorize them.

Selecting Text and Graphics

Every time you want to do something with text or graphics within PageMaker, you must first select it — that is, highlight it or form a selection box around it. Depending on what you want to do, you first choose the correct tool and then select the text or graphics.

SELECTING TEXT You can select text with either the text tool or the pointer tool, depending on what you want to do. For example, if you want to move an entire block of text from one spot on the page to another, you would use the pointer tool. However, if you want to change the type specification for the text, you would highlight it with the text tool.

If you're selecting text with the pointer tool, simply place the pointer on the text and click the mouse button. The text will be enclosed in a selection box.

If you're selecting text with the text tool, you must first drag over the text with the I-beam to highlight it. Then you specify what you want done with the text.

If you repeatedly try to select some text and cannot, or can only select something else, "something else" is getting in the way. For example, if the block of text is not on the top layer, you may have to bring it to the front in order to work with it. You can see the various selection areas by choosing "Select all" from the Edit menu. It allows you to see whether the "something else" is on the top layer or whether you're not placing the pointer in the correct spot. If the text you want was created on the master page and you're currently trying to select it on a regular page, you'll have to return to the master page to select it.

SELECTING LINES OR GRAPHICS If you have just created a line or box, it may still be selected if you have not deselected it by clicking the mouse button somewhere else. You can tell by the tiny boxes that appear at the ends or around the item. If the item has been deselected, you'll have to reselect the graphic or line with the pointer tool.

You place the tip of the pointer on the line or graphic and click the mouse button. The selected item will be displayed with two tiny boxes on the ends or eight tiny boxes around it.

To select a line or graphic, you may have to work around other items that get in the way. You may have a column or margin guide, for instance, that is repeatedly selected instead of the line you want. To select a line that lies over or near it, try turning on "Lock guides in the Options menu," or, as a final means, you may have to move the guide to get at the line you want. Alternatively, you may use the "Bring to front" command to bring the graphic to the front in order to select it, or use the "Send to back" command if text or other graphics are interferring with the selection.

DESELECTING SELECTED TEXT OR GRAPHICS To deselect anything, simply click your pointer on something else — it can be on other text you want to select or on the Pasteboard. You can select an item after it has been deselected by following the rules just outlined.

Moving Text or Graphics

Moving text or graphics is a three-step process: (1) select the item with the pointer tool; (2) press and hold the mouse button until the pointer becomes a four-headed arrow, and (3) drag the item wherever you want it on the screen.

Copying Text or Graphics

Copying text or graphics with the pointer tool is a five-step process: (1) highlight or select the item with the pointer tool; (2) copy it by pressing COMMAND + C or F3; (3) find the page where you want the item inserted; (4) press COMMAND + V or F4 to paste the copy on the screen; and (5) press the mouse button with the pointer tool and drag the item where you want it.

If you want multiple copies, you can continue with step 3 because the copy remains available to you on the clipboard until you cut or copy something else.

Copying text with the text tool is done when you want to copy and then insert the text into another text block. In this case you click the insertion point to indicate where the text is to be placed before pressing COMMAND + V or F4.

SETTING UP A DUMMY PUBLICATION

PageMaker's ability to create a dummy publication saves you an enormous amount of time by providing a standard framework within which you can build all the issues of a newsletter. Essentially, you create a newsletter with all the standard and recurring portions; then you load that publication and customize it for the specific issue you're building.

The newsletter has two recurring page formats, as shown in Figure 7-10. The first page has three columns, the title, and a standard graphic between two columns. The three remaining newsletter pages contain four columns with a smaller title and page numbers. Because the last three pages have the same basic layout, you can use PageMaker's master page facility to create them.

Master pages allow you to set up a standard look for the newsletter and replicate that throughout the publication. You create a standard grid, or layout, and then format it only once rather than for each page that is the same.

Constructing master pages is appropriate for pages 2 through 4. The first page is unique to the newsletter, though it appears the same for all issues. You will build a "custom" page for it. Pages 2 through 4, although identical per the master page layout, will have varying features unique to one particular page but constant from issue to issue. For example, an ad for the printer of *The Orator* always appears in the same spot on page 3. The unique features are developed on individual page layouts that are copies of the master pages. Together, the customized page 1 and individualized master pages make up the dummy publication.

The first step is to construct the master pages.

Constructing Master Pages

There are several tasks to building the master pages. First, reset the zero point. There is a zero point on both the

THE ORATOR
Volume 4, Issue 4—November 1989

*The Orator is
published quarterly by
The Churchill Club.
Subscriptions are
guaranteed
free of charge
to all corporate and
individual members.
Printing of The Orator
is donated
by Pandick Press,
San Francisco.*

*Editor: Richard Karlgaard
Historian: Michael Perkins
Cartoonist: Kurt Peterson*

FIGURE 7-10 Complete dummy publication (1 of 4)

THE ORATOR

The nonprofit Churchill Club
provides a nonpartisan forum
for public discourse on timely
issues, particularly those in
which business and politics
converge. The Club is named
after Winston Churchill, whose
character and career personify
the democratic values of open
discourse, diversity and
freedom. Accordingly, Club
membership is without regard
to sex, lifestyle, legitimacy,
sobriety, race, color, creed,
physical or mental disposition,
or origin.

FIGURE 7-10   Complete dummy publication (2 of 4)

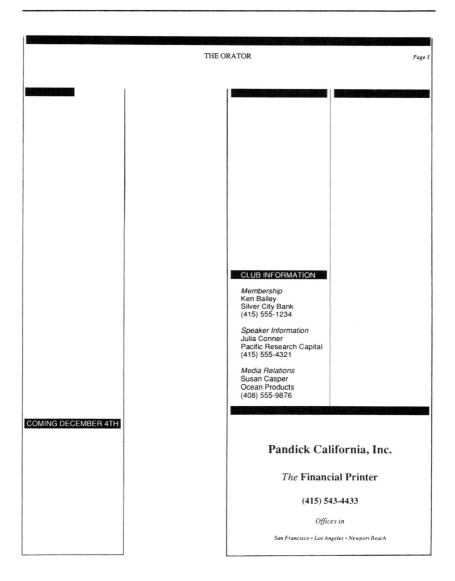

THE ORATOR   *Page 3*

CLUB INFORMATION

Membership
Ken Bailey
Silver City Bank
(415) 555-1234

Speaker Information
Julia Conner
Pacific Research Capital
(415) 555-4321

Media Relations
Susan Casper
Ocean Products
(408) 555-9876

COMING DECEMBER 4TH

Pandick California, Inc.

The **Financial Printer**

(415) 543-4433

Offices in

San Francisco • Los Angeles • Newport Beach

FIGURE 7-10 Complete dummy publication (3 of 4)

Board of Directors

Chairman
Co-Founder
Anthony DeVoe
Silver City Bank

Director of Marketing
Co-Founder
Richard Karlgaard
Opinion Movers

Director of Finance
Edward Hecht
PX, Inc.

Director of Speakers
Susan Casper
Ocean Products

Director of Membership
Ken Bailey
Silver City Bank

Director of Operations
Edward Osborne
Reiley Aerospace

Director, Scholarship Committee
William Shelly
Nordic Distributors

Club Historian
Michael Rains
South Port Cold Storage

Corporate Secretaries
Frederick Shelly
Scott Katz
Shelly, Katz, & Greenlee

Tom Cook
Cook Corporation

Barry Burton
Standard Computer

Marjorie Walters
South American Importers

Diane Graves

Robert Lusk
Graves, Lusk, Meadows, & Thomas

Timothy Lamson
Lamson Associates

James North, Jr.
Technology Consultants, Inc.

Stephen Petosa
RotoGraphic Corporation

Alex Lange
Pacific Imports

Grant Strom
Strom Computer

Peter Dayton
Creative Designs

Doug Hendrix
Strom Computer

Steve Masion
Pacific Southern

Michael Boggs
New Toy Corporation

Cordell Tucker
Tucker Steel Pipe

Michael Jones
Smith and Jones

Senior Advisory Board

Roger Weiss
President and CEO
Silver City Bank

Ed Adams
U.S. Congressman

Norm Browning
U.S. Congressman

Judy Carlson
President
Carlson Associates

Robert Wohlers
Chairman
New Toy Corporation

Robert Freeland, Jr.
President
Robert Freeland Associates

Larry Meadows
Partner
Graves, Lusk, Meadows, & Thomas

Samuel Robinson
General Partner
Robinson Venture Partners

William Dunn
Chairman
Leader Corporation

Joe Parsons
Managing Partner
Springtime Capital

Richard Van Waters
President
Vanguard Trucking

James Johnston
President and CEO
Northern Metal Fabricators

Robert Dyer
Vice President
Pacific Imports

Consuelo Martinez
Director
Center for Better Learning

Lorayne Easton
Political Consultant

Ryland Keeney
Managing Partner
Thomas and Keeney

George Maynard
President & CEO
Micro Corporation of America

Rob Younger
Editor
Silver City Evening News

Walter A. McIntyre
Professor of Political Science
Northern University

Corporate Members

ABC Corporation
American Consultants
Arrow Brothers
Art Treasures
Avery Products
Barringer, Easter, & McGrath
Bayside Interiors
Berg Equipment
Bergman Communications
Central Area Bank
Commercial Bank
Dick Shepard & Co.
Doolittle, Peters, & Curfman
Edwards and Rogers
EG Enterprises
Electronic Instruments
Everett Anchor & Chain
First East/West Bank
Formal Technology
Foster Homes, Inc.
Frank Reiley & Co.
Frankel and Associates
Graves, Lusk, Meadows, & Thomas
Gregory Dunn Ventures
Gunderson, Dimple, & Eagen
Hamlin National
KRGT Silver City
KSAB Bayside
KTZZ Silver City
Leader Corporation
Management Services
McKen Engineering
Micro Corporation of America
Network Ventures
New Technology Consultants
New Toy Corporation
Northern Ventures Partners
Opinion Movers
Pacific Construction
Pacific Press
Pacific Research Capital
Pacific Systems Corp.
Pacific Technology Review
Pauley Furniture
Personal Technology
Peterson Bailey Co.
Philips Manufacturing
Platis, Hawkins, & Grant
Plum Warehouse
Plywood Fabricators
Quantum Research
Que Technology
Reiley Aerospace
Richards Hotels
Ricker & Ricker
Sierra Partners
Silver City Bank
Silver City Entrepreneurs Club
Silver City Evening News
Silver City Journal
Small Properties
Smith and Jones
South American Imports
Tanquery and Noilly
Thomas Insurance
Travel Partners
Tyler, Funk, & Bailey
Warehouse Furniture
Western Bank
Western Taxi
Williams, Anderson Associates

FIGURE 7-10 Complete dummy publication (4 of 4)

horizontal and vertical rulers. Reset this so you can accurately measure the positions on a page. Second, install several horizontal ruler guides to help you place the headings and the top of the text. Third, type in the name of the newsletter. Fourth, install the four columns with minimal space between them. Next, draw in lines along the left and right margins and between the column guides. To do this, you will draw one line and then copy it to the other places so that you can be sure that the lines will all be exactly the same length. Finally, place an automatic page number on the pages.

SETTING UP THE ZERO POINT AND HORIZONTAL RULER GUIDES After bringing up the image of the left and right master pages, you'll reset the zero point. You want the point to be at the intersection of the top and left margins. Then, to position the title correctly, you'll place four horizontal ruler guides.

When you have facing pages on the screen, the zero point on the horizontal ruler is initially in the center, and the ruler marks go in both directions. Therefore, you have two 6s, two 2.5s, and so forth on the horizontal ruler. To clarify which marks you are using, the instructions will state "left" or "right" for the side of the horizontal ruler currently being used—for example, "left 6H" or "right 42.5H."

Follow these steps to set the zero point and horizontal ruler guides:

1. Click the master page icons (L,R). Two facing pages will appear on your screen.

2. Place your pointer at left 36H/12V and COMMAND+ OPTION+ click for an "Actual size" view.

3. Place the pointer in the intersection of the horizontal and vertical rulers (slightly to the left and below the publication window close box) and drag the zero point to the intersection of the left and top margins (not the top of the page) of the left master page, as shown in Figure 7-11.

4. Drag two horizontal ruler guides down to 2.5 and 6 picas on the vertical ruler.

5. Return to "Fit in window" view.

ENTERING THE DESIGN LINE AND THE TITLE   Now you'll draw the 12-point line along the top margin so that the title can be placed with it in sight.

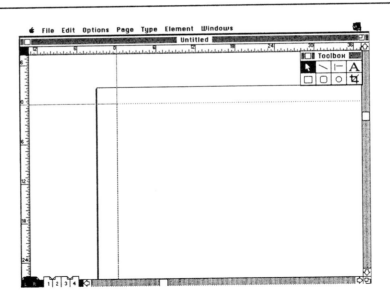

FIGURE 7-11   Resetting the zero point on the left master page

1. Using the perpendicular-line tool (SHIFT + F3), draw a line on the top margin of the left master page from the left to the right margin.

2. While the line is still selected, choose "12 pt" from the Line option of the Element menu.

Before the line is deselected, verify that it is correctly drawn in an "Actual size" view. Then you'll draw an identical line on the top margin of the right master page. Before you can place the line accurately, you'll have to hide the Toolbox. From now on, if possible, use the shortcut keys to get the tools you need.

3. While the line is selected, place your pointer at 12H/6V, press COMMAND + OPTION + click, and verify that the line is between the left and right margins and that it hangs down from the top margin. Use the horizontal scroll bar to adjust the screen.

4. Hide the Toolbox by clicking on its close box.

5. Return to the "Fit in window" view by pressing the mouse button and, using the perpendicular-line tool, draw a second line on the top margin of the right master page.

6. While the line is selected, choose "12 pt" from the Line option of the Element menu.

You may have to use the "Actual size" view to place it perfectly. To do this, place your pointer between the left and right master pages and click COMMAND + OPTION + click. Your screen will look like the one shown in Figure 7-12.

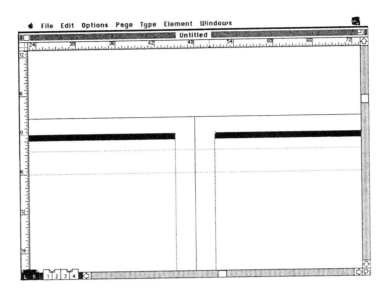

FIGURE 7-12   Two 12-point lines on the master pages

You can scroll back and forth with the horizontal scroll bar to see the whole top line. The line should be placed exactly between the left and right margins and should hang down from the top margin.

7. When you are satisfied with the line placement, return to the "Fit in window" view.

   Now you will type the heading on the left master page and then copy it to the right master page.

8. With the text tool (SHIFT + F4) place the I-beam at 24H/12V and COMMAND + OPTION + click. Then place the I-beam at 1H/2.5V and click the mouse button.

9. Press COMMAND + T for the Type specifications dialog box and type **8** for "Size" and click on "Italic" for "Type style." Click on "OK" when you're finished.

10. Type **Page**, insert a space, and press COMMAND + OPTION + P to place PageMaker's automatic page numbering character.

When you press COMMAND + OPTION + P all at the same time on a master page you are telling PageMaker that you want the automatic page counter to locate its results at that location. LM (for Left Master) will appear where you pressed COMMAND + OPTION + P on the master page. On the regular pages, however, the actual page number will appear. Next you will type the title.

11. Press TAB and COMMAND + T. Choose "10" points and "Normal" style and press RETURN.

12. Press CAPS LOCK and type **THE ORATOR**.

13. Press COMMAND + I to open the Indents/tabs dialog box. Select the centering tab, (lower left box) and click at 22.5 on the ruler as shown here:

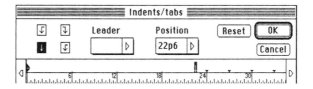

14. Click on "OK." When your screen is redisplayed you will see that the page number is left aligned and that "THE ORATOR" is centered, as shown in Figure 7-13.

To reproduce the title and page number on the right master pages, proceed as follows:

15. Return to "Fit in window" view.

16. With the text tool (SHIFT + F4), place the pointer at 74H/12V and COMMAND + OPTION + click. Then place the pointer at 52H/2.5V and click the mouse button.

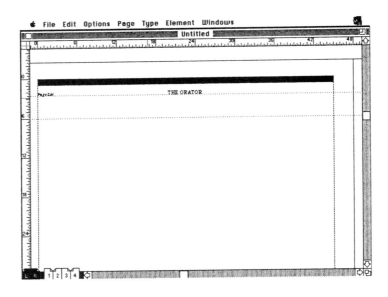

FIGURE 7-13   Page number left-aligned and title
centered

17. Press COMMAND + SHIFT + R to right align the title, press
    TAB, type **THE ORATOR**, and press TAB again.

18. Press CAPS LOCK to turn it off. Then press COMMAND + T
    and choose "8" points, "Italic," and click "OK."

19. Type **Page**, a space, and press COMMAND + OPTION + P.

20. Press COMMAND + I to open the Indents/tabs dialog box.
    Select the centering tab, click at 22.5 on the ruler, and
    click on "OK."

21. Return to "Fit in window" view.

Figure 7-14 shows the titles and page numbers correctly
placed on the master pages. Next you will set up the
columns and draw the column dividers.

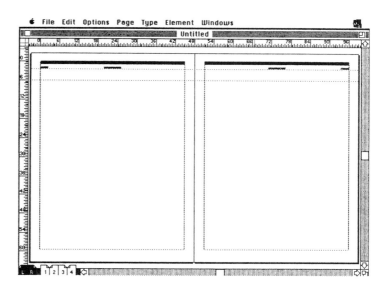

FIGURE 7-14 Titles and page numbers placed on both master pages

SETTING UP COLUMNS Except for the first page, the newsletter pages contain four columns. Spacing between the columns is 0.75 pica, or 9 points (since there are 12 points per pica). This can be typed either as ".75" or as "0p9." The latter is the standard display in PageMaker, 0 representing the number of picas and 9 representing the number of points. After you have built the columns, you will draw lines down the center of the column guides to separate the columns, and along the margins. Then you will copy the first line and drag it to the other column guides on both pages.

If the original line is too short or too long, delete it by pressing DELETE while it is still selected and draw another line. If the line is not centered between the column guides or is too high or too low, reposition it by selecting it with the pointer tool and pressing the mouse button until the four-headed arrow allows you to move it exactly where you want it.

To set up the columns and column dividers, follow these steps:

1. Choose "Column guides..." from the Options menu.

2. Type **4**, press TAB, type **.75** or **0p9** (for 9 points), and press RETURN, to specify four columns and the dividing space between them.

3. Turn off "Snap to guides" by pressing COMMAND + U and turn off "Snap to rulers" by pressing COMMAND + [.

4. Select the perpendicular-line tool by pressing SHIFT + F3.

5. Draw a vertical line down between the leftmost set of column guides (at about 11H) from the horizontal ruler guide at 6V to the bottom margin.

6. While the line is selected, verify in "Actual size" view that the top and bottom of the line are exactly on the horizontal ruler guides and in the center between the column guides.

7. If the line is incorrectly placed, select the pointer tool (SHIFT + F1) and drag the line so that it is correctly placed.

See Figure 7-15 for the "Actual size" view of the top of the column. Notice how the line is reasonably close to the center of the column guides although not perfectly in the center, and against the horizontal ruler guide.

8. While the line is selected, copy it by pressing COMMAND + C or F3.

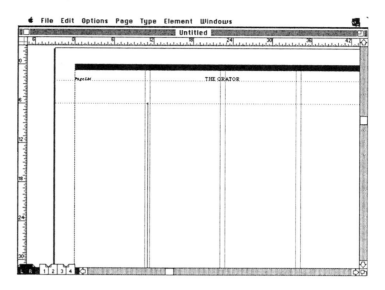

═══ **FIGURE 7-15** Top of the column with the new dividing
line

9. Arrange your screen so that the first, second, and third
   sets of column guides are visible on the screen; then
   select the pointer (SHIFT + F1) and press COMMAND + V or
   F4.

   A copy of the line will be inserted in the middle of the
   screen. If you're in "Actual size" view, the top of the line
   will be off the screen. You can move it with the pointer tool
   by dragging it down (or up, if you are looking at the
   bottom). You may have to drag it several times to pull the
   top of the line within the image area.

10. Drag the line down to the second set of column guides
    and place it between them with the top of the line
    against the horizontal ruler guide.

Until you copy or cut something else, you can access the copied line by pressing COMMAND + V or F4. You needn't copy it again and again. If you must delete a line and start over, you'll have to select the original line with the pointer tool (probably moving the column guides to do it) and copy it again.

11. In the same way, install the column dividers for the rest of the columns on both the left and right master pages.

The final task in setting up the master pages is to draw the lines on the left and right margins, from the top to the bottom margins. You'll draw them slightly outside of the left and right margin guides.

12. Restore the "Snap to rulers" by pressing COMMAND + [.

13. In the "Fit in window" view with the perpendicular-line tool (SHIFT + F3), draw a vertical line from the top margin (0V) to the bottom (59.5V) along the left margin guide.

14. In "Actual size" view, verify that it is the proper length and accurately placed. If it's not, either delete it and start again or drag it to a better location.

15. With the pointer tool (SHIFT + F1), in "Actual size" view, drag the line to left .25H (1/4 pica, or 3 points, which is the smallest mark in the "Actual size" view). See Figure 7-16.

16. When it is acceptable, and before it is deselected, copy it by pressing COMMAND + C or F3.

17. Place the copies in the right margin on the left master page and the left and right margins on the right master page. Do this by pressing COMMAND + V or F4 and drag-

ging the line to each site. Place the lines 1/4 pica outside of the margin guides. You'll find that it's easier to both place and verify in the "Actual size" view.

18. Return to "Fit in window" view.

SAVING THE DUMMY PUBLICATION   The final step in setting up a master page is to save it on disk.

1. Choose "Save as. . ." from the File menu.

2. When the Save as dialog box is displayed, open the Publications folder.

3. Type the filename **dummy** as shown on the next page, and press RETURN.

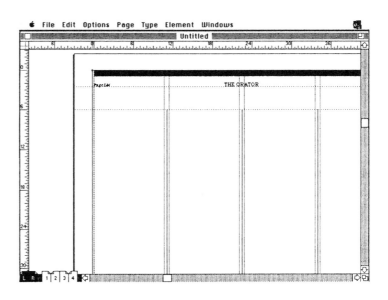

FIGURE 7-16   Actual size view of line outside margin

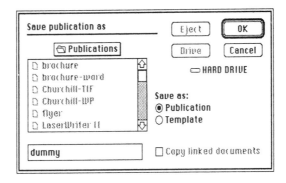

For now, save this as a publication. When you have finished creating the dummy, you will save it as a template. Saving a publication as a template tells PageMaker to open a copy instead of the original when you call it up.

Now where are you? You have created the master pages for pages 2 through 4 of the newsletter, and they will be of enormous benefit to you. Now you must customize page 1. Then you will individualize a copy of the master pages for the dummy pages 2 through 4.

Customizing Page 1

Page 1 will not use the elements of the master pages that you'll use for the other three pages. However, you will create a custom page for the dummy publication to set the standard for page 1 in all future issues.

Page 1 contains some fancy design elements that you'll have fun creating. As you saw in Figure 7-10, the title is contained in a box with a shaded background. After you build the three columns on the page, you will place a second box for the Churchill Club logo between columns 1 and 2.

First, you'll place the ruler guides.

PLACING HORIZONTAL AND VERTICAL GUIDES When you bring up page 1 on the screen, you'll see that it echoes the master page format with four columns. Because you cannot change the master format except on the master pages, you'll have to cancel the master format for page 1 and construct a new one specifically for it. Even after you cancel the master format, the unprintable lines will remain. You'll delete these by temporarily specifying that the page will have only one column.

To cancel the master page format and to install the guides, follow these instructions:

1. Click on the page 1 icon.

2. Choose "Display master items" from the Page menu to turn off the display.

3. Choose "Column guides..." from the Options menu, type **1**, and press RETURN.

4. Move the zero point to the intersection of the left and top margins, approximately at 51H/0V.

5. Press COMMAND + V or F4 to bring on the outside line created on the master page. In "Actual size" view, position the line at left .25H/0V.

6. Press COMMAND + V or F4 again to bring in a second outside line. Position it at 45.25H/0V.

7. Drag horizontal ruler guides to 3V and to 5.5V.

8. Drag five new horizontal ruler guides to 8, 10, 23, 34, and 42 picas on the vertical ruler. Use the vertical scroll bar to adjust the view.

9. Drag two vertical guides to 7 and 15.5 picas on the horizontal ruler.

10. Return to "Fit in window" view.

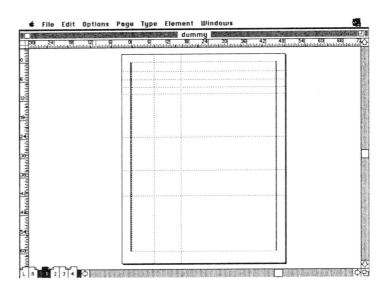

FIGURE 7-17 Ruler guides installed on page 1

Your screen should look like that shown in Figure 7-17.

ENTERING THE TITLE Before entering the title, you'll draw the line on the top of the page because placing the title depends to some extent on that. You will then center-align, select the type, and type the title. After you have ensured that the title is placed correctly, you will build a box around it, filling the box with 10 percent shading and sending it to the back so that the title can be seen.

Follow these instructions for installing the title:

1. Restore "Snap to guides" by presing COMMAND + U.

2. Using the perpendicular-line tool (SHIFT + F3), draw a line along the top margin from the left to the right margin.

3. Choose "12 pt" from the Line option of the Element menu.

4. Select the text tool (SHIFT + F4), place it at 22H/12V, press COMMAND + OPTION and click for an "Actual size" view.

5. Place the I-beam at 20H/4.5V and click the mouse button to reposition the insertion point.

6. Center the text by pressing COMMAND + SHIFT + C.

7. Press COMMAND + T for the Type specifications dialog box and type **48** for the Size. Then click "Bold" Type style to turn it on, and click "OK" to close the dialog box.

8. Press CAPS LOCK.

9. Type **THE ORATOR**.

Without breaking the line, you'll enter the type specifications for the rest of the title information. (When developing the dummy for an actual newsletter, you would not specify an actual volume or issue, as you will here. Instead, you might type **Volume 0, Issue 0**, creating a placeholder for the numbers, which would be entered later when you customize the dummy for a specific newsletter.)

10. Press CAPS LOCK to release it.

11. Press COMMAND + T and type **10** for the size, and click on "Bold" to turn it off; click "Italic" to turn on italic, and then click on "OK."

12. Type a space, and type **Volume 4, Issue 4**, press OPTION + SHIFT + - for an em-dash, and then type **November 1989**.

13. Using the pointer tool (SHIFT + F1), select the title text and drag it so that the center bars of the H, E, and R are on the horizontal ruler guide at 5.5V.

    Your screen will look like that shown in Figure 7-18.
    Now you are ready to draw the box around the title. To do this, you will use the square-corner tool and drag the box from the left-hand margin above the title to the right-hand margin below the title. Then you will fill the box with shading and send it to the back.

14. If necessary, adjust the screen so that you can see the left-hand margin and all of the title in "Actual size" view.

FIGURE 7-18   Title as entered, before box surrounds it

15. Select the square-corner tool (SHIFT + F5) and place it at 0H/3V.

16. Drag the box to 45H/8V and release the mouse button.

17. If the box is not correctly placed on the margin and guides, drag it with the pointer tool (SHIFT + F1) until you are satisfied with its placement.

18. Select "10%" from the Fill option of the Element menu.

19. Send the box to the back by pressing COMMAND + B.

Your screen will look like that shown in Figure 7-19. Now you will set up the columns for page 1.

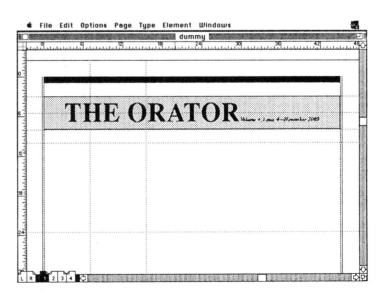

FIGURE 7-19   Title with shaded box behind it

SETTING UP COLUMNS FOR PAGE 1 Page 1 has three columns. They will use the same separation space as the master pages, 3/4 pica (9 points). After PageMaker places the column guides on your page, you will move them so that the center column is the widest. It will contain the lead article for all issues. Then you will draw the column divider lines, using the copy function to replicate them.

Follow these steps to set up the columns:

1. Return to the "Fit in window" view.

2. Choose "Column guides..." from the Options menu and type **3** columns and verify that the column separation of "0p9" picas has carried over from the master pages. Click on "OK."

3. With the pointer (SHIFT + F1), move the right guide line of the left pair of column guides from 15.5 to 11.5 picas on the horizontal ruler.

4. Move the right guide line of the right pair of column guides from 30.5 to 33.5 picas on the horizontal ruler.

5. Turn off "Snap to guides" by pressing COMMAND + U. You may also want to turn off the "Snap to rulers" by pressing COMMAND + [.

6. Select the perpendicular-line tool (SHIFT + F3) and draw a vertical line down the center of the left column guides (at about 62.25H), from 10V to the bottom margin.

7. Before the line is deselected, verify its position and length in "Actual size" view.

If the line is too short or too long, delete it with the DELETE key and draw another. If the line is the correct length but is placed too close to one of the guide lines or is too high or too low, reposition it by dragging it to the correct place with the pointer tool.

8. When the line is correct, copy it by pressing COMMAND + C or F3.

9. Adjust the screen so that the top of column 2 is visible in the "Actual size" view.

10. Press COMMAND + V or F4 and drag the line between the right set of column guides.

11. Verify the line placement and correct it if necessary.

12. Return to the "Fit in window" view.

The Churchill logo is still to be added to page 1.

INSTALLING GRAPHIC PLACEHOLDERS AND DESIGN LINES Two design elements on page 1 need to be handled in the dummy. First, all issues have a silhouette of Winston Churchill between the first and second columns, as shown in Figure 7-10. You'll draw a box to mark its position, over which the actual graphic will be placed — either by you or by a commercial printer. Second, a 12-point line always marks the top of the third column, the secondary article for the newsletter. You'll draw a line and make it 12 points wide.

Follow these steps to draw the line:

1. Restore "Snap to guides" by pressing COMMAND + U and restore "Snap to rulers" by pressing COMMAND + [.

2. Select the perpendicular-line tool (SHIFT + F3).

3. Place it at 22H/18V and press COMMAND + OPTION + click for "Actual size" view.

4. Draw a line from the left column guide of column 3 to the right margin, over the horizontal ruler guide at 10V.

(It should not touch either the solid column divider or the outer right line.)

5. Choose "12 pt" from the Line option of the Element menu.

You should now have a 12-point line. If you want to reposition the line, drag it to where you want it.

6. Return to the "Fit in window" view.

7. Select the square-corner tool (SHIFT + F5).

8. Draw a box from 7H/23V to 15.5H/34V. (It covers the box created by the horizontal and vertical ruler guides.)

9. Choose "10%" from the Fill option.

Your screen will look like that shown in Figure 7-20.

Now you want to get rid of the two vertical ruler guides that you are finished with. You'll keep the horizontal ruler guides.

10. With the pointer (SHIFT + F1), remove the two vertical ruler guides by dragging them off the page.

PLACING THE SCANNED GRAPHIC While you're on page 1, you can now place the Churchill graphic on the placeholder. Because of the layers that you're working with (currently two—the column dividers and the shaded box), you'll have to manipulate the graph a bit. First, place the file Church.TIF on page 1 to the side of the placeholder. Then draw a smaller box by tracing over part of the graphic and filling the box with "paper." Drag the filled box over to the placeholder and then drag the actual graphic. Because you can see through the graphic to the shaded placeholder, the white box is necessary to maintain the contrast of the graphic to the shaded background.

Follow these steps to install the graphic:

1. Return to the "Fit in window" view, if you're not there.

2. Place your pointer at 22H/32V and COMMAND + OPTION + click for an "Actual size" view.

3. Press COMMAND + D and double-click the filename Churchil.TIF (or the name of the file you're using if you're using clip art instead of the scanned Churchill graphic).

4. Place the TIFF icon at 24H/24V, to the side of the placeholder.

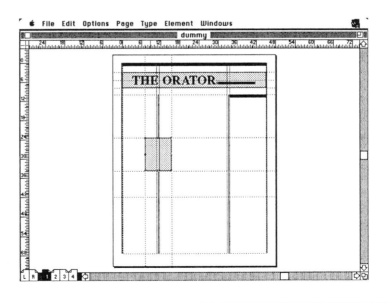

FIGURE 7-20   Page 1 with the line and graphic placeholder

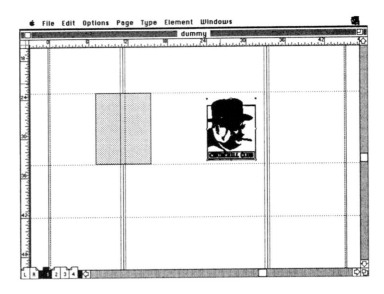

FIGURE 7-21   Graphic placed next to placeholder

5. Drag the icon to 31.5H/33.5V and release the mouse button.

6. Your graphic should look like that shown in Figure 7-21.

7. Using the square-corner tool (SHIFT + F5), draw a box on top of the graphic on the border lines, from 24H/25V to 31.5H/33.5V

8. Choose "Paper" from the Fill option of the Element menu.

9. With the pointer tool (SHIFT + F1), select the box and drag it over the placeholder so that it looks like Figure 7-22. The horizontal alignment should be at 7.5 and 15, and the vertical alignment should be at 25 and 33.5.

10. Choose "None" from the Line option.

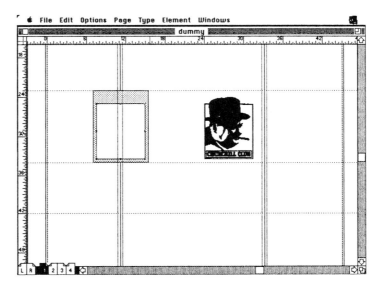

FIGURE 7-22 White box placed over graphic placeholder

11. Click the graphic to select it and drag it over the white box on the placeholder.

The resulting graphic should look like this:

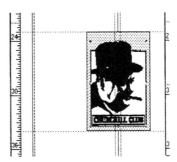

12. Return to the "Fit in window" view.

13. Save the file by pressing COMMAND + S.

Next, you will flow the masthead text through the dummy publication.

Flowing the Masthead Text

The text, now contained in the Microsoft Word file Masthead-Word, is part of every issue. From issue to issue, some of the text is always placed in the same location, such as the general information about *The Orator* contained on page 1. Other text is placed around the issue-specific articles and may vary in location from one issue to the next, such as the "Club Information." You will still flow all the standard information into the dummy publication, realizing that since you are preparing a specific issue, some of the masthead text may have to be moved in other issues.

POINTERS ON FLOWING TEXT When you name the file you want to place, in this case the Masthead-Word file, the pointer becomes the text icon, which is used to flow the text. You place the icon, flow as much text at a time as you want, manipulate the text, and then flow the next batch. Correctly deciding how much text to flow can save you much time. You will want to flow all the text in a file if you don't know how long it is or if it requires much editing. This is because PageMaker treats the file as one long, continuous string of characters. Some types of editing changes will reverberate throughout the file. For example, if on page 3 you increase the size of the space required for an article (perhaps through a change in type size or leading), the increase will cause changes from page 3 to move forward as the text is pushed ahead. You may have to flow text several times to get it just right. Careful editing of text in the word processor will reduce the effort of flowing your text.

For this newsletter, you are saved the steps of flowing and reflowing text because this preliminary work has already been done for you. You will be able to flow the text a bit at a time.

You will place some standard text on each page.

FLOWING PAGE 1 The first page contains some general information about the newsletter, plus the names of primary individuals working on it. Figure 7-10 shows that the first part of the information is narrower than the three names. You will achieve this effect by creating two text blocks, squeezing one to half a column width and then flowing the second block at normal column width.

Follow these steps to place the first page:

1. Place the pointer at the intersection of 22H/48V and press COMMAND + OPTION + click.

You will be looking at the lower part of page 1. Adjust the screen so that you can see both the horizontal ruler guide at 42 picas and the bottom margin.

2. Press COMMAND + D to enter the name of the file to place.

3. Double-click Masthead-Word. Use the horizontal scroll bar to find the filename if necessary.

4. Place the text icon against the left margin at 42V and click the mouse button.

Your screen should look like that shown in Figure 7-23.

5. Place the pointer on one of the tiny boxes on the right end of the top line and drag it toward the center of the column, squeezing the box, until reaching 7.75 picas on the horizontal ruler.

Some of the text will disappear because the column is now narrower.

6. Drag the bottom handle up until only the first paragraph is displayed.

7. Click the bottom handle for the text icon.

8. Place the icon against the left margin at 54V and click the mouse button.

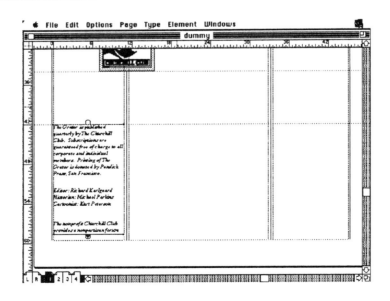

FIGURE 7-23 Flowing the first segment of the masthead text

9. If necessary, again roll up the handle so that only the three names appear.

10. Arrange both text blocks so that the names rest on the bottom margin and the top of the upper text block is on 44V, as shown in Figure 7-24. You do this by clicking on each of the text blocks to select them and then dragging them to their respective locations. You may want to use the text tool, SHIFT + F4, to insert carriage returns to get better line endings.

11. Return to the "Fit in window" view.

12. Select the bottom text block and then click on the bottom handle for the text icon.

You'll handle page 2 in much the same way.

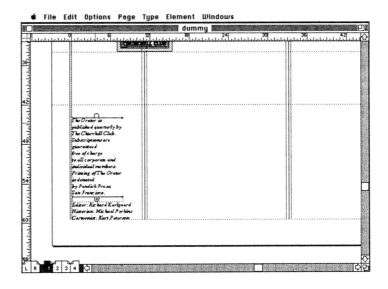

FIGURE 7-24 Flowing masthead text on page 1

FLOWING MASTHEAD TEXT ON PAGE 2   Page 2 contains a small paragraph that briefly explains the function and background of the Churchill Club, sponsors of *The Orator.* You will place it on the page much as you did with page 1. Above the text is a 12-point line across two thirds of the column.

Notice that the horizontal ruler's zero point is still placed on the right page's top and left margins. This results in a split ruler — pages 2 and 3 have common ruler scales such that 30 picas may be found on either page. Assume, if you're working on page 2, that the measurements given will be for the left side of the zero point. That will be reversed when you work on page 3, of course.

Follow these steps for page 2:

1. Click the page 2 icon.

2. Drag a horizontal ruler guide to 42V.

3. Place the text icon in the first column on the new guide and the left margin; then click the mouse button.

4. Place the pointer at 28.5H/46V and press COMMAND + OPTION + click for the "Actual size" view.

5. Adjust the text handle until one full paragraph shows.

6. Drag the text block so that the bottom line rests on the bottom margin.

7. Using the perpendicular-line tool (SHIFT + F3), draw a line above the text at 42V from the left margin to 45H, as shown in Figure 7-25.

8. Select "12 pt" from the Line option.

9. Select the text block with the pointer tool (SHIFT + F1) and click the bottom handle for the text icon.

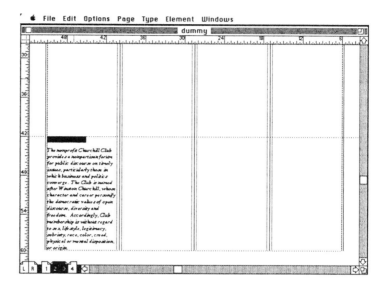

FIGURE 7-25   Page 2 masthead text placed on the
bottom margin

Page 2 is completed. In certain issues you may want to
move this masthead text elsewhere on the page, but you
will usually find it here. Page 3 is next.

FLOWING MASTHEAD TEXT ON PAGE 3   The third
page contains a small block of "Club Information," which
you must treat slightly differently. First, you want the text
squeezed vertically rather than horizontally, as you did on
the first page. To do this, you will change the leading from
"Auto" to "11" points, which for this text is one point less
than the default. As you'll recall, the leading is the space
between the lines. You will be reducing this space.

In addition, you have a design element in the title. It is a
dark bar with white letters—reverse type. To achieve this
effect, you'll draw a box around the title of the block, fill it
with solid shading, and send it to the back layer. The

black letters of the title will then be reversed (made white) and will stand out against the black background.

Remember that since you're working on page 3, you'll be using the horizontal ruler to the right of the zero point.

Follow these steps to flow the standard text onto page 3:

1. Return to the "Fit in window" view.

2. Drag a horizontal ruler guide to 27V.

3. Place the text icon in the third column, on the new guide and the left column guide (23H/27V); then click the mouse button.

The text will flow into the third column. About halfway down the text you see the words "Board of Directors," or perhaps just a thicker line, which is the title for the next segment of the masthead text. You can verify this by placing the pointer next to the title, pressing COMMAND + OPTION + click for an "Actual size" view, and then returning to the "Fit in window" view.

4. Drag the bottom text handle up above the heading, as shown here:

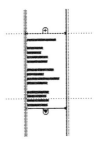

Now you will change the leading for the text block.

5. Place the pointer at 22H/36V and COMMAND + OPTION + click to get the "Actual size" view.

6. Select the text tool (SHIFT + F4) and highlight the whole text block.

7. Open the Type specifications dialog box by pressing COMMAND + T.

8. Drag the text tool across the "Auto" in the Leading text box.

9. Type **11** and press RETURN.

The tightened text will be shorter on the screen.

10. With the pointer (SHIFT + F1), drag the text block until the bottom telephone number rests on the horizontal ruler guide at 42V and is slightly in from the left column guide, at about 24H. The title will appear to be roughly centered between the two column guides, as shown in Figure 7-26, and should be slightly below the horizontal ruler guide at 27V.

Now you'll reverse the type, then build the box around the title, fill it with shading, and send it to the back.

11. With the text tool (SHIFT + F4), drag across the heading "CLUB INFORMATION." Then, from the Type style option of the Type menu, select "Reverse." The words "CLUB INFORMATION" will disappear — they have become white on a white background.

12. Verify that the "Snap to guides" option is on.

13. Select the square-corner tool (SHIFT + F5) and place it on the left column guide and horizontal ruler guide, slightly above the title text, at about 23H/27V.

14. Drag a box diagonally across the name until it rests on the right column guide, slightly below the name, at about 28.75V.

15. Choose "Solid" from the Fill option menu.

16. Send it to the back by pressing COMMAND + B.

When you have completed building and filling the box, the text on page 3 should look like this:

17. Return to "Fit in window" view by pressing COMMAND + OPTION + click.

18. With the pointer tool (SHIFT + F1), select the page 3 text and then click the bottom handle for the text icon.

The last page contains the remaining text of Masthead-Word.

FLOWING MASTHEAD TEXT ON PAGE 4   Page 4 contains solely masthead text. It lists officers, members of the Board of Directors and Senior Advisory Board, and, finally, Corporate Members. You will flow the text over the entire page, using PageMaker's Autoflow feature. You will then

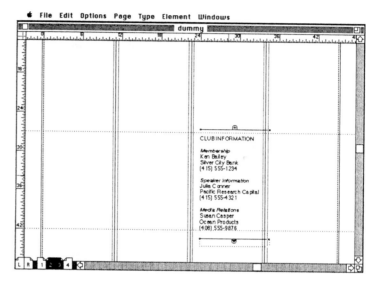

═══════ **FIGURE 7-26**   Placing the masthead text on page 3

adjust the text to better fit the page. In addition to flowing the text, you will be inserting some design elements in the form of lines to separate the categories. Figure 7-27 shows the completed page 4.

Follow these steps for page 4.

1. Select "Autoflow" from the Options menu and click the page 4 icon.

2. Place the text icon in the first column, at the left margin and 7V, below the horizontal ruler guide at 6V, and click the mouse button. The remaining text will fill the page, as shown in Figure 7-28.

3. Select the perpendicular-line tool (SHIFT + F3) and draw a line across the top of column 1, on the horizontal ruler guide at 6V.

4. Choose "12 pt" from the Line option.

Page 4 THE ORATOR

Board of Directors

Chairman
Co-Founder
Anthony DeVoe
Silver City Bank

Director of Marketing
Co-Founder
Richard Karlgaard
Opinion Movers

Director of Finance
Edward Hecht
PX, Inc.

Director of Speakers
Susan Casper
Ocean Products

Director of Membership
Ken Bailey
Silver City Bank

Director of Operations
Edward Osborne
Reiley Aerospace

Director, Scholarship Committee
William Shelly
Nordic Distributors

Club Historian
Michael Rains
South Port Cold Storage

Corporate Secretaries
Frederick Shelly
Scott Katz
Shelly, Katz, & Greenlee

Tom Cook
Cook Corporation

Barry Burton
Standard Computer

Marjorie Walters
South American Importers

Diane Graves

Robert Lusk
Graves, Lusk, Meadows, &
Thomas

Timothy Lamson
Lamson Associates

James North, Jr.
Technology Consultants, Inc.

Stephen Petosa
RotoGraphic Corporation

Alex Lange
Pacific Imports

Grant Strom
Strom Computer

Peter Dayton
Creative Designs

Doug Hendrix
Strom Computer

Steve Masion
Pacific Southern

Michael Boggs
New Toy Corporation

Cordell Tucker
Tucker Steel Pipe

Michael Jones
Smith and Jones

Senior Advisory Board

Roger Weiss
President and CEO
Silver City Bank

Ed Adams
U.S. Congressman

Norm Browning
U.S. Congressman

Judy Carlson
President
Carlson Associates

Robert Wohlers
Chairman
New Toy Corporation

Robert Freeland, Jr.
President
Robert Freeland Associates

Larry Meadows
Partner
Graves, Lusk, Meadows, &
Thomas

Samuel Robinson
General Partner
Robinson Venture Partners

William Dunn
Chairman
Leader Corporation

Joe Parsons
Managing Partner
Springtime Capital

Richard Van Waters
President
Vanguard Trucking

James Johnston
President and CEO
Northern Metal Fabricators

Robert Dyer
Vice President
Pacific Imports

Consuelo Martinez
Director
Center for Better Learning

Lorayne Easton
Political Consultant

Ryland Keeney
Managing Partner
Thomas and Keeney

George Maynard
President & CEO
Micro Corporation of America

Rob Younger
Editor
Silver City Evening News

Walter A. McIntyre
Professor of Political Science
Northern University

Corporate Members

ABC Corporation
American Consultants
Arrow Brothers
Art Treasures
Avery Products
Barringer, Easter, & McGrath
Bayside Interiors
Berg Equipment
Bergman Communications
Central Area Bank
Commercial Bank
Dick Shepard & Co.
Doolittle, Peters, & Curfman
Edwards and Rogers
BG Enterprises
Electronic Instruments
Everett Anchor & Chain
First East/West Bank
Formal Technology
Foster Homes, Inc.
Frank Reiley & Co.
Frankel and Associates
Graves, Lusk, Meadows, & Thomas
Gregory Dunn Ventures
Gunderson, Dimple, & Eagen
Hamlin National
KRGT Silver City
KSAB Bayside
KTZZ Silver City
Leader Corporation
Management Services
McKee Engineering
Micro Corporation of America
Network Ventures
New Technology Consultants
New Toy Corporation
Northern Ventures Partners
Opinion Movers
Pacific Construction
Pacific Press
Pacific Research Capital
Pacific Systems Corp.
Pacific Technology Review
Paisley Furniture
Personal Technology
Peterson Bailey Co.
Philips Manufacturing
Platia, Hawkins, & Grant
Plum Warehouse
Plywood Fabricators
Quantum Research
Que Technology
Reiley Aerospace
Richards Hotels
Ricker & Ricker
Sierra Partners
Silver City Bank
Silver City Entrepreneurs Club
Silver City Evening News
Silver City Journal
Small Properties
Smith and Jones
South American Imports
Tanquery and Noully
Thomas Insurance
Travel Partners
Tyler, Punk, & Bailey
Warehouse Furniture
Western Bank
Western Taxi
Williams, Anderson Associates

FIGURE 7-27 Printout of final version of page 4

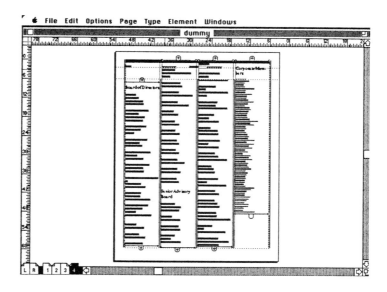

FIGURE 7-28 Page 4 as it is Autoflowed

5. Place the pointer at 29H/16V and COMMAND + OPTION + click for an "Actual size" view.

6. With the pointer tool (SHIFT + F1), drag a horizontal ruler guide down to 8.5 on the vertical ruler. Then select and drag the text in the first column until the heading is sitting on the new ruler you placed, like this:

7. Return to the "Fit in window" view.

8. With the text tool (SHIFT + F4), drag across and highlight the first and second columns from just beneath the heading "Board of Directors" to just above the heading "Senior Advisory Board."

9. Press COMMAND + T, drag across "Auto," type **11.5**, and press RETURN to change the leading.

10. Beginning just after the heading "Senior Advisory Board," drag across the remainder of column 2, all of column 3, and possibly (depending upon how the text flows) the very top of column 4, stopping just before the heading "Corporate Members," so that all of the Senior Advisory Board is highlighted.

11. Press COMMAND + T, drag across "Auto," type **11.5**, and press RETURN.

12. In a similar fashion, highlight the remainder of column 4 beneath the headline "Corporate Members" and change its leading to 7.5 points.

13. With the pointer (SHIFT + F1), point on 28H/45V and press COMMAND + OPTION + click to go to "Actual size" view.

14. Click on the first column and pull the bottom text handle down until "Diane Graves" is the last item in the column.

15. In "Fit in Window" view, click on the second column and drag the text down until it is just under the horizontal ruler guide at 6V.

16. Pull the bottom text handle up until it reaches the lower margin. "Carlson Associates" should be the last line in the column.

17. Similarly, drag down and adjust the bottom of columns 3 and 4 so that they line up like this:

18. In "Fit in window" view, press COMMAND + OPTION + click at 32H/44V.

19. Drag a horizontal ruler guide down to 41V and, with the perpendicular-line tool (SHIFT + F3), draw a line across the second column on the new horizontal ruler guide.

20. Choose "12 pt" from the Line option.

21. Remove the horizontal ruler guide.

22. With the text tool (SHIFT + F4), place the insertion point just to the left of the "A" in "Advisory." Press DELETE, or BACKSPACE, and RETURN to move "Advisory" down to the second line.

23. In "Fit in window" view, COMMAND+OPTION+click at 28H/18V.

24. Drag the horizontal ruler guide at 8.5V down to 9V and, with the perpendicular-line tool (SHIFT + F3), draw a line across the fourth column on the new horizontal ruler guide.

25. Choose "12 pt" from the Line option.

26. Remove the horizontal ruler guide.

27. With the text tool (SHIFT + F4), place the insertion point just to the left of the "M" in "Members." Press DELETE, or BACKSPACE, and RETURN to move "Members" down to the next line.

Figure 7-29 shows what the finished page 4 now looks like.

28. Save your work by pressing COMMAND + S.

Finishing the Dummy

There are some other tasks to be included in the dummy publication. First, an advertisement must be placed on page 3. Second, a graphic placeholder is needed on page 3. Finally, some design lines must be placed.

PLACING AN ADVERTISEMENT The advertisement spans two columns. You will draw a small narrow box over the column dividers, fill it with "Paper" shading, and then

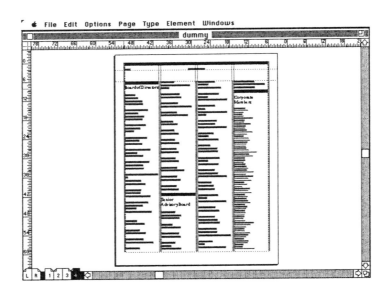

FIGURE 7-29 Screen showing page 4 complete

type in the text. Each line of the ad will vary in type size, so you will specify the type size for each line. For some you'll use the shorthand method of pressing COMMAND + OPTION + SHIFT + < to decrease the type size to the next smaller size. Also, the text must be centered.

Follow these steps to complete the advertisement:

1. Click on the page 3 icon.

2. Place your pointer at 22H/46V and COMMAND + OPTION + click for an "Actual size" view.

3. Drag the horizontal ruler guide from 42V to 42.5V.

4. Using the square-corner tool (SHIFT + F5), draw a box around the column guides, from 33H/42.5V to the bottom margin guides at 35H/59.5V. The box should encompass the column guides, as shown in Figure 7-30.

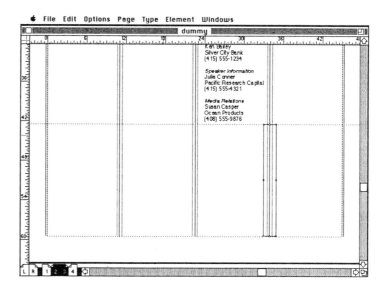

FIGURE 7-30 Box around the column dividers

5. Choose "Paper" from the Fill option while the box is selected.

6. Choose "None" from the Line option.

7. Using the perpendicular-line tool (SHIFT + F3), draw a line at 42.5V from the left column guide in column 3 to the right margin guide.

8. Choose "12 pt" from the Line option.

9. Draw another line across the bottom margin connecting the two existing vertical lines, so that a solid line connects the left, right, and bottom sides of the box.

10. Select the text tool (SHIFT + F4) and click it in the box at 24H/47V.

11. Press COMMAND + SHIFT + C to center the text.

12. Press COMMAND + T for the Type specifications dialog box, type **16** for the "Size," click on "Bold," and click on "OK."

13. Type **Pandick California, Inc.,** and press RETURN twice.

    The line will wrap around, but you'll straighten it out in a moment.

14. Press COMMAND + OPTION + SHIFT + < twice to reduce the point size by two points (to 14 points). Press COMMAND + SHIFT + B to turn off bold and press COMMAND + SHIFT + I to turn on italic.

15. Type the word **The**, press COMMAND + SHIFT + I to turn off italic; press COMMAND + SHIFT + B to turn on bold, type **Financial Printer**, and press RETURN twice.

16. Press COMMAND + OPTION + SHIFT + < twice to again reduce the point size by two points (to 12 points).

17. Type **(415)543-4433** and press RETURN twice.

18. Press COMMAND + T, type **10** for the "Size," click on "Bold" to turn it off, click on "Italic" to turn it on, and click on "OK" to close the dialog box.

19. Type **Offices in** and press RETURN twice.

The list of office locations contains a bullet between each of the cities. You get a bullet by pressing OPTION + 8, simultaneously.

20. Press COMMAND + OPTION + SHIFT + < twice to reduce the point size to 8 points.

21. Type **San Francisco**, press SPACEBAR, OPTION + 8, press SPACEBAR, type **Los Angeles**, press SPACEBAR, OPTION + 8, press SPACEBAR, type **Newport Beach**, and press RETURN.

Now you will straighten the text by selecting it with the pointer tool and stretching the selection box across the fourth column. The text will be rearranged as you intended.

22. Select the pointer (SHIFT + F1) and click on the text you've just typed.

23. Drag one of the tiny boxes on the right end of the text selection box to the right margin, as shown in Figure 7-31.

24. Return to the "Fit in window" view.

25. Press CTRL + S to save the newsletter.

Next you'll build a placeholder for the graphic that is always placed on page 3.

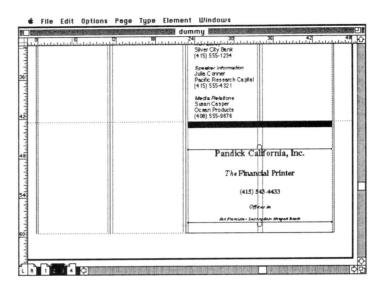

FIGURE 7-31 The finished ad on page 3

BUILDING A GRAPHIC PLACEHOLDER The graphic placeholder will contain a graphic that varies with each issue. Follow these steps to establish the placeholder with a reverse type title:

1. Drag the horizontal ruler guide at 42.5V to 44V.

2. Place the pointer at 22H/46V and press COMMAND + OPTION + click for an "Actual size" view.

3. Click the text tool (SHIFT + F4) at 0.5H/45V.

4. Press COMMAND + SHIFT + C to center the text.

5. Press COMMAND + T and choose "Helvetica," "10" points, and "Reverse." Click on "OK."

6. Type **COMING DECEMBER 4TH**. (Since you are typing white on white you won't be able to see what you are typing.)

7. With the square-corner tool (SHIFT + F5), build a box from the left margin guide at 0H/44V to the left column guide at 10.75H/45V.

8. Choose "Solid" from the Fill option.

9. Send the box to the back by pressing COMMAND + B.

10. With the perpendicular-line tool (SHIFT + F3), draw a line connecting the line at left 0.25H to the column divider at 11H, along the bottom margin at 59.5V.

Your screen should look like the one shown in Figure 7-32.

11. Return to the "Fit in window" view.

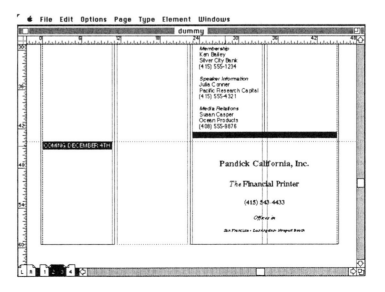

FIGURE 7-32 Graphic placeholder with title

DRAWING DESIGN LINES   There are three lines to be drawn on page 3. To enter them you will reset the publication default from "Hairline" to "12 pt," enter the three lines, and then reset the default to its original "Hairline" setting. The three 12-point lines mark the heads of columns 1, 3, and 4. The lines are shown in Figure 7-33.

Follow these quick steps to draw them:

1. With the pointer tool (SHIFT + F1), choose "12 pt" from the Line option of the Element menu.

2. Place the pointer at right 22H/12V and press COMMAND + OPTION + click for an "Actual size" view.

3. With the perpendicular-line tool (SHIFT + F3), draw a line across the horizontal ruler guide at 6V in the left column, for half of the column width, from the left margin to right 5.5H.

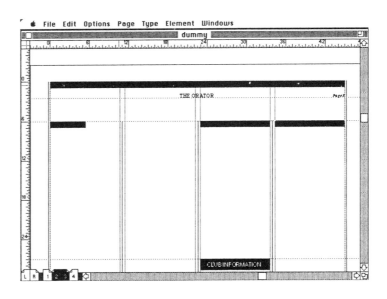

FIGURE 7-33   Design lines on columns 3 and 4, page 3

4. In the third column, draw a line from the left column guide at 23H to the right column guide at 33.5H on the horizontal ruler guide at 6V.

5. In the fourth column, draw a line from the left column guide at 34.25H to the right margin on the horizontal ruler at 6V.

6. With the pointer (SHIFT + F1), choose "Hairline" from the Line option of the Element menu.

7. Return to "Fit in window" view.

The results are shown in Figure 7-33. The first and most exacting part of building the newsletter is over. Now you must save and print your work.

Saving and Printing the Dummy Publication

This completes construction of the dummy publication. You must now save it as a template, knowing that you will be saving yourself all this work each time you publish another issue of your newsletter.

1. From the File menu, choose "Save as...," click on "Template," and click on "OK."

Also, print the file so that you can see exactly how the pages look at this point. You'll want to correct any major problems that you may have with the dummy. It should look like Figure 7-10.

2. Print the file by pressing COMMAND + P and then clicking on "OK" on the Print dialog box.

Now you can begin Volume 4, Issue 4, of *The Orator.*

CONSTRUCTING A SPECIFIC ISSUE OF THE NEWSLETTER

Constructing a specific issue of any newsletter is really a trial-and-error process. First you place graphics on the dummy publication and then you flow one text file, page by page, line by line, adjusting and enhancing it until the page is the way you want it to appear. Then you go on to the next page. After you finish with one file, you then go to the next and flow it, until the whole text file is flowed.

You must have a good idea how long the articles will be and how much space you have in each column of the newsletter. Space depends to a great extent on the number of columns, the type sizes, and the special graphics and design elements you use. You may not know exactly what length articles you can work with until you have experimented with PageMaker.

When you are dealing with unknown newsletter capacities and article lengths, it is important first to flow the higher priority articles in total. Then you will know what text you have and what you will have to cut or add in order to complete the newsletter.

Creating Page 1 of the Newsletter

You'll build Issue 4 of *The Orator* page by page. First, you will flow the lead article from the Vol4Issue4-Word file, followed by the first part of the Churchill-WP file. You can mix files in this way, flowing one before you have finished with another when you know the length of the files and have edited them. You will insert several design elements, such as an emphasized quote from the Churchill article.

You will finish the page by filling in "Continued on page 2" at the end of column 3. When you are finished, your page should look like that shown in Figure 7-34.

HANDLING THE LEAD ARTICLE　The lead article in this newsletter exactly fits in the middle column on page 1. With the text wrap feature of PageMaker, flowing the text around the graphic is completely automatic. As before, you will switch between the "Fit in window" and "Actual size" views to place the text and verify its placement.

Follow these steps to complete the lead article:

1. Select "Save as. . ." from the File menu and type **nov89nl** in the Name text box. This will make sure that the dummy is preserved.

2. Click on the page 1 icon.

3. In "Actual Size" view, click on the outer box around the Churchill Club logo.

4. Select "Text wrap. . ." from the Element menu and then click on the middle wrap option ("All sides icon") to flow text around the graphic. The far right text flow option will automatically highlight, as will the 1-pica default separation as shown here:

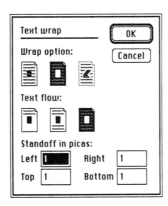

THE ORATOR
Volume 4, Issue 4—November 1989

SOUTH AFRICA'S BUTHELEZI TO ADDRESS CHURCHILL CLUB ON DECEMBER 4TH

The Churchill Club will sponsor its eighth and final event of 1989 on Thursday, December 4th, at the Santa Clara Marriott. The guest: Gatsha Buthelezi, Chief Minister of the Kwa-Zulu homeland in South Africa. The event starts at 6 P.M.

Chief Gatsha Buthelezi claims the support of South Africa's six million Zulus, the nation's largest ethnic group. Despite his moderate voice (or perhaps because of it), this makes him a powerful voice in this turmoiled region. Tom Lodge, a political-science professor at the University of Witswatersrand, says, "It is a dangerous situation to leave Buthelezi out of the equation." Chief Buthelezi himself asserts, "There can't be a successful negotiation without me."

Chief Buthelezi comes across to many white South Africans as comfortably moderate. To them, he embodies the hope for the future. He speaks about whites' fears without fanning them. He says he doesn't want to overthrow white South Africa's values and aspirations. Rather, he says, he wants blacks to be able to share them.

A more serious difference is between Chief Buthelezi and the African National Congress, the broadly based antiapartheid organization that has recently espoused violence. The ANC (and its leader, the jailed Nelson Mandela) quietly supported Buthelezi in the 1970s, recognizing his ability to mobilize people from the rural areas. But in the 1980s the ANC became impatient with Buthelezi's pleas for peaceful change. The group now espouses violence as a necessary catalyst for change in South Africa.

Ennui and the brush-Winston as the artist

Broadly speaking, human beings may be divided into three classes: those who are toiled to death, those who are worried to death, and those who are bored to death.

Churchill himself, of course, was by no means immune to these afflictions about which he wrote. But what was he to do about it?

Churchill typically sought surcease in a number of activities, including reading, fencing, swimming, riding, hunting, flying, polo, horse racing, gardening, and bricklaying. He was also a collector of butterflies and tropical fish and had a number of pets.

Further, Churchill was something of the big kid indulging in everything from toy trains, tin soldiers, and erector sets to

"The tired parts of the mind can be rested and strengthened, not merely by rest, but by using other parts"

building sandcastles and snowmen.

The common denominator in all this activity was change. As Churchill himself writes,

Continued on page 2

The Orator is published quarterly by The Churchill Club. Subscriptions are guaranteed free of charge to all corporate and individual members. Printing of The Orator is donated by Pandick Press, San Francisco.

Editor: Richard Karlgaard
Historian: Michael Perkins
Cartoonist: Kurt Peterson

FIGURE 7-34 Printout of completed page 1

5. Click on "OK" and a boarder will appear around the graphic.

6. Select "Autoflow" from the Options menu to turn it off.

7. Press COMMAND + D for the Place dialog box and double-click on Vol4Issue4-Word. The pointer will become a text icon.

8. Place the text icon on top of column 2 (11.5H/10V) and click the mouse button to flow the text.

The text will flow around the graphic and continue to the bottom of the column. Your screen should look like Figure 7-35.

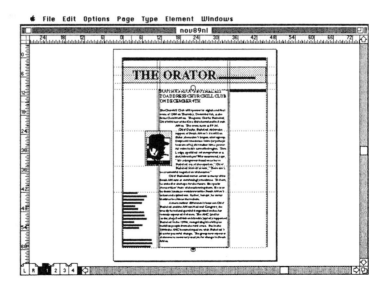

FIGURE 7-35 Leading article placed on page 1

PLACING THE SECOND ARTICLE ON PAGE 1 The second article is several columns long, and only the first part fits on page 1. In addition, you must emphasize a quote from the article by specifying a different type font and setting it off between lines.

Follow these steps to complete page 1:

1. Press COMMAND + D for the Place dialog box.

2. Double-click the filename Churchill-WP. The pointer will become the text icon.

3. Place the icon in the top of the third column at 33.5H/12V and click it.

4. In "Actual size" view, look at the placement and drag the text block so that it is aligned properly below the 12-point line, as shown here:

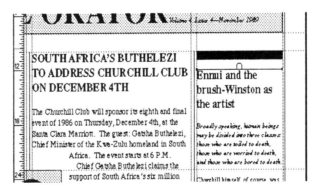

5. Select the pointer (SHIFT + F1) and, in "Fit in window" view, verify that you have a horizontal ruler guide at 42V.

6. Select the text in column 3 and pull the handle up to the horizontal ruler guide at 42V.

7. Verify in "Actual size" view that the last line of the text block is "tin soldiers, and erector sets to."

8. Choose "None" (the leftmost) text wrap icon from the Text wrap dialog box, accessed from the Element menu.

9. Using the perpendicular-line tool (SHIFT + F3), draw a line from the left column guide to the right margin guide, on the horizontal ruler guide at 42V.

10. Choose "6 pt" from the Line option.

11. Select the text tool (SHIFT + F4) and click it at 43.5V, below the new line.

12. Press COMMAND + SHIFT + L for left align.

13. Press COMMAND + T for the Type specifications dialog box, choose "Helvetica" and "12" points and click on "OK."

14. Type "**The tired parts of the mind can be rested and strengthened, not merely by rest, but by using other parts**" (include the quotation marks).

15. With the pointer (SHIFT + F1), drag a horizontal ruler guide just below the newly typed text (to 50V).

16. Using the perpendicular-line tool (SHIFT + F3), draw a line from the left column guide to the right margin guide.

17. Choose "6 pt" from the Line option.

18. With the pointer (SHIFT + F1), select the newly typed quote and center it between the lines. The top should be at about 43.25V, as shown here:

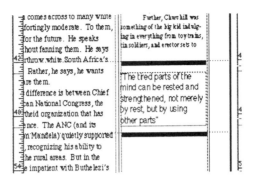

19. With the pointer (SHIFT + F1), select the text block above the new insert and click the bottom handle of the text block.

20. In the "Fit in window" view, place the text icon just below the new line at 51V and click.

21. Look at the text in "Actual size" view and drag it to a better location if necessary. The last line should be the single word "writes."

22. Pull the handle up or down so that your screen looks like that shown in Figure 7-36.

While you're in the third column, you can type the last line.

23. Using the text tool (SHIFT + F4), click the I-beam at 34H/58V.

24. Press COMMAND + SHIFT + R to right-align the next text.

25. Press COMMAND + T for the Type specifications dialog box and choose "8" points, and "Italic" and click on "OK."

26. Type **Continued on page 2**.

27. If the line is not placed correctly, switch to the pointer tool (SHIFT + F1), click it, and drag it to where you want.

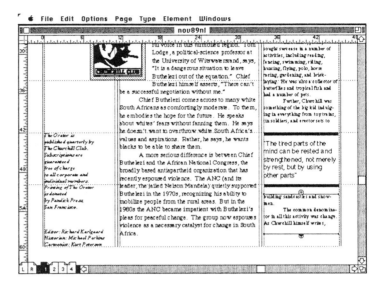

FIGURE 7-36 Bottom of column 3 on page 1

28. Return to the "Fit in window" view.

Your screen should look like that shown in Figure 7-37.

SAVING AND PRINTING PAGE 1 This is a good time to save and print your work, using the following instructions:

1. Press COMMAND + S to save the newsletter.

2. Press COMMAND + P for the Print dialog box.

3. Drag across the "From" text box and type **1**.

4. Drag across the "to" text box and type **1**.

5. Click on "OK."

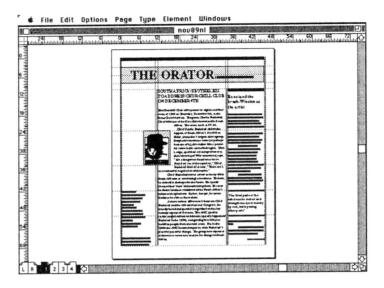

FIGURE 7-37 Completed page 1

Your printed copy should look like Figure 7-34. Now you can work on page 2.

Creating Page 2 of the Newsletter

Page 2 is somewhat more complex, with three files placed within it, as seen in Figure 7-38. First, you will prepare page 2 for the text, building a box to hold the Martini-WN file and placing some design element lines. You will handle the rest of the text, column by column, and flow the remaining Churchill-WP file into the first three columns. Then you will place the Martini-WN file into a box that spans columns 2 and 3, changing the type font for the italic portions. Finally, you will place the next segment of the Vol4Issue4-Word file.

Change is the master key. A man can wear out a particular part of his mind by continually using it and tiring it. The tired parts of the mind can be rested and strengthened, not merely by rest, but by using other parts. It is only when new cells are called into activity, when new stars become lords of the ascendant, that relief, repose, refreshment are afforded.

At age 40 Churchill found himself out of political office for the first time in fifteen years and he needed to discover a new way to creatively fill up the hours.

Exercise, travel, solitude, light socializing, even golf (which he likened to chasing a pill around a cow pasture) did not suffice. It was then, with a friend's encouragement, that he took up painting.

Intensity, Relish and Audacity
Painting at once provided Churchill an opportunity to use his hands as well as a different part of his brain. The "muse of painting" had come to his rescue.

▬▬▬▬▬

The nonprofit Churchill Club provides a nonpartisan forum for public discourse on timely issues, particularly those in which business and politics converge. The Club is named after Winston Churchill, whose character and career personify the democratic values of open discourse, diversity and freedom. Accordingly, Club membership is without regard to sex, lifestyle, legitimacy, sobriety, race, color, creed, physical or mental disposition, or origin.

When Churchill took up the brush, he did it with the same intensity, relish, and audacity as everything he undertook, and he was not discouraged by the results. Painting also proved to be the perfect diversion. In Painting as a Pastime he writes,

I know nothing which, without exhausting the body, more entirely absorbs the mind. Whatever the worries of the hour or the threats of the future, once the picture has begun to flow along, there is no room for them in the mental screen. They pass out into shadow and darkness. All one's mental light, such as it is, becomes concentrated on the task. Time stands respectfully aside.

Churchill chose to devote his painting to landscapes and still lifes in an impressionist style. His brilliant colors became a type of trademark: "I cannot pretend to be impartial about the colours," he wrote. "I rejoice with the brilliant ones and am genuinely sorry for the poor browns."

In search of beautiful scenes, Churchill took his easel with him wherever he traveled including the Middle East and North America. On a trip to Scotland he wrote to his wife, "In the afternoon I went out and painted a beautiful river in the afternoon light with crimson and golden hills in the background."

From the Riviera he writes of a villa that he painted "all in shimmering sunshine and violet shades."

Antidote to Melancholy and Ennui
In the end, painting was to

▬▬▬▬▬

There is something about a martini —a tingle remarkably pleasant

Thus began poet Ogden Nash in *A Drink with Something in It.*

The perfect dry martini contains gin, vermouth, and a twist of lemon. It must be very cold, but not contain ice or water, so keep your gin in the freezer and vermouth in the refrigerator. The especially discriminating may use Tanqueray gin and Noilly extra dry vermouth.

Polish a martini glass and put it in the freezer along with your jigger and stirring rod. The glass should be large, but light, with a feathered rim and a long stem to keep the martini cold. With a sharp knife, cut a generous twist from a ripe, fresh lemon. Be careful to separate the yellow peel from the white pulp, as the peel contains the lemon oil and the pulp would impart a bitter flavor to the martini.

Take the glass from the freezer. Twist the lemon peel to release its oil. Rub the oily surface around the inside of the glass and along its rim, then drop the twist in the glass. Take the gin from the freezer (or Stolichnaya vodka if you feel diffident about gin) and measure two jiggers into the glass. Take the vermouth from the refrigerator and measure a third of a jigger into the glass. Stir vigorously, but do not shake. Remove to a pleasant setting and enjoy.

by "Christopher Russell"

prove one of the chief antidotes to Winston's sometime melancholy and ennui. It also served to deepen Churchill's powers of observation, so much that he had come to see that "the whole world is open with all its treasures, even the simplest objects have their beauty."

Like the poet and artist William Blake, Churchill had learned not only to see with, but through the eye.

Contributed by
Michael Perkins
Club Historian

MY EARLY LIFE

It took me three tries to pass into Sandhurst. There were five subjects, of which Mathematics, Latin and English were obligatory, and I chose in addition French and Chemistry. In this hand I held only a pair of Kings--English and chemistry. Nothing less than three would open the jackpot. I had to find another useful card.

W.S. CHURCHILL

FIGURE 7-38 Completed printout of page 2

PREPARING PAGE 2 You have several tasks to perform to prepare page 2 before flowing the text. You must reset the zero point so that it is located where the top and left margins meet. You must drag another horizontal ruler guide to mark the location of the bottom of a box. Then you will draw the box that spans columns 3 and 4 and holds the Martini-WN text. You will fill the box with "Paper" to cover the column guides and line. Then you will draw a line to mark the bottom of the box. You will also draw a 12-point line on the top of the two columns to highlight this article.

Follow these steps to prepare the page:

1. Click the page 2 icon and return to "Fit in window" view, if you are not already there.

2. Reset the zero point by placing the pointer where the horizontal and vertical rulers meet and dragging the zero point to the top and left margins on page 2. (Make sure that the horizontal zero point is on the margin, not the line outside the margin. You may want to go to "Actual size" view to verify this.)

3. Using the pointer tool (SHIFT + F1), drag the 44H horizontal ruler guide to 37.5V.

4. Using the square corner tool (SHIFT + F5), draw a box from the upper left column guide in column 3 at 33H/6V to 35H/37.5V. The lines of the box should just enclose the column guides between columns 3 and 4.

5. Choose "None" from the Line option of the Element menu.

6. Choose "Paper" from the Fill option of the Element menu.

7. Using the perpendicular-line tool (SHIFT + F3), draw a line across the bottom of the box over the horizontal ruler guide from the left column guide in column 3 to the right margin guide in column 4 (from about 23H/37.5V to 45H).

8. Draw another line at the head of the columns over the horizontal ruler guide at 6V, from the left column guide to the right margin guide (23H/6V to 45H).

9. Choose "12 pt" from the Lines menu.

Now you can flow the Martini-WN file.

PLACING THE MARTINI-WN FILE The text will be placed on top of the box you've just created. It will fit perfectly.
Follow these steps to place the WriteNow file:

1. If you are in "Actual size," return to the "Fit in window" view.

2. Press COMMAND + D to specify the filename to place.

3. In the Place dialog box, double-click the filename Martini-WN. You may need to use the horizontal scroll bars to find it. The pointer will become the familiar text icon.

4. To force the text to span columns, place the icon at 23H/8V, next to the left column guide under the line marking the top of columns 2 and 3, and drag the pointer to 45H/37.5V. Then release the mouse button.

The lower loop of the selection box will be empty, indicating that the entire file has been placed.

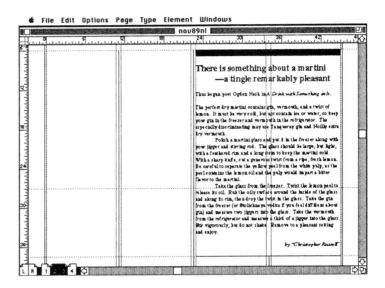

FIGURE 7-39   Martini article placed

5. Place the pointer at 22H/22V, and COMMAND + OPTION + click for an "Actual size" view.

6. Examine the text and make any necessary adjustments.

Your screen should look like that shown in Figure 7-39.

7. Return to the "Fit in window" view.

Next, you will finish placing the CHURCHILL-WP file.

COMPLETING THE WORDPERFECT FILE   Page 1 contains the first part of the Churchill-WP file. To continue placing it, simply click the text handle on the bottom of the text on page 1 to get the text icon. Then you can automatically flow the text into the first three columns of page 2.

Follow these steps to flow the rest of the file:

1. Click the page 1 icon.

2. To reselect the CHURCHILL-WP file, select the pointer (SHIFT + F1) and click the last paragraph of text in column 3 (just above "Continued on page 2").

3. Click the bottom handle for the text icon, click the Page 2 icon, and select "Autoflow" from the Options menu.

4. On page 2, place the text icon at 0H/6V at the top of column 1 and click the mouse button.

5. In "Actual size" view, with the pointer (SHIFT + F1) look at the top of the text in column 1 and place it just below the horizontal ruler guide at 6V.

6. Using the horizontal scroll bar to reposition your screen image, look at the bottom of the text in column 1, and, if necessary, drag it up so that the last line reads "rescue."

7. In the "Fit in window" view, pull down the text in the second column until it is just below the horizontal ruler guide at 6V.

8. In "Actual size" view, look at the top of the column and drag the text block so that the first line in column 1 is lined up with the first line in column 2, like this:

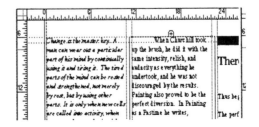

9. Look at the bottom of the column and drag the text handle up so that the last line reads, "In the end, painting was to."

10. Return to the "Fit in window" view and pull down the text in the third column until the top is at 38.5V.

11. In "Actual size" view, examine the top of the column and adjust its position if necessary.

12. Drag up the bottom handle so that the three lines of the author's identification are the last lines showing.

   The author's name should be centered.

13. With the text tool (SHIFT + F4), highlight the three lines of the author's identification.

14. Press COMMAND + SHIFT + C to center it.

   Figure 7-40 shows the results.

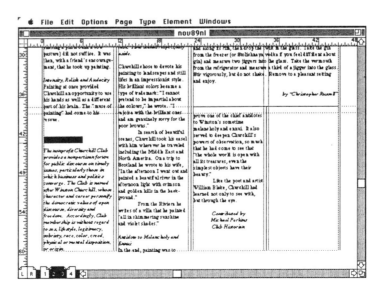

FIGURE 7-40   Last three lines of column 3 centered

15. Return to the "Fit in window" view and, with the pointer tool (SHIFT + F1) pull down the text in the fourth column, so that the top line ("MY EARLY LIFE") is just beneath the horizontal ruler guide at 37.5.

Your final task on page 2 will be to enhance the text segment in column 4.

ENHANCING COLUMN 4 Column 4 contains a short insert, a sort of filler article, that quotes Winston Churchill. It is the last article on the Churchill.WP file. You will emphasize the insert by building a box around the title and Churchill's name, filling it with shading, sending it to the back, and reversing the type. You did this before for the "Club Information" on page 3.

Follow these steps to build the insert:

1. Drag a horizontal ruler guide to 38.5V.

2. Place the pointer at 39H/44V and click the mouse button for an "Actual size" view.

3. Drag the text block so that the title is placed in the middle between the new horizontal ruler guides, at 39 and 38.5, like this:

Keep in mind that you will be building a box around the title and position it to account for the box, as described in the following instructions:

4. Squeeze the text block by dragging the right end of the text selection box from 45H to 44H and the left end from 34.24H to 35H.

5. If necessary, drag the bottom handle down until all text is displayed.

6. With the text tool (SHIFT + F4), highlight the whole text block.

7. Press COMMAND + T for the Type specifications dialog box and choose the "Helvetica," "10" points, and "Normal" options. Click on "OK."

8. Highlight the title.

9. Center it by pressing COMMAND + SHIFT + C. Also, reverse the title by selecting "Reverse" as the "Type style" option of the Type menu.

10. Highlight Churchill's name.

11. Center it by pressing COMMAND + SHIFT + C. Also, reverse Churchill's name by selecting "Reverse" as the "Type style" option of the Type menu.

12. Using the square-corner tool (SHIFT + F5), draw a box around the title, from the right column guide of the left column guide to the right margin (from 34.25H/37.5V to 45H/38.5V).

13. Shade the box by choosing "solid" from the Fill option.

14. Copy the box by pressing COMMAND + C or F3.

15. Send the box to the back by pressing COMMAND + B.

The box and type will then look like this:

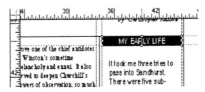

The bottom line should be moved down. You'll do this by adding space before the start of the paragraph of text and before the byline at the end.

16. Highlight the first line of the paragraph of text (beginning with "It took me three tries to.") Press COMMAND + M to open the Paragraph specifications dialog box. Drag across the "Before" text box and type **Op6** to add 6 points or 1/2 pica of space before the paragraph. Click on "OK."

17. Beginning just below the word "card" (the last word in the text paragraph), highlight "W.S. Churchill" at the bottom of column 4. Press COMMAND + M, drag across the "Before" text box, and type **1p4** to add 16 points or 1 1/3 picas before the byline. Click on "OK."

18. Press COMMAND + V or F4 to paste the copy of the box.

19. Using the pointer (SHIFT + F1), drag the box over Churchill's name so that it rests on the bottom margin.

20. Press COMMAND + B to send the box to the back.

The screen should look like that shown in Figure 7-41.

21. Return to the "Fit in window" view.

22. Save the file by pressing COMMAND + S.

You may want to print page 2 to see how it compares to Figure 7-38.

23. Press COMMAND + P for the Print dialog box.

24. Drag the Page range "From" text box and type **2**.

25. Drag the "to" text box, type **2**, and click on "OK."

Only page 3 remains to be done.

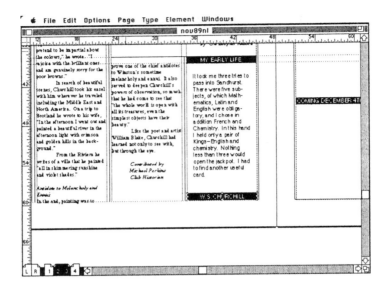

_____ **FIGURE 7-41**   Insert with highlighted title and name

Completing Page 3 of the Newsletter

You'll finish page 3 by drawing some design element lines and then flowing the rest of the Vol4Issue4-Word file. The file contains five more articles that flow one after the other.

FLOWING THE FIRST COLUMN   The first column consists of a heading, one article, and a graphic with a highlighted title, as shown in Figure 7-42.

Follow these steps to flow the text:

1. Reset the zero point to the top and left margins on page 3.

2. Verify that "Snap to guides" is on and that "Autoflow" is off, both from the Options menu.

THE ORATOR   *Page 3*

Members Only

GOVERNOR DEUKMEJIAN INTRODUCES CHILDREN'S INITIATIVE AT 10-9-89 MEETING

Governor George Deukmejian proposed a $5 million program to bolster statewide child care and medical services at a joint meeting of the Churchill Club and Commonwealth Club on October 9, 1989.

Before 500 people at the San Jose Hyatt, the governor outlined a seven-point "children's initiative" that included a call for expanded drug abuse prevention programs and a crackdown on parents who evade payment of child support.

He also promised to hire more senior citizens to work in child care centers and offered to write legislation providing incentives for drug companies to produce vaccines for childhood diseases.

The Churchill Club thanks the Commonwealth Club for co-sponsoring this fine event.

COMING DECEMBER 4TH

"IMMIGRATION OUT OF CONTROL," COLORADO'S LAMM TELLS CLUB

Warning that the United States is at a crossroads, Colorado Governor Richard Lamm called for stronger border control measures during an address to the Churchill Club on October 16, 1989.

"The creativity and capital of this country, for all its genius, cannot keep pace with the demands put on it if we have to solve not only our own unemployment rate, but that of Mexico, Guatemala, and El Salvador," said the four-term governor.

CLUB MEMBERS IN THE NEWS

Board member Bill Reichert is now vp/marketing at The Learning Company, a Menlo Park-based educational software firm. Reichert's alma mater, New Venture Consultants, is the newest corporate member of the Club...John Sewell, former vice president and general manager of Kodak's largest division, joined the board of Redlake Corporation, a Morgan Hill company that manufactures and sells photo-instrumentation equipment. Redlake is also a Club corporate member...Bob Hansens of Business Solutions Consultants is forming the Silicon Valley Entrepreneur's Club. First meeting is scheduled for January 24th at the San Jose Hyatt. Call Bob at (408) 458-1303 for more information...Club chairman Tony Perkins has returned to Silicon Valley Bank as vice president of SVB's technology group. Also new with SVB are Club members Henry Kellog and Eric Jones.

T.J. Rodgers confirmed for late January

Semiconductor entrepreneur T.J. Rodgers will address the Churchill Club in late January.

Founder and CEO of Cypress Semiconductor, Rodgers has engineered one of Silicon Valley's brightest stories of late. Cypress went public last summer at a valuation of $270 million.

Invitations to a *Night with T.J. Rodgers* will be mailed in early January.

CLUB INFORMATION

Membership
Ken Bailey
Silver City Bank
(415) 555-1234

Speaker Information
Julia Conner
Pacific Research Capital
(415) 555-4321

Media Relations
Susan Casper
Ocean Products
(408) 555-9876

Former H&Q president Tom Volpe on February 19th

Tom Volpe, founder of Volpe Covington, a new investment banking firm that includes Arthur Rock and Warren Hellman as major investors, will address the Churchill Club on Thursday, February 19th.

Volpe has had a meteoric career in investment banking. After taking his AB and MBA from Harvard —with a one-year stopover at the London School of Economics—he began his career with White, Weld & Company, later moving to Blyth, Eastman, Dillon.

At age 30 Volpe joined Hambrecht & Quist as a general partner and opened the investment banking firm's New York Office. In 1984 he became president and CEO of H&Q.

Invitations to *A Night with Tom Volpe* will be mailed to all Club members in early January.

Pandick California, Inc.

The Financial Printer

(415) 543-4433

Offices in

San Francisco · Los Angeles · Newport Beach

FIGURE 7-42 Printout of completed page 3

3. With the pointer (SHIFT + F1), click the page 1 icon and then the lead article in the middle column so that the article is enclosed in the selection box.

4. Click on the bottom handle of the selection box.

5. Click on the page 3 icon.

6. Place the text icon at the top of the first column of page 3 just under the line at 7V and click the mouse botton.

7. In "Actual size" view, look at the top of the text block and, if necessary, drag it so that the heading is just under the line at the head of the column, as shown in Figure 7-43.

The text block will have flowed until it encountered the graphic box. You want the text to end in the fourth paragraph, with the words "this fine event."

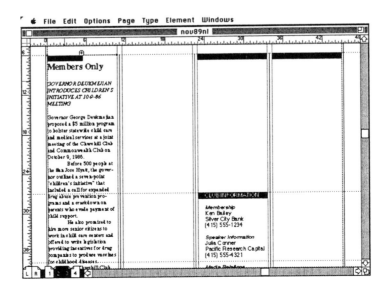

FIGURE 7-43 Column 1, page 3, headline aligned

8. Using the horizontal scroll bar, peruse the column in "Actual view" until you reach the bottom of the flowed text.

9. Drag the text handle up (or down) until it ends after the fourth paragraph. You may have to move the whole text block up closer to the top line.

The next column is very straightforward, except that you must change the leading to get all of the two articles to fit in the column. In this column, the text begins at the same level as the top of the design line, on the horizontal ruler guide.

10. Click the handle for the text icon and return to the "Fit in window" view.

11. Place the icon at the top of column 2 and click the mouse button.

12. In "Actual size" view, look at the bottom of the column. Pull the text handle down and drag the text block higher in the column until "Club members Henry Kellog and Eric Jones." is the last line of text in column 2.

You'll be switching between dragging the text block higher in the column and dragging the handle down so that more text can flow. You'll see that to fit all text in column 2, you'll have to drag the lower handle almost off the page. Figure 7-44 shows the results.

13. In the "Fit in window" view and with the text tool, highlight the whole column of text (including the headlines).

14. Press COMMAND+T, to display the Type specifications dialog box.

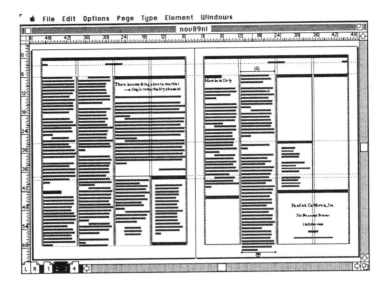

FIGURE 7-44   Column 2, page 3, before leading is reduced

15. Drag across the Leading text box, type **11.5**, and then click on "OK."

The text will shrink so that it can be contained in the one column. Now you need to adjust the position of the text block.

16. Place your pointer at 23H/16V and press the mouse button for an "Actual size" view.

17. With the pointer tool (SHIFT + F1), click somewhere in column 2 to get the selection box.

18. Drag down a new horizontal ruler guide so that it is just beneath the title in column 1, as shown in Figure 7-45.

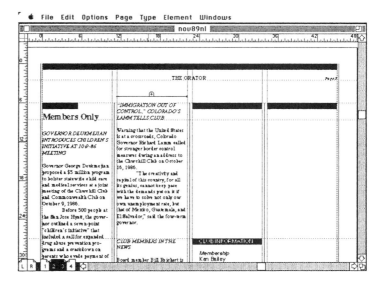

FIGURE 7-45   Headlines for columns 1 and 2 of page 3 aligned

19. Drag the title text block in column 2 so that the title spans from the top of the design lines in the other columns to the new horizontal line placed in step 18. You can move the article in column 1 down a bit, if necessary, to accomplish this. If there is not enough space in column 2 to position the title text block between the two guidelines, you may have to move down the column 1 text and horizontal ruler guide beneath the column 1 title to a position at which you can fit in the column 2 title.

20. When the positioning is as you want it, click the bottom handle for the text icon.

Flowing the next two columns will be much easier.

COMPLETING THE PLACEMENT OF THE TEXT The last two columns each contain one article that fits in the space available. You will flow the text, verify that it is correctly positioned at the top of the column, drag the text handle down to get all of the text in the article, and then flow the next column.

Follow these steps to finish this task:

1. Place the text icon at the top of column 3, under the heavy line, and click the mouse button.

2. In "Actual size" view, look at the top of the column and adjust it if necessary.

3. Drag the text handle down so that all the text in the article appears in column 3, ending with the line "mailed in early January."

4. With the pointer tool (SHIFT + F1), click the bottom text handle to get the text icon.

5. Place the icon at the head of column 4 and click the mouse button.

6. In "Actual size" view, line up the headline with the article in column 3, as shown in Figure 7-46.

7. In the "Fit in window" view, drag down the handle so that all text appears. (The handle will be empty.)

8. Verify the results with the "Actual size" view.

9. With the text tool (SHIFT + F4), highlight the body of text (not the title) in column 4. Press COMMAND + T, drag across the "Leading" text box, and click on "OK."

10. With the text tool, click an insertion point to the left of the "c" in "confirmed" in the column 3 title. Press DELETE (or BACKSPACE) and RETURN to move "confirmed"

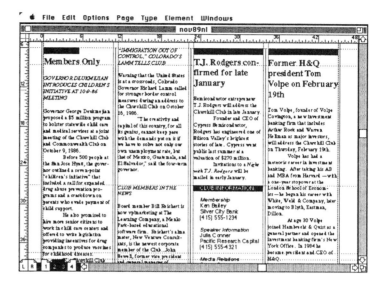

FIGURE 7-46 Heading for columns 3 and 4 aligned

to the next line. In a like manner, move the word "late" to the next line.

11. Move the word "Tom" in column 4 down to the next line. Your final screen should look like Figure 7-47.

12. Return to the "Fit in window" view. Figure 7-48 shows how your screen should look if you turn off "Guides" from the Options menu.

13. Save your work by pressing COMMAND + S.

Having successfully flowed all the text, you are ready to complete the final step—perusing your publication and adding final touches. You will want to examine the typing, looking for misspellings and typos. Look at the inserts, lines, and design elements. Are they placed exactly right? Do they meet the column dividers or margins where they

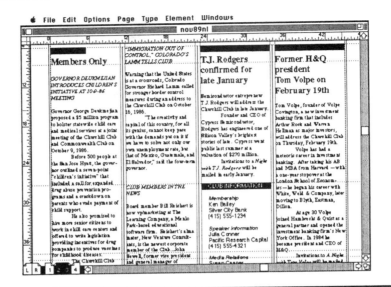

FIGURE 7-47 Headlines for columns 3 and 4 with proper line breaks

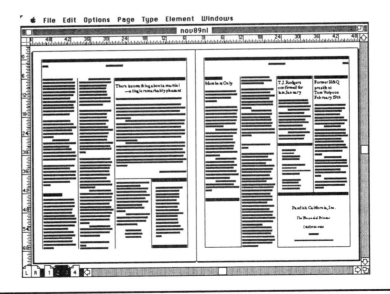

FIGURE 7-48 Finished pages 2 and 3 with "Guides" turned off

should? Are your boxes long enough? Too long? This is the time to be very critical and to perfect your work. Final editing is often a repetitive process of examining the newsletter on the screen, printing it, examining the printout, correcting any errors, and reprinting it.

USING THE STORY EDITING FEATURES

In looking through your newsletter, you will find several references to 1986 that should be 1989. Suppose, also, that you are unsure about the spelling of several words. To handle these problems, you'll use PageMaker 4's story editing features.

The story editor provides a means of editing stories placed in a PageMaker publication, similar to what you can do in a word processing package. In this case, you want to use the search and replace feature, called "Change. . .", to change 1986 to 1989, and the spelling checker, called "Spelling. . ." to find and correct problem words. Follow these instructions:

1. Click on the page 1 icon and then click with the pointer (SHIFT + F1) on the article in column 2—the Buthelezi address.

2. From the Edit menu, choose "Edit story." The story window will open as shown in Figure 7-49.

As you can see, the story view provides a perspective different from the normal PageMaker layout view. Your

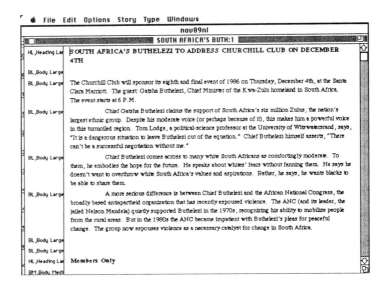

━━━━ **FIGURE 7-49**   The story view of Vol4Issue4-Word

original layout has not changed; you are just looking at it in another view. The story view window includes a different set of menus. You'll use some of the menu options to edit the newsletter.

The left column in Figure 7-49 displays the style names. You can turn these off through the Options menu. With the Options menu you can also turn on the display of hidden characters, such as carriage returns (which are indicated by paragraph marks) and tabs at the end of the line (which are indicated by arrows). Do that next and then search and replace (or "Change") 1986.

3. From the Options menu, choose "Display ¶." You will see where your paragraph and tab characters are.

4. From the Edit menu, choose "Change. . . ." The Change dialog box will open as shown here:

```
 ▤☐▤▤▤▤▤▤▤▤▤▤ Change ▤▤▤▤▤▤▤▤▤▤▤▤
 Find what: [                          ]    ╭────────╮
                                            │  Find   │
 Change to: [                          ]    ╰────────╯
                                            ╭────────╮
 Options: ☐ Match case  ☐ Whole word        │ Change  │
                                            ╰────────╯
 Search:  ○ Selected text ⊙ Current story   ╭──────────────╮
          ○ All stories                     │ Change & find │
                                            ╰──────────────╯
                                            ╭────────────╮
                                            │ Change all  │
                                            ╰────────────╯
                                            ╭────────────╮
                                            │ Attributes… │
                                            ╰────────────╯
```

5. Type **86** in the "Find what:" text box.

6. Press TAB, type **89** in the "Change to:" text box, and click on "Find." The first occurrence in the first line of the article will be highlighted.

7. Click on "Change & find" to change the first occurrence and find the next one.

8. The second occurrence, which appears in the "members only" article, will be found. Again, click on "Change & find."

9. Repeat step 8. PageMaker will find two more occurrences of "1986"—one again in the "members only" article and the other in the subsequent article. When you see the message "Search complete!", click on "OK" and click on the close box of the Change dialog box.

Next, move the insertion point back to the top of the story and run the spelling checker.

10. Press COMMAND + 9 on the numeric keypad and click the insertion point before "South" in the title, as shown in Figure 7-49.

11. Choose "Spelling. . ." from the Edit menu. A dialog box will be displayed. Click on "Start." PageMaker will begin to search the text and to highlight words that are not in its dictionary.

12. The first word that PageMaker will highlight is Buthelezi. It will also appear in the dialog box with alternative spellings and a text box in which you can type a revised spelling. In this case, click on "Ignore."

13. PageMaker will continue to highlight and display unknown words. Click on "Ignore" or correct the spelling as needed until you have reached the end of the article.

14. When you have finished checking the spelling, click on the close box on the Spelling dialog box.

You are now ready to return the corrected story to the layout view.

15. From the Story menu, choose "Close story." You will be returned to the layout view.

Save and Print the Finished Newsletter

Once you are satisfied with its content, you need only print the final newsletter. But first you should save your work again.

16. Press COMMAND + S to save the file.

17. Press COMMAND + P for the Print dialog box.

18. Click "All" to print pages 1 to 4. Click on "OK."

This concludes the newsletter project. It has been challenging and time-consuming, as you would expect with a task of this size. You will be able to use many of the techniques you've used here with your own newsletters or similar work.

Chapter 8 presents you with another challenge, that of creating a catalog. You'll continue to advance your skills in the next chapter.

chapter **8**

BUILDING A
CATALOG

Planning and Designing the Catalog
Creating Text and Graphics for the Catalog
Setting Defaults
Important Techniques Used in This Chapter
Constructing the Master Pages
Building the Title Page
Constructing the Detail Catalog Pages

In this chapter, you will create the title page and two regular pages of a catalog, as shown in Figure 8-1. Catalogs are usually built from a repetitive layout within which changing contents are placed. The emphasis of the chapter is therefore in building the master pages. The two regular catalog pages are constructed to represent how the bulk of the catalog is built. A title page is also prepared to give you an opportunity to use and place graphics. A complete catalog, of course, would contain many more pages and numerous other layouts.

Wholesale Art Supplies
Graphic Arts, Drafting, and Engineering
1327 Park Avenue
Emeryville, CA 94608
(415) 428-9011

FIGURE 8-1   The title page of the catalog (1 of 3)

The catalog that served as a model for this chapter is published by MacPherson's wholesale art supply store in Emeryville, California. MacPherson's built the catalog using PageMaker on the Macintosh. In so doing, they saved considerable time and money compared with the traditional method of manual layout and typesetting.

MacPherson

Watercolor Paint Sets

Prang Watercolor Sets (American Crayon)
Oval-8 Set contains 8 oval semi-moist half pan colors with No. 7 brush. No. 16 Set contains 16 semi-moist half pan colors, a No. 1 and 4 brush. Oval 16 Set contains the same colors and brushes as No. 16 Set, except with oval half pans. No. 8 Set contains 8 semi-moist half pan colors with No. 7 brush. (Qty = Each)

Order No.	Item
AC16	Prang Watercolor Set
AC16-OVL	Prang Watercolor Set
AC8	Prang Watercolor Set
AC8-OVL	Prang Watercolor Set

Artista Watercolor Sets (Binney & Smith)
No. 080 set contains 8 oval half pans and a No. 7 brush. No. 08 contains 8 half pans and a No. 7 brush. No. 016 contains 16 half pans and a No. 7 brush. (Qty = Each)

Order No.	Item
BS016	W/C Half Pan Set
BS08	W/C Half Pan Set
BS080	W/C Oval Pan Set

Gouache Sets (Caran D'Ache)
Highly concentrated light-resistant watercolors for opaque painting. The No. 10308 Set contains 7 pans of assorted colors and one tube of white. (Qty = Each)

Order No.	Item
CD10308	Pan Set 8 Colors with Brush
CD20313	Tube Set 13 Colors with Brush

Licolette Gouache Sets (Loew-Cornell)
Set 500-12 contains 10 opaque colors, white, and black. Set 500-24 contains 22 opaque colors, white, and black. (Qty = Each)

Order No.	Item
LK500-12	Licolette Gouache Set/12 Colors
LK500-24	Licolette Gouache Set/24 Colors

Radiant Concentrated Sets (Dr. Ph. Martin)
Each set is comprised of 14 colors to cover the entire range as listed in groups, corresponding to the open-stock radiant colors. DRA Set is all "A" colors. DRB Set is all "B" colors. DRC Set is all "C" colors. DRDST is all "D" colors. 1/2 oz. bottle size. (Qty = Each)

Order No.	Item
DRA	Radiant CNC Set/14 All A
DRB	Radiant CNC Set/14 All B
DRC	Radiant CNC Set/14 All C
DRDST	Radiant CNC Set/14 All D

2

FIGURE 8-1 Page 2 of the catalog (2 of 3)

The MacPherson catalog was constructed by pulling together and organizing the literature of a number of different vendors. The creators scan the artwork and photographs from the vendor's literature to convert them to

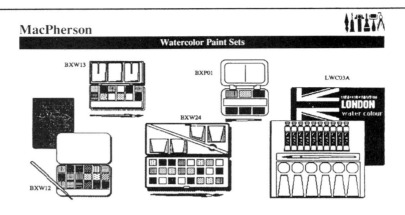

MacPherson

Watercolor Paint Sets

The Bijou No. 3 (Winsor & Newton)
The ideal companion for the traveling watercolorist.
Made of strong die-cast metal finished in black enamel
and packed in an attractive carrying case. Contains 18
semi-moist pans of Artists' Water Color and a sable brush
in a metal holder with protective cap. Size 2" x 5". (Qty
= Each)

Order No.	Item
WNBXW12	No. 3 Bijou

The Bijou No. 2 (Winsor & Newton)
Same as Bijou No. 3, but contains 12 colors. Size 2" x 3-
1/4". (Qty = Each)

Order No.	Item
WNBXW11	No. 2 Bijou

Sketchers Pocket Box (Winsor & Newton)
A compact white plastic box containing 12 square pans of
transparent watercolor and a pocket sable brush with a
protective cap. Size 4" x 2" x 1/2". (Qty = Each)

Order No.	Item
WNBXW13	W/C Pocket Box

Sketchers Box #24 (Winsor & Newton)
A black plastic box containing 24 square pans of economical watercolor and a Series 33 sable brush. Refill
pans not available. Size 8-1/2" x 4-1/2" x 1/4". (Qty =
Each)

Order No.	Item
WNBXW24	W/C Set - 24 Colors

London Water Color Set #3A (Winsor & Newton)
Contains 10 London Water Colors in 7.5 ml. tubes.
Includes a watercolor brush, a six well/six slant tile plastic
palette, color chart and painting techniques leaflet. (Qty =
Each)

Order No.	Item
WNBXLW03A	London W/C Set #3A

London Water Color Set #4 (Winsor & Newton)
Contains 12 London Water colors in 7.5 ml. tubes in an
aluminum box with white enameled palette/lid, two water
color brushes, a color chart and a painting techniques
leaflet. (Qty = Each)

Order No.	Item
WNBXLW04	London W/C Set #4

Page Water Color Sets (Winsor & Newton)
This range represents excellent value in inexpensive water
color sets for young artists. Colorfully designed boxes
make these sets ideal as gifts. Each set comes with a
brush and all are shrink-wrapped for protection except
#01 (Qty = Each)

Order No.	Item
WNBXP01	6 Pan Water Color Set
WNBXP05	12 Pan Water Color Set
WNBXP10	20 Pan Water Color Set
WNBXP15	30 Pan Water Color Set
WNBXP20	40 Pan Water Color Set
WNBXP25	50 Pan Water Color Set
WNBXP30	60 Pan Water Color Set
WNBXP35	78 Pan Water Color Set

3

FIGURE 8-1 Page 3 of the catalog (3 of 3)

computer-readable form, and they type the text into a word
processor to give it a consistent format and font.

In this chapter you will follow a similar procedure. You
will scan the artwork for the two regular pages and will

enter the text in Microsoft Word. If you do not have a scanner, use one of the compatible graphics programs, such as Adobe Illustrator, Aldus FreeHand, DeskPaint, and Super-Paint, to prepare a graphic, or use commercially available clip art instead of a scanned image. Then follow the instructions for placing the graphic, changing the filename as necessary.

If you use a word processor other than Microsoft Word, review the Microsoft Word instructions and then adapt them to your word processor.

PLANNING AND DESIGNING THE CATALOG

The planning and design of a catalog are essential to a successful publication, as you have seen in the other publications in this book.

Planning the Catalog

The primary concern when planning a catalog is is determining what will be included — which products from which vendors. Once you have determined that, you must consider how to get the latest literature, how to organize it, and who will scan the art and enter the text. Depending on the size of the catalog, this may be a one-person job, or many people may be involved. The larger the catalog and the more people involved, the more planning must be done.

Printing a catalog, like most desktop-published projects, ranges from simply reproducing what is generated by the laser printer to having the catalog commercially printed and bound. MacPherson took the latter approach, using a beautiful, multicolored cover and simple black-and-white printing for the regular pages.

Planning the schedule for the catalog depends largely on whether the catalog is aimed at a particular buying season, such as Christmas, or must be produced within some other time frame. If there is a deadline, the schedule obviously takes on greater significance. In budgeting, you must similarly consider the size of the publication and how sophisticated the printing and binding will be. Furthermore, distributing the catalog by mail can add substantially to the budget and can dictate the weight and subsequent size of the catalog.

Designing the Catalog

In designing the catalog, strive to create an attractive and functional layout that can be used for most of the content. The ease of placing numerous graphics and text blocks is important and precludes undue customization of individual pages. At the same time, the design must accommodate a wide variety of items. MacPherson's catalog, for instance, covers art supplies from pencils and tubes of paint to easels and drafting tables.

The master page layout, then, takes on considerable significance for most catalogs. As you will see, all the design elements are placed on the master pages, and little, if any, customization is done.

LINES Lines are used in the catalog to create highlights and to define areas of the page. Most of the lines are 1/2-point wide and are used to define margins and columns or to separate graphics from text. In addition, there is a

1/4-inch line across the top of each page that has the section name in it. You create this line by drawing a box, filling it with shading, and using reverse type.

FONTS   The catalog uses only the Times typeface in four fonts. The company name, on the inside of each catalog page, is 18-point bold; the page number and section name are 12-point bold; and the text is 10-point with headings in bold and the body in normal weight. The section name at the top of each page is in reversed type (white letters on a black background).

SHADING   Shading is used in the catalog as the background of the section name in the box across the top of each page. "Solid" fill is applied. You could choose, in adddition, to shade your graphics or some of the text.

LEADING   In the example pages produced in this chapter, only "Auto" leading is used. PageMaker assumes 120 percent leading as its default "Auto" leading setting. The 10-point type used in the catalog text, therefore, has 12 points of leading, expressed as 10/12. You may want to vary the leading on pages you produce to squeeze additional text onto a page or to expand text to fill a page.

GRAPHICS   Four separate graphics are used in the catalog. The title for the catalog is produced directly with Aldus FreeHand. The other three, two sets of products and the logo, are scanned and produce TIFF files.

LAYOUT   The layout for the catalog will be in decimal inches, often the easiest system with which to work. You will use a standard 8.5 x 11-inch format, with a 1-inch inside margin and 0.75-inch top, outside, and bottom margins. The wider inside margin is for binding purposes. The regular pages will have two columns with 0.25-inch spacing between columns, although the first page has only one column.

The next step is to create the text and graphics.

CREATING TEXT AND GRAPHICS FOR THE CATALOG

You will create the catalog text and graphics outside Page-Maker with graphics and word processing packages that interface with it. As mentioned earlier, the catalog text is produced with Microsoft Word. The graphics come from various sources: a company name graphic created in Aldus FreeHand, a company logo, and the catalog product drawings created from scanned art. You can select your own word processor (if it works with PageMaker) and your own means of producing graphics if you prefer.

If you are not using Word, check to see if your word processor is covered in this book and read about any restrictions you may have with it. (WordPerfect and WriteNow are covered in Chapter 7, and MacWrite is discussed in Chapter 6.)

Another alternative for both the text and graphics is to purchase the companion disk for this book and use the files on that disk. Use the coupon included in the front of this book to order it.

If you don't have a scanner or Aldus FreeHand, you can use clip art or any of the several painting and drawing programs supported by PageMaker. It is recommended that you do create some graphics. It will allow you to experiment with placing graphics, even if they aren't exactly right for the publication. However, if you elect to forego the graphics part altogether and simply establish the placeholders in PageMaker, you'll still gain valuable experience.

Creating Text with Microsoft Word

You will build only one file with Microsoft Word. In a full catalog you would normally create several files and might use more than one word processor. Figure 8-2 contains the text that you will enter with Microsoft Word.

The text consists of several paragraphs, each describing a product. Fortunately, with Microsoft Word you can transfer everything you need in the catalog to PageMaker—the typeface, type sizes, bold, and italics. This considerably reduces the work in PageMaker.

Load Microsoft Word or the word processing program you want to use. Place two tabs, one at 1.25 and one at 1.75 inches. Set your default formatting to 10-point Times, left aligned, with "Auto" leading. If you wish, you can create a style sheet with two styles: a body medium (BM) that is 10-point Times, left aligned, with "Auto" leading; and a heading medium (HM) that is body medium with bold.

Type the text shown in Figure 8-2. For the heading, or the first line of each product description, use bold or HM style. For all the remaining text and numbers, use the default formatting or BM style. Place two tabs between the "Order No." and "Item" column heads and one tab between the actual product number and the product description. Leave two blank lines between products.

When you have completed typing the file, save it in the Publications folder with the filename Catalog-Word.

If you are using a different folder for the PageMaker files created in this book, change the folder name here accordingly.

Prang Watercolor Sets (American Crayon)
Oval-8 Set contains 8 oval semi-moist half pan colors with No. 7 brush. No. 16 Set contains 16 semi-moist half pan colors, a No. 1 and 4 brush. Oval 16 Set contains the same colors and brushes as No. 16 Set, except with oval half pans. No. 8 Set contains 8 semi-moist half pan colors with No. 7 brush.
(Qty = Each)

Order No.	Item
AC16	Prang Watercolor Set
AC16-OVL	Prang Watercolor Set
AC8	Prang Watercolor Set
AC8-OVL	Prang Watercolor Set

Artista Watercolor Sets (Binney & Smith)
No. 080 set contains 8 oval half pans and a No. 7 brush. No. 08 contains 8 half pans and a No. 7 brush. No. 016 contains 16 half pans and a No. 7 brush. (Qty = Each)

Order No.	Item
BS016	W/C Half Pan Set
BS08	W/C Half Pan Set
BS080	W/C Oval Pan Set

Gouache Sets (Caran D'Ache)
Highly concentrated light-resistant watercolors for opaque painting. The No. 10308 Set contains 7 pans of assorted colors and one tube of white. (Qty = Each)

Order No.	Item
CD10308	Pan Set 8 Colors with Brush
CD20313	Tube Set 13 Colors with Brush

Licolette Gouache Sets (Loew-Cornell)
Set 500-12 contains 10 opaque colors, white, and black. Set 500-24 contains 22 opaque colors, white, and black. (Qty = Each)

Order No.	Item
LK500-12	Licolette Gouache Set/12 Colors
LK500-24	Licolette Gouache Set/24 Colors

Radiant Concentrated Sets (Dr. Ph. Martin)
Each set is comprised of 14 colors to cover the entire range as listed in groups, corresponding to the open-stock radiant colors. DRA Set is all "A" colors. DRB Set is all "B" colors. DRC Set is all "C" colors. DRDST is all "D" colors. 1/2 oz. bottle size. (Qty = Each)

Order No.	Item
DRA	Radiant CNC Set/14 All A
DRB	Radiant CNC Set/14 All B
DRC	Radiant CNC Set/14 All C
DRDST	Radiant CNC Set/14 All D

The Bijou No. 3 (Winsor & Newton)
The ideal companion for the traveling watercolorist. Made of strong die-cast metal finished in black enamel and packed in an attractive carrying case. Contains 18 semi-moist pans of Artists' Water Color and a sable brush in a metal holder with protective cap. Size 2" x 5". (Qty = Each)

Order No.	Item
WNBXW12	No. 3 Bijou

The Bijou No. 2 (Winsor & Newton)
Same as Bijou No. 3, but contains 12 colors. Size 2" x 3-1/4". (Qty = Each)

Order No.	Item
WNBXW11	No. 2 Bijou

FIGURE 8-2 Text created with Microsoft Word (1 of 2)

Sketchers Pocket Box (Winsor & Newton)
A compact white plastic box containing 12 square pans of transparent watercolor and a pocket sable
brush with a protective cap. Size 4" x 2" x 1/2". (Qty = Each)
Order No.   Item
  WNBXW13   W/C Pocket Box

Sketchers Box #24 (Winsor & Newton)
A black plastic box containing 24 square pans of economical watercolor and a Series 33 sable brush.
Refill pans not available. Size 8-1/2" x 4-1/2" x 1/4". (Qty = Each)
Order No.   Item
WNBXW24   W/C Set - 24 Colors

London Water Color Set #3A (Winsor & Newton)
Contains 10 London Water Colors in 7.5 ml. tubes. Includes a watercolor brush, a six well/six slant tile
plastic palette, color chart and painting techniques leaflet. (Qty = Each)
Order No.   Item
WNBXLW03A   London W/C Set #3A

London Water Color Set #4 (Winsor & Newton)
Contains 12 London Water colors in 7.5 ml. tubes in an aluminum box with white enameled palette/lid,
two water color brushes, a color chart and a painting techniques leaflet. (Qty = Each)
Order No.   Item
WNBXLW04   London W/C Set #4

Page Water Color Sets (Winsor & Newton)
This range represents excellent value in inexpensive water color sets for young artists. Colorfully
designed boxes make these sets ideal as gifts. Each set comes with a brush and all are shrink-wrapped for
protection except #01 (Qty = Each)
Order No.   Item
WNBXP01   6 Pan Water Color Set
WNBXP05   12 Pan Water Color Set
WNBXP10   20 Pan Water Color Set
WNBXP15   30 Pan Water Color Set
WNBXP20   40 Pan Water Color Set
WNBXP25   50 Pan Water Color Set
WNBXP30   60 Pan Water Color Set
WNBXP35   78 Pan Water Color Set

FIGURE 8-2 Text created with Microsoft Word (2 of 2)

Using Graphics Within the Catalog

You have several options for using graphics within Page-
Maker. You can create a graphic using one of the painting
or drawing programs, such as Adobe Illustrator, Aldus
FreeHand, DeskPaint, and SuperPaint. You can create a
graphic file by scanning a photo or line drawing with a
scanner. Or you can have a commercial printer photo-
graphically place and size the graphic in the catalog before
it is printed.

MacPherson chose to scan the graphics for their catalog,
as is done in this chapter. If you have a scanner, the
graphics are reproduced in Appendix D and can be removed from the book for use here. If you don't have a
scanner and wish to learn to place a graphic, draw a quick
substitute or use clip art.

Creating the Title Page Name with Aldus FreeHand

The title page contains a stylized company name as shown
in Figure 8-3. You'll produce this in Aldus FreeHand and
then load it in PageMaker.

Load Aldus FreeHand or the graphics program you
want to use. Set the typeface to Times bold italic. The first
letter of the name is a different type size than the rest of
the letters. The first letter should be set to 150 points and
the remaining letters to 96 points. To begin, enter the
name **MacPherson** in black type.

Then draw nine 12-point lines with 10 points of space
between them, stepped from left to right in 20-point increments. FreeHand provides a very easy way to do this. Draw
one 12-point line. Then use the "Duplicate" option of the

Edit menu or press COMMAND+D eight times. "Duplicate" is different from "Copy" in that "Duplicate" will slightly off-set the copy it makes. The "Duplicate" option immediately places the copies on the drawing instead of on the Clip-board. The offset that "Duplicate" creates is exactly what you want.

After completing the lines, select the name, reverse it or color it white, and bring it to the top or front layer. In FreeHand this is done by selecting "Character Fill. . ." from the "Effect" option of the Type menu and choosing "White" from the Color option box. Then select "Bring to front" from the "Arrange" option of the Element menu.

Finally, arrange the name in the center of the lines as shown in Figure 8-3. When your drawing looks like Figure 8-3, save it in the Publications folder with the filename

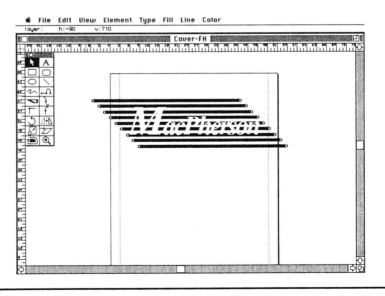

FIGURE 8-3 Company name graphic created in Aldus FreeHand

Cover-FH and convert the file to the EPS (Encapsulated PostScript) format by using the "Export" option from the File menu and placing it in the Publications folder with the name Cover.eps. You can also print the graphic if you wish.

Next you will scan the catalog art to get the product pictures and the company logo.

SCANNING THE CATALOG ART   If you have a scanner and want to produce the catalog with scanned graphics, turn on your scanner and load its driver software.

From your scanner software, set your resolution to "300x300," brightness and contrast to "Normal" or "Automatic," mode to "Drawing," and file type to "TIFF." These options and settings differ among scanners and their respective types of driver software. Set yours as close to these as possible. If you are using a flatbed scanner instead of hand-held scanner, define the smallest area of the page possible to scan just the object you want. This will keep your scanned files as small as possible.

There are three pieces of art to be scanned: one for page 2 of the catalog as shown in Figure 8-4, another for page 3, and the MacPherson logo. The latter two are shown in Figure 8-5. All three pieces of art are contained in Appendix D. Remove Appendix D from the book now and scan each piece. Save the scanned images in the Publications folder with the names Page2.tif, Page3.tif, and Logo.tif.

Now that the text and graphics for the catalog have been created, you can begin to build the catalog. The first thing you'll do is set defaults within PageMaker.

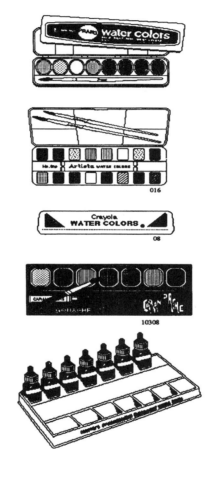

FIGURE 8-4   Art for page 2 of the catalog

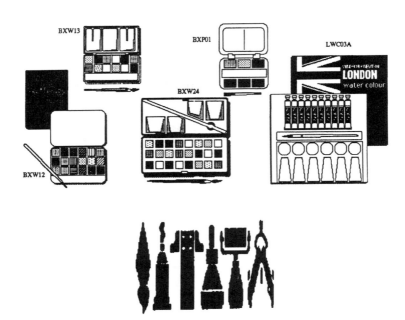

FIGURE 8-5   Art for page 3 and the logo for the catalog

SETTING DEFAULTS

As you have done in other chapters, your first task within PageMaker will be to set the defaults. For the catalog, you will change both startup defaults (those that remain from one PageMaker session to another) and publication defaults (those that are unique to a publication).

Startup Defaults

The startup defaults you will set are the preferences for measurement. This is done to assure that the page setup (a publication default) is correctly initiated.

If you are using PageMaker, close any active publication so that you have no publications open for the next few steps. If PageMaker is not active, load it now.

SETTING PREFERENCES For the catalog, you'll use decimal inches for units of measurement. Verify that the scale is set for those units in this way:

1. Choose "Preferences. . ." from the Edit menu.

2. Drag on the option boxes for both the "Measurement system" and "Vertical ruler" to select "Inches decimal" and then click on "OK."

With the startup defaults set, you can now establish the publication defaults.

Publication Defaults

The publication defaults consist of the page setup, the line and type specifications, and the selection of several other options you will want – all routine by now.

PAGE SETUP For the first time in this book, you will use the standard page setup defaults, including the standard margins, with which PageMaker is shipped. Therefore, unless you have changed the startup defaults in the page setup (by setting the page setup without a publication open), the only default you will need to change is the number of pages. Do this and check the other page settings with the following instructions:

1. Choose "New. . ." from the File menu.

2. Verify that "Letter" Size, "Tall" Orientation, "Double-sided" and "Facing pages" are all checked.

3. Type **3** in the "# of pages" option.

4. Verify that the following margins are set: "1" for "Inside," and "0.75" for "Outside," "Top," and "Bottom," as shown in Figure 8-6.

5. Press RETURN to complete the dialog box.

SETTING THE LINES AND SHADES DEFAULTS All the lines within the catalog are half a point in width. The only use of shading is the Solid fill in the box at the top of the page. Set these as defaults in this way:

1. Choose ".5 pt" from the Line option of the Element menu.

2. Choose "Solid" from the Fill option of the Element menu.

ESTABLISHING TYPE SPECIFICATIONS The text in the catalog is 10-point Times. Even though Microsoft Word will determine the font, set the default to 10-point Times so

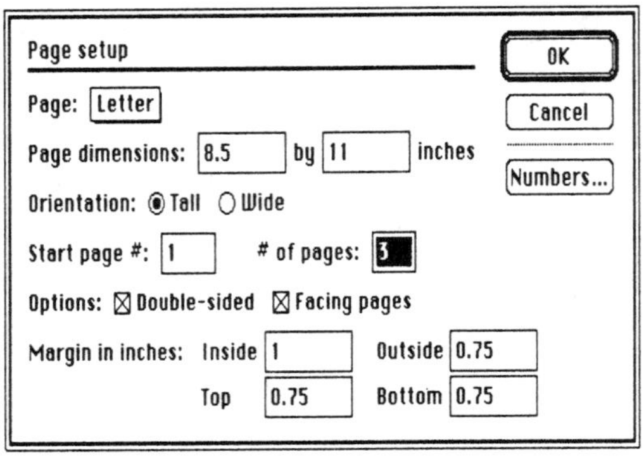

FIGURE 8-6 Page setup settings for the catalog

that any last-minute editing you do will be correct. Set the type specifications accordingly.

1. Press COMMAND+T for the Type specifications dialog box.

2. Type **10** and verify that "Times," "Auto" leading and "Normal" Style, Position, and Case are all set.

3. Click on "OK" to complete the dialog box.

All of the text in the body of the catalog will be left-aligned, so set that now.

4. Choose "Align left" from the "Alignment" option of the Type menu.

This completes setting the type defaults.

SETTING OTHER OPTIONS The other options to choose or verify are using "Rulers," "Guides," "Snap to rulers," and "Snap to guides," and *not* using the "Toolbox." Follow these steps to make those choices.

1. Verify that "Rulers," "Guides," "Snap to rulers," and "Snap to guides" are checked on the Options menu. If any are not, choose them.

2. If you have an extended keyboard and "Toolbox" is checked on the Windows menu, click on it to turn it off.

Horizontal and vertical rulers should be on the screen, and the Toolbox should not.

IMPORTANT TECHNIQUES USED IN THIS CHAPTER

Several techniques for working with text and graphics are repeatedly used in this chapter. Rather than repeating the explanation each time, we will describe the techniques now.

Switching Between "Actual size" and "Fit in window"

To accurately place the text, graphics, and lines, you'll have to switch between "Actual size" and "Fit in window" many times. Quickly switching between these two views of a page is a very efficient way to place and then verify your work. To do this, press and hold COMMAND+OPTION while clicking the mouse button.

The command you use to switch between "Fit in window" and "Actual size" views is presented, in abbreviated form, as COMMAND+OPTION+click in the remainder of this chapter.

If you are in "Fit in window" and want the "Actual size" view, position your pointer on what you want to appear in the middle of the screen and COMMAND+OPTION+click. To help you place the pointer, you will be given the horizontal and vertical ruler coordinates, in this format: 6H/2.5V; this should be read "6 inches on the horizontal ruler and 2.5 inches on the vertical ruler." When you are in "Actual size" and want to move to the "Fit in window" view, simply

COMMAND+OPTION+click or press COMMAND+W. To simplify this, when you are to go from "Actual size" to "Fit in window" in this chapter, you will be told to "Return to the 'Fit in window' view."

The Toolbox

The Toolbox obscures a corner of your work area when you are using facing pages. For this reason, you've turned it off. To select the necessary tools, if you have an extended keyboard, you'll use shortcut keys, such as SHIFT+F1 for the pointer. You'll be reminded of which keys to use when you need them—although you'll soon memorize them.

Selecting Text and Graphics

Every time you want to work on your text or graphics within PageMaker, you must first select the text or graphics—that is, highlight it or put a selection box around it. Depending on what you want to do, you first choose the correct tool, then select the text or graphics, and finally carry out the task.

SELECTING TEXT You can select text with either the text tool or the pointer tool, depending on what you want to do. If you want to move a block of text from one spot on the page to another, you would use the pointer. However, if you want to change the type specifications for text, you would highlight it with the text tool.

If you're selecting text with the pointer tool, simply place the pointer on the text and click the mouse button. The text will be enclosed in a selection box. If you're selecting text with the text tool, you must first drag over the text with the I-beam. It will be highlighted. Then you specify what you want done with the text.

SELECTING LINES OR GRAPHICS   If you have just created a line or box, it may still be selected if you have not deselected it by clicking the mouse button on something else. You can tell if it is selected by the tiny boxes that appear on the item. If the item has been deselected, then you can select a graphic or line again with the pointer tool.

Place the tip of the pointer on the line or graphic and click the mouse button. The item selected will be displayed with tiny boxes around or on the ends of it.

To select a line or graphic, you may have to work around other items that get in the way. A column or margin guide, for instance, may get selected instead of the line you want. To select a line that lies over or near it, you may have to move the line or guide to get at the one you want. Choosing "Lock guides" from the Options menu allows you to select a line that is on a ruler guide. Or you can use the "Send to back" feature when other items are preventing you from selecting something.

DESELECTING SELECTED TEXT OR GRAPHICS   To deselect anything, simply click your pointer on something else—either on other text or graphics that you want to select, or elsewhere on the pasteboard.

Moving and Copying Text or Graphics

Moving text or graphics is a three-step process: (1) select the item with the pointer tool; (2) press and hold the mouse button until the pointer becomes a four-headed arrow; and (3) drag the item wherever you want it on the screen.

Copying text or graphics requires three more steps: (1) select the text or graphics as in step 1 in the previous list; (2) copy it by pressing COMMAND+C or F3; (3) find the area or page where you want the item inserted; (4) press COMMAND+V or F4 to get the copy back on the publication (the item will be inserted on the center of the screen); (5) press and hold the mouse button until the pointer becomes a four-headed arrow; and (6) drag the item wherever you want it on the screen.

If you want multiple copies, press COMMAND+V or F4 again (assuming that you have not copied or deleted anything else in the meantime) because the copy remains on the Clipboard until you delete or copy something else.

Use the text tool to copy text and then insert it into another text block. In this case you click the insertion point to indicate where the text is to be placed before pressing COMMAND+V or F4.

CONSTRUCTING THE MASTER PAGES

The master pages, an example of which is shown in Figure 8-7, contain five design elements common to both facing pages: (1) a 1/4-inch-wide box at the top of each page filled with "Solid" shading; (2) the company name just above the box on the inside of the page; (3) a logo also just above the box on the outside of the page; (4) a 1/2-point line across the bottom margin; and (5) a page number in the lower outside corner of each page. There is also a vertical 1/2-point line of varying length down the middle of each page

MacPherson

RM

FIGURE 8-7 Master page layout with common design elements

and a 1/2-point line across the right-hand page. You'll first produce the common elements and then add the unique lines.

Producing the Common Master Page Elements

You will produce each of the common master page elements by following the instructions in the next four sections.

BUILDING THE BOXES The boxes at the top of each page, along with the logo and company name, tie the catalog together. Build the boxes with these instructions:

1. Click on one of the master page icons (L or R) to bring them on the screen.

The master pages are displayed as two facing pages on the screen. You'll notice on the horizontal ruler that the zero point is between the two pages. From that point the ruler's scales go in both directions, so there are two of each scale mark. You will be told which ruler mark to use — the left or the right — by the word in front of the coordinates, for example, "right 5H/3V," unless it is obvious.

2. Drag a horizontal ruler guide down to 1V.

3. Press SHIFT+F5 to select the square-corner tool.

4. Place the crossbar at left 7.75H/.75V (the intersection of top and left margins) and drag it to left 1H/1V (the intersection of right margin and the new horizontal ruler guide).

5. Place the crossbar at right 1H/.75V and drag it to right 7.75H/1V.

Two filled boxes should appear, as shown in Figure 8-8.

ENTERING THE NAME The second common element on the master pages is the company name on the inside of each page, immediately above the box that you just drew. You will enter the name on the left page, position it cor-

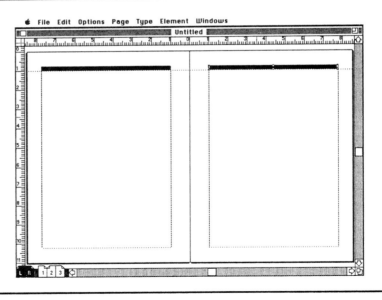

FIGURE 8-8 Two shaded boxes at the top of the master pages

rectly on the page, copy it to the Clipboard, and then paste it on the right page. The instructions for this are as follows:

1. Place the pointer at left 1H/1V and COMMAND+ OPTION+click for "Actual size."

2. With the pointer tool (SHIFT+F1), drag the horizontal ruler guide at 1V up to .7V.

3. Press SHIFT+F4 to select the text tool.

4. Click the mouse button at left 3H/.6V.

5. Press COMMAND+T for the Type specifications dialog box.

6. Type **18** points in the Size text box and click on the "Bold" Type style. Click on "OK."

7. Type **MacPherson**.

8. Press SHIFT+F1 to select the pointer.

9. Click on the company name and drag it so that it sits on the horizontal ruler guide at .7V and the right end of the selection box is against the right margin at left 1H, as shown in Figure 8-9. (You may need to be in "Fit in window" view to do this.)

10. Press COMMAND+C or F3 to copy the name to the Clipboard.

11. Press COMMAND+V or F4 to paste the name back on the publication.

12. Drag the second copy over to the right page so that it sits on the line at .7V and is aligned against the left margin at right 1H, as shown in Figure 8-10.

13. Press SHIFT+F4 to select the text tool.

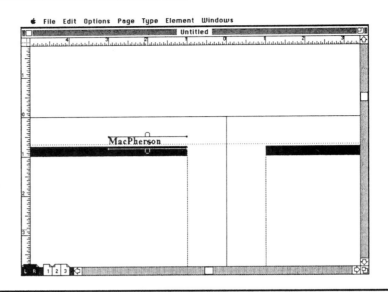

FIGURE 8-9 The company name on the left master page

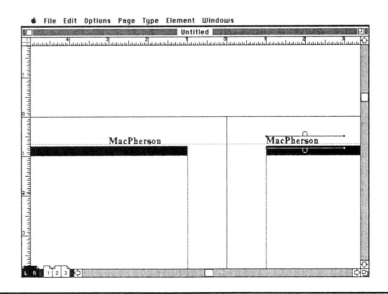

FIGURE 8-10 The company name on both master pages

14. Drag across the company name on the left page to highlight the name.

15. Press COMMAND+SHIFT+R to right-align the name.

When both company names are properly aligned, your screen should look like that shown in Figure 8-11.

PLACING THE LOGO   You will place the company logo just above the box on the outside of the page, horizontally aligned with the company name. Figure 8-12 shows how it will look when properly placed. Do this with the following instructions:

1. Press SHIFT+F1 to select the pointer.

2. Return to the "Fit in window" view.

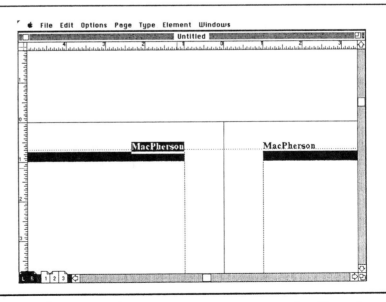

═══ **FIGURE 8-11**   The company name properly aligned on both master pages

3. Place the pointer at left 7.5H and 1V and COMMAND+ OPTION+click for "Actual size."

4. Drag a vertical ruler guide over to left 7.75H (on the left margin).

5. Press COMMAND+D to open the Place dialog box.

6. Scroll the list box until Logo.tif appears. Double-click on it, and the TIFF icon will appear.

7. Place the icon on the left master page at left 7.75H/.3V and drag it to left 7H/.7V.

8. Adjust the logo until it is placed as shown in Figure 8-12.

9. Press COMMAND+C or F3 to copy the logo to the Clipboard.

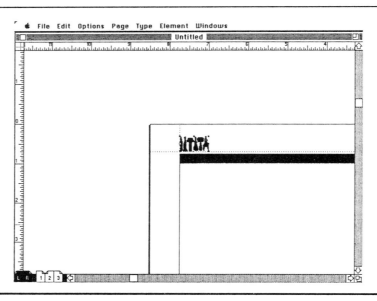

FIGURE 8-12   The logo in final position on the left master page

10. Return to the "Fit in window" view.

11. Press COMMAND+V or F4 to paste the logo back on the publication.

12. Drag the second copy over to the upper right corner of the right page.

13. Place the pointer at right 7.5H/1V and COMMAND+OPTION+click for "Actual size."

14. Drag a vertical ruler guide over to right 7.75H (the right margin).

15. Drag the logo on the right page so that it sits on the line at .7V and is aligned against the right margin at right 7.75H, as shown in Figure 8-13.

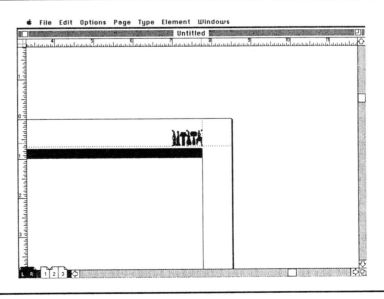

FIGURE 8-13 The logo aligned on the right master page

ADDING THE PAGE NUMBER PageMaker will automatically insert the correct page number on the regular pages if you place a COMMAND+OPTION+P code on the master pages where you want a page number to appear. Do that with the following instructions:

1. Return to the "Fit in window" view.

2. Place the pointer at left 7H/10V and COMMAND+OPTION+click for "Actual size."

3. Press SHIFT+F4 to select the text tool.

4. Click the text tool at left 7.7H/10.4V.

5. Press COMMAND+T for the Type specifications dialog box, type **12** for the Size click "Bold" for the Type style, and click on "OK."

6. Press COMMAND+OPTION+P to place the page number on the left master page, and LM (Left Master) will appear.

7. Press SHIFT+F1 to select the pointer.

8. Click on the page number and drag it so that the top is at 10.3V and against the left margin at left 7.75H, as shown in Figure 8-14.

9. Press COMMAND+C or F3 to copy the page number to the Clipboard.

10. Return to the "Fit in window" view.

11. Press COMMAND+V or F4 to paste a copy of the page number on the page.

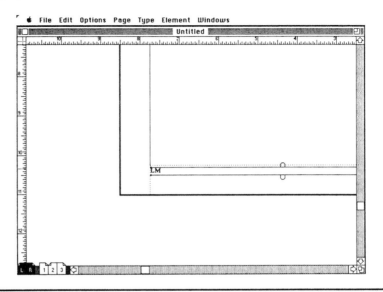

FIGURE 8-14 The page number on the lower left
master page

12. Drag the second page number to the right master page
    below the lower margin, as shown in Figure 8-15.

13. Press SHIFT+F4 to select the text tool.

14. Drag across the page number on the right page to
    highlight it.

15. Press COMMAND+SHIFT+R to right-align the page number
    on the right page.

16. Place the I-beam at right 7H/10V and COMMAND+
    OPTION+click for "Actual size."

17. Press SHIFT+F1 to select the pointer.

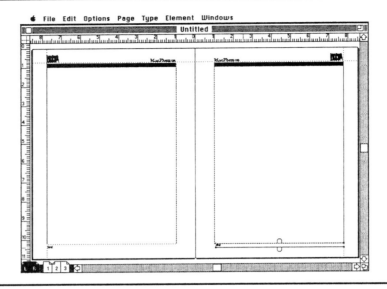

FIGURE 8-15 The page number on the right page as it is originally placed

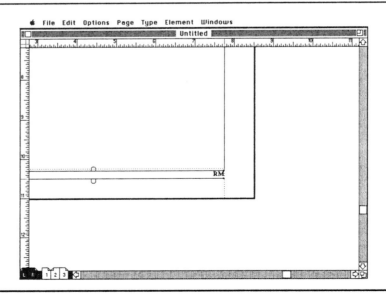

FIGURE 8-16 The page number on the lower right master page in final position

18. Click on the page number and align it so that the top is at 10.3V and the right side is against the right margin at right 7.75H, as shown in Figure 8-16.

19. Return to the "Fit in Window" view.

Drawing the Lines

You will add two lines to the left page and three to the right page. This provides two different basic layouts and the opportunity to vary the layout with a little customization. This layout is based on a two-column page. On the left page, you have two vertical columns with a line separating them. On the right page, the top is left open across both columns so that a graphic can span the page. The lower part of the page reverts to the two-column layout. The right page should therefore include a horizontal line in the middle and a vertical line down the lower part. Both pages have a line across the bottom margin. When you have completed the final line, your master pages should look like those shown in Figure 8-17.

The instructions for drawing these lines are as follows:

1. Choose "Column guides. . ." from the Options menu.

2. Type **2** for the number of columns, press TAB, type **.25** for the space between columns, and press RETURN.

3. Press SHIFT+F3 to select the perpendicular-line tool.

4. Press COMMAND+U to turn the "Snap to guides" off.

5. Draw a vertical line from left 4.4H/1V down to 10.25V.

6. Drag a horizontal ruler guide down to 4.5V.

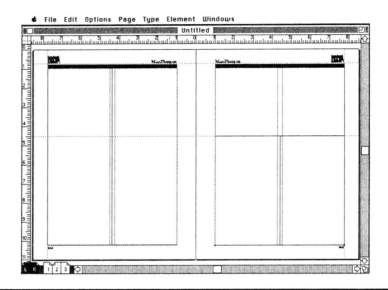

FIGURE 8-17 The completed master pages

7. Draw a vertical line from right 4.4H/4.5V down to 10.25V.

8. Press COMMAND+U to turn the "Snap to guides" back on.

9. Draw a horizontal line from right 1H/4.5V over to right 7.75H.

10. Draw a horizontal line from left 7.75H/10.25V over to left 1H.

11. Draw a horizontal line from right 1H/10.25V over to right 7.75H.

12. Press COMMAND+S to open the Save dialog box.

13. Drag the Open folder list box to highlight the Publications folder, type **catalog** for the filename, and press RETURN to complete saving the file.

This would be a good time for a break. If you leave PageMaker, remember to check the defaults on reentering.

BUILDING THE TITLE PAGE

The title page is composed of three parts: the graphic title created with Aldus FreeHand, the company logo captured with the scanner, and the company address entered directly as text, as shown in Figure 8-18. Because most of the work is in preparing the graphics, assembling the title page is simple and quick.

Bringing in the Graphic from Aldus FreeHand

First, bring in the company name graphic from Aldus Free-Hand and size it as shown in Figure 8-19.

Follow these instructions to place the company name:

1. Click the page 1 icon.

2. Choose "Display master items" from the Page menu to turn the options off.

3. Choose "Column guides. . ." from the Options menu, specify **1** column, and press RETURN to get rid of the column guides.

4. With the pointer tool (SHIFT+F1), move the horizontal ruler guide from 4.5V to 4.0V.

5. Press COMMAND+D to open the Place dialog box.

Wholesale Art Supplies
Graphic Arts, Drafting, and Engineering
1327 Park Avenue
Emeryville, CA 94608
(415) 428-9011

FIGURE 8-18 The final printout of the title page

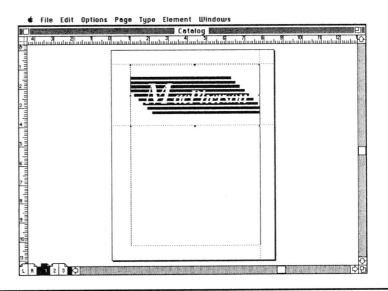

FIGURE 8-19   The company name for the title page

6. When the Place dialog box is displayed, choose the filename Cover.eps. You may have to use the horizontal scroll bar to find it.

7. Place the icon in the upper left corner at right 1H/.75V and drag it to right 7.75H/4.0V.

Your screen should now look like the one shown in Figure 8-19.

Placing the Company Logo

Next, place the company logo and then stretch it, just as you did with the company name.

1. Drag two horizontal ruler guides to 4.7V and 6.5V.

2. Drag two vertical ruler guides to 3H and 5.75H.

3. Press COMMAND+D to open the Place dialog box.

4. When the Place dialog box is displayed, click on the filename Logo.tif. You may have to use the horizontal scroll bar to find it.

5. Place the icon at 3H/4.7V and drag the selection box to 5.5H/6.5V.

6. With the pointer tool (SHIFT+F1), adjust the logo's position on the page until it looks like Figure 8-20.

Next, you'll type in the address.

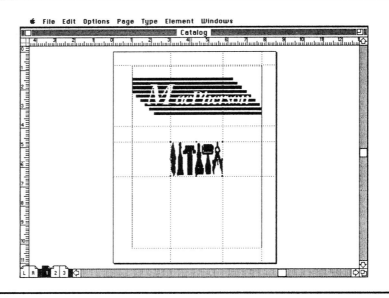

FIGURE 8-20   The title page with logo placed

Entering the Company Address

The last step in creating the title page is to enter the company address. You'll use the text tool and type in several lines in varying type sizes.

Follow these instructions to enter the address:

1. Place your pointer at 4H/8.5V and COMMAND+OPTION+ click for an "Actual size" view.

2. Select the text tool (SHIFT+F4) and click the mouse button at 4H/8.5V.

3. Press COMMAND+T for the Type specifications dialog box, and type **14** points. Click on "OK."

4. Press COMMAND+SHIFT+C to center the address.

5. Type **Wholesale Art Supplies** and press RETURN.

6. Press COMMAND+OPTION+SHIFT + < for the next smaller type size.

7. Type **Graphic Arts, Drafting, and Engineering** and press RETURN.

8. Press COMMAND+OPTION+SHIFT + < for the next smaller type size.

9. Type **1327 Park Avenue** and press RETURN.

10. Type **Emeryville, CA 94608** and press RETURN.

11. Type **(415) 428-9011** and press RETURN.

Your screen will look like that shown in Figure 8-21.

12. Return to the "Fit in window" view.

13. Press COMMAND+S to save the catalog.

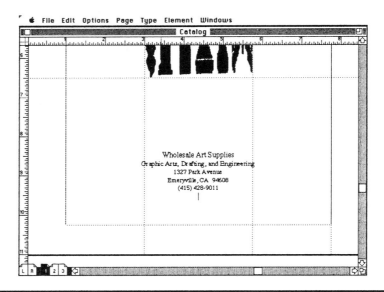

Wholesale Art Supplies
Graphic Arts, Drafting, and Engineering
1327 Park Avenue
Emeryville, CA 94608
(415) 428-9011

FIGURE 8-21 The screen image with the address

You have now completed the title page. The final printed version of it can be seen in Figure 8-18. Now you will handle the detail catalog pages.

CONSTRUCTING THE DETAIL CATALOG PAGES

A catalog would normally have many detail pages. To see how to build a catalog, you will build two of the detail pages. These detail pages, pages 2 and 3 of your publication, will mirror the master pages. That is, all the elements of the master pages will remain unchanged.

Assembling Page 2

You will place three items on page 2, as shown in Figure 8-22: the art for the products being described, the text of the description, and the title of the current section of the catalog. The following paragraphs describe how each item is built.

PLACING THE ART   Earlier you scanned the art for page 2 and then saved it in a file called Page2.tif. Your task here is to place and size that art so that it fits the layout for page 2. The instructions to do that are as follows:

1. Press SHIFT+F1 to select the pointer.

2. Click on the page 2 icon.

3. From the Options menu, verify that "Snap to guides" is on.

4. Press COMMAND+D to open the Place dialog box.

5. Scroll the list box until Page2.tif appears. Double-click on Page2.tif, and the TIFF icon will appear.

6. Place the TIFF icon on page 2 at left 7.75H (left margin)/1.5V and drag it to left 4.5H (right column guide)/9.5V.

   Your screen should look like that shown in Figure 8-23.

7. Place the pointer at left 6.H/2.5V and COMMAND+ OPTION+click for "Actual size."

8. Look at the placement of the art and compare it to Figure 8-24. Adjust it as necessary by using the pointer tool to drag the graphic up or down on the page.

MacPherson

Watercolor Paint Sets

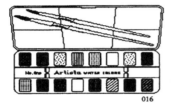

016

08

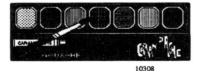

10308

Prang Watercolor Sets (American Crayon)
Oval-8 Set contains 8 oval semi-moist half pan colors
with No. 7 brush. No. 16 Set contains 16 semi-moist half
pan colors, a No. 1 and 4 brush. Oval 16 Set contains the
same colors and brushes as No. 16 Set, except with oval
half pans. No. 8 Set contains 8 semi-moist half pan colors
with No. 7 brush. (Qty = Each)

Order No.	Item
AC16	Prang Watercolor Set
AC16-OVL	Prang Watercolor Set
AC8	Prang Watercolor Set
AC8-OVL	Prang Watercolor Set

Artista Watercolor Sets (Binney & Smith)
No. 080 set contains 8 oval half pans and a No. 7 brush.
No. 08 contains 8 half pans and a No. 7 brush. No. 016
contains 16 half pans and a No. 7 brush. (Qty = Each)

Order No.	Item
BS016	W/C Half Pan Set
BS08	W/C Half Pan Set
BS080	W/C Oval Pan Set

Gouache Sets (Caran D'Ache)
Highly concentrated light-resistant watercolors for opaque
painting. The No. 10308 Set contains 7 pans of assorted
colors and one tube of white. (Qty = Each)

Order No.	Item
CD10308	Pan Set 8 Colors with Brush
CD20313	Tube Set 13 Colors with Brush

Licolette Gouache Sets (Loew-Cornell)
Set 500-12 contains 10 opaque colors, white, and black.
Set 500-24 contains 22 opaque colors, white, and black.
(Qty = Each)

Order No.	Item
LK500-12	Licolette Gouache Set/12 Colors
LK500-24	Licolette Gouache Set/24 Colors

Radiant Concentrated Sets (Dr. Ph. Martin)
Each set is comprised of 14 colors to cover the entire
range as listed in groups, corresponding to the open-stock
radiant colors. DRA Set is all "A" colors. DRB Set is all
"B" colors. DRC Set is all "C" colors. DRDST is all "D"
colors. 1/2 oz. bottle size. (Qty = Each)

Order No.	Item
DRA	Radiant CNC Set/14 All A
DRB	Radiant CNC Set/14 All B
DRC	Radiant CNC Set/14 All C
DRDST	Radiant CNC Set/14 All D

2

≡≡≡ **FIGURE 8-22** The final page 2 printout

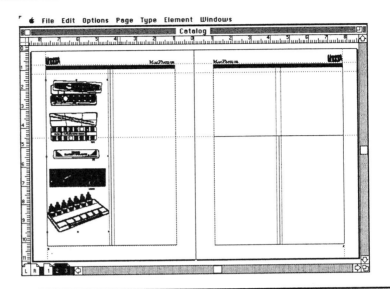

FIGURE 8-23 Art in place on page 2

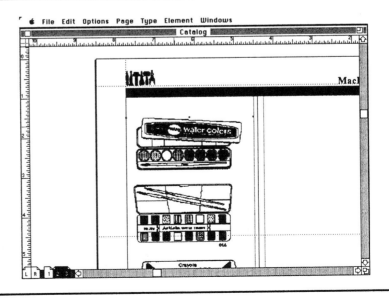

FIGURE 8-24 Detail of art on page 2

ADDING THE TEXT The text for both page 2 and page 3 was created using Microsoft Word and was saved in a file named Catalog-Word. You will place the first part of that file here and then place the balance on page 3. The instructions to place the text on page 2 are as follows:

1. Return to the "Fit in window" view.

2. Drag a horizontal ruler guide down to 1.2V.

3. Press COMMAND+D to open the Place dialog box.

4. Double-click on Catalog-Word, and the text icon will appear.

5. Place the text icon on page 2 at left 4.25H/1.2V and click the mouse button.

6. Place the pointer at left 4.4H/2V and click the mouse button for "Actual size."

7. If the upper part of your text is not aligned as shown in Figure 8-25, adjust it as necessary by dragging it with the pointer.

8. Use the vertical scroll bar to position the screen so that you can see the lower part of the text on page 2. Your screen should look like that shown in Figure 8-26.

9. If the lower part of your text is not aligned as shown in Figure 8-25, adjust it as necessary. Drag the handle down so that the fourth item under "Order No." (DRDST) shows on the screen.

INSERTING THE TITLE Your final task on page 2 is to add the section name in the box at the top of the page. You will type the name in the box after setting the font to

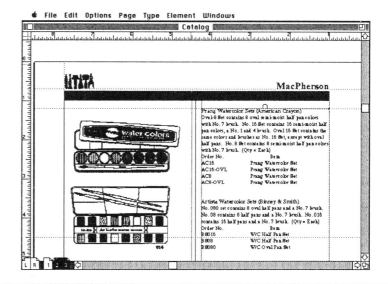

═══ **FIGURE 8-25** The upper part of text on page 2

═══ **FIGURE 8-25** The upper part of text on page 2

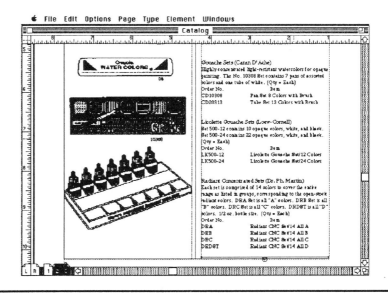

═══ **FIGURE 8-26** The lower part of text on page 2

bold, 12-point Times reverse type, and then center it in all four directions. The instructions for this are as follows:

1. Return to the "Fit in window" view.

2. Place the pointer at left 4.4H/2V and COMMAND+ OPTION+click for "Actual size."

3. Press SHIFT+F4 to select the text tool.

4. Click the text tool at left 7H/.9V.

5. Press COMMAND+T to open the Type specifications dialog box.

6. Type **12** points in the Size list box, and click on "Bold" for the Type style, "Reverse" to reverse the color, and "OK."

7. Press COMMAND+SHIFT+C to center the section name.

The insertion point will move to the center of the left column. You will adjust this shortly.

8. Type **Watercolor Paint Sets**.

9. Press SHIFT+F1 to select the pointer.

10. Click on the section name to form the selection box around it.

11. Drag one of the tiny boxes on the right end of the selection box to the right margin at left 1H.

12. If necessary, drag one of the tiny boxes on the left end of the selection box to the left margin at left 7.75H.

13. With the pointer, center the section name vertically in the box as shown in Figure 8-27.

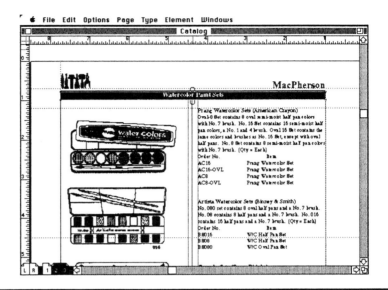

FIGURE 8-27   The section name centered in the box on page 2

14. Press COMMAND+C or F3 to copy the section name for use on page 3.

15. Press COMMAND+S to save the catalog.

You have now completed page 2. When it is printed, it will look like Figure 8-22.

Assembling Page 3

Page 3 is shown in Figure 8-28. The steps to assemble it are very similar to those for page 2 except that you will do them in a different order. Because the section name is on the Clipboard, you will place it first before it gets written

MacPherson

Watercolor Paint Sets

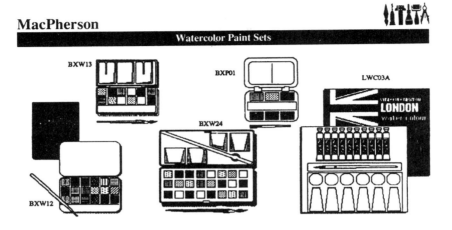

The Bijou No. 3 (Winsor & Newton)
The ideal companion for the traveling watercolorist.
Made of strong die-cast metal finished in black enamel
and packed in an attractive carrying case. Contains 18
semi-moist pans of Artists' Water Color and a sable brush
in a metal holder with protective cap. Size 2" x 5". (Qty
= Each)

Order No.	Item
WNBXW12	No. 3 Bijou

The Bijou No. 2 (Winsor & Newton)
Same as Bijou No. 3, but contains 12 colors. Size 2" x 3-
1/4". (Qty = Each)

Order No.	Item
WNBXW11	No. 2 Bijou

Sketchers Pocket Box (Winsor & Newton)
A compact white plastic box containing 12 square pans of
transparent watercolor and a pocket sable brush with a
protective cap. Size 4" x 2" x 1/2". (Qty = Each)

Order No.	Item
WNBXW13	W/C Pocket Box

Sketchers Box #24 (Winsor & Newton)
A black plastic box containing 24 square pans of economical watercolor and a Series 33 sable brush. Refill
pans not available. Size 8-1/2" x 4-1/2" x 1/4". (Qty =
Each)

Order No.	Item
WNBXW24	W/C Set - 24 Colors

London Water Color Set #3A (Winsor & Newton)
Contains 10 London Water Colors in 7.5 ml. tubes.
Includes a watercolor brush, a six well/six slant tile plastic
palette, color chart and painting techniques leaflet. (Qty =
Each)

Order No.	Item
WNBXLW03A	London W/C Set #3A

London Water Color Set #4 (Winsor & Newton)
Contains 12 London Water colors in 7.5 ml. tubes in an
aluminum box with white enameled palette/lid, two water
color brushes, a color chart and a painting techniques
leaflet. (Qty = Each)

Order No.	Item
WNBXLW04	London W/C Set #4

Page Water Color Sets (Winsor & Newton)
This range represents excellent value in inexpensive water
color sets for young artists. Colorfully designed boxes
make these sets ideal as gifts. Each set comes with a
brush and all are shrink-wrapped for protection except
#01 (Qty = Each)

Order No.	Item
WNBXP01	6 Pan Water Color Set
WNBXP05	12 Pan Water Color Set
WNBXP10	20 Pan Water Color Set
WNBXP15	30 Pan Water Color Set
WNBXP20	40 Pan Water Color Set
WNBXP25	50 Pan Water Color Set
WNBXP30	60 Pan Water Color Set
WNBXP35	78 Pan Water Color Set

3

FIGURE 8-28   The final printout of page 3

over. Also, having done page 2, you will find page 3 a little easier. Use the following instructions to assemble page 3:

1. Return to the "Fit in window" view.

2. Press COMMAND+V or F4 to paste the section name back onto the page.

3. Drag the section name into the box at the top of the right page.

4. Place the pointer at right 4.4H/1V and COMMAND+ OPTION+click for "Actual size."

5. Position the section name so that it is centered both vertically and horizontally in the box, as shown in Figure 8-29.

6. Return to the "Fit in window" view.

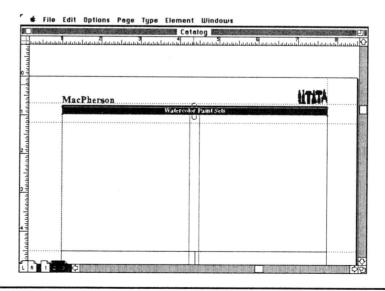

FIGURE 8-29   The section name centered on page 3

7. Click on the text on page 2 and then click on the loop in the handle at the bottom of the page. A text icon will appear.

8. Place the text icon at right 1H/4.2V (above the line at 4.5V) and click the mouse button.

9. Click on the loop in the handle at the bottom of the page.

10. Place the text icon at right 4.5H/4.4V and click the mouse button.

11. Drag a horizontal ruler guide down to 4.7V.

12. Place the pointer at right 4.4H/7V and COMMAND+ OPTION+click for "Actual size."

13. Align both columns of text on page 3 so that the top line of the text is setting on the new horizontal ruler guide at 4.7V, as shown in Figure 8-30.

14. Return to the "Fit in window" view.

15. Drag a horizontal ruler guide down to 4.2V.

16. Press COMMAND+D to open the Place dialog box.

17. Scroll the list box until Page3.tif appears. Double-click on Page3.tif, and the TIFF icon will appear.

18. Place the TIFF icon on page 3 at right 1H/1.2V and drag it to right 7.75H/4.2V.

19. Place the pointer at right 4.4H/2.8V and click the mouse button for "Actual size."

20. Adjust the art on page 3 until it is aligned as shown in Figure 8-31.

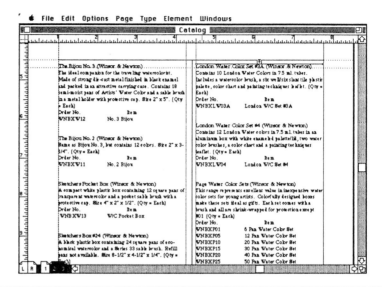

FIGURE 8-30 The text properly aligned on page 3

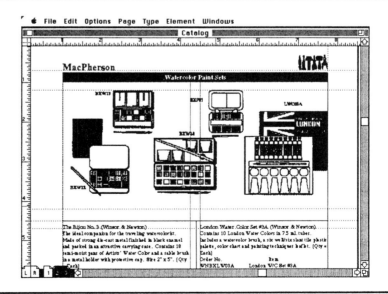

FIGURE 8-31 The art properly aligned on page 3

21. Press COMMAND+S to save the catalog.

22. Press COMMAND+P to open the Print dialog box. Make any necessary changes and click on "Print" to print the catalog.

23. Choose "Quit" from the File menu.

This completes the construction of the sample catalog. Your printed page 3 should look like Figure 8-28.

The sum of all the chapters in this book should leave you with a significantly improved ability to plan, design, and build your own publications with PageMaker. Happy publishing!

appendix A

INSTALLING AND STARTING PAGEMAKER 4

What do You Need?
Copying Your Disks
Using the Aldus Installer
Storing Your Publications
Starting and Leaving PageMaker

With the Installer feature, Aldus has made installing PageMaker 4 almost automatic. You still need to make several decisions and answer a few questions, so it's not quite as easy as clicking the mouse button and walking away. This appendix will provide some assistance on the choices you need to make and the questions that need to be answered. It will also describe the equipment that you need, how to start and leave PageMaker, and where to store the work or publications that you produce with Page-Maker.

WHAT DO YOU NEED?

PageMaker 4 will run on any model of Macintosh computer with the following minimum configuration:

Memory   You must have a minimum of 1 MB to run PageMaker 4. If you want to use the Apple Macintosh MultiFinder, you must have a minimum of 2 MB and must allocate 1.5 MB to Page-Maker.

Disk   You must have a hard disk with 6.5 MB free if you want to install absolutely everything in the program. If you remove the templates, tutorial, Installer, and ReadMe files (none of which affect the operation of Page-Maker) you can get by with slightly less than 5 MB of usable hard disk space.

Display   Virtually every display available for the Macintosh can be used with Page-Maker. If you have an unusual display, check with Aldus, but it is a very good bet that it will work.

Printer   Aldus supplies printer drivers— programs that allow PageMaker to talk to specific printers—for a number of printers. Aldus calls these programs APD (Aldus Printer Description) files. As you install PageMaker, you will see a list of available APD files. If you want to use a printer that is not on the list, check with Aldus to see if there are additional APD files available or if you can substitute another APD for your printer.

System

You must have the Apple Macintosh System, Version 6.03 or later and the Apple Macintosh Finder, Version 6.1 or later. You should only have one System folder, and that folder should have only one System file and one Finder file.

Other Programs

While PageMaker (and especially PageMaker 4 with the story editor) will run without other programs, it is recommended that you also have at least a word processing program and a graphics program with which to feed text and graphics files to PageMaker. Examples are Microsoft Word, MacWrite II, WriteNow, and Word-Perfect for word processing programs; and Aldus Freehand, Adobe Illustrator, DeskPaint, SuperPaint, and MacDraw II for graphics programs.

COPYING YOUR DISKS

To protect yourself in case you accidentally destroy the original floppy disks that contain the PageMaker programs, you need to make a copy or backup of these disks before installing the program. (The Aldus license allows you to make one copy for this express purpose.) There are four PageMaker disks named Disk 1, Disk 2, Disk 3, and Disk 4. Make a copy of each of them and give the copies the same name as the original disks. You will copy the PageMaker programs onto four blank or newly *initialized* (or formatted) disks.

You can copy floppy disks in one of two ways, depending on whether you have two floppy disk drives. Since you must have a hard drive to run PageMaker, instructions will first be given for using one floppy drive and one hard drive. Following that are the somewhat easier instructions for using two floppy drives. Included in the first set of instructions is how to initialize or format a new floppy disk.

Copying with a Hard Drive and a Floppy Drive

To copy a floppy disk with one hard drive and one floppy drive, you must first copy the files *from* the original disk in the floppy drive *to* the hard drive, and then copy those same files to a new floppy disk in the floppy drive. Use these instructions:

1. Turn on your computer either with the switch on the back of the Macintosh Plus or SE or by pressing POWER ON on the Macintosh II family keyboards. You should already have installed the Macintosh System on the hard drive and have run through the tutorial contained in the *Open Me First* portfolio that came with your Macintosh.

2. A window labeled HARD DRIVE should be open, displaying the contents of your hard drive. It should contain at least a System folder and a Utilities folder. If

the window isn't open, double-click (press and release
the mouse button twice in rapid succession while using
the mouse pointer) on the HARD DRIVE icon in the
upper right of your screen.

You should also be in icon view, as shown in Figure A-1,
which displays drawings of file folders with their names
beneath them. If you are not in icon view, drag the View
menu (place the pointer on "View" at the top of your
screen and press and hold the mouse button while pulling
the mouse toward you) until "by Icon" is highlighted, and
then release the mouse button.

Finally, make sure you have enough empty space in the
HARD DRIVE window. If your HARD DRIVE window
does not have space for at least one more folder icon, drag

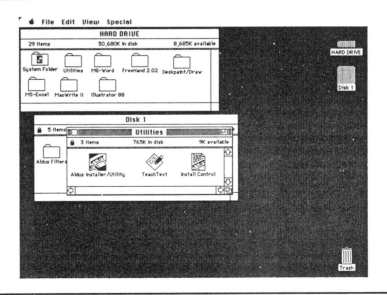

═══ **FIGURE A-1**   The Hard Drive, Disk 1, and Utilities
Windows open

the size box in the lower right corner (press and hold the mouse button while pointing on the size box and move the mouse to the lower right) until you have the needed space.

3. Insert the first PageMaker disk, labeled Disk 1 of 4, into your floppy drive. The Disk 1 and Utilities folders should open, as shown in Figure A-1. If these folders did not open, skip step four.

4. If your Disk 1 and Utilities folders opened, click (press and release the mouse button while using the mouse pointer) on the close box (the small white square in the upper left corner) of the Utilities window and the Disk 1 window. The Disk 1 and the Utilities windows will close, leaving only the HARD DRIVE window open.

5. Drag the Disk 1 icon on the right of the screen (place the mouse pointer on the floppy disk icon and press and hold the mouse button while moving the mouse) to the empty space in the HARD DRIVE window. Be sure not to place the floppy disk icon on top of a folder icon. When you have the Disk 1 icon in place, this warning message will appear:

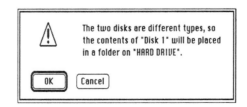

6. The System will begin copying the contents of the floppy drive onto the hard drive. It will take a couple of minutes. When the copying is complete, click on "OK." You

will have a new folder in your HARD DRIVE window labeled Disk 1.

7. Drag the Disk 1 icon on the right (*not* the folder in the HARD DRIVE window) to the Trash icon. This will cause the floppy disk to be ejected from the floppy drive.

8. Insert a new or blank floppy disk into the floppy drive on which to copy what you have just copied.

9. If the floppy disk has never been formatted, you will get this message:

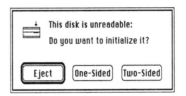

10. This means that the disk needs to be initialized or formatted to prepare it to receive information. If you get this message, click on "Two-Sided." A second message will appear saying that all of the information on the disk will be erased. Click on "Erase."

Next, the System will display the message "Please name this disk." Type in **Disk 1**. The name of the copy must be exactly the same as the original disk. When you have finished typing, click on "OK." You will get the message "Formatting disk. . . ."

11. When the initialization or formatting is complete, (it will take several minutes) double-click on the Disk 1

folder in the HARD DRIVE window. The folder will open, and the contents of Disk 1 will be displayed in a window.

12. Place the mouse above and to the left of the upper leftmost item in the Disk 1 window. Press and hold the mouse button while dragging the mouse below and to the right of the lower and rightmost item. A box will encompass all of the items in the window, as shown in Figure A-2. The purpose of this is to select all of the items in the window.

13. Drag all of the items in the folder to the Disk 1 floppy disk icon by dragging on any one item. All of the items will be copied to the new floppy disk—a several minute process.

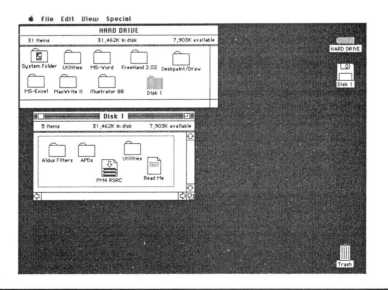

FIGURE A-2   Selecting all items in the Disk 1 folder window

14. When the copying is complete, first drag the Disk 1 floppy disk icon to the Trash icon to eject it, and then drag the Disk 1 folder to the Trash icon to dispose of it.

15. Place a label on the new disk that identifies it as Page-Maker 4, Disk 1 of 4.

16. Repeat these steps for Disks 2 through 4.

When you have completed copying all four disks, lock the new disks to prevent them from being written on or infected with a virus. To lock a floppy disk, turn it on its back so you can see the metal hub in the center. Then, with the metal end away from you, slide the small black plastic rectangle in the lower right corner toward you, toward the outer edge of the disk. This will leave a hole you can see through. Once you have done this, the disk cannot be written on until you slide the small plastic rectangle back to its original position.

Place your original PageMaker disks in a safe location and use the copies you made for the installation to follow. Use the original disks only to make additional copies.

Copying with Two Floppy Drives

If you have two floppy drives, the copying process is simpler but similar. Use these instructions. (Read the previous instructions if you are unfamiliar with the terms "click on," "drag," and "double-click on.")

1. Eject any disks currently in the drives by dragging their icons to the Trash icon.

2. Insert the PageMaker Disk 1 of 4 in one of the floppy drives and insert a new or blank disk in the other drive.

3. If the new or blank disk needs to be initialized or formatted, you will get a message to that effect. If so, follow instructions 9 through 11 in the section "Copying with a Hard Disk," being sure to name the disk Disk 1.

4. When both floppy disk icons are on the screen, drag the PageMaker Disk 1 icon to the other disk icon (called the Destination Disk). A message will appear, asking you if you want to completely replace the contents of the Destination Disk. Click on "OK."

5. When the copying is complete, and if you did not just format and name the Destination Disk, click on the Destination Disk icon to select it, press DELETE to remove the current name, and type **Disk 1** to rename it.

6. Drag both disk icons to the Trash icon to eject them and then label the copy as PageMaker 4, Disk 1 of 4.

7. Repeat steps 2 through 6 for the other three disks.

When you have completed copying all four disks, you will need to lock the new disks to prevent them from being harmed. See the discussion at the end of the section "Copying with a Hard Disk," to learn how to do this.

Place your original PageMaker disks in a safe location and use the copies you made for the installation that follows. Use the original disks only to make additional copies.

USING THE ALDUS INSTALLER

The Aldus Installer feature provided with PageMaker 4 copies the various PageMaker files to your hard disk. Some of the files are always required and are copied in every instance. Other files are dependent on the printer and word processing package you will be using. A third set of files are completely optional. Each of these will be discussed as they come up in the installation. The key is that most of the work, the copying, is done automatically for you. All you have to do is make decisions, answer questions, and change disks. Begin now with these instructions:

1. Insert the copy of PageMaker 4 Disk 1 of 4 into a floppy disk drive. The Disk 1 icon will appear on the right of your screen.

2. If Disk 1 did not open automatically, double-click on the Disk 1 icon. The Disk 1 window will open and display five items, including a folder labeled Utilities.

3. If the Utilities folder does not open automatically, double-click on the Utilities folder icon. The Utilities window will open and display three items, including the Aldus Installer. Your screen should look like Figure A-3.

4. Double-click on the Aldus Installer/Utility icon. A copyright screen will appear briefly, followed by the Aldus Installer Main window with three text windows, as shown in Figure A-4.

The Aldus Main Installer window allows you to choose the items you want to install: "PageMaker 4" itself, "Templates" which are sample publications built with PageMaker, and "Tutorial Files," which are publications built with PageMaker that are used with the lessons in the *Getting Started* manual. Initially, all three items are checked, assuming as the default that you want them all installed.

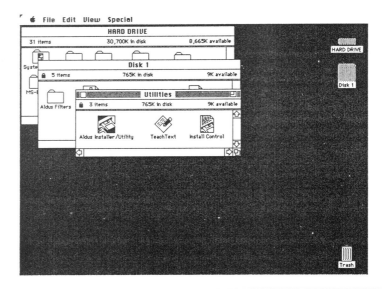

Two of the three text windows, Aldus Installer History and Aldus Installer Diagnostics, are initially blank. The text files displayed in these two windows are used as a log of the Installer's activity. If you have a problem during installation or want to find out later if you installed a particular file, you can come back and read these files after installation.

The third text window displays the Read Me file. This is a very important file because it contains last minute information not included in the PageMaker manuals. To read this file:

5. Click on the title bar at the top of the Read Me window to select it.

6. Click on the zoom button in the upper right corner to expand the window to fill the screen.

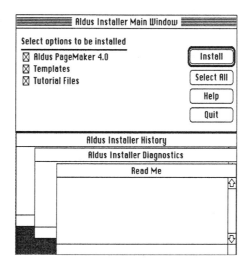

FIGURE A-4   Installer Main window and text windows

7. Scroll the text in the window by clicking on the downward-pointing scroll arrow on the right side of the window.

8. When you have completed reading the Read Me file, close its window by clicking on the close box in the upper left corner.

Next, you need to decide which files to install. If you are installing PageMaker 4 for the first time, you need to install the PageMaker 4 files. If you want to use the lessons in the *Getting Started* manual, you also need to install the Tutorial Files. The Templates provide many sample publications that are often helpful as idea starters.

9. Click on the check box for the item(s) you do *not* want installed. If you want all three items installed, leave the

check boxes as they are. Then click on "Install." The Aldus APD (Aldus Printer Description) installation dialog box will open, as shown in Figure A-5.

The Aldus APD installation dialog box allows you to tell PageMaker which printer or printers you want to use. For the printer(s) you select, an APD file will be copied to the hard disk. If your hard disk does not have this file, PageMaker cannot use your printer.

10. Click on the downward-pointing scroll arrow on the right side of the list box to scroll through the list of printers.

11. When you see the printer you want to use, click on its name in the list box. If you want to select several

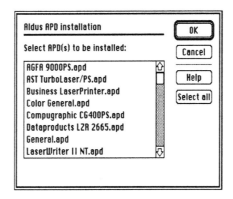

FIGURE A-5 Aldus APD installation dialog box

printers, press and hold SHIFT while clicking on the several printers.

If your printer isn't listed, contact Aldus to see if there are additional APD files available or if you can substitute another APD file.

12. When you have selected the printer you want to use, click on "OK." The Aldus filter installation dialog box will open, as shown in Figure A-6.

The Aldus filter dialog box lists the *filters* that allow PageMaker to read and write to the files produced by various word processing programs. These filters are for both *importing* (reading and placing a word processing file in a PageMaker publication), and *exporting* (writing changes

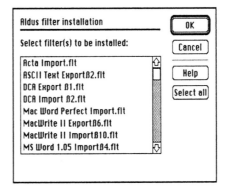

FIGURE A-6 Aldus filter installation dialog box

made in PageMaker back *out* to the original word processing file). In order to read a file produced by a word processing program, you must install its import filter. If you also want to write changes made in PageMaker back out to the original file, you must install an export filter.

13. Scroll through the list of filters by clicking on the downward-pointing scroll arrow.

14. When you see the filter you want to use, click on its name in the list box. If you want to select several filters, press and hold SHIFT while clicking in several filters.

15. When you have selected the filters you want to use, click on "OK."

In the next steps, several diagnostics will be run, and then you will be asked to enter your name, company name, and PageMaker serial number in the box shown in Figure A-7. If you upgraded from an earlier version of PageMaker, your serial number is the same as it was in the earlier version. (In earlier versions, the serial number is located on your original program disk, in the *User Manual,* or on the bottom of the box). If you just purchased PageMaker 4, your serial number is on the registration card and on the bottom of the box. Exclude any letters at the beginning of the serial number but include all numbers and hyphens.

16. Type your name, company name, and serial number in the fields indicated, pressing TAB to move from field to field. When you are done, click on "OK." The Installer will repeat what you typed and ask you to confirm it. If the information is correct, click on "OK." If it is incorrect, click on "Change," make the necessary changes and then click on "OK."

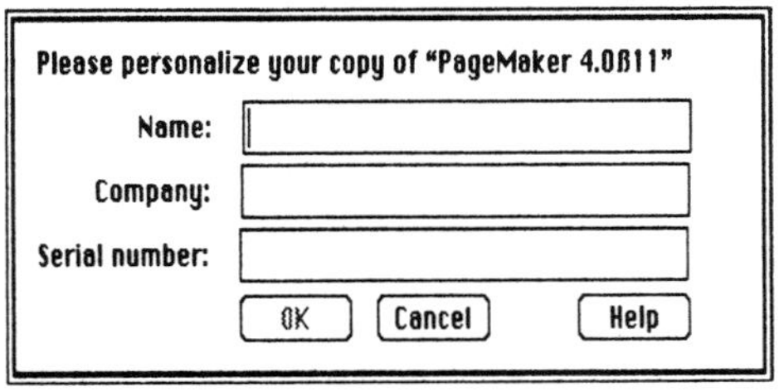

Please personalize your copy of "PageMaker 4.0B11"

Name: [   ]

Company: [   ]

Serial number: [   ]

[OK] [Cancel] [Help]

FIGURE A-7 Name and serial number entry screen

The Installer will then check to see if there is enough room on your disk to install PageMaker and all of the files you have requested.

17. If there isn't enough room, the Installer will display a message. Click on "Cancel." This will cancel the entire installation procedure you have just followed. You will be returned to the Installer Main window. If you need only a small amount of additional space, follow the installation process again and choose only the Page-Maker 4 files, only one printer APD, and only one word processing filter. If you need quite a bit of disk space, click on "Quit" from the Installer Main window and make the necessary space on your hard disk by removing unused files. Then restart the installation.

18. If there is enough room on your hard drive for all the files you have requested, you will be asked where to install those files. The Installer will suggest as the default that they be placed in a folder named Aldus PageMaker 4.0 on your hard drive. See Figure A-8.

19. Unless you have an unusual configuration, such as two hard drives, accept the suggested folder name and drive location by clicking on "Install."

The actual copying of files will begin. You can follow what is being copied by watching the thermometer box at the top of the screen and the Aldus Installer History text box at the bottom. When necessary, you will be asked to change the floppy disk in the drive, as shown in Figure A-9.

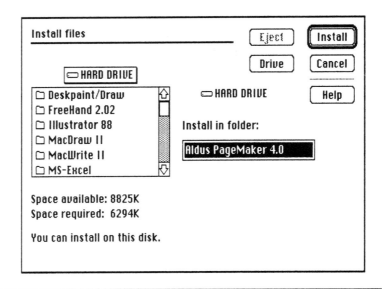

FIGURE A-8 The Installer asking where to install

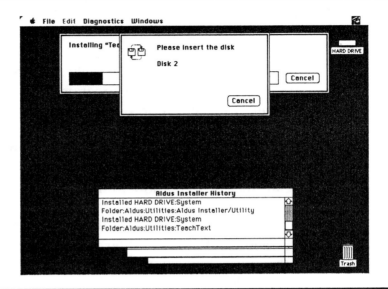

FIGURE A-9   The Installer asking to change disks

When all of the requested files have been copied, you will see the message "Assembling PageMaker." When that is completed, you will see a brief message that will tell you the installation was successfully completed and you will be returned to the Macintosh desktop.

In addition to placing the PageMaker files in the Aldus PageMaker 4.0 folder, the Installer placed a number of files in a folder named Aldus within the System folder. The Aldus folder, which is referenced by other Aldus programs such as FreeHand and Persuasion, contains the APD files, filters, dictionaries, and other files. For PageMaker to operate correctly, the Aldus folder should not be removed or renamed, and none of the files or folders in the Aldus folder should be moved or renamed.

STORING YOUR PUBLICATIONS

When you use PageMaker to create publications, you could store them in the Aldus PageMaker 4.0 folder that you just created for the PageMaker program files. It is a better idea, however, to store your publication files in one or more folders separate from the program files. In this way, you can delete your old program folder when you upgrade it without accidentally deleting any of your publication files. Create such a folder now with these instructions:

1. Drag on the File menu in the menu bar at the top of the screen until "New Folder" is highlighted, then release the mouse button. An "Empty Folder" will be created as shown here:

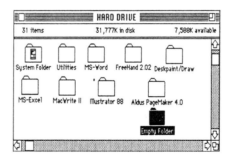

2. Press the DELETE or BACKSPACE key to remove the name "Empty folders" and then type **Publications** as the new name of the folder.

STARTING AND LEAVING PAGEMAKER

Test your PageMaker installation by starting it now with these instructions:

1. If your HARD DRIVE window is not open, double-click on the HARD DRIVE icon.

2. Double-click on the Aldus PageMaker 4.0 folder to open it.

3. Finally, double-click on the PageMaker icon to start PageMaker.

Upon starting PageMaker, you will see first a copyright notice, then a confirmation of the name and serial number

FIGURE A-10 PageMaker desktop

you entered, then the PageMaker desktop shown in Figure A-10.

Chapter 3, "Getting Started with a Flyer," discusses the PageMaker desktop and each of the menus shown across the top of the screen. For now,

4. Leave PageMaker by pressing and holding the COMMAND key while pressing **Q**.

5. If you wish to turn off your computer, do so now by either turning off the switch if you have a Macintosh Plus or SE or, for the Macintosh II family, by dragging on the Special menu until "Shut Down" is highlighted.

USING FONTS AND
LASER PRINTERS

PostScript and the Apple LaserWriter IINT
Alternative Laser Printers
Font Alternatives

Laser printers and the type fonts that they use are two major components of desktop publishing. In this book, it is assumed that you are using the Apple LaserWriter IINT with its 35 internal Adobe Postscript fonts. There are, of course, a number of alternatives for both printers and fonts. This appendix takes a brief look at some of these alternatives and examines how they relate to the rest of the book.

The Apple LaserWriter IINT is the industry standard for laser printers for the Macintosh. The original Apple LaserWriter and LaserWriter Plus have the capability to print the combined text and graphics that are the hallmark of desktop publishing. Several other, more recent laser printers emulate the Apple LaserWriter IINT.

The Adobe PostScript internal fonts are used in this book because they are part of the printer and include the sizes and styles needed to build the publications described. Times and Helvetica are used because they are the industry standards for serif and sans serif typefaces (see the typeface discussion in Chapter 1, "Desktop Publishing and PageMaker"), but there are numerous other options.

POSTSCRIPT AND THE APPLE LASERWRITER IINT

PostScript is a page description language (PDL) used by a program that runs in the LaserWriter IINT. Using a PDL leaves to the printer the task of how to place an image on a page. The computer and its applications, such as Page-Maker, need only describe the procedures and parameters necessary for PostScript to calculate where to place the image.

There are some obvious benefits to this. First, work is transferred to the printer, freeing the computer for other tasks. Second, less information is transferred from the computer to the printer, saving time. And third, storing a PostScript file of what is to be printed on disk takes much less space than storing a complete print image.

A less obvious benefit concerns how PostScript works with fonts. PostScript uses fonts that are in outline form—a series of instructions that trace a particular character. In contrast, the fonts on an HP LaserJet or an Apple Laser-Writer SC are in bit-mapped form—a series of dots that produce a character of a particular size and weight. The outline form allows PostScript to scale, in the printer, a given character from very small to very large point sizes, to rotate a character, and to compress or squeeze a character.

This saves time in communicating with the printer and saves memory in the printer. (Although an additional Post-Script font does require additional memory, it requires less than an additional bit-mapped font.)

Finally, a number of devices use PostScript, including several professional imagesetting devices. This means that you can build a publication in PageMaker, print it on the Apple LaserWriter IINT for proofing purposes, and then print the final copy on a Linotronic 100P or 300P to get full typeset quality. The highest resolution on the Apple Laser-Writer is 300 dpi (dots per inch); on most imagesetters it is 1200 dpi, and on some it is even higher.

The Apple LaserWriter IINT includes 11 Adobe Post-Script typefaces with 35 fonts: Avant Garde, Bookman, Courier, Helvetica, Helvetica Narrow, New Century Schoolbook, Palatino, and Times, each in medium weight (roman), italic, bold, and bold italic. Additionally, there are Symbol and Zapf DingBats in medium weight and Zapf Chancery in medium italic.

The Apple LaserWriter IINT has 2 MB of memory. Since the fonts take up so little memory on the Laser-Writer, you have more memory remaining than you would if the same fonts were used on a bit-mapped laser printer. The LaserWriter IINT has a Diablo emulation mode and both an AppleTalk and serial interface.

The LaserWriter IINTX is faster than the NT, can emulate an HP LaserJet, and can be connected directly to a disk drive for fonts. (It also has a considerably higher price.)

The third member of the family is Apple LaserWriter IISC. The LaserWriter IISC does not include PostScript, uses bit-mapped QuickDraw fonts, and is priced less than the IINT.

ALTERNATIVE LASER PRINTERS

In the Macintosh world, alternative laser printer means, with a few exceptions, alternative PostScript printer. Most alternative PostScript printers have capabilities similar to the Apple LaserWriter IINT, sometimes with an added feature or two, and often at a slightly lower price.

Two examples of alternative PostScript printers are the QMS PS-810 and the NEC SilentWriter LC890. Both of these printers are equipped with the same 35 Adobe PostScript fonts, AppleTalk ports to connect directly to a Macintosh, 300 dpi resolution, and eight page-per-minute print speed, exactly like the LaserWriter IINT.

The QMS PS-810 uses the same Cannon SX printer engine as the LaserWriter IINT. Unlike the Apple LaserWriter IINT, both the QMS PS-810 and the NEC LC890 have HP LaserJet+ emulation and a parallel port for connection to IBM PC-compatible computers. Also, the QMS printer has slightly faster processing speed and HP plotter emulation.

The NEC printer has two 250-sheet paper trays that you can switch between, whereas both the Apple and QMS printers have a single 200-sheet tray. The NEC printer, however, uses a different technology for producing the image on the page that does not provide the clarity available on either the Apple or QMS printers. Also, the NEC is ranked lower in reliability compared to either the Apple or QMS printers, while the QMS is ranked equal to or slightly above the Apple.* Both the QMS and NEC printers are priced lower than the Apple printer.

*"Buyers Praise QMS, Apple PostScript Laser Printers," *PC Week,* (October 23, 1989).

In the class of non-PostScript laser printers, two new entries are of real interest: the GCC Technologies PLP II and the Hewlett Packard (HP) LaserJet Series III. The GCC PLP II uses Apple's QuickDraw font technology in outline form (unlike the bit-mapped Apple LaserWriter IISC) to produce a 300-dpi laser printer with 22 scalable fonts for about a third of the price of an Apple Laser-Writer IINT. When System 7 comes out with the Royal font technology (see "Font Alternatives" later in this appendix), all the outline fonts available in System 7 will be directly usable on GCC PLP II. The price for getting so much at so little cost is that the GCC PLP II is less than half as fast as the LaserWriter IINT.

The HP LaserJet Series III costs less than half as much as the Apple LaserWriter IINT, uses the same Cannon SX 300-dpi engine, and has 14 fonts, 8 of which are scalable from 4-points up, rotatable, and can be outlined, shadowed, or reversed just like PostScript fonts. The Series III also has a resolution enhancement technology that varies the size and placement of the dots that form the image to smooth curves and fill in white space to reduce the jaggedness of the type. Unlike the GCC PLP II, the Series III has the same rated speed (eight pages-per-minute) as the LaserWriter IINT and is considerably faster in terms of *throughput* (time from initiating the print command to getting the printed page). Options for the HP Series III include an AppleTalk port and a plug-in cartridge that contains PostScript with the standard 35 fonts.

There is one other class of laser printer—those that use a PDL other than PostScript to place an image on a page but are PostScript-compatible. Outstanding in this group is LaserMAX Systems, which produce controller boards and printers that are not only much faster than the LaserWriter IINT but also have several times the resolution of the Apple printer. The LaserMAX 1000 printer provides a resolution of 1000 dpi, 135 built-in fonts, and throughput speeds several times faster than the LaserWriter IINT even though it uses the same Cannon SX engine. The Laser-MAX 1000 costs about twice as much as a LaserWriter IINT, but that is still about half what a 1200 dpi commercial imagesetter costs. The LaserMAX controller boards work with any existing Apple LaserWriter printer to increase resolution to 400 dpi, 600 dpi, or 800 dpi, and supply 135 fonts. A 600 dpi controller board costs about the same as a LaserWriter IINT, which means that the LaserMAX controller and a LaserWriter IINT together cost about the same as a LaserMAX 1000.

Both the LaserMAX controller boards and the Laser-MAX 1000 printer require one of the Macintosh II family of computers and will use one of the expansion slots. The printer and the controller boards provide all of the features of PostScript and are fully PostScript compatible. In other words, any program that can print with a PostScript printer, such as PageMaker, can print with a LaserMAX printer or controller.

FONT ALTERNATIVES

In addition to the 35 internal or resident fonts available on the Apple LaserWriter IINT, you can *download* (copy from your computer to your printer) fonts stored on the hard disk in your computer. These fonts are called *soft fonts* because they are distributed on floppy disks and are not hard-wired into a printer as are the 35 internal LaserWriter fonts. Soft fonts are available from a number of sources. Adobe sells over a 100 different soft font packages, each with a different typeface, and Bitstream sells a similar number. Besides Adobe and Bitstream, a number of other vendors sell soft fonts. Consult any Macintosh or desktop publishing publication for more on this.

While soft fonts provide a great variety of typefaces and sizes, they also take up valuable room on your hard disk and in your printer's memory that could otherwise be used for text and graphics. You'll quickly develop a love/hate relationship with soft fonts, and you may initially hate them because they are difficult to install.

The real alternative to Adobe PostScript fonts is still in development at the time this book is being written. It is the Apple Royal font technology, which will add fonts directly to the Macintosh System 7 to be released sometime in 1990.

Initially these fonts will only be for the screen — providing high-resolution, scalable screen fonts similar to Adobe's Type Manager but without the added cost and the need for the Font/DA Mover utility to install them. When still another line of Apple laser printers that use the Royal font technology is available, you will be able for the first time to truly achieve a "what you see is what you get" (WYSIWYG, pronounced "wizzy-wig") relationship between the fonts on your screen and the fonts produced by your printer. While you are waiting for the new laser printers, you will be able to use the Royal font technology directly with QuickDraw-based printers without storing the bit maps on your hard disk, and you can use PostScript printers by using the System 7 translator to convert Royal to PostScript fonts.

SCANNER GRAPHIC
FOR CHAPTER 7

Remove this page and scan the image of the Churchill
Club's logo.

SCANNER GRAPHICS
FOR CHAPTER 8

To use the illustrations that appear in Chapter 8 in your own work, cut the following page along the broken line and scan both sides into your machine.

016

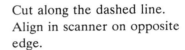

Cut along the dashed line. Align in scanner on opposite edge.

08

10308

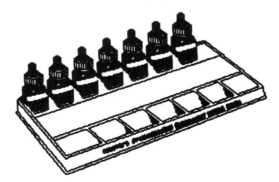

BXW13

 BXP01

 BXW12

 BXW24

Cut along the dashed line.
Align in scanner on opposite edge.

LWC03A

VENDOR ADDRESSES AND PHONE NUMBERS

Software Vendors
Hardware Vendors
Other Vendors

L isted below are the names, addresses, and telephone numbers of the main vendors mentioned in this book.

SOFTWARE VENDORS

Desktop Publishing Programs

PageMaker
Aldus Corporation
411 First Avenue South
Seattle, WA 98104-2871
(206) 622-5500

Graphics Programs

Adobe Illustrator
Adobe Systems, Inc.
1585 Charleston Road
P.O. Box 7900
Mountain View, CA 94039-7900
(800) 833-6687 or (415) 961-4400

Aldus Freehand
Aldus Corporation
411 First Avenue South
Seattle, WA 98104-2871
(206) 622-5500

DeskPaint and DeskDraw
Zedcor, Inc.
4500 E. Speedway, Suite 22
Tucson, AZ 85712-5305
(800) 482-4567 or (602) 880-8101

MacDraw II
Claris Corporation
440 Clyde Avenue
Mountain View, CA 94043
(415) 960-1500

SuperPaint
Silicon Beach Software, Inc.
P.O. Box 261430
San Diego, CA 92126
(619) 695-6956

Spreadsheet Programs

Microsoft Excel and Microsoft Works
Microsoft Corporation
16011 NE 36th Way
P.O. Box 97019
Redmond, WA 98073-9719
(800) 426-9400 or (206) 882-8080

Word Processing Programs

MacWrite II
Claris Corporation
440 Clyde Avenue
Mountain View, CA 94043
(415) 960-1500

Microsoft Word and Microsoft Works
Microsoft Corporation
16011 NE 36th Way
P.O. Box 97019
Redmond, WA 98073-9719
(800) 426-9400 or (206) 882-8080

WordPerfect
WordPerfect Corporation
1555 N. Technology Way
Orem, UT 84057
(801) 225-5000

WriteNow
T/Maker Company
1390 Villa Street
Mountain View, CA 94041-9908
(415) 962-0195

Other Programs

Capture
Mainstay
5311-B Derry Avenue
Agoura Hills, CA 91301
(818) 991-6540

HARDWARE VENDORS

Printers

Apple LaserWriter IINT
Apple Computer, Inc.
20525 Mariani Avenue
Cupertino, CA 95014
(408) 996-1010

GCC PLP II
GCC Technologies
580 Winter Street
Waltham, MA 02154
(800) 422-7777

HP LaserJet Series III
Hewlett-Packard Company
19319 Pruneridge Avenue
Cupertino, CA 95014
(800) 752-0900

LaserMAX 1000
LaserMAX Systems, Inc.
7156 Shady Oak Road
Eden Prairie, MN 55344
(612) 944-9696

QMS PS-810
QMS, Inc.
One Magnum Pass
P.O. Box 81250
Mobile, Alabama 36689
(800) 631-2692 or (205) 633-4300

Scanners

Apple Scanner
Apple Computer, Inc.
20525 Mariani Avenue
Cupertino, CA 95014
(408) 996-1010

HP ScanJet
Hewlett-Packard Company
19319 Pruneridge Avenue
Cupertino, CA 95014
(800) 752-0900

OTHER VENDORS

Clip Art

ClickArt
T/Maker Company
1390 Villa Street
Mountain View, CA 94041-9908
(415) 962-0195

Fonts

Adobe Type Library
Adobe Systems, Inc.
1585 Charleston Road
P.O. Box 7900
Mountain View, CA 94039-7900
(800) 833-6687 or (415) 961-4400

Fontware
Bitstream, Inc.
Athenaeum House
215 First Street
Cambridge, MA 02142
(617) 497-6222

MENU OPTIONS AND KEYBOARD COMMANDS

Menu Options
Keyboard Commands
Special Characters
Toolbox Tools

Appendix F provides a complete listing of each of the menu options and keyboard commands in addition to the tools in the Toolbox and some of the special characters PageMaker can produce. In all applicable cases, the keyboard shortcut is shown and a brief description is provided. This appendix is meant as a quick reference when you need to look something up quickly. Toward that end, the menu options also appear on a tear-out command card at the back of the book.

MENU OPTIONS

In PageMaker 4, options can be selected in two ways: by selecting the menu and choosing the option with the mouse, or by pressing the shortcut keys. The following table lists the alternate methods for selecting each Page-Maker option.

Option	Menu	Shortcut keys	Description
25% size	Page	COMMAND + 0	Changes display size to 25% of actual
50% size	Page	COMMAND + 5	Changes display size to 50% of actual
75% size	Page	COMMAND + 7	Changes display size to 75% of actual
200% size	Page	COMMAND + 2	Changes display size to 200% of actual
400% size	Page	COMMAND + 4	Changes display size to 400% of actual
Actual size	Page	COMMAND + 1	Changes display size to actual size
Align center	Type	COMMAND + SHIFT + C	Aligns text at center
Align left	Type	COMMAND + SHIFT + L	Aligns text on left
Align right	Type	COMMAND + SHIFT + R	Aligns text on right
Alignment	Type		Sets how text will be aligned
Auto leading	Type	COMMAND + SHIFT + A	Applies 120% leading to text
Autoflow	Options		Toggles[1] flowing entire story
Bold	Type	COMMAND + SHIFT + B	Sets bold type style
Book. . .[2]	File		Groups several PageMaker publications

Option	Menu	Shortcut keys	Description
Bring to front	Element	COMMAND + F	Moves text/graphics layer to top of stack
Change. . .	Edit	COMMAND + 9	Searches for and replaces text, fonts, styles
Clear	Edit	DELETE[3]	Deletes selection — not to Clipboard
Close	File		Closes current publication
Close story	Story	COMMAND + W	Closes current story window
Color palette	Windows	COMMAND + K	Toggles display of color palette
Column guides. . .	Options		Sets up columns and their spacing
Copy	Edit	COMMAND + C or F3	Copies selection to Clipboard
Copy master guides	Page		Copies guide lines from master pages
Create TOC. . .	Options		Creates a table of contents
Create index. . .	Options		Creates an index from a set of entries
Cut	Edit	COMMAND + X or F2	Deletes selection to Clipboard
Define colors. . .	Element		Creates colors to apply to text or graphics
Define styles. . .	Type	COMMAND + 3	Defines paragraph styles
Display master items	Page		Toggles display of master page items
Display style names	Options		Toggles display of style names in Story view

Option	Menu	Shortcut keys	Description
Display ¶	Options		Toggles display of special characters in Story view
Edit story/ layout	Edit	COMMAND + E	Toggles between Layout view and Story view
Export...	File		Saves text in word processing file
Fill	Element		Sets fill density and pattern
Find...	Edit	COMMAND + 8	Searches for text, fonts, or styles in Story view
Find next...	Edit	COMMAND + ,	Searches for next occurrence in Story view
Fit in Window	Page	COMMAND + W	Changes display size to fit in window
Font	Type		Sets typeface
Force justify	Type	COMMAND + SHIFT + F	Spreads text evenly between margins
Go to page...	Page	COMMAND + G	Displays another page
Guides	Options	COMMAND + J	Toggles display of guide lines
Help...	Windows	HELP or COMMAND + ?	Opens online Help system
Hyphen- ation...	Type	COMMAND + H	Determines if and how words will be hyphenated
Image control...	Element		Sets contrast, density, and pattern of graphic
Import...	Story		Imports text in Story view
Indents/ tabs...	Type	COMMAND + I	Sets indent and tab positions

Option	Menu	Shortcut keys	Description
Index entry...	Options	COMMAND + ;	Creates an index entry
Insert pages...	Page		Adds one or more pages
Italic	Type	COMMAND + SHIFT + I	Sets italic type style
Justify	Type	COMMAND + SHIFT + J	Aligns text on both left and right
Leading	Type		Sets amount of space between lines
Line	Element		Sets line width and style
Link info...	Element		Supplies information on file links
Link options...	Element		Determines how linked items are stored and updated
Links...	File	COMMAND + =	Manages links with text or graphics files
Lock guides	Options		Locks guide lines in place
New story	Story		Creates new, untitled story window
New...	File	COMMAND + N	Creates new publication
No track	Type	COMMAND + SHIFT + Q	Turns off any kerning
Normal style	Type	COMMAND + SHIFT + SPACE	Sets normal type style
Normal width	Type	COMMAND + SHIFT + X	Sets normal character width
Open...	File	COMMAND + O	Opens existing publication
Outline	Type	COMMAND + SHIFT + D	Sets outline type style

Option	Menu	Shortcut keys	Description
Page setup...	File		Sets margins and other page options
Paragraph...	Type	COMMAND + M	Sets paragraph specifications
Paste	Edit	COMMAND + V or F4	Inserts contents of Clipboard
Place...	File	COMMAND + D	Places text or graphics in publication
Preferences...	Edit		Sets unit of measure, placement of guides, and resolution of graphics
Print...	File	COMMAND + P	Prints current publication
Quit	File	COMMAND + Q	Leaves PageMaker
Remove pages	Page		Deletes one or more pages
Replace	File	COMMAND + D	Closes story window and reflows story in Layout view
Reverse	Type		Sets reverse type style
Revert	File		Restores last save of current publication
Rounded corners...	Element		Sets degree of roundness
Rulers	Options	COMMAND + R	Toggles the display of rulers
Save	File	COMMAND + S	Saves current publication
Save as...	File		Saves publication with new name
Scroll bars	Windows		Toggles display of scroll bars

Option	Menu	Shortcut keys	Description
Select all	Edit	COMMAND + A	Selects an entire story or page
Send to back	Element	COMMAND + B	Moves text/graphics to bottom of stack
Set width	Type		Sets width of characters
Shadow	Type	COMMAND + SHIFT + W	Sets shadow type style
Show Clip-board	Edit		Displays contents of Clipboard
Show index. . .	Options		Allows review and edit of an index
Size	Type		Sets type size
Snap to guides	Options	COMMAND + U	Aligns items to guide lines
Snap to rulers	Options	COMMAND + [	Aligns items to ruler marks
Spelling. . .	Edit	COMMAND + L	Checks and corrects spelling in Story view
Strikethru	Type	COMMAND + SHIFT + /	Sets strikethru type style
Style	Type		Sets paragraph style
Style palette	Windows	COMMAND + Y	Toggles display of style palette
Text rota-tion. . .	Element		Rotates selected text
Text wrap. . .	Element		Sets how text wraps around graphics
Toolbox	Windows	COMMAND + 6	Toggles display of Toolbox
Track	Type		Sets amount of space between characters

Option	Menu	Shortcut keys	Description
Type specs. . .	Type	COMMAND + T	Sets all type specifications
Type style	Type		Sets type style such as bold or italic
Underline	Type	COMMAND + SHIFT + U	Sets underline type style
Undo	Edit	COMMAND + Z or F1	Reverses last action
Zero lock	Options		Locks rulers zero point

KEYBOARD COMMANDS

Keyboard commands are actions that you can take to control PageMaker exclusive of the menus and sometimes in conjunction with the mouse.

Command	Key Combination	Description
All caps	COMMAND + SHIFT + K	Sets all caps type style
Beginning of line	keypad[4] 7	Moves to beginning of line
Beginning of paragraph	COMMAND + keypad 8	Moves to beginning of paragraph
Beginning of sentence	COMMAND + keypad 7	Moves to beginning of sentence
Beginning of story	HOME or COMMAND + keypad 9	Moves to beginning of story
Beginning of word	COMMAND + keypad 4	Moves to beginning of word
Bottom of story	END or COMMAND + keypad 3	Moves to bottom of story

Command	Key Combination	Description
Clear manual kerning	OPTION + CLEAR or COMMAND + OPTION + K	Removes kerning in selected text
Down a line	DOWN ARROW or keypad 2	Moves down one line
Down a paragraph	COMMAND + DOWN ARROW or COMMAND + keypad 2	Moves down to start of next paragraph
Down a screen	PAGE DOWN or keypad 3	Moves down one screen in text mode or Story view
End of line	keypad 1	Moves to end of line
End of sentence	COMMAND + keypad 1	Moves to end of sentence
End of story	END or COMMAND + keypad 3	Moves to end of story in text mode or Story view
Fit in window/ Actual size	COMMAND + OPTION + click	Toggles between Fit in window and Actual size
Kern apart — coarse	COMMAND + SHIFT + DELETE or COMMAND + RIGHT ARROW	Adds 1/24 em between characters
Kern apart — fine	OPTION + SHIFT + DELETE or COMMAND + SHIFT + RIGHT ARROW	Adds 1/100 em between characters
Kern together — coarse	COMMAND + DELETE or COMMAND + LEFT ARROW	Removes 1/24 em between characters
Kern together — fine	OPTION + DELETE or COMMAND + SHIFT + LEFT ARROW	Removes 1/100 em between characters
Larger point size	COMMAND + OPTION + SHIFT + >	Increases point size by one point

Command	Key Combination	Description
Larger standard point size	COMMAND + SHIFT + >	Increases point size per menu
Left a character	LEFT ARROW or keypad 4	Moves left one character
Left a word	COMMAND + keypad 4	Moves left one word
Move publication	OPTION + drag	Moves publication in its window
Next line	DOWN ARROW or keypad 2	Moves to next line
Next page	COMMAND + TAB	Moves to next page
Next paragraph	COMMAND + DOWN ARROW or COMMAND + keypad 2	Moves to start of next paragraph
Next word	COMMAND + keypad 6	Moves to start of next word
Previous page	COMMAND + SHIFT + TAB	Moves to previous page
Right a character	RIGHT ARROW or keypad 6	Moves right one character
Right a word	COMMAND + keypad 6	Moves right one word
Select character left	SHIFT + LEFT ARROW or SHIFT + keypad 4	Selects character to left
Select character right	SHIFT + RIGHT ARROW or SHIFT + keypad 6	Selects character to right
Select down a line	SHIFT + DOWN ARROW or SHIFT + keypad 2	Selects text down one line
Select paragraph	Triple-click	Selects paragraph with mouse
Select range	Drag	Selects range with mouse

Command	Key Combination	Description
Select to line beginning	SHIFT + keypad 7	Selects text to beginning of line
Select to line end	SHIFT + keypad 1	Selects text to end of line
Select to paragraph beginning	COMMAND + SHIFT + UP ARROW or COMMAND + SHIFT + keypad 8	Selects text to beginning of paragraph
Select to paragraph end	COMMAND + SHIFT + DOWN ARROW or COMMAND + SHIFT + keypad 2	Selects text to end of paragraph
Select to sentence beginning	COMMAND + SHIFT + keypad 7	Selects text to beginning of sentence
Select to sentence end	COMMAND + SHIFT + keypad 1	Selects text to end of sentence
Select to story beginning	SHIFT + HOME or COMMAND + SHIFT + keypad 9	Selects text to beginning of story
Select to story end	SHIFT + END or COMMAND + SHIFT + keypad 3	Selects text to end of story
Select up a line	SHIFT + UP ARROW or SHIFT + keypad 8	Selects text up one line
Select word	Double-click	Selects word with mouse
Select word left	COMMAND + SHIFT + keypad 4	Selects word to left
Select word right	COMMAND + SHIFT + keypad 6	Selects word to right
Small caps	COMMAND + SHIFT + H	Sets small caps type style
Smaller point size	COMMAND + OPTION + SHIFT + <	Decreases point size by one point
Smaller standard point size	COMMAND + SHIFT + <	Decreases point size per menu

Command	Key Combination	Description
Subscript	COMMAND + SHIFT + -	Sets subscripted type style
Superscript	COMMAND + SHIFT + +	Sets superscripted type style
Top of story	HOME or COMMAND + keypad 9	Moves to start of story in text mode or Story view
Up a line	UP ARROW or keypad 8	Moves up one line
Up a paragraph	COMMAND + UP ARROW or COMMAND + keypad 8	Moves up one paragraph
Up a screen	PAGE UP or keypad 9	Moves up one screen in text mode or Story view

SPECIAL CHARACTERS

Numerous special characters can be generated with Page-Maker and a PostScript printer. Some of the more useful English language special characters are shown here:

Character	Key Combination	Description
British pound	OPTION + 3	Adds £ character
Bullet	OPTION + 8	Adds ● character
Cent sign	OPTION + 4	Adds ¢ character
Closing double quotes	OPTION + SHIFT + [	Adds " character
Closing single quote	OPTION + SHIFT +]	Adds ' character
Copyright mark	OPTION + G	Adds © character
Dagger	OPTION + T	Adds † character

Character	Key Combination	Description
Discretionary hyphen	COMMAND + -	Adds hyphen if word breaks
Double dagger	OPTION + SHIFT + 7	Adds ‡ character
Ellipsis	OPTION + ;	Adds . . . character
Em-dash	OPTION + SHIFT + -	Adds dash equal to current point size
Em-space	COMMAND + SHIFT + M	Adds space equal to current point size
En-dash	OPTION + -	Adds 1/2 em dash
En-space	COMMAND + SHIFT + N	Adds 1/2 em space
Fixed space	OPTION + SPACE	Adds fixed-width space character
Japanese yen	OPTION + Y	Adds ¥ character
Nonbreaking hyphen	COMMAND + OPTION + -	Adds a nonword-breaking dash or hyphen
Nonbreaking slash	COMMAND + OPTION + /	Adds a nonword-breaking slash
Opening double quotes	OPTION + [	Adds " character
Opening single quote	OPTION +]	Adds ' character
Page number marker	COMMAND + OPTION + P	Adds page number marker to master pages
Paragraph mark	OPTION + 7	Adds ¶ character
Registration mark	OPTION + R	Adds ® character
Section mark	OPTION + 6	Adds § character
Thin space	COMMAND + SHIFT + T	Adds 1/4 em space
Trademark	OPTION + 2	Adds ™ character

554 ≡≡≡ PageMaker for the Macintosh Made Easy

TOOLBOX TOOLS

If the Toolbox is on the screen, it is easy to click on the tool you want. If, for some reason, you need to remove the Toolbox to see your publication, you can still change tools if you have an Apple extended keyboard. The key combinations you use to do this are shown here:

Tool	Key Combination	Description
Box tool	SHIFT + F5	Draws boxes with square corners
Circle tool	SHIFT + F7	Draws circles or ovals
Cropping tool	SHIFT + F8	Trims graphics
Line tool	SHIFT + F2	Draws any type of line
Oval tool	SHIFT + F7	Draws ovals or circles
Perpendicular-line tool	SHIFT + F3	Draws lines at 45-degree increments
Pointer tool	SHIFT + F1 or COMMAND + SPACE[5]	Selects and drags text and graphics
Rounded-corner tool	SHIFT + F6	Draws boxes with rounded corners
Square-corner tool	SHIFT + F5	Draws boxes with square corners
Text tool	SHIFT + F4	Enters or edits text

Footnotes

[1] "Toggle" means that the current state is reversed. If a setting is "on," it will be turned "off" by selecting the toggle, and vice versa.

[2] An ellipsis (. . .) means that this command opens a dialog box.

[3] DELETE refers to the key in the upper right corner of the typewriter keyboard, sometimes labeled BACKSPACE.

[4] "Keypad" refers to the numeric keypad on the right of your keyboard.

[5] COMMAND + SPACE will toggle you between any other tool and the pointer tool. If you are using the Text tool, for example, and press COMMAND + SPACE, you will get the Pointer tool; then if you press COMMAND + SPACE again you will be returned to the Text tool.

TRADEMARKS

Adobe Illustrator®	Adobe Systems, Inc.
Aldus FreeHand™	Aldus Corporation
Apple®	Apple Computer, Inc.
Apple LaserWriter®	Apple Computer, Inc.
Bitstream®	Bitstream, Inc.
CA-Cricket Graph®	Computer Associates
Capture™	Mainstay
Clickart®	T/Maker Company
DeltaGraph™	DeltaPoint, Inc.
DeskDraw™	Zedcor, Inc.
DeskPaint™	Zedcor, Inc.
DEST®	DEST Corporation
Finder™	Apple Computer, Inc.
Helvetica®	Linotype Company
Hewlett-Packard®	Hewlett-Packard Company
HP LaserJet®	Hewlett-Packard Company
HP ScanJet®	Hewlett-Packard Company

LaserMAX Sytems™	LaserMAX Systems, Inc.
Lotus 1-2-3®	Lotus Development Corporation
MacDraw™	Claris Corporation
Macintosh®	Apple Computer, Inc.
MacPaint®	Apple Computer, Inc.
MacWrite®	Claris Corporation
Microsoft Excel™	Microsoft Corporation
Microsoft Works®	Microsoft Corporation
MultiFinder®	Apple Computer, Inc.
MultiMate®	Multimate International Corporation
NEC SilentWriter LC890®	NEC Corporation
PageMaker®	Aldus Corporation
Palatino®	Linotype Company
Persuasion®	Aldus Corporation
PostScript®	Adobe Systems, Inc.
QMS PS 810®	Quality Micro Systems
QuickDraw™	Apple Computer, Inc.
SuperPaint™	Silicon Beach Software, Inc., an Aldus Corporation company
Times®	Linotype Company
WordPerfect®	WordPerfect Corporation
WriteNow™	T/Maker Company
XyWrite™	XYQuest, Inc.

INDEX

PageMaker 4 Menu Options
(arranged alphabetically)

Option[1]	Menu	Shortcut keys	Description
25% size	Page	COMMAND + 0	Changes display size to 25% of actual
50% size	Page	COMMAND + 5	Changes display size to 50% of actual
75% size	Page	COMMAND + 7	Changes display size to 75% of actual
200% size	Page	COMMAND + 2	Changes display size to 200% of actual
400% size	Page	COMMAND + 4	Changes display size to 400% of actual
Actual size	Page	COMMAND + 1	Changes display size to actual size
Align center	Type	COMMAND + SHIFT + C	Aligns text at center
Align left	Type	COMMAND + SHIFT + L	Aligns text on left
Align right	Type	COMMAND + SHIFT + R	Aligns text on right
Alignment	Type		Sets how text will be aligned
Auto leading	Type	COMMAND + SHIFT + A	Applies 120% leading to text
Autoflow	Options		Toggles[2] flowing entire story
Bold	Type	COMMAND + SHIFT + B	Sets bold type style
Book. . .[3]	File		Groups several PageMaker publications
Bring to front	Element	COMMAND + F	Moves text/graphics layer to top of stack
Change. . .	Edit	COMMAND + 9	Searches for and replaces text, fonts, styles
Clear	Edit	DELETE[4]	Deletes selection — not to Clipboard
Close	File		Closes current publication
Close story	Story	COMMAND + W	Closes current story window
Color palette	Windows	COMMAND + K	Toggles display of color palette
Column guides. . .	Options		Sets up columns and their spacing
Copy	Edit	COMMAND + C or F3	Copies selection to Clipboard
Copy master guides	Page		Copies guide lines from master pages
Create TOC. . .	Options		Creates a table of contents
Create index. . .	Options		Creates an index from a set of entries
Cut	Edit	COMMAND + X or F2	Deletes selection to Clipboard
Define colors. . .	Element		Creates colors to apply to text or graphics

Option[1]	Menu	Shortcut keys	Description
Define styles. . .	Type	COMMAND + 3	Defines paragraph styles
Display master items	Page		Toggles display of master page items
Display style names	Options		Toggles display of style names in Story view
Display ¶	Options		Toggles display of special characters in Story view
Edit story/layout	Edit	COMMAND + E	Toggles between Layout view and Story view
Export. . .	File		Saves text in word processing file
Fill	Element		Sets fill density and pattern
Find. . .	Edit	COMMAND + 8	Searches for text, fonts, or styles in Story view
Find next. . .	Edit	COMMAND + ,	Searches for next occurrence in Story view
Fit in Window	Page	COMMAND + W	Changes display size to fit in window
Font	Type		Sets typeface
Force justify	Type	COMMAND + SHIFT + F	Spreads text evenly between margins
Go to page. . .	Page	COMMAND + G	Displays another page
Guides	Options	COMMAND + J	Toggles display of guide lines
Help. . .	Windows	HELP or COMMAND + ?	Opens online Help system
Hyphenation. . .	Type	COMMAND + H	Determines if and how words will be hyphenated
Image control. . .	Element		Sets contrast, density, and pattern of graphic
Import. . .	Story		Imports text in Story view
Indents/tabs. . .	Type	COMMAND + I	Sets indent and tab positions
Index entry. . .	Options	COMMAND + ;	Creates an index entry
Insert pages. . .	Page		Adds one or more pages
Italic	Type	COMMAND + SHIFT + I	Sets italic type style
Justify	Type	COMMAND + SHIFT + J	Aligns text on both left and right
Leading	Type		Sets amount of space between lines
Line	Element		Sets line width and style
Link info. . .	Element		Supplies information on file links
Link options. . .	Element		Determines how linked items are stored and updated
Links. . .	File	COMMAND + =	Manages links with text or graphics files

© 1990 McGraw-Hill

Option[1]	Menu	Shortcut keys	Description
Show Clipboard	Edit		Displays contents of Clipboard
Show index. . .	Options		Allows review and edit of an index
Size	Type		Sets type size
Snap to guides	Options	COMMAND + U	Aligns items to guide lines
Snap to rulers	Options	COMMAND + [	Aligns items to ruler marks
Spelling. . .	Edit	COMMAND + L	Checks and corrects spelling in Story view
Strikethru	Type	COMMAND + SHIFT + /	Sets strikethru type style
Style	Type		Sets paragraph style
Style palette	Windows	COMMAND + Y	Toggles display of style palette
Text rotation. . .	Element		Rotates selected text
Text wrap. . .	Element		Sets how text wraps around graphics
Toolbox	Windows	COMMAND + 6	Toggles display of Toolbox
Track	Type		Sets amount of space between characters
Type specs. . .	Type	COMMAND + T	Sets all type specifications
Type style	Type		Sets type style such as bold or italic
Underline	Type	COMMAND + SHIFT + U	Sets underline type style
Undo	Edit	COMMAND + Z or F1	Reverses last action
Zero lock	Options		Locks rulers zero point

[1] Options are selected in two ways:
   a. by selecting the menu and choosing the option with the mouse, or
   b. by pressing the shortcut keys shown.

[2] "Toggle" means that the current state is reversed. If a setting is "on," it will be turned "off" by selecting the toggle, and vice versa.

[3] An ellipsis (. . .) means that this command opens a dialog box.

[4] DELETE refers to the key in the upper right corner of the typewriter keyboard, sometimes labeled BACKSPACE.

Option[1]	Menu	Shortcut keys	Description
Lock guides	Options		Locks guide lines in place
New story	Story		Creates new, untitled story window
New...	File	COMMAND + N	Creates new publication
No track	Type	COMMAND + SHIFT + Q	Turns off any kerning
Normal style	Type	COMMAND + SHIFT + SPACE	Sets normal type style
Normal width	Type	COMMAND + SHIFT + X	Sets normal character width
Open...	File	COMMAND + O	Opens existing publication
Outline	Type	COMMAND + SHIFT + D	Sets outline type style
Page setup...	File		Sets margins and other page options
Paragraph...	Type	COMMAND + M	Sets paragraph specifications
Paste	Edit	COMMAND + V or F4	Inserts contents of Clipboard
Place...	File	COMMAND + D	Places text or graphics in publication
Preferences...	Edit		Sets unit of measure, placement of guides, and resolution of graphics
Print...	File	COMMAND + P	Prints current publication
Quit	File	COMMAND + Q	Leaves PageMaker
Remove pages	Page		Deletes one or more pages
Replace	File	COMMAND + D	Closes story window and reflows story in Layout view
Reverse	Type		Sets reverse type style
Revert	File		Restores last save of current publication
Rounded corners...	Element		Sets degree of roundness
Rulers	Options	COMMAND + R	Toggles the display of rulers
Save	File	COMMAND + S	Saves current publication
Save as...	File		Saves publication with new name
Scroll bars	Windows		Toggles display of scroll bars
Select all	Edit	COMMAND + A	Selects an entire story or page
Send to back	Element	COMMAND + B	Moves text/graphics to bottom of stack
Set width	Type		Sets width of characters
Shadow	Type	COMMAND + SHIFT + W	Sets shadow type style

© 1990 McGraw-Hill